The Development of American Prisons and Prison Customs, 1776-1845

With Special Reference to Early Institutions
in the State of New York

By ORLANDO F. LEWIS, Ph.D.
*Late General Secretary, American Prison Association
and the Prison Association of New York*

With a New Introduction by
DONALD H. GOFF
General Secretary, The Correctional Association of New York

Originally Published 1922 by the Prison Association of New York

*Reprinted with the Cooperation of
The Correctional Association of New York*

PATTERSON SMITH
Montclair, New Jersey, 1967

365.973
L587d

*New introduction copyright 1967
by Patterson Smith*

INTRODUCTION TO THE NEW EDITION

Forty-four years ago, The Correctional Association of New York (then known as the Prison Association of New York) published *The Development of American Prisons and Prison Customs, 1776-1845, With Special Reference to the State of New York*. This work presented the results of an historical research project by the Association's General Secretary, Dr. Orlando F. Lewis. Like most original studies, it was not widely circulated —only five hundred copies were printed by the Association. Despite this limited distribution, the work was early recognized as one of fundamental importance to the history of American correction, a position it still holds today. (Students of criminological history might be interested to note that Dr. Lewis's work stands at the chronological midpoint between the present writing and the publication in 1877 of another report by the Prison Association of New York that had far-reaching influence on popular thought and criminological theory—namely, Richard L. Dugdale's study in family degeneracy, *The Jukes.*)

The history of American correction might be viewed as falling into three periods. In the first, individual reformers like Dorothea Dix and prominent "thinkers" like Francis Lieber brought the subject of penal treatment into the public consciousness and made of it a social issue. Then followed a century of "professionalization" in which men like Enoch Cobb Wines, general secretary of the Prison Association of New York, worked through voluntary non-profit organizations to put into practice some of the more settled principles of correction. In recent years attacks on the problems of the treatment of the criminal have come more and more from a new quarter—the university, now the chief supplier (often with government and foundation aid) of wealth and manpower for the research so necessary to the understanding of problems that are essentially at the root of human behavior.

Dr. Lewis's work is representative of all three eras. The first, of course, is the period under his review, ranging from the origins of the American prison system ("systems" is perhaps better) to the founding of the Prison Association of New York in 1844. Dr. Lewis's writing took place during the second period under the auspices of the Association, which has been pursuing its labors for over one hundred years with less public attention than was attracted in the early nineteenth century, when advocates of the Auburn and Pennsylvania systems warred upon each other in public print. Dr. Lewis himself was a harbinger of the third period. Academically trained (though not in criminology), he wrote at a time when there were probably no more than a dozen academic criminologists and penologists in America. In more recent years not only have sociologists, psychologists, and psychiatrists been working energetically in correction, but social historians have also begun to give merited attention to the history of our country's penal methods. Modern scholarship in this field is heavily indebted to Dr. Lewis's work.

Just as the agencies of correctional reform have been shifting, so has their orientation. Reports of the Prison Association of New York from the 1840's up to Dr. Lewis's own time reflect emphasis upon the physical aspects of prison life. These reports contain many pages of descriptions of the structures in which offenders were housed and worked as well as frequent comments on the need for new buildings—a concern with the "prison plant" that shows clearly in Dr. Lewis's writings. By the time that *Development of American Prisons* was published, correctional emphasis had shifted to administrative aspects of the prison environment—prison management, forms and functions of state regulatory bodies, and establishment of standards to protect the welfare of inmates. Attention at that time was directed much more toward the amelioration of personal inmate hardships resulting from imprisonment than toward a search for alternatives to imprisonment itself. To be sure, incarceration had never been viewed as the sole means of handling the crime problem, for the Association had in the late 1800's helped introduce into the United States the concepts of the indeterminate sentence and parole and in the early 1900's had supervised on a voluntary basis probationers in New York City. Nevertheless, correctional reform in the 1920's remained essentially "prison reform."

A re-orientation from penal and prison to correctional and rehabilitation is now with us. "Prisons" in many states are now officially "correctional institutions," and a similar terminological substitution graces the names of our New York and national correctional associations. What once were "guards" or "keepers" are now "correctional officers." But shifting activities go beyond mere terminology. The Correctional Association of New York, for example, no longer concentrates upon the welfare of the inmate within the institution but concerns itself equally with more removed aspects of the administration of justice, such as the penal law, crime prevention, and alternatives to imprisonment. An example can be seen in the treatment of the alcoholic. Recognizing that to end the jailing of alcoholics for public intoxication would reduce the jail population of the United States by upwards of 50%, the Association has acted upon its belief in the injustice, inefficacy and futility of this type of handling by attacking its constitutionality through the filing of an *amicus curiae* brief with the United States Supreme Court.

Occupying the same position in The Correctional Association of New York as did Dr. Lewis half a century before me and working in the same office where he worked, I am sure that the many pressures, dilemmas, and frustrations that I have experienced must also have confronted him. Did he, I wonder, find in his dispassionate chronicling of a by-gone era release from the very personal anxieties that beset the criminologist in his day-to-day encounters with the stubborn problems of effective reform? Or did he see the past inadequacies and injustices of our penal system as goads to future exertions against unchanging human deficiencies? Whatever the source of his devotion, to Dr. Lewis goes the gratitude not only of the Association for which he labored but also of everyone who recognizes the necessity for building a factual basis upon which any efforts toward social reform must rest.

DONALD H. GOFF

The Correctional Association of New York
September, 1966

TABLE OF CONTENTS.

		PAGE
Foreword		6

Chapter		
I.	The Beginnings of American Prison Reform	7
II.	Planning a Prison System	16
III.	The Walnut Street Prison	25
IV.	Early European Influences	33
V.	The Breakdown	38
VI.	Newgate Prison in New York	43
VII.	Newgate of Connecticut	64
VIII.	The Massachusetts State Prison	68
IX.	The Development of the Auburn System	77
X.	The Early Years of Mount Pleasant Prison (Sing Sing)	107
XI.	The Western and the Eastern Penitentiaries of Pennsylvania	118
XII.	The Early Development of Prison Labor in New York	130
XIII.	Other Early Prisons in New England	147
	Maine	
	New Hampshire	
	Vermont	
XIV.	The Massachusetts State Prison	158
XV.	Connecticut	175
XVI.	New Jersey	189
XVII.	Maryland	204
XVIII.	Virginia	210
XIX.	The Eastern Penitentiary of Pennsylvania	217
XX.	Kentucky	253
XXI.	Other Early American Prisons	260
	Ohio	
	Washington, D. C.	
	Georgia	
	Tennessee	
XXII.	County Jails	269
XXIII.	The Rev. Louis Dwight	289
XXIV.	The Early Juvenile Reformatories, 1824-1844	293
XXV.	The State of Prisons in 1845	323
	Bibliography	347

FOREWORD

Dr. Orlando F. Lewis, the author of this book, spent some five years in gathering material for it. He died before it was completed, and, therefore, was unable to make a final revision of the manuscript, or to complete one or two of the chapters, which unfortunately are left in an unfinished state. The book represents an earnest scholarly effort on the part of a man unusually well qualified to prepare such a history. For some twelve years before his untimely death, Dr. Lewis was the General Secretary of the Prison Association of New York. He brought to the discharge of his duties in that position exceptional qualifications, the product of unusual training. After graduation at Tufts College in 1895, he taught in that institution for about two years, earning the degree of Master of Arts. For three years afterwards, he pursued his studies abroad at the University of Munich and at the Sorbonne, in Paris, thus qualifying for the degree of Ph. D., which was conferred upon him by the University of Pennsylvania in 1900. For the next five years, he was Professor of Modern Languages at the University of Maine. In 1905, he accepted appointment with the Charity Organization Society in the City of New York, and in that position he was brought into direct contact with the varied problems of delinquency and offenders against the law and the manifold variety of organized eleemosynary and benevolent effort in the metropolitan region of New York. In that field, he acquired an experience which peculiarly fitted him for the service of the Prison Association, by which he was chosen General Secretary in 1910. His services in that capacity were characterized by rare address, great devotion, intelligent and sympathetic effort. Under his direction, the Association during that period fully maintained its traditions of helpful service to the cause for which it exists, and its present high position in that field in no small measure is due to Dr. Lewis' character and labors. The Association feels that this volume will constitute the best lasting memorial to Dr. Lewis' life and work. He was cut off in the prime of his life, and when his capacity for intelligent labor was very high. Some comprehension of his labors in the field of penology may be derived from a reading of the ensuing pages.

GEORGE W. WICKERSHAM,
*Chairman, Executive Committee of the Prison
Association of New York.*

CHAPTER 1

THE BEGINNINGS OF AMERICAN PRISON REFORM

The traveler who passes Ossining, New York, upon the train can hardly fail to note the gray, bastile-like prison of Sing Sing, looming like a monolith beside the railroad track. Its many small windows, that look like loop-holes; its cheerless granite walls, worn by the elements during an entire century; its extraordinary architectural construction, and its notorious history as a place of punishment, all lead the mind of the traveler to ponder upon the prison as a necessary institution in our American life.

But Sing Sing is passing. Built in 1825, by 1925 it will undoubtedly have been superseded by the most modern, most humane and most scientific institution for the treatment of delinquents yet projected upon the North American continent. A receiving and classification prison is now under construction, upon the hill above the old prison. To this new prison will come all felons sentenced to the State prisons of New York. From it the newcomers will be sent, after the most careful study of their individual treatment-needs, to the institutions in which they may find the best and most permanent curative and reformatory treatment.

A new day has indeed arrived in American penological methods. Throughout the last half century, with rapidly increasing momentum, corrective social agencies other than the prison have developed in the constant and always necessary battle of society against crime. The reformatory movement, typified by the founding of Elmira Reformatory in the seventies of the nineteenth century; the development of the so-called indeterminate sentence; the growth of the application of parole after imprisonment; the remarkable rise of probation, as a form of substitute for the prison term; the marvellous spread of juvenile courts; the growth of farm prisons and specialized institutions; the organization of Big Brother and Big Sister work, enlisting the philanthropic and devoted services of volunteers; the introduction into penal and reformatory institutions of the scientific minds of the psychologist and the psychiatrist, whereby methods of treatment of inmates have become materially changed; and the nation-wide attention given in most recent years to the institutional problems of feeblemindedness and diminished responsibility—all these factors in so-called "prison reform" have, as it were, been cumulatively reducing the original functions and methods of the American prison to something quite different. And all of these social efforts to humanize, and to make more just, the treatment by society of the prison inmate have brought increased hope of success into the prison problem.

But how did the American prison come to be what, for a century, it has been—a highly individual, unique, and not infrequently notorious institution? What were its chief origins? Who played a part in devising this extraordinary social instrument of alleged justice? How came it, that there solidified in the midst of our American civilization this social mechanism of punishment that, with few deviations, from type, rose in each State of the Union during the early nineteenth century, or sprang into being shortly after Statehood was achieved? Upon what models rose these early prisons? From what minds, and because of what philosophies of justice and of punishment, came the origins of American penal institutions?

It is exactly these origins that have been largely veiled or hidden to the student of prison reform. There has been much assumption on the part of writers relative to our earliest prisons. The so-called "Auburn" and "Pennsylvania" prison systems, each springing up in the third decade of the nineteenth century, have been rather generally assumed to be the chief sources of our traditional prison methods. Exceedingly little attention has been given to still earlier efforts in the first American States to deal institutionally with the problems of crime.

Yet there lies back there, beginning with the birth of the American republic, and extending through a period of a half-century, a development of penal philosophies and of accompanying institutions that in many respects is not only of great historical interest, but also of highest significance in the development of our American systems of dealing with offenders. The writer has been led to explore this region because of the absence of available material in readily accessible form. The results of this exploration he now presents in this volume, emphasizing however with frankness that this is but an excursion into a little known land, and not a comprehensive survey and charting of the entire territory.

There has been a certain zest in this pioneering exploration of the period between 1776 and 1845. If what the writer may be able to present shall add to and clarify our general knowledge of our earlier prison methods, and explain much that is still found as survivals of earliest methods, the intermittent study of several years will be more than repaid.

The birth of the American republic and the birth of an organized prison system in this country occurred practically simultaneously. It was actually in the first year of American independence, 1776, that an early act of the newly-formed State of Pennsylvania provided, in its constitution, that the Legislature

"proceed, as soon as might be, to the reform of the penal laws, and invent punishments less sanguinary, and better proportioned to the various degrees of criminality."[1]

We shall constantly see the relatively prominent and progressive position of Pennsylvania in the development of more humane methods of dealing with criminals. The colonial period of American history had been marked by the prevalence of corporal and of capital punishment. Even at the time of the emancipation of the Colonies from British domination, the punitive methods of the Old Country prevailed in the new world. A distinguished Quaker

---

[1] Turnbull's visit to the Philadelphia Prison, p. 8.

philanthropist, Thomas Eddy, living in New York city at the period of the beginnings of American independence, wrote of the age:

> "The tears of the sympathetic, and the voice of the benevolent, had made but slow progress against the apathy of the great mass of mankind, and the vindictive spirit of a few, who believe, or profess to believe, that the world should be governed by a rod of iron. The hearts of the people were made callous by the sight of stocks, whipping posts, pillories in every shire town or considerable village. Flagellation with the cat-o'-nine tails, burning in the hand or forehead with a hot iron, cropping the ears of prisoners in the pillory, were all common sights to the youngest as well as the oldest portion of the community." [2]

The Colonial period of our American history was characterized by a free employment of capital punishment for offenses that to-day are followed by no such treatment. Even at the close of the eighteenth century, the English penal code still retained the death penalty for 160 offenses. And the policy of England had been to superimpose upon the Colonies her own methods of punishment.

Methods of punishment, once established and practiced, tend by their very existence and continuance to justify themselves. When Thomas Mott Osborne campaigned at Auburn Prison in 1913 and 1914 against "medieval prison methods," both in housing prisoners and in their daily routine, he was combatting many traditional customs handed down by almost a century of practice from the early "Auburn System." To-day the whipping post is still used in Delaware, and its very presence leads not only to its justification by a portion of the population of that State, but gives opportunity to residents of other States to argue, from its presence, the necessity of severer punishments in their own States.

Moreover, tradition ultimately often gives sanction to that which at first seemed unjustified, or improper, or only an emergency measure. Edward Livingston, the noted American jurist, wrote that in this manner

> "The English nation have submitted to the legislation of its courts, and seen their fellow subjects hanged for constructive felonies; quartered for constructive treasons; and roasted alive for constructive heresies, with a patience that would be astonishing, even if their written laws had sanctioned the butchery." [3]

The gradual emancipation of the Colonies, and later of the States, from the sanguinary and horrible tyranny of mutilation of offenders, branding, ear-cropping, flogging, and the like, came about through the growing realization of the leaders in social and political life of the communities that the barbarous and debasing physical punishments failed to check crime or solve the problems of its reduction. If such realization seemed to be of slow growth, one has but to contemplate the present reactionary attitude toward the treatment of the offender. Throughout the land there is in this year (1921) a marked trend toward far greater severity of punishment for crime, and a growing inclination to attribute the

---

[2] Life of Thos. Eddy, p. 56.
[3] Livingston, Vol. 1, p. 13.

failure to reduce crime to excessive leniency of judicial and institutional treatment of criminals and other offenders. Throughout the history of penal treatment we find the pendulum swinging from extremes of opinion, and often of treatment.

It was recognized by William Bradford, a Quaker of Philadelphia, who became in 1794 the Attorney General of the United States, that

"on no subject has government in different parts of the world discovered more indolence and inattention than in the construction or reform of the penal code. Legislators feel themselves elevated above the commission of crimes which the laws prescribed, and they have too little personal interest in a system of punishments to be critically exact in retaining its severity. The degraded class of men, who are the victims of the laws, are thrown at a distance that obscures their sufferings, and blunts the sensibilities of the legislator. Hence, sanguinary punishments, contrived in despotic and barbarous ages, have been continued when the progress of science, freedom and morals renders them unnecessary and mischievous; and laws, the offspring of a corrupted monarchy, are fostered in the bosom of a youthful republic."[3]

We turn naturally, not only to the State and earlier Colony of Pennsylvania, but of course also to William Penn, to discover early enlightened efforts to mitigate the severities of the criminal code, and to introduce into existing punitive methods the qualities of greater mercy. When William Penn, arriving in the Delaware River in 1682 from England, with a charter from Charles the Second, founded the province of Pennsylvania, he brought from the British monarch permission to establish a penal code of most exceptional mildness, which retained the death penalty only in cases of homicide,[4] and which allowed the substitution of imprisonment at hard labor for former bloody punishments.

William Bradford wrote, a hundred years afterwards, of this great forerunner of the Quaker humanitarianism:

"The founder of the province of Pennsylvania was a philosopher whose elevated mind rose above the errors and prejudices of his age, like a mountain, whose summit is enlightened by the first beams of the sun, while the plains are still covered with mists and darkness."[5]

Penn's outstanding purpose in the treatment of criminals and offenders was clemency and, when possible, rehabilitation. He had been in prison. He had been a martyr. He had endured six months of the promiscuous horrors of Newgate in London, because he had refused to take an oath, which was an act contrary to his religious convictions. In a tour of Holland, he had inspected the Dutch workhouses, which even in those earliest times in rational institutional management were well-developed institutions for the amendment of lawbreakers through compulsory labor. He became deeply impressed with the industrial features of these workhouses, and when he came to America, he brought the purpose with him of substituting the prison for the gallows, labor for bloody punishments, and workshops for the idleness and debauchery of the jail yard.[7]

---
[4] Gray, F. C. Prison Discipline in America. Boston, 1847, or Bradford, p. 16.
[5] Bradford, p. 14.
[6] Bradford, p. 5.
[7] Krohne. Geschichte des Gefangniswesens, Vol. 1, p. 92.

The temptation of the student of prison history is, constantly, to contrast the dim past with the vivid present. To-day, in the length and breadth of our land, idleness, promiscuity, and individual demoralization of the individual are salient characteristics of the county jails of the United States. Over two hundred years after Penn, we still fight for workshops, and compulsory labor, and the abolition of the herding of human beings in our jails and local places of correction. Penn's penal philosophy is applicable to-day —and he towers in history as one of the great reformers in the penal field—one whose work soon was dissipated in the sands of inertia, reaction and traditional adherence to man's penal inhumanity to man.

Yet, at the time, despite the policy of Great Britain to keep the laws of the Colonies in unison with the Mother Country's laws, and to overwhelm an infant country with a mass of sanguinary laws, Penn, in his Frame of Government, abolished tortures and bloody punishments, and substituted therefor the penalties of imprisonment at hard labor, stripes (i. e., flogging), fines and forfeitures. As Bradford put it, his penal code was brief but complete,

"animated by the pure spirit of philanthropy. Punishments were calculated to tie up the hands of the criminal, to reform, to repair the wrongs of the injured party, and to hold up an object to terror sufficient to check a people."[8]

A reform is to be judged, of course, not by what to-day would be considered adequate as the substitute for an evil, but in the light of its relative progressiveness as a substitute for existing conditions, in an existing state of public opinion and of prevailing customs. William Penn substituted for extreme penalties physical punishments that to-day would be turned from in horror by the most enlightened minds. With the purpose of modifying so far as possible the vindictive and retaliatory features of then existing laws, punitive measures were to be employed for the reformation of the offender, and not for his extermination. Reparation of wrongs was instituted in favor of the injured party, and a chief object of his code was the deterrence from crime of those who might be tempted, in the absence of severe treatment, to commit crime.

To cite several specific illustrations: He provided that all prisoners should be bailable on sufficient securities, thus enabling the miserable offender, when possible, to avoid the long and debauching imprisonment, prior to trial, in the local jail or institution. An exception to admission to bail was such a capital crime as seemed to bear its own evident proof, or in which the presumption was great. To prevent false imprisonment, all persons wrongfully imprisoned or prosecuted at law were to recover double damages against the informer or prosecutor. All prisons were to be free as to fees, food and lodging, thus eliminating the extortion of jailers.[9] To make crime still more unattractive, all lands and goods of felons should be liable to make satisfaction to the parties wronged, to

[8] Bradford, p. 15.
[9] Carson, H. L. "Wm. Penn as a Lawgiver." Pa. Mag. of Hist. and Biography, Vol. 30.

the limit of twice the value; and for want of lands or goods, the felons should be bondmen, to work in the common prison or workhouse until the injured party was satisfied.

These features were substantially enacted in the Great Law of Pennsylvania in 1682.[10] Penn provided also for a new institution that was to supersede in large measure the public summary punishments of the past, namely, the stocks, the pillory, the branding iron, and the gallows. In short, the counties were each to

"build a sufficient house, at least twenty feet square, for restraint, correction, labor and punishment of all such persons as shall be thereunto committed by law."[11]

The basic purpose of these new institutions was that law-breakers should be made to work, and to learn the habits of labor.

In Penn's project of his code of laws, it was expressly declared that "all prisons shall be workhouses for felons, vagrants, and loose and idle persons." The Great Law of 1682 contained a similar provision, the stock, according to George W. Smith in 1829, upon which all subsequent legislation in Pennsylvania was grafted. From the year 1682 to 1717, labor formed an invariable part of the punishments of those sentenced to the prisons of Pennsylvania.[12]

In our present day, much stress is laid upon "prevention" as the most constructive method of checking and reducing delinquency. We emphasize the far-reaching influences of the church, the school and the home as prime factors in maintaining good conduct among the young. We advocate the establishment and support of boys' clubs, girls' clubs, social centers, the Scout movement, settlements, and the like. We repeat the old adage that an ounce of prevention is worth a pound of cure in the treatment of crime. But Penn's mind, over two centuries ago, had traveled also along the practical road of prevention. He aimed by law to provide for the prevention of crime among the young, by making it mandatory that all children of the age of twelve years should be taught some useful trade or skill,

"to the end that none might be idle, but that the poor might work to live, and that the rich, if they became poor, might not want."

And, in order that the citizens of Pennsylvania while still young might learn the laws, it was provided that the laws should be studied as a text-book in the common schools.

However, the principles underlying Penn's effort for the transformation of the penal practice of the time were much too far in advance of their time to receive the sanction of Queen Anne, who succeeded Charles the Second.[13] The laws were repealed by the Queen in council, only to be re-enacted by the Province of Pennsylvania, where they continued in force until the death of Penn in 1718. It was written that during this period of thirty-five years, it did not appear that Pennsylvania was the theatre of more atrocious crimes than other Colonies.[15]

---

[10] Charter to Wm. Penn, and Laws of Prov. of Pa., p. 100.
[11] Charter to Wm. Penn, p. 1139.
[12] Geo. W. Smith, in R. Vaux. Brief Sketch of the Origins, etc., p. 28.
[13] Vaux. Roberts' Notices, etc. Phila., 1826.
[15] Bradford, p. 16.

The sanguinary laws, restored in 1718, continued in force until the period of the American Revolution.[14] During this time the following offenses were again capital crimes:

High treason; petty treason; murder; burglary; rape; sodomy; buggery; malicious maiming; manslaughter by stabbing; witchcraft by conjuration; arson;

and every other felony was made capital in the case of a second conviction.[20] Later, there was added counterfeiting. All these crimes, with the possible exception of witchcraft, were capital at the time of the Revolution.[18]

We come to the first year of American independence, 1776. It was in this year that in Philadelphia the first prison reform society of America or Europe[16] was founded—the "Philadelphia Society for Assisting Distressed Prisoners." The name of the organization was significant. Emphasis was laid upon the succoring of the unfortunates in prison. The society was the result of private initiative. The membership was small, and the life of the society was extremely brief, for after some nineteen months the British entered Philadelphia, and took possession, among other things, of the local jail.[17]

However, after the Revolution, the society was revived on May 8th, 1787, at the German Schoolhouse on Cherry street, by the surviving members of the first society. It was now called "The Philadelphia Society for Alleviating the Miseries of Public Prisons."[19] As the Pennsylvania Prison Society this society still exists, and plays an influential role in the prison reform field of Pennsylvania. Its last annual meeting was the one hundred and thirty-third.

The new title of the reorganized society of 1787 indicated that the attention of the members was now to be directed in greater measure toward the miserable physical and social conditions of the public jails. The principal duties of the society were, to visit the public prisons at least once every week, through members of its managing committee; to inquire into the circumstances of persons confined therein; to report abuses discovered, and to examine into the influence of confinement or punishment upon the morals of society.[21]

The purposes of the newly-formed society were, according to Caleb Lownes, somewhat different. Founded mainly because of the gross excesses arising from the employment of prisoners from the jail at labor upon the public streets—which we shall shortly describe—the new society appointed a committee of six members

---

[14] Vaux, p. 7. Notices.
[16] Smith, G. W. "Defense of the Pa. System of Solitary Confinement." Quoted by Vaux, Richard, in "Origin and History," etc., p. 29.
[17] Vaux, p. 8ff.
[18] Bradford, p. 19.
[19] Julius. "Sittleche Zusbaende, Vol. II, p. 122.
[20] Bradford, p. 16.
[21] Vaux, pp. 8ff.

to visit the prison, to furnish bread when necessary, clothe the naked, accommodate differences, discharge those confined for small debts, and generally to mitigate the sufferings of prisoners.

We should, at this point, pause to recognize clearly the remarkable and ever-active interest and work of the Society of Friends, commonly called Quakers, in prison reform. It would have been a far different and more backward America, penologically, had it not been for the activity and initiative of the Quakers. Theirs was the great service of devising, in large measure, the first American State prison, on Walnut street, which we shall shortly describe. Theirs was the leavening philanthropic influence in Pennsylvania during the period under discussion. And, indeed, theirs is still, in 1921, a persistent, sober, constructive interest and activity in penological matters. To early prisons they contributed wardens of high integrity. They philosophized upon the criminological problems of the day. They conditioned in large measure, not as a sect, but as individuals, the development of the earlier American prisons, and their daily routine.

Particularly in Pennsylvania and in New York were the Quakers persistent in efforts to abolish the death penalty and sanguinary punishments, to improve the conditions of prisons, and, wherever possible, to achieve the reformation of the inmate. We cite at this point the noteworthy description by Edward Livingston (1822) of the participation of the Quakers in public affairs:

"Happily for Pennsylvania, and perhaps for the world, she had enlightened men to frame her penal laws; and happier still, she had a class of citizens admirably calculated to execute them with the zeal of enthusiasm.

"The founder of that State, and his first associates, belonged to a sect which fitted them, by its principles, and by the habits and pursuits which it created and prescribed, to be the agents of a reform in jurisprudence similar to that which they adopted, and perhaps carried to excess, in religion. Their descendents, with less of that enthusiasm which in their ancestors was exalted by persecution, had all the active benevolence and Christian charity necessary to prompt, and the perseverance and unwearied industry to support, their exertions.

"Abstracted by their tenets from the pleasures which occupy so large a portion of life among other sects; equally excluded from other pursuits in which so many find occupation; freed from the vexations of mutual litigation by submitting every difference to the umpirage of the elders, and from the tyranny of fashion by an independent contempt for its rules, the modern Quakers devote all the time which others waste in dissipation, or employ in intriguing for public employment, to the direction of charitable institutions, and that surplus wealth which others dissipate in frivolous pursuits, to the cause of humanity.

"In every society for promoting education, for instructing or supporting the poor, for relieving the distresses of prisoners, for suppressing vice and immorality, they are active and zealous members; and they indemnify themselves for the loss of the honors and the pleasures of the world by the highest of all honors, the purest of all pleasures, that of doing good."[23]

The Quakers held that the prevention of crime was the sole end of punishment, a most advanced attitude for the time. They held further that every punishment that was not absolutely necessary to

---

[23] Works of Edward Livingston, Vol. I. p, 508

that end was a cruel and tyrannical act. Every penalty should be apportioned to the offense.[22] Punishment should not be such as to plunge the criminal still deeper into destruction. The prison should make better instead of worse.

With these extremely advanced penological ideas, the Quakers, strongly represented in the newly-formed prison reform society of Philadelphia, faced the practical problem of bettering the conditions of public prisoners, and of establishing a humane and reasonable system of prison treatment.

---

[22] Bradford, p. 3.

CHAPTER II

PLANNING A PRISON SYSTEM

In 1786, the Pennsylvania Legislature, influenced largely by the penal principles of the Quakers, reduced materially once more the extent of the application of the death penalty, reserving now the infliction of capital punishment only for treason, murder, rape and arson,[1] while other offenses were to be punished by whipping, imprisonment, and by hard labor in public.

If, now, the gallows were to be less frequently used, what should take the gallows' place? Thus was the practical problem of a suitable place and mode of imprisonment forced upon the advocates of a more lenient treatment of criminals. The Quakers were thus obligated to devise a prison system, or "prison discipline," as it was more commonly called.

They faced a situation almost without precedents. The influence of the great English prison investigator and reformer, John Howard, was but beginning to reach across the Atlantic. There were no prison structures in other States that might serve as examples to imitate, or to copy in part. To be sure, jails had long existed in the American Colonies, because there had to be places in which to lock people up, but they were local institutions, used in general either for brief detention or for short terms of imprisonment. Obviously, so long as physical punishments in the open, before the public, were common forms of penalty, or so long as the execution of the criminal was frequent, or at least provided in the laws with frequency, the use of the prison as a place of permanent punishment, or of actual reformation, was hardly in the contemplation of the people. And the jails were, moreover, the centers of promiscuous herding of prisoners of all descriptions.

The Quakers were confronted with just such a condition, in the existence of the old jail at the corner of Third and High streets. This prison was all that Howard could have described or Hogarth depicted. It was the "scene of promiscuous and unrestricted intercourse, and of universal riot and debauchery."[2] There was no separation of prisoners by sex. Keepers locked up the male and female prisoners in the same rooms at night. When the Philadelphia Society had successfully memorialized the Legislature, and that body had enacted a law for the separation of sexes in this jail, the number of female prisoners soon averaged four or five, instead of between thirty and forty.[3]

This Philadelphia jail was a typical catch-all of miserable persons, criminals, lesser offenders, debtors and others. In this building, the young and old, the white and the colored, the depraved and

---
[1] Gray. Prison Discp. in America.
[2] Vaux, p. 8ff.
[3] Vaux, p. 24.

the relatively innocent were indiscriminately herded. Liquor was freely sold at a bar, kept by one of the prison officers. Jail fees were required even of those who had been tried and acquitted. From the windows of the jail the inmates were wont to push out bags and baskets, imploring alms from the passers-by, and roundly reviling them if they refused to give.[4] The prison was of the kind that Penn, a century earlier, had sought to supplant by his provision of county workhouses.

The first individual, unconnected with the administration of the criminal laws, who appears to have given attention to the inhabitants of the jail, was Richard Wistar, who died in 1781 at the age of 54, and who lived in that neighborhood. Before the Revolution he was in the habit of causing wholesome soup, prepared in his own dwelling, to be distributed among the prisoners.[5]

One of the oldest of the evils of the prison was, according to Caleb Lownes, the gaol fees. "Guilty or innocent, able or unable, strip or pay, was the first salutation."

An effort to remedy conditions by a form of compulsory labor was attempted by the Legislature of 1786. The employment of prisoners upon the public roads of the city of Philadelphia was made mandatory. The prisoners should meet the expenses of their keep through their labor.

That prisoners can be employed on roads, and in general in the open air, outside the limits of prisons, is in the year 1921 an established fact, so fully accepted to-day as to be no longer debatable. In gangs and squads, without the wearing of stripes, and often actually without guards, such squads of prisoners can be found in many parts of the United States. Road work in northern States is often regarded by the prisoners as a great privilege, in comparison with work within the institution, and "honor camps" are frequently filled with convicts who thus labor, generally in full view of the passers-by.

Yet this condition has been arrived at only gradually, and after many trials. This early experiment on the roads of Philadelphia bore deplorable results. The public of the period 1786 to 1790, feared these malefactors, thus employed in public places, and the jail authorities, on their side, feared that the convicts would escape. Consequently, the prisoners thus working were weighted down with iron collars and chains, and they dragged these clankingly as they worked.[7] They were garbed in an "infamous dress,"[8] and their heads were shaved, that they might be easily identified if they should run away. In short, they were public exhibitions of a wild human animal, called a convict, restrained by chains and arms in the hands of the guards from escaping to prey further upon society.

The picture is of intense interest in comparison with present road-work methods in convict camps. To-day the prisoners labor, in northern States, without ball and chain. They enjoy unre-

---
[4] Gray. Prison Discp. in America.
[5] Vaux, p. 8.
[7] Crawford.
[8] Vaux, p. 21.

stricted freedom of motion. The stripes are almost entirely gone in northern States. There is no "infamous dress," but a gray uniform of unobjectionable pattern and hue. The workers from the prison are not thus designated as pariahs and outcasts, and one of the strong temptations to escape — namely, the avoidance of such pitiless pillorying in conspicuous places before the eye of the public — has been done away with. In southern States the chain and the striped suit are still more or less customary.

In the Philadelphia of 1786-1790, the results were inevitable. "The drunkenness, profanity and indecencies of the prisoners on the streets were in the minds of almost all of the citizens," wrote Caleb Lownes, one of the leading Quaker prison reformers of the period.[6] And, said Lownes:

"The number of criminals increased to such a degree as to alarm the community with fears. The keepers (on the streets) were armed with swords, blunderbusses and other weapons of destruction. The prisoners were secured by iron collars, and chains, fixed to bombshells . . . The old and hardened offenders were daily in the practice of begging and insulting the inhabitants, collecting crowds of idle boys, and holding with them the most indecent and improper conversations."[9]

It is often asked why a method that, when tried at one time, proves successful, could not have been tried and used successfully long before. Road-work is a case in point. To-day, the general attitude of the public is to give the prisoner a "square deal" and another chance prepares, so to speak, an environment for his work that is favorable. To-day, also, the use of the indeterminate sentence makes good work and good behavior an inducement to the parole board to lessen the period of imprisonment. Honor systems have instituted a sense of responsibility among prisoners who enjoy the greater privileges of that system. Neighborhoods in which prisoners work on roads have discovered the "humanness" of prisoners. The idea of the innate or irremediable depravity of the convict is passing away. In short, both prison and public to-day give the prisoner a chance to make good.

The attitude of the Philadelphia public was an admixture of terror, of belief in the total depravity of the convict, and of conviction that he had few or no common characteristics with the "good," that is, those not in prison. As we shall see later, the line of cleavage between the good and the bad was sharp, and the jail or prison was one of the most vivid symbols of the great "badness" of the people imprisoned therein. The old prison above cited in Philadelphia was an example of this public attitude of mind. A clergyman, William Rogers, announced in this period that he intended upon a certain Sunday to hold a divine service for all the prisoners. The jailer, fearful of the loss of some of his perquisites and "vested interests," should the conditions within the jail become too publicly known, claimed the danger to the minister to be such that on the appointed Sabbath the jailer introduced a

[6] Account of Alterations and Present State of the Penal Laws of Pa., etc., Phila., 1793.
[9] Lownes. Acct. of Alterations, etc., p. 84.

cannon into the jail, which he installed in front of the pulpit, pointing it at the herded convicts, and stationed beside it a man with a lighted torch, so that at the first sign of outbreak among the prisoners they might be shot down.[10]

But the service went on to completion, nevertheless. It is said that this service was the first that had ever been held before all the prisoners in Philadelphia at one time.[11, 12]

We turn now to an incident that will be recognized by the student of penology and criminology in this country as little short of amazing. There are in the biological field what are called "sports," or unexpected deviations from type, occurring not in systematic sequence, or in frequent succession, but intermittently, and apparently unrelated to what has gone before.

There occurred, in an address given by Dr. Benjamin Rush of Philadelphia, at the home of Benjamin Franklin in that city in March, 1787, a "sport" among theories of penal administration. We present here the theories of Dr. Rush at some length, because in many ways his suggested system of prison administration echoed in that far-off time many of the principles that even to-day are considered advanced in the penological field. And, so far as the writer has been able to discern, there were no clear results from Dr. Rush's paper, nor did the eminent physician in later life take a specially active part in penal philanthropy.

Doctor Rush presented a lengthy paper upon the effects of public punishments upon criminals and upon society. In his opinion, as we summarize it from his article, buried in a series of miscellaneous papers on subjects other than prisons, the design of the punishment of criminals was threefold:

1. To reform the person who suffers punishment.
2. To prevent the perpetration of crimes, by exciting terror in the minds of spectators.
3. To remove those persons from society who have manifested by their tempers and crimes, that they are unfit to live in society.

In short, Doctor Rush has expressed practically the penological program of the present day, for he maintained that the prison must serve three purposes: Reformation, the deterrence of others from crime, and the protection of society from crime.

We are accustomed to regard the principle of "reformation" as a modern matter — one, say, of the last half century, since the establishment of the so-called State reformatories, beginning with the New York State Reformatory at Elmira, which opened in 1876. In the popular mind, the prisons, through the first century since 1776 to 1876 — exactly a hundred years from the first prison society in Philadelphia to the opening of Elmira — were places of strict and forbidding deterrence and punishment. The "reformatories" were founded, that the younger prisoners in State prisons might be transferred, or from that time on committed, to correctional institutions primarily reformative and educational in their scope and

---

[10] Rochefoucauld-Liancourt.
[11] Vaux, p. 8ff.
[12] The death of the author is responsible for the absence of a statement on the repeal of the Law of 1790.

purpose. The very term "reformatories" has set the prisons apart in the popular mind, and even to-day, when honor systems and self-government, as well as extended systems of education, are found in many a prison, it still devolves upon the prison to emphasize the fact that its purpose is not primarily repressive and punitive, but curative and reformatory, in so far as these results can be achieved.

Doctor Rush wished to deter from crime by exciting terror of the prison in the minds of the spectators. Throughout the following century we shall find this purpose uppermost, even in the minds of those who sought reformation in the criminal's heart. It was generally accepted as sound penology, in the early days, that terrorism within the institution would accomplish good ends. We shall see clearly manifested, somewhat later in our study, that "reformation" among the earlier philanthropists connoted much more than at present the actual saving of the criminal's soul. Therefore, with so mighty a stake, those effects must be employed that would be most striking, impressive and potent. In an age when even the infliction of capital punishment for over a dozen crimes seemed fruitless, it was not unnatural that the substitute therefor, the prison, should shape itself in the minds of the theorists as a place where most forbidding influences and methods must prevail.

Yet Doctor Rush, in his article, held that all public punishments — that is, punishments in the open, before the eyes of the onlookers, — tended to make bad men worse, and to increase crimes, by the noxious influences of such punishments upon society. At this time, 1787, the working of the prisoners publicly upon the roads of Philadelphia must have been in the minds of all. Moreover, as we have seen, the instruments of public punishments, which we have referred to in our first chapter, were a frequent sight. Public punishments, maintained the young surgeon, destroyed the sense of shame in those punished, and made them hard. Of relatively short duration, publicity of punishment produced no permanent changes in the sufferers. And when a man had been thus humiliated, he had nothing more to lose, and would, in Doctor Rush's opinion, be driven toward repeated crime.

A century and a half of penal administration has seemingly proved the soundness of the then exceedingly radical views of Doctor Rush. To-day the whipping post survives only in Delaware. Corporal punishment in prison administration is forbidden by the laws of most States. Stripes have passed, as we have seen, in most Northern prisons. Brutality has yielded to deprivations of privileges, and to moral suasion. And in Delaware itself, where the court sentences to prison, and often lays an additional penalty of so and so many lashes at the whipping post, located at the prison — the Newcastle County Workhouse in Wilmington — the warden of the prison lays on the lashes in such fashion as at least not grievously to pain the man at the post.

Moreover, according to Doctor Rush, the fortitude and pseudo-martyrdom produced in the criminal by public punishments stiffened the resistance of criminals to the law. And so, in time, these public punishments produced a moral and mental insensibility to punishment. Upon the spectator, also, the effects were bad, because distress thus publicly and repeatedly seen — whether in the public employment of prisoners, or in the stocks, or the pillory, or in more brutal forms — worked in the spectator an increasing indifference to the sufferings of others, and an increased familiarity with the brutality of the law. The young and the innocent were hardened, and became acquainted with spectacles of human criminality that would have been spared most of them during their entire lives, had the punishments been private. But, maintained Doctor Rush, sympathy and pity ought to stir the minds and hearts of citizens for those steeped in crime, instead of the indignation and contempt toward the criminals that were engendered by such public exhibitions.

One has, in our own century, but to read the papers to discover the false heroism and pseudo-martyrdom attending punishments that, although within prison walls, as in the case of executions, are nevertheless more public in many ways than were ever the public punishments of the era of Doctor Rush. Where, at that time, hundreds may have seen the flogging, or thousands the execution, to-day millions read, in the State of New York for instance, of the last moments of the newest victim of the chair. When the four gunmen were executed, several years ago, for the murder of Herman Rosenthal, the entire State of New York was given columns of minutest details of the preparations for the execution, and the execution itself, and the subsequent disposition of the bodies in the undertakers' establishments in New York city was the occasion for the thronging of thousands to the morbid viewing and acclaiming of the young men as — at least — not deliberate and wretched criminals.

It was the insight of Doctor Rush as to this deep-lying trait of the human mind that led him to seek a solution of the problem of public punishments and of a substitute therefor. He maintained that a system of imprisonment should be developed along the following lines. A large "house should" be constructed in a convenient portion of the State, the house to be divided into a number of apartments, and with cells for the solitary confinement of refractory criminals. There should be developed at this house those industries that were capable of putting the institution on a financially sound basis. There should be gardens, which would provide, by the labor of the prisoners, food for the inmates, and which should be also places of exercise.

The name of this institution should convey an idea of its benevolent and salutary design, and it should *not* be called a prison. The direction of the institution should be committed to persons of high character, amenable at all times to the Legislature or to the courts.

Let us seek to appreciate fully this project of Doctor Rush, in the light of present-day efforts for the betterment of prisons. Let us ask ourselves what general reception such a project would meet, even to-day, at the hands of those who still claim that the "prison is for punishment." This Philadelphia physician, knowing nothing save a local prison that was a center of debauchery, proposed an institution that would embody:

(a) classification of offenders,
(b) a rational system of prison labor,
(c) a productivity that should meet the expenses of the institution,
(d) outdoor employment of prisoners, for the raising of food for their own consumption,
(e) a kind of institution that should be a reformative institution.

There is surprisingly close analogy here with the "farm colony" plan of prison or penal institution that in recent years has taken root in many States. But the genius of the physician was also most surprisingly manifest in his further proposition that the various methods of treatment to be visited upon the inmates should not be specified by the committing court, and that there should not be in the law any notice of the kind of punishment that awaited any crime.

In short, the public mind should not become accustomed to think of crime in terms of the possible punishment that might be meted out to the offender in the penal institution. The kinds of punishment that *might* be employed should be specified in the law, but their duration should not be fixed, save as to a possible maximum. The limitations of punishment in specific cases within the prison should not be known to the prisoners.

Said Doctor Rush:

"I consider that this secret will be of the utmost importance in reforming criminals and in preventing crime. The imagination, when agitated with uncertainty, will seldom fail of connecting the longest duration of punishment with the smallest crime".

The historian of penal progress, looking in future years most carefully over the entire field of American penology and criminology for the first hundred years from 1776, will dwell with increasing admiration upon this little brochure of Doctor Rush, for we cannot escape the conviction that in the physician's mind was a clear foreshadowing of an indeterminate sentence — the practical working out of which was conspicuously the contribution of Enoch C. Wines, Zebulon R. Brockway, and Frank Sanborn in the days of the organization of the National Prison Association in 1870 at Cincinnati, and in the solidification of their theories in the first State reformatory at Elmira a few years later.

Indeed, the often quoted "Declaration of Principles," promulgated and adopted at Cincinnati on the occasion of the first gathering of that body which has become the large "trade-congress" of those dealing with the institutional treatment of criminals and other delinquents, the American Prison Association, contains certain paragraphs that are interesting to set along side the theories of Doctor Rush, advocated over eighty years before.

From the "Declaration of Principles":

I. . . . Punishment is suffering inflicted on the criminal for the wrongdoing done by him, with a special view to secure his reformation.
II. . . . The supreme aim of prison discipline is the reformation of criminals, not the infliction of vindictive punishment.

III. The progressive classification of prisoners, based on character and worked on some well-adjusted mark system, should be established in all prisons above the county jail.
IV. . . . Rewards rather than punishments, are essential to every good prison system.
VIII. Peremptory sentences ought to be replaced by those of indeterminate length. Sentences limited only by satisfactory proof of reformation should be substituted for those measured by mere lapse of time.
XVI. . . . Steady, active, honorable labor is the basis of all reformatory discipline.

In the essay of Doctor Rush, he suggests nowhere a definite sentence for crimes. His "punishments" include "painfulness, labor, watchfulness, solitude, and silence." These were in his mind evidently the component parts of a prison sentence. The word "punishment" may well have connoted for him what we to-day understand by "imprisonment." To him, "imprisonment" connoted such idleness, debauchery, and filth, as existed at the old jail on High street. We shall trace, from 1790 on, a succession of "systems" of prison discipline, but not until the above-mentioned development of the seventies of the nineteenth century is reached will there probably be found a more broad-minded, liberal and daring plan than that which, with some natural vagueness, was presented by Doctor Rush.

Indeed, the physician seems to have embodied in his plan also the conception of a "court," quite distinct from any then existing body, that should visit the "receptacle of crime" twice a year and determine the nature, degree and duration (beyond a certain degree) of all punishments. No more power than was at the time vested in existing courts was suggested by Doctor Rush for the new court, save that it should at intervals visit the institution for the above purposes.

The theory of a "court of parole" or of a "court of rehabilitation" is relatively modern. The establishment of the indeterminate sentence in connection with the operation of Elmira Reformatory necessitated the determination by some legal authority as to the time when an inmate should be released from the institution. Consequently, in most recent years, boards of parole, distinct from the governing bodies of the institutions operating under an indeterminate sentence, have been constituted by law, such as the Board of Parole for State Prisons in the State of New York, and the Parole Commission of New York city. It should be clearly understood that at the time of conviction the sentencing court imposes an indeterminate sentence, with a definite maximum not greater than the maximum provided in law for the specific crime. Within the maximum at one extreme, and whatever minimum the court may have imposed — or if the court has not imposed any minimum, at any time within the maximum sentence, the separate board or court of parole may release the prisoner upon "parole." Such is, in general, the present-day procedure.

In Doctor Rush's mind, his "court" should operate distinct from the board of managers of the proposed institution. As a physician, he was hostile to any uniform or wholesale punitive treatment of criminals. Punishments, he contended, should be adapted to the constitutions and tempers of prisoners. The nature, degrees and duration of punishments should be adapted to crimes, as they arose from passion, habit or temptation. In short, the physician urged, as a general principle of penal treatment, the individualization of punishment.

Again, the physician pointed out that the degree, nature and duration of pain, as a punishment, would require some knowledge of the principles of sensation and of the "sympathies" that occur in the nervous system:

"In the application of punishments, the utmost possible advantages should be taken of the association of ideas, of habit and of imitation. . . . I have no more doubt of every crime having its cure in moral and physical influences than I have of the efficacy of the Peruvian bark in curing the intermittent fever. . . . The great art of surgery has been said to consist in saving, not in destroying or amputating the diseased parts of the human body. Let governments learn to imitate, in this respect, the skill and humanity of the healing art."

In short, the physician here regarded the individual prisoner as a "case," each differing from the other. Somewhere there was a cure for every criminal, but the medicine for one was not necessarily the medicine for his fellow. In the diagnosis, prognosis and treatment of the imprisoned criminal, the physician would employ the principles of physiology and psychology as then known to specialists.

But, so far as we have learned in our study of this period, the chief interests of the Quaker physician were in the line of his professional speciality. In the development of the first prison system of Philadelphia, which was to become the early model for other American States, it was other men — perhaps more "practical"— like Caleb Lownes, also a Quaker, who were to play the constructive part, and we do not now know whether the essay of Doctor Rush, read not in a meeting of the Philadelphia prison society, but before another group, ever gained much circulation.

To-day, however, his long-forgotten essay brings him before us as a brilliant theorist, possessing almost uncanny prescience, joining him closely with the "pioneers" of eighty years later — linking us, in a way, with the far earlier William Penn in the breadth of his vision — and making the present-day program of the extension of the indeterminate sentence, the individual treatment of the prisoner, and the rational and scientific administration of prisons seem not so strongly "modern" in its conception or execution.

CHAPTER III

THE WALNUT STREET PRISON

We come to the year 1790, a noteworthy year in the history of prison reform. The Pennsylvania Legislature provided in this year that a certain prison, located in Walnut street, Philadelphia, and which had been begun in 1773, should be remodeled, after which it should receive the prisoners from the old High Street Prison.[1] In this renovated prison on Walnut street there should be confined two classes of prisoners, those who had been convicted of the more serious offenses, and those who had committed crimes of lesser severity.

We find thus the law now providing a certain rough basis of classification — which is in a way the beginning of the rational treatment of prisoners. The more serious offenders were to be confined in sixteen solitary cells, each 6 feet wide, 8 feet long, and 9 feet high, a total of 432 cubic feet. The less "hardened and dangerous" convicts were to be lodged in large rooms, approximately 20 by 18 feet in size. The convicts in the solitary cells were to be absolutely without labor; the other convicts were to work in shops during the day, in association with each other.[2]

We should pause here to emphasize the fundamental importance of the proper housing of prisoners, from several standpoints — safety, moral health and comfort. In this planned renovation of the Walnut Street Prison we face for the first time in our historical survey the cellular problem. Shall prisoners be housed separately or in association? Shall the separate housing of prisoners be for purposes of punishment? Shall prisoners be always separately housed, or shall they be allowed to be at any time in association? If at any time, shall they work in association and be housed separately when not working? Shall prisoners be housed, if in association, in large dormitory groups, or in small groups? If housed in association, what degree of guarding and supervision will be necessary or advisable?

The provisions for housing the inmates of a prison are a vital matter. Lodging, meals and treatment are fundamental problems of any prison. The Walnut Street Prison became of nation-wide significance not because of any extraordinary conception in its development, but because, for lack of any other model, it became the pattern upon which numerous other State prisons were built and administered in the succeeding thirty years — until the far more noteworthy development of the competing prison systems of Auburn and Pennsylvania rose suddenly, in the twenties of the nineteenth century. In short, what was done at Walnut Street conditioned practically absolutely the prison system, so far as there was a system, in the United States for nearly forty years.

[1] Vaux, p. 31.
[2] La Rochefoucauld-Liancourt, p. 8.

It is worth while, therefore, to dwell in some detail upon this device of the Quaker philanthropists to combine effective custody and punishment of criminals with humane treatment. The Walnut Street Prison started with the proposition of segregating its supposedly most difficult and dangerous cases. The single cells were thus at the outset branded in the public mind as punishment cells, for the protection of society and for the infliction of the hardest endurable conditions.

In this respect, the single separate cells were the very extreme antithesis of the crowded promiscuous living rooms of the old — and standard — local jail. Half-way between the old crowded jail room and the separate cell were the rooms in Walnut street for the lesser offenders. It seemed to be believed that a number of prisoners, less dangerous so far as known, might be housed in one room.

Herein the first prison system committed a fundamental error, which led only too soon, among other causes, to the absolute and deplorable breakdown of the first system of prison administration. For we shall shortly see how, as the population of the prisons increased, there grew up the constant temptation and even necessity for the prison authorities to crowd more and more prisoners into the so-called "night rooms," where the bulk of the inmates not only slept, but also passed their leisure time. Amid naturally contaminating surroundings, inmates almost invariably corrupt each other, and undermine prison discipline and authority.

What opportunities did the Walnut Street Prison afford for the classification of prisoners? The old High Street Prison had collected its inmates in a general mass. The Walnut Street Prison consisted of several buildings, housing not only convicts but lesser offenders (called vagrants), witnesses and debtors.

The total area of the prison enclosure was 400 by 200 feet.[9] The prison building for those convicts who worked in association during the day was a large stone structure, 184 feet long, on the north side of the enclosure, two stories high, and divided into the above-mentioned night-rooms. These rooms were separated from each other by a central hallway, extending the length of the building, and 11½ feet wide. There were eight lodging or night-rooms, approximately 18 feet by 20 feet, of this kind on each of the two floors.

On the east and west ends of the buildings were two wings, extending 90 feet south, 2 stories high, containing 4 rooms on each floor, nearly the size of those in the large building. On the south side there was a large stone building designed as a workhouse, where the debtors were confined.

Three hundred feet of the north part of the enclosure were divided off for the use of the convict population, and 100 feet of the south end of the yard for the debtors. The female prisoners used a yard 90 by 32 feet, and the vagrants one of similar size.

The building that contained the 16 solitary or separate cells, which was called the "penitentiary house" after the term intro

---

[9] General Description from Lownes. Acct. of Alterations, etc., pp. 88ff.

duced into England by John Howard,[5] was of plain brick, and 160 feet by 80 in size. Each cell was 8 feet long, 6 feet wide, and 10 feet high, had two doors, an outer wooden one, and an inside iron door.[4] A passage ran through the middle of the floor, separating the cells, just as in most buildings for the lodging of any considerable number of persons the interior hall runs down the center of the floor, with rooms on each side of the corridor. A stove in the corridor was to warm the rooms. Each cell had a large leaden pipe that led to the sewer, and thus formed a very primitive kind of a closet. The window of the cell was secured by blinds and wire, to prevent anything being passed in or out. The convicts in the solitary cells were not to labor; the other convicts worked in shops during the day.

That this "penitentiary house" was the "cradle of the American system of reformative prison discipline" was the assertion of Doctor Julius, the noted Prussian prison student and investigator, who visited this country in the early thirties of the nineteenth century, and published the above statement in 1839. Dr. Julius laid stress on the fact that this prison for the dangerous offenders embodied the principle of a separate cell for each inmate, which became ultimately the controlling factor in the erection of American prisons. Persons who had been convicted of crimes that were formerly punishable by death were to spend from one-twentieth to one-half of their term in solitary confinement.

The yard surrounding the building containing the solitary cells was used as a garden, and was managed by some of the orderly convicts. Here we may perhaps find the echo of one of the propositions of Doctor Rush. The large yard in which was located the other prison building was used as a place of labor of convicts, and also as an exercise yard.[6]

It was probably not much of a step in the course of time from these solitary cells for the worst offenders to the "dark cell" and the "dungeon." At any rate, here was the prototype. In administering these cells as definite places of punishment, the tendency would grow to make them as forbidding and repellent as possible. An easy development caused such cells to be used as the severest form of punishment except corporal punishment.

By the transfer of the prisoners from the High Street Prison to Walnut street, three great evils of the former prison were abolished, namely, the commingling of the sexes, the use of spirituous liquors, and the indiscriminate confinement of debtors and witnesses with those confined for criminal offenses. The new prison made as clean a sweep as possible of the old customs. The convicts at Walnut street were to be clothed in suits of uniform color and make. Labor was the prominent feature of the routine. Eight hours of work were required daily in November, December and January,

---

[4] Julius. "Sittleche Zusbaende," Vol. II, p. 124.
[5] A phrase current by 1779 in English law. Julius. "Sittleche Zusbaende," p. 132.
[6] Lownes. Acct. of Alterations, etc., pp. 88ff.

nine hours in February and October, and ten hours in the other months. Strenuousness and strictness of routine were fundamentals of the new system.[7]

The government of the prison was vested in a board of twelve managers, called "inspectors," who were appointed from among the citizens by the mayor and two aldermen of Philadelphia. Seven members of the board constituted a quorum. A sub-committee of two members were to make weekly, or even more frequent, visits to the prison in order to supervise the details of management in all particulars. Most of the members of the board were of the Society of Friends. The prison was also to be visited every day by one or more of the inspectors, "who all took great delight and were indefatigable in the execution of the humane task allotted to them."[8]

Throughout our study we naturally find it of interest to trace the origins of methods that later become custom. Here in the Philadelphia prison of 1790, and from then on, we find at the outset the theory that an unpaid board of managers, having the appointment of a superintendent or warden, enlists volunteer service of a high quality from among the citizens. The power that appoints such a board becomes in time generally the Legislature or the governor. The board of managers or directors, or "inspectors" determines the general policies of the institution, and through a sub-committee supervises the administration. The executive power is vested in one official, the warden, or superintendent (or, as he was early called in New York, the "agent and warden") who is a paid officer, and is responsible to the board of managers. This general form of management of American prisons has varied little since its initiation at Walnut street.

The new board of managers, among whom the dominant figure was Caleb Lownes,[9] a Quaker, had solicitude for many things in the convict's life. Moral and religious instruction was to be provided through the Bible and other religious books. Divine service was to be held weekly. So humane, by comparison with the earlier methods of dealing with criminals, were the new projects and proposals of law, that a time limit of five years was set upon the new law, and at the end of the time only a distinct success of the new methods, achieved in the meantime, would warrant a continuation of the system.[11] Yet, by 1794, the results were so remarkable that the Legislature went still further and reduced the infliction of capital punishment to premeditated murder alone.[10]

Over the new system at Walnut street there was in Philadelphia the greatest enthusiasm. Out of jail chaos seemed to have come prison order. The results appeared almost miraculous. In 1790 the law relative to the employment of prisoners upon the public

---

[7] Gray. Prison Discipline in America, p. 20.
[8] Wm. Roscoe. "Observations on Penal Jurisprudence," p. 88.
[9] Roche-Lian. Voyage, etc.
[10] Turnbull, p. 11.
[11] Buxton.

roads had been repealed, and labor within the prison substituted.[12] The new board of managers had made known to the prisoners at the outset

"that the new system would be carried into full effect; that their treatment would depend upon their conduct, and that those who evinced a disposition which would afford encouragement to the inspectors to believe that they might be restored to their liberty should be recommended to the governor for a pardon, as soon as circumstances would permit; but if they were convicted again, the law in its fullest vigor would be carried into effect against them. A change of conduct was early visible. They were encouraged to labor. Many were pardoned, and before a year had expired their behaviour was almost without exception decent, orderly and respectful."[13]

What were the apparently practical, statistical results?

There was proclaimed a noteworthy diminution of crime in Philadelphia in the first years of the new system. Convictions for crime and commitments to the prison, amounting to 131 in 1789, had fallen by 1793 to 45. The prison was called a school of reformation and a place of public labor.[14] In the four years preceding the beginning of the new system at Walnut street, 104 prisoners had escaped from the High Street Prison; not a prisoner escaped in the four succeeding years at Walnut street, save the fourteen prisoners who ran away on the opening day, when a plot to discredit the innovation was engineered by the hostile jailer.[15]

Many of us are familiar with certain extraordinary apparent successes that have attended in recent years the introduction of new and bold methods, in prisons and other institutions, in the treatment of prisoners. We have heard of and seen, the remarkable results of the application of the "honor system" in a score of prisons. We have heard of the best days of self-government at Sing Sing, under Thomas Mott Osborne. We have seen road-work conducted under almost unbelievably liberal conditions, with apparent success. We know the "thrill" of a successful new method, that seems almost to challenge the traditional "laws of penological gravitation" as one friendly critic has put it.

We can, therefore, sense the carrying power of the words of Caleb Lownes, writing in Philadelphia in 1797 of the new prison:

"Our streets meet with no interruption from those characters that formerly rendered it dangerous to walk out of an evening. Our roads in the vicinity of the city, so constantly infested with robbers, are seldom disturbed by these dangerous characters. . . . Our houses, stores and vessels, so perpetually disturbed and robbed, no longer experience these alarming evils. We lie down in peace, we sleep in security. There have been but two instances of burglaries in this city and county for near two years. Pickpockets, formerly such pests to society, are now unknown. . . . Out of near 200 persons pardoned by the governor, only four have been recommitted. If the discharged prisoners have returned to their old courses, they have chosen the risk of being hanged in other States, rather than encounter the certainty of their being confined in the penitentiary cells of this."[16]

We come now upon one of the earlier evidences of the mutual influencing of Europe and America in penitentiary matters. The

---
[12] Vaux.
[13] Lownes. Alterations, p. 91.
[14] Gray. Prison Discipline in America.
[15] Buxton, pp. 91-98.
[16] Lownes. Alterations, etc., p. 100.

Walnut Street Prison began to be known in Europe. In 1794 the Duc de La Rochefoucauld-Liancourt, after visiting the prison, proclaimed its excellences on the other side of the Atlantic.

Robert Turnbull, visiting the prison in 1796 from the south, called it in a pamphlet a "wonder of the world."[17] De Beaumont and de Tocqueville, forty years later, reported that "all the world repeated the praise of La Rochefoucauld."

It was natural that other States, seeking a model for their own new prison construction, should follow the lead of such an enlightened commonwealth as Pennsylvania, particularly since that State was the first to seek a modern solution of the problems of dealing institutionally with convicts. New York built a prison in 1796, Virginia in 1800, Massachusetts in 1804, Vermont in 1808, Maryland in 1811, New Hampshire in 1812 and New York a second prison in 1816, the latter at Auburn, in the western part of the State. All of these earliest State prisons were constructed upon the general lines of the Walnut street institution, with large common lodging or night-rooms for the prisoners, and with large rooms for their associated labor.

Most of these prisons copied also the system of solitary cells for major offenders. Into the laws of the above-mentioned States were written, more or less literally, the laws of Pennsylvania regulating the administration of the Walnut Street Prison. The rules and regulations of the board of inspectors were likewise frequently copied. There was a striking absence of initiative on the part of other States.

We have said that the basic principles of the new prison were labor and humane treatment. Whereas the prisoners in solitary confinement saw their keepers but once a day, and were then served with a coarse pudding of maize and molasses, and whereas these same convicts could acquire only after a certain time the privilege of working in their cells, and of reading therein, not being permitted to emerge from these cells except when ill, the ordinary convicts, not sentenced to solitary confinement, presented such a spirit of industry that it was difficult for Turnbull, visiting the prison in 1796, to divest himself of the idea that these were surely not convicts at all, but accustomed to labor from their infancy.[19]

The inmates worked at carpentry, joinery, weaving, shoemaking, tailoring, and the making of nails — all of them occupations that later became stock industries in American prisons. The unskilled convicts, and the group classified as "vagrants," were employed in beating hemp and picking moss, wood or oakum. The female convicts worked at spinning cotton, yarn, carding wool, picking cotton, preparing flax and hemp, and washing and mending.[18]

In this earliest prison we find the complex problem rising of a wage incentive for the efficient labor of the prisoners. Throughout all prison administrations, it is found that two motives above all others actuate the prisoner to industrial effort: The hope of

[17] Turnbull, p. 4.
[18] Turnbull, p. 16.
[19] Turnbull, p. 6.

earlier release from prison for good work, and the hope of some financial recompense for his work. Perhaps no more difficult problem still presents itself in American prisons than an equable wage scale and an equable commutation table. After maintaining State prisons in New York for over a century, since 1796, the Empire State has as yet been able to concede to the prisoners as a daily wage only one cent and a half! And in other States, under different systems of labor and of marketing the products of labor, there is little uniformity or adequacy in the wages granted. The prison wage and prison labor problems are still in 1921 unsolved in this country.

Therefore, it is of special interest to see the manner in which the problems were attacked in this earliest State prison. Each male prisoner at Walnut street was said to be credited with fair pay for his labor, and was debited with the cost of his daily maintenance, which is still a favorite and reasonable method in theory, though not in practice. Moreover, the hope of an ultimate pardon was held always before the prisoners' minds. Approximately 15 cents a day was charged to the individual prisoner for board, and his share of the tools, and his earnings depended upon his ability and the nature of his task. Some prisoners earned more than a dollar a day, and went out of the prison with more than fifty dollars to their credit.[20] All prisoners, it was said, were released well clothed, and mostly with money in their pocket. The discharged prisoner in need was assisted by the Philadelphia Prison Society.

The wages paid to the prisoners were the same as, or somewhat lower than, those paid for similar work on the outside. The law required that the prisoner should pay the costs of his trial, and generally also a fine. If there was a balance against the prisoner at the time of the expiration of his sentence, he was retained until it was liquidated. If the balance was in his favor, he received it.[24]

That the convicts might know both their earnings and their obligations, they carried their accounts in little books. The women prisoners had similar chances to earn small sums, and were debited for each day's maintenance about seven cents.[25] Untried prisoners were not forced to work, but those who desired work were given work to do.[23]

Naturally, this chance to earn wages proved a powerful stimulus, and gave to the prison administration a chance to hold over the convicts the constant threat, not only of the solitary cell in cases of serious disobedience, but also of a cessation of wages during that period, accompanied by a continuation of the daily maintenance expenses.

The obedient convict fared relatively well. No irons or chains were allowed in the prison. The guards were forbidden to use sabres, pistols, or even canes.[21] Corporal punishment was said to be unknown within the prison. Moreover, while silence was the

---
[20] Lownes. Alterations, p. 98.
[21] Turnbull, p. 48.
[23] Buxton, p. 92.
[24] Buxton, p. 93.
[25] Lownes, pp. 92-93.

inflexible rule in the shops and at table, the convicts were allowed to converse in their lodging rooms at night, in low tones, until ordered to bed.[22] It might be stated, parenthetically, that the rule of silence was not imposed upon the female prisoners.

"The orderly prisoners, who by their industry earn a sufficiency for the purpose, are allowed a better suit to attend public worship. . . . No provisions are allowed besides the prison allowance, except to the more laborious part of the prisoners, while orderly, who are allowed to get some of the heads of the sheep from the butcher at their own expense; this is esteemed an indulgence, and is attended with good effects, both physical and mental. . . . The orderly women are sometimes indulged with tea."[26]

This absence and virtual prohibition of deadly weapons, or of any weapons of defense whatsoever, was an extraordinary feature of this first prison system. We find here, at the outset, a series of regulations, and a method of attempting a humane and considerate treatment of prisoners, that are a revelation to those who have assumed that efforts at honor systems, equable wages, reasonable hours of labor, and government without the use of deadly weapons are new ideas. In a word, the earliest prison system started upon a high plane that has seldom been reached in any succeeding generation.

Throughout the hundred and thirty years or more since the Walnut street institution began its career, there have been only a few years at the beginning and at the end of this span of more than a century and a quarter when it has been held that prisons can be largely governed without weapons of any sort. When revolvers were abolished at Sing Sing prison in 1916 it was regarded as not only revolutionary, but dangerous. Indeed, during the period of the preparation of this study, residents of Ossining, the city in which Sing Sing is located, appealed to the prison authorities asking that revolvers be restored to the guards who were supervising the prisoners engaged in excavating upon the site of the new prison.

There is, in this twentieth century, a popular idea that such institutions as the honor system, the outdoor employment of convicts, the classification of offenders, self-government, and such principles as the indeterminate sentence are essentially the outgrowth of recent experiments by daring prison wordens. But, without detracting from the fine initiative that has led modern wardens or superintendents to undertake new methods, where politics or precedents were averse to such enterprises, we must nevertheless have recourse to the old adage that there is nothing new under the sun, and in justice to the "old days" thus outline in considerable detail these earliest efforts to conduct a penal institution with high intelligence and deep interest in the welfare of the prisoner.

[22] Turnbull, p. 26.
[26] Lownes, pp. 92, 93.

CHAPTER IV

EARLY EUROPEAN INFLUENCES

In seeking for the explanation of such apparently immediate enlightenment on the part of the pioneer penologists, we find that the Friends who largely developed this earliest system were not without a well-grounded knowledge of the penological principles of the times. There was constant intercourse in literature between the old world and America. Shipments of the latest books were eagerly awaited and perused. William Bradford's little book, from which we have several times quoted, carried as the motto on the title page the statement of Montesquieu:

"If we inquire into the cause of all human corruptions, we shall find that they proceed from the impunity of crime, and not from the moderation of punishment".[1]

And Bradford himself held that

"it is from the ignorance, wretchedness and corrupted manners of a people that crimes proceed. In a country where these do not prevail, moderate punishments, strictly enforced, will be a curb as effective as the greatest severity. A mitigation of punishment ought, therefore, to be accompanied as far as possible by a diffusion of knowledge, and strict execution of laws.[2]

In 1773, three years before the first prisoners' aid society in Philadelphia was founded, John Howard, an English gentleman, had begun to visit English prisons as a horrified yet careful and balanced observer of the gross evils of those institutions. From 1773 until the publication of his monumental work on the "State of Prisons in England and Wales," in 1777, he was an indefatigable, painstaking investigator, visiting the principal European countries, and inspecting scores of prisons, jails and lazarettos. Howard's work stands out in spectacular singleness during this period, and when his work was published,

"there was a universal outcry of horror and indignation which was heard throughout the civilized world, when he disclosed the misery everywhere suffered by the prisoners."[3]

It was inevitable that he should soon become known in the new and pioneering republic across the Atlantic as the great authority on prison discipline and prison construction. It is likely that ultimately, when this early period of our penal history is fully explored, it will be found that John Howard was in many respects a founder of our American prison system. He was not, to be sure, the direct incentive to prison reform in this country, because "prison reform," as we have seen, has already organized a charitable society in Philadelphia by 1776. Yet he was unquestionably a substantial influence. It is a curious coincidence, perhaps, that

[1] Bradford. Enquiry, p. ...
[2] Bradford. Enquiry, p. 43.
[3] Encyclopedia Americana, 1832, Vol. X, p. 342.

Howard's first book on prisons appeared almost contemporaneously with the founding of the first prison reform society in America in the republican era, and that his death occurred in 1790, the very year of the opening of the first State prison managed in accordance with a highly humane plan of prison discipline.

Caleb Lownes, William Bradford, and others of the Society of Friends became early acquainted with Howard's views, which were in part summarized by Bradford, and which we have still further summarized below: [4]

Prisons for convicts at labor ought to be in or near a large town or city, and easily accessible to inspection.

Inspection — that is, direction — should not be assumed from any mercenary views, but solely from a sense of duty, and the love of humanity.

Steady, lenient and persuasive measures have always been found the best means of preventing escapes.

The great object of prisons ought to be to reclaim and reform prisoners.

The earnings of the prisoners, from their labor, ought to be a secondary consideration to the State.

Young offenders ought to be separated from older offenders.

Solitary confinement, on coarse diet, should always be the inevitable portion of every old or great offender. But such punishment is best inflicted at intervals, seldom more than 20 or 30 days at a time.

Howard's untiring investigations in England and on the continent brought relatively quick results. In 1779, the English parliament passed an act establishing "penitentiary houses" near London, the objects of which were:

"To seclude the criminals from their former associates; to separate those of whom hopes might be entertained from those who were desperate; to teach them useful trades; to accustom them to habits of industry; to give them religious instruction, and to provide them with a recommendation to the world, and the means of obtaining an honest livelihood after the expiration of the term of their punishment."

It is more than probable that this law was known by 1790 to the Pennsylvania Quakers, and that it was a material guide in the establishing of the first State prison of Pennsylvania. Moreover, we find in Howard's "Account of the Principal Lazarettos in Europe," published in London in 1789, the following analysis of the receptivity of desperate convicts to humane methods, which must have struck a most responsive chord in the hearts of such men as Lownes and Bradford:

"There is a mode of managing some of the most desperate convicts with ease to yourself, and advantage to them. Many such are shrewd and sensible. Let them be managed with calmness, yet with steadiness. Show them that you have humanity, and that you are to make them useful members of society; and let them see and hear the rules and orders of the prison, that they may be convinced that they are not defrauded in their provisions or clothes, by contractors or jailors.

"When they are sick, let them be treated with tenderness. Such conduct would prevent mutiny in prisons, and attempts to escape; which I am fully persuaded are often owing to prisoners being made desperate, by the profaneness, inhumanity and ill usage of their keepers." [5]

There were, apparently, rather close relations between the Philadelphia Society and John Howard. On January 14, 1788, the

---

[4] Bradford. Enquiry.
[5] Howard. Account, etc., p. 222.

Society wrote to Howard, sending him a copy of their constitution, and asking communications from Howard on the designs of the Society. . . . Howard expressed himself in one of his public works to the effect that he wanted in England a Society like that of Philadelphia, and that he would subscribe £500 to it, if other annuities were obtained.

An illuminating statement was made some thirty years later, in 1821, by a Vermont lawyer, Daniel Chipman, relative to the reform movement of the period we are now considering:[6]

"The penitentiary system was introduced into the United States when there was a rage for improvement. It was supposed by many, that the world, or rather some individuals, had been suddenly enlightened; that the dictates of experience were only so many more obstacles to the perfectibility of human nature, of which they talked so much, and to which they really believed they had arrived; and that they could, by a mighty effort, bring the darkened and lagging world up to their own elevation. . . .

"The projectors of the penitentiary system were peculiarly exposed to an enthusiasm which led them to expect beneficial effects, which could never be realized. Every feeling of humanity was enlisted — it was so pleasant and satisfying, to think not only of saving the life of the offender, but of reforming him, and restoring him to society a useful member. It was also calculated that the punishment would strike a dread upon the vicious, equal to an ignominious death upon the scaffold''.

Now, Daniel Chipman wrote the above lines when the first prison system, undertaken in high philanthropic enthusiasm, had broken down deplorably, and when there was actual and serious thought of reverting by law and by practice to the old sanguinary and capital punishments once more. He wrote:

"This day of enthusiasm (above described) has passed away, and we find ourselves in the position in which imperfect man has ever been; knowing but very little which it is useful to know, but what was known before; and indeed, it requires labor to keep the stock good, if I may so say, and transmit as much to posterity as we might learn from those who have gone before us''.

Yet, in the pessimistic reasoning of the "hard-headed" New Englander from the Green Mountains, writing almost in phrases that to-day can still be frequently heard, there was at least a partial fallacy. We shall very likely come to believe, as we pursue this study, that the early penal philosophy of the Philadelphia group was "before its time," and consequently could not last, but we shall also see that it was not solely the enthusiasm or the visionary nature of the early reformers, or their belief in the perfectibility of human nature that brought about the collapse of the first prison system. Failure came quickly enough from the combination of a number of causes, among which were politics, the withdrawal of the originators of the movement from further active participation in its continuance, and above all, from the fundamental error with which the system started, namely, the physical impossibility of meeting with adequate separation and classification of individuals the increasing population of the prison. Architectural blunders, inherent in the housing provisions of the Walnut Street Prison, made inevitable the break-down and the final disgrace attendant upon the first attempt to rationalize and humanize the treatment of convicts.

---

[6] Report on the Penitentiary System. Appendix, p. 64.

Yet, before that period arrived, with the turn of the century, we find the prison presenting an example most surprising to visitors. Turnbull, an interesting reporter of his own observations, discovered that some of the convicts even developed a real liking for their keepers, which he said was as surprising to him as that there should be crocodiles in Greenland.[7]

A striking manifestation of a primitive form of honor system was recorded in 1793, when on the occasion of an epidemic of yellow fever, a number of convicts responded to the call for volunteers to fill the places of attendants at the Bush Hill Hospital. They acquitted themselves well, none leaving the hospital until all were ready to go back to the prison, when the need of further service was past. One of the convicts subsequently married an attendant whom he met at the hospital. Another convict, imprisoned for robbery, was employed in the transportation of provisions from the city to the hospital, returning ultimately to prison, after excellent services. He finally received a pardon.[9]

A variant of this tale, given by William Roscoe in 1819,[10] in his "Observations on Penal Jurisprudence," was as follows:

"At the time of the yellow fever at Philadelphia in 1793, great difficulty was found in obtaining nurses for the sick at Bush Hill Hospital. Recourse was had to the prison; as many of the female convicts offered as were wanted; they continued faithful until the dreadful scene was closed. In another instance, when request was made to them to give up their bedsteads for the use of the sick at the hospital, they cheerfully offered even their bedding etc. When a similar request was made to the debtors, they all refused."

In this same period of the prison, we find a trace of primitive self-government, developed by the convicts, who established rules for their more harmonious living with each other:

"One of their principal regulations relative to cleanliness was that no one should spit elsewhere than in the chimney. The punishment was simply an exclusion of the convict from the society of his fellow convicts; and this is found to be sufficient."[8]

A century and a quarter later, at Auburn and Sing Sing Prisons, the self-governing Mutual Welfare League, composed of prisoners, employed somewhat similar ostracism as their chief form of punishment. And, just as in the most modern days it has been found that participation of the prisoners in their own government has in the main resulted in decreased necessity for watchfulness by guards, so in the Walnut Street Prison. In 1794 the Duc de La Rochefoucauld-Liancourt discovered that 280 convicts were governed by only 4 officers, the women prisoners being under the control of a woman.[11]

"To be told that a turnkey would be beloved by criminals would have been as much believed as that Reynard would be attached to a hound. I have been in a prison (Walnut Street) where the heart of the turnkey is like that of another man, and where humanity is the standing order of the day."[15]

[7] Turnbull, p. 35.
[8] Turnbull, p. 30.
[9] Buxton quoted in notes sur les Prisons de la Suisse, by Francis Cunningham. Génève, 1828, p. 153.
[10] Roscoe. Observations on Penal Jurisprudence, London, 1819, p. 57, footnote.
[11] La Rochefoucauld-Liancourt.
[15] Turnbull, p. 35.

The health of the convicts was excellent. The physician's annual bill, which before the new system has been $1,280 a year — a sum suggestive of the ancient possibilities of "honest graft"— seldom exceeded under the new regime $160 a year.[13] The convicts' food was held to be adequate. For breakfast and supper a pudding of maize and molasses was served. Dinner consisted of one-half pound of meat, vegetables and one-half pound of bread.[12]

What were the general results of this first prison system, in its period of rise and greatest efficiency, from 1790 to 1800? Summarizing the analysis of an early critic, in the Encyclopaedia Americana of 1832:[14]

It saved the lives of many who otherwise would have suffered capital punishment.

It saved many prisoners from the infliction of gross and unwise corporal punishment.

The new system was much dreaded by the prisoners, and for a few years it seems to have reduced crime materially, and also the number of commitments to prison.

The labor of the prisoners relieved the State of a considerable portion of the expense of maintaining the prison.

Many men, formerly lost to society, were made useful and were trained to work.

It set an advanced standard of prison discipline.

That this radical attempt at the amelioration of the conditions of prisoners should receive criticism was to be expected. Incredulity was expressed at the time as to the truth of the amazing statements emanating from the friends of the new system. It was alleged, among other things, that the convicts at Philadelphia had been forcibly tamed into going through their routine like dumb wild beasts. But to this, La Rochefoucauld-Liancourt replied:[16]

"Recall Doctor Hunter of York, in England, who of all other physicians has cured most lunatics, by striking off their chains, and leading them back by gentleness and reason. No one needs to be shocked by the comparison of fool and criminal."

---

[12] La Rochefoucauld-Liancourt.
[13] Turnbull, p. 30.
[14] Encyclopedia Americana, Vol. X, 1832, p. 342.
[16] Voyage, p. 43.

CHAPTER V

THE BREAKDOWN

By the year 1800 there was apparent an ominous relaxation of discipline within the Philadelphia prison. The prison society warned against any abatement of any part of the period of solitary confinement, and against increasing the hitherto infrequent attempts of the board of managers to secure pardons for deserving prisoners.[1]

These warnings deserve our attention. The Friends introduced rigid severity into the prison for those who had forfeited the right to benevolent clemency. Just as mildness was to be a persuasive factor in the reform of the budding criminal, so was a drastic solitary confinement to deter by its rigors the dense and calloused malefactor from further crime. These two extreme methods were thus employed to achieve the same end, the further cessation of criminal acts.

At the very outset of the new methods, pardons had been promised, as something to be hoped for in return for good labor and good conduct. Thus was the ground laid for what has always been one of the grievous abuses, and one of the most ready temptations to the breakdown of morale, in American prison administration. Freedom is the constant craving of the prisoner. The "intellectual" and the illiterate will both affirm that it is primarily the loss of liberty that is the chief punishment of the prison sentence. And, since the prisoner's mind is ever centered on the day when he is to come out, the pardon — and in later years the parole — have been constant inducements, or constant possible means, to stimulating the inmate to hard work and good behavior.

Yet in the granting of pardon, as an act of grace and not of justice, there lies inherent the great possibilities of apparent favoritism. The fortunate man was lucky — the one who did not get a pardon was discriminated against, in the opinion of the disappointed. Politics could "get" to the governor of the State, for it was only by the governor that a pardon could be given. And in the first century of our American prison systems, when as yet the indeterminate sentence had not placed upon the prisoner a considerable responsibility for his own release from prison through his own good conduct and good work, it was the governor's pardon, that was the only means of earlier emergence from the bastile-like prison.

Hence the abuse of the pardoning power was to become flagrant in many States. A reasonable incentive when sparingly used, and when grounded in justice and legitimate mercy, pardons became only too often a sop to the discouraged convicts, a method of achieving outward order in the prison by easy means, and they

---

[1] Vaux, pp. 31ff.

were fundamentally a body-blow at the efficacy of the penal law, which prescribed a definite duration of sentence, only to be vitiated by the interposition of the pardoning power, often within a space of time that tended to make the sentence, the courts and the purposes of the prison appear absurd. The strength of the pardoning power lay in its opportunity to provide an incentive to prisoners to behave and to work. The weakness of the pardoning power lay in its ready and tempting abuse.

The chief cause of the ultimate demoralization of the Walnut Street Prison system lay, however, in the increasingly crowded condition of the institution. Persistent increase of commitments to the prison broke the system down. Much of the success of the system lay in the personal attention that could be given to prisoners by humanely minded officers. This was possible in a prison of small numbers. But, whereas in 1793 the commitments to the prison had been but 43, in 1801 the commitments had risen to approximately 150, with no increased accommodations in shops or cells. Moreover, this prison was the sole place of confinement in the entire State for convicts. In addition, the substitution of solitary confinement for the death penalty was increasing not only the number of commitments to the prison, but also, naturally, was increasing the number of prisoners in the institution, because many of the terms of the prisoners were long.[2]

Moreover, the number of "vagrants" was increasing. There was also much more crime, apparently, in the city than in the early years of the prison. Probably the institution was no longer an object of alarm among the criminals "on the outside." Familiarity had bred contempt. The natural growth of the city and State population was bringing its proportional increase to the prison. A larger jail population meant increased administrative difficulties, both in lodging the prisoners and in working them. Silence and good order, at the prescribed hours, could be preserved only with greater difficulty. The natural tendency of the administration was to relax, and then to allow the discipline to slump. The expenses of the prison increased, both through the numerical increase in population, and because the consequent labor output was hindered by inmate congestion. Labor became less productive. Arrangements for the disposal of the manufactured product were less readily made. There was an outbreak of jail fever in 1802. There must be additional buildings, or a new prison. Even the present buildings were of faulty construction.

The violent political strife in the city had its effect upon the personnel and the morale of the board of managers of the prison. Party politics led to the replacement, by other persons, of the original Quakers upon the board. The Philadelphia Society for Alleviating the Miseries of Public Prisons became gradually no longer an intimate co-operator with the prison board of managers, but an organization of protest and of opposition, as the policies

---

[2] Vaux, p. 31ff.

of the prison changed.³ Undoubtedly, the personal devotion of the early members of the board ceased to control the affairs of the institution.

Some physical alleviation came, for a time, when the Bridewell was built, on Mulberry and Broad streets.⁴ To this institution were sent henceforth those lesser offenders whom we to-day classify as misdemeanants, or as violators of local ordinances. Nevertheless, the Walnut Street Prison continued to be congested with felons, for from 1807 on, the convict population increased out of all proportion to the increase of the State's population. The methods of the government of the prison underwent many changes. Shifting of managers and officers was frequent. Laxity, favoritism, and politics continued. Responsibility for administration was divided. The labor of the prisoners was increasingly exploited to the detriment of the possibilities of reformation.

The former rigorous system of seclusion of the more hardened prisoners was relaxed or abandoned. The frequent recommendations of the boards of managers for the pardon of prisoners became a serious abuse, and those who had been judicially committed to suffer the greatest punishment generally gained ultimately a pardon. Convicts were discharged from the prison without money or friends, and in many instances soon followed the line of least resistance, or of actual temptation, and reverted to crime.¹⁰ Of 451 convicts in the Walnut Street Prison in January, 1817, 162 had been previously convicted or pardoned.

It was a time of increasing discouragement for the friends of a reformed prison discipline, but they were not shaken in their belief as to the validity of the principles they had espoused. By 1817, the Philadelphia Society was forced to announce that the demoralization of the now famous system had proceeded so far that 10 to 40 prisoners were lodged in rooms 18 feet square, and that the prison had already begun to assume the character of a European prison, and that instead of being longer a school of reformation, it was now a seminary of vice.⁵ The solitary cells were wholly abandoned before the year 1820.⁶

In this period the Society's activities took on several broader aspects. There was correspondence with the executives of penitentiaries in other States; also with the London Society for the Improvement of Prison Discipline, relative to the failure of the Walnut Street Prison system. The Society was planning for a house of reformation for juvenile offenders, seeking thus to eliminate them from the prisons where adults were confined — a movement that found its fruition first in New York city in 1824 and in Philadelphia in 1828. The Society also planned an asylum for the temporary employment of convicts discharged from prison or jail without employment, but this movement does not seem to have eventuated in a building.⁹

---

³ Life of Thomas Eddy, p. 204.
⁴ Vaux, p. 39.
⁵ Roscoe's Inquiry. Appendix, p. 23.
⁶ Julius. Sittleche Zusbaende, Vol. II, p. 125.
⁹ Vaux, p. 46.
¹⁰ Vaux, p. 57.

The period, from the standpoint of prison progress, became crucial. The danger of a complete breakdown of humane principles and beneficent legislation was a real one. In this crisis, the Prison Society urged, in 1818, that there be erected in the State two penitentiaries, one in the eastern and one in the western part of Pennsylvania. This proposal was adopted by the Legislature of 1818, which authorized the establishment of a new prison in Pittsburg, on a new basis of construction. The plan here adopted became later, in Pennsylvania, of the highest importance and should be especially noted. The prison was to be so designed that not only should *each* prisoner be in solitary confinement during his incarceration, but he should also, throughout his entire prison term, be *without work*.[7] The act of 1818 also authorized the sale of the Walnut Street Prison, and the erection of a new prison in Philadelphia, on the same general plan.

We meet here developing the famous and fearfully drastic principle of *imprisonment in solitude without work,* which, sanctioned by leading philanthropists of the times, shows to what desperate straits of thinking and of penal philosophy the abhorrent disintegration of their first prison system had brought them. It was a leap into an unknown possible method of saving the "cause." To us of to-day there would seem to be hardly a severer punishment than continued solitary confinement without employment, or one more fruitless of good results. Indeed, we should confidently expect degeneracy, insanity and general collapse of the individual to follow in time. We shall see what the actual results were in Pennsylvania. Yet the Philadelphia Society believed that in that direction lay reformatory possibilities.

William Roscoe of Scotland was an attentive student of the development of penal philosophy in the United States and especially in Philadelphia. In his "Additional Observations on Penal Jurisprudence," published in 1823, he gives what may have been the echo of an ingenious argument in favor of solitary confinement without labor: "Since the labor of prisoners is not profitable, there will be no loss but perhaps a gain in keeping them in solitary confinement without labor. And since work diminishes to a very great degree the tediousness of confinement, and thus mitigates the punishment, it may become a question whether work ought not to be abandoned altogether except as an indulgence to the prisoner."[8]

Doctor James Mease, an authority in Philadelphia on prison matters at this period, wrote:

"The only good effect which religious public exercises have on convicts is in keeping them quiet, and inducing them to hope for a mitigation as to the period of confinement, by observing the religious routine prescribed. Reformation is out of the question. They are 'desperately wicked', and there is nothing left for us but to frighten them away from the land, or to send them to distant sections of the globe. Solitary confinement will have the effect first mentioned; whether I shall succeed in persuading any of our legislatures to try transportation remains to be ascertained."[11]

---

[7] Vaux.
[8] Roscoe. Additional Observations on Penal Jurisprudence, 1823.
[11] Roscoe. Body and Appendix.

The fearful conditions in the local prison may well have stampeded them, so to speak, into the adoption of the above standpoint. They were swung into an extreme position by the occurrences in the Walnut Street prison, thus described in a legislative document in 1821:

"There were in confinement, on the first of January, 424 men and 40 women convicts. For want of room to separate them, the young associate with the old offenders; the petty thief becomes the pupil of the highway robber; the beardless boy listens with delight to the well-told tale of daring exploits, of hoary-headed villiany; and from the experience of age derives instruction, which fits him to be a pest and a terror to society. Community of interest and design is excited among them, and instead of reformation, ruin is the general result."

In short, the position relative to prisons was approximately that preceding the first reform developments between 1787 and 1790, except that humane methods had been tried, and by caustic critics might have been cited as one of the causes of breakdown. The pendulum was ready to swing to an opposite extreme. Again the Philadelphia Society felt in duty bound to devise a new system of prison administration.

CHAPTER VI

NEWGATE PRISON IN NEW YORK

In the years 1794 and 1795, Thomas Eddy, a New York philanthropist and Quaker, visited the Walnut Street Prison several times for purposes of study. A prison was being planned for the State of New York. The New York Quakers had heard of the remarkable success of the Philadelphia prison. In the year 1788, thirteen crimes were still punishable by death in New York. Even felonies that for the first offense were punishable by fine, imprisonment or corporal punishment, were, on conviction of a second offense, followed by the death penalty. The capital crimes at the time were:

Treason, murder, rape, sodomy, burglary, robbery, arson, maiming and wounding, forgery, counterfeiting.

Many of these crimes were capital only in certain more serious forms.

Thomas Eddy was often in the later years of his life called the "John Howard of America."[1] He was the dominant figure in the introduction of the humane methods of prison discipline into New York. He was a business man, and a philanthropist who devoted his life, so far as his means would permit, to works of charity. He was, apparently, the first American philanthropist to urge the erection of prisons in which all prisoners should be lodged in separate cells.[2] His vision of a reasonable and humane prison system for New York led him, six years after the establishment of the first State prison in New York, to recommend for the *city* of New York the erection of a prison with a cell for each prisoner. He recommended for each county of the State the establishment of similar prisons. But at the time of urging, and later of designing, the first New York State prison, Eddy had not come to recognize the imperative necessity of providing a separate cell for each prisoner, or of providing for the ultimate serious increase in the prison population, and so the New York prison fell at last into the same deplorable plight as the prison in Walnut street.

"The plan of the present prison (the State Prison) was entirely my own, and though I visited Philadelphia and examined many of Howard's plans and was furnished with several by William W. Pitt, a member of Parliament from Dorchester, of prisons in England, yet a most striking error was committed — it should have contained 500 rooms, 7 feet by 9, to keep the prisoners separate at night."

Eddy was a most diligent student of penal principles. His own philosophy of criminal treatment was based upon Beccaria, Montesquieu, Penn, Howard and other writers.[4] He sought a system of penal treatment that would be both disciplinary and humane.

[1] Life of Thomas Eddy, p. 41.
[2] Same, p. 76.
[4] Same, p. 57.

With European philanthropists he maintained a diligent correspondence, and while receiving the documents sent him in abundance on European charitable and correctional activities, he exchanged persistently American publications with his European friends. Without question, he contributed much in this manner to establish the cross-currents of penological influence between Europe and America that marked the first thirty years of the nineteenth century.

In 1796, Eddy induced General Philip Schuyler, a senator of New York, and Ambrose Spencer to introduce into the Legislature at Albany a bill "for making alterations in the criminal law of the State, and the erecting of State prisons." By the passage of this bill in March, 1796, a radical amelioration of the penal code was effected. Only two capital crimes, murder and treason, were retained.[3, 5] And, as in Philadelphia, so now in New York a prison system must be devised and installed.

With an imitativeness characteristic of the early American States in penal matters, New York adopted almost bodily the Philadelphia system. And, for the first time, a prison was designed "to order," to fit the new penal code and prison discipline.

The building commission and the first board of governors of the prison were composed mainly of Quakers.[6] Indeed, Eddy was said to have built the prison, and he became its first warden. During 1796 and 1797 the State erected on Greenwich street, about two miles from the New York City Hall, and where now, only a block away, the Christopher Street Ferry slip stands, a prison, on the east bank of the Hudson River, which was called Newgate, after the famous London prison. To-day the remains of a brewery occupy the site of the ancient prison. Massive walls surrounded the four acres of prison land. Within these walls rose a building 204 feet long and two stories high. From each end of this edifice there extended at right angles, toward the Hudson, a wing containing rooms for prisoners, and again from each of these wings a further wing, in the same direction, each containing seven solitary cells. Back toward the river, and parallel with the main building, was a two-story structure, 200 feet long, and two stories high, containing the workshops. In the central yard was a substantial vegetable garden. The first prisoners were admitted on November 28, 1797.[8] The prison cost when completed about $200,000.[7]

The chief characteristic of this prison was its 54 rooms, each room measuring 12 by 18 feet, sufficient to accommodate in each case 8 persons.[9] We see in this arrangement the ultimate doom of the prison foreshadowed. Thomas Eddy, writing prophetically even in 1801, said:

"Had the rooms for the prisoners been so constructed as to lodge but one person, the chance of their corrupting each other would have been

---
[3] View of New York State Prisons.
[5] Corporal punishments were prohibited.
[6] Life of Thomas Eddy, p. 19.
[7] Account of the State Prisons.
[8] View of New York State Prisons.
[9] Report of Society for Prevention of Pauperism, p. 19.

diminished, and escapes would have been more difficult. The prison need not, in that case, have been made so strong or so expensive. Absolute reliance ought not to be placed on the strength of any prison. Nothing will probably prevent escapes but the unremitting vigilance of the keepers, and a strict watch day and night.''[10]

Eddy's vision was clear upon two points. Ultimately the discipline of the prison would require the separation of prisoners from each other, and secondly, prisons were safe about in proportion to the success of the methods of prison discipline employed, and not in proportion to the stone and iron of the structure. In 1910, Joseph P. Scott, long the superintendent of Elmira Reformatory, stated to the writer that the weakest prison, structurally, is the strongest, because of the necessity of unremitting vigilance of supervision. And in those prisons that to-day utilize the methods of self-government or of the honor system, the safety of the prison rests less than ever upon structural strength, and more than ever upon the ethical responsibilities of the inmates.

The bulk of the inmate population of the New York Newgate was, therefore, to be lodged in large night-rooms, while only those condemned to separate confinement or under punishment for prison offenses were to occupy the solitary cells. In the large rooms, two persons slept in each bed, an unspeakably demoralizing practice in many institutions.[11] Prisons are under any circumstances the centers of abnormal life, and the proximity of two prisoners, when not under supervision, and not restrained by strong motives of honor, is recognized by intelligent prison executives as predisposing to vice and degradation.

The beds at Newgate were made of tow cloth, stuffed with straw, enclosed in a kind of wooden frame or box that folded up during the day. The living rooms were located on each side of a central corridor. From their iron-grated windows the prisoners gained views of the green fields and of the river. The keeper and his family resided in the central building.

The custom, at this time begun, of thus forcing the chief officer of the prison to be housed at the prison has endured to this day. In the earlier systems of prison discipline, we shall find there were frequent emergencies such as seemingly to require the warden to be constantly on hand to check riots or to enforce discipline. In later days, with the advent of more reformatory measures, the custom of housing the warden and his family at the prison has still endured. Only in most recent times has it been realized that the warden deserves the same opportunity that other officers of the prison have to get away from the prison for a certain number of hours a day. The injustice to the warden's family, and to the warden himself, of enforced constant proximity to the prison atmosphere becomes more apparent, and the emergencies that require the presence of a warden, or control by brute force, become increasingly rare.

The prisoners at Newgate ate their meals in silence in the corridor, or in a dining room, at large tables. We shall see throughout

[10] Account of State Prisons, p. 18.
[11] Account of State Prisons, p. 18.

the nineteenth century almost inflexible adherence to the principle of silence at meals in prison, and, with the advent of the Auburn system from 1823 on, silence at all times when prisoners are in contact with each other. The principle of silence as a penological means of discipline we shall discuss at length in connection with the establishment of the Auburn system of prison management.

Special attention was given in the New York prison to the dietary and to the cost of food, Count Rumford's studies in dietetics being regarded as authoritative. In the light of present food prices, we cannot refrain from citing the three following sample bills of fare at the New York prison in 1800: [12]

BREAKFAST, AUGUST 3RD, 1800

1 peck of rye	$0 25
6½ quarts of molasses	1 02
130 pounds of bread of rye and Indian	1 95
Fuel used in cooking	08
Total for 235 persons	$3 30

DINNER, JULY 28TH, 1800

17 ox hearts	$0 93
7 ox heads	1 09
6 lamb plucks	19
1 peck of potatoes	15
3 pounds of Indian meal	46
3 pounds salt	05
¼th pound pepper	10
110 pounds bread	1 65
Fuel	24
Sundry herbs from garden	00
Total for 225 persons	$4 45

SUPPER, AUGUST 6TH, 1800

36½ pounds Indian meal for mush	$0 54
1 1/12 pound salt	03
61 pounds of bread	91
2 gallons, 3 quarts, and 7 gills molasses	1 79
Fuel	08
Total cost	$3 36

The dietary was changed somewhat from day to day, and according to season. The inspectors took pride in their food experiments, which they regarded as a laboratory contribution to the State's knowledge of dietetics.[13]

We have seen how in Philadelphia the prisoners were employed at the Walnut Street Prison. In every prison there exists the problem of properly employing the inmates. The abolition of capital and sanguinary public punishments suggested inevitably, in connection with imprisonment, the necessity of employing labor as a substitute for the previous pains and tortures. Work, which is what man lives by, has been turned, in prison, into a punishment

---

[12] Account of State Prison, pp. 40-41.
[13] Account of State Prison.

in itself, and distorted often into torture. The sentencing to hard labor has conventionalized the idea of the association of work within prison walls with punishment. Hence the reformative and vocational possibilities of the use of work were barely emphasized, and labor, hard by command of the law, has been from the first assumed to be an integral part of the prison sentence, and therefore not carrying with it any obligation on the part of the State to pay the inmate for what he does. Labor was, in other words, a part of the legitimate sentence of the criminal to prison.

Whatever the prisoner might thus, by his labor, earn for the State would reduce by so much the expenses of the institution. The hours of labor were not a subject of concern to the State. In the free life of the "mechanic," labor from sun-up to sun-down was sufficiently common to cause similar rules within the prison to be considered not only legitimate, but self-evident. The Newgate prison was distinctly in the country, in unsettled territory, and away from whatever police or military protection the city might otherwise offer. Hence, to ward against the danger of outbreaks under cover of the dark, it was not deemed wise or safe to let the prisoners out of their rooms before six in the morning in summer, or before daybreak in winter.

The problem of employing the prisoners at Newgate was beset with difficulties from the first. After four years from the founding of Newgate in 1801, the labor of the inmates had not yet met the expenses of the institution. The first occupation, established two years after the opening of the prison, was the making of boots and shoes, which trade a life prisoner taught the other inmates. Blacksmithing, the cutting of nails, carpentry, weaving, cooperage, and tailoring were other trades, in each of which inmates supervised the work of others. All the linen and woolen cloth and the stockings of the convicts, were manufactured in the prison.[14]

The conditions in determining the occupations pursued were, so far as possible:

Those requiring least capital;
Those productive of profit;
Those most consistent with health of the convicts and the general security of the prison.

A system of crediting and debiting the inmates was introduced on lines similar to the procedure in Walnut Street Prison. On discharge, the prisoner was given his net earnings, if in the opinion of the inspectors he would make good use of the same. Otherwise, the earnings were calmly withheld, an act that surely must have turned the convict out into the world with no gentle thoughts regarding the justice of prison life. Sometimes the payment of earnings was delayed for three months, and the discharged prisoner must at the end of that time bring a certificate from his employer of his industriousness and good conduct. As at Philadelphia, the convict was debited for his clothes, and the expenses of his transportation, and was charged fifteen cents a day for board and lodging.

---

[14] Account of the State Prison.

The method adopted of witholding a portion of the prisoner's earnings, during a post-prison period of proving his good conduct and industry, had an element in it of the later methods of conducting parole, which is the generally accepted term for the period of conditional release after a term of imprisonment, during which period the released inmate is under the supervision of a parole officer, and subject to such regulations as the institution or the duly appointed parole board may set. Parole came into practice in this country with the establishment of the indeterminate sentence and the State reformatories. But, whereas under the parole system, the prisoner released on parole must satisfy the authorities of his good conduct and his industry, it has not been customary to withhold from him any part of his earnings within the prison. Therefore, in the early methods of the New York Newgate, the withheld earnings acted in a way as under the parole system the rules and regulations of the paroling authorities. It tended to keep the released inmate "straight."

The State of New York, by introducing industries into Newgate, went thus into the business of manufacturing for the "open market"— a system which in later years was called the "State Account System." The prison bought the raw materials, made them up by the labor of prisoners, and sold them without the intervention or assistance of contractors or middlemen. The board of directors —"Inspectors"— were empowered to employ the prisoners, and to credit them for their labor, as they might in their discretion decide. A significant law of 1801 provided that boots and shoes made by the convicts must be branded with the words: "State Prison." There lay probably in this legislation the first feeble attempts of the "honest mechanics," whose activities in later years we shall follow in detail, to reduce the newly threatening competition of prison-made goods with those produced by so-called "free labor." In 1804, a further law provided that not more than one-eighth of the convicts should be employed in the making of boots and shoes, excluding women or men who had learned the trade before commitment. This was clearly a move to limit the production of a commodity which could be readily manufactured in prison. The female convicts occupied a separate wing, and were employed at washing, spinning and weaving.

The convicts were garbed in summer in jacket and trousers of brown linen, and in a similar but heavier costume in winter.[16] The convict who had previously served a term in prison wore a garb half red and half blue. It must have early suggested itself that by clothing the convict in a conspicuous and unusual costume, he would be more easily distinguished if he should escape from the prison. This is probably mainly the origin of the marked garb of the convict, and the general adoption later of the stripes, alternately black and white and running on jacket and trousers in a horizontal direction.

The government of the prison was vested in a board of seven inspectors, unsalaried, and appointed by the governor and council.

[16] Account of State Prison, p. 19ff.

Their frequency of meetings, and their methods of visiting the prison, were largely copied from the methods of the Philadelphia board. Certain State officials and ministers of the Gospel having churches or congregations in the neighborhood, were eligible to visit the prison.[15] We note already a certain semi-official authority or legal permission for specific persons not of the prison administration to visit the prisoners. In the earlier years, as in Philadelphia and at Newgate, such permission granted to the Philadelphia Society and to the nearby ministers was primarily for the purpose of spiritual help to the inmates. The idea of an outside body inspecting the work of the prison authorities seemed not thus early to be planned, although later the various prison associations and prisoners' aid organizations secured in some instances the power of inspection and of reporting to the legislature on the conditions of prisons, as in the case of the Prison Association of New York, founded in 1844. We shall find in the State prison at Auburn in the late twenties of the nineteenth century, the question arising in marked degree as to the relation of the prison visitor, the clergyman, to the warden and to the administration of the prison.

The chief officer of the prison was the agent, who served as financial and industrial manager. He received a salary of $1,500. The second in command was the principal keeper (a name that has survived in many prisons to-day, shortened in the prison vocabulary to "P. K."), who had charge of the general discipline and routine of the institution. Under him were the assistant keepers. The salary of the principal keeper was $875, including his board and the necessary apartments for himself and family.[17]

One deputy keeper received about $400 a year; the assistant keepers $250, with diet, lodging and washing.[17]

By 1815 the salary of the agent (warden) had been advanced to $2,000. The principal keeper still received $875, and the additional perquisites; the deputy keeper received $600, and the assistant keepers $365, with meals, lodging and washing. The clerks received $600.[18]

Apparently it was at first intended that the principal keeper should command the prison discipline — an office that ultimately fell to the warden of all prisons. Here were the attributes that Thomas Eddy stated a principal keeper should possess — a list that to-day would qualify the fortunate possessor for positions paying much more than do many present-day wardenships:

"A keeper should be a person of sound understanding, quick discernment, and ready apprehension; of a temper cool, equable, and dispassionate; with a heart warmed with the feelings of benevolence, but firm and resolute; of manners dignified and commanding, yet mild and conciliating; a lover of temperance, decency and order; neither resentful, talkative, nor familiar; but patient, persevering and discrete in all his conduct.

"While the unhappy wretches committed to his care and subjected to his power are regarded as susceptible of being influenced by their fellow men, and capable of reformation, he should never treat them with harshness, cruelty or caprice, nor thwart or irritate them in trivial matters; but on all

---
[15] Account of State Prison, p. 19ff.
[17] Account of the State Prison.
[18] View of the State Prison.

occasions, while he makes himself feared, he should by a mild and temperate behaviour, by visiting the sick, inquiring into their wants, and occasionally supplying them with little comforts, and speaking kindly to those at work, endeavor to gain their affection and respect.

"Though, in order that he may be on his guard against their machinations, he should consider them as wicked and depraved, capable of every atrocity, and ever plotting some means of violence and escape; yet he should always be convinced of the possibility of their amendment, and exert himself in every way to promote it; . . . In the infliction of punishment he should be calm and inflexible without anger, so that he may convince the offender that he acts, not from passion or vengeance, but from justice."[19]

We see here Thomas Eddy laying down the first standards for a new profession, that of the executive officer of a new kind of institution, a prison, and undoubtedly outlining in summarized form his own efforts as warden of the institution to deal justly and humanely with the inmates in his charge. These are specifications for a warden who would govern his prison mainly through personality. No warden with the above attributes could act comfortably within the limits set by hard and fast rules, nor would he establish a routine. Breadth of vision, ingenuity, high-mindedness and persevering charity characterize this list of human attributes presented by Thomas Eddy. And to-day, in the frequent discussion in conventions and conferences like the American Prison Association and the National Conference on Social Work, we find insistent stress still upon the commanding role of "personality" in the management of correctional institutions. Only as late as 1920 did Dr. Katharine Bement Davis, long the superintendent of the New York State Reformatory for Women at Bedford Hills, and with ripe experience in all phases of work with women offenders, state publicly that practically the only permanent reformations that she had observed in the course of her professional career had come from the influence of a dominant personality upon an inmate.

As in Philadelphia, so at New York, the effort was made by the first board of managers to bar from the prison all corporal punishments, nor were arms allowed. The keepers must bar profanity among themselves, and be gentlemanly. The punishment of the inmates was not to be physical, but by means of solitary confinement. Differing from the practice in Pennsylvania, in New York the judges did not — though the law permitted it — commit the convicted offender to solitary confinement as a part of his sentence. The solitary cells were used, therefore, as punishment for infractions of prison rules. As an inducement to good conduct within the prison, well-behaved inmates might see their wives and connections once in three months.[20]

There was a hospital ward, with an attending physician, at an annual salary of $200. His assistant, called "apothecary," received only board and lodging. Prisoners acted as nurses. There was a chapel seating 600, but up to 1801 there was no chaplain, divine service being conducted on the Sabbath by ministers from the outside.

---

[19] Account of State Prison, p. 25.
[20] Account of State Prison.

The law of 1796 not only made two crimes alone capital, namely, treason and murder, but it also made punishable by life imprisonment, with the additional penalty of hard labor, or solitude, or both, those crimes formerly designated as capital offenses. Fourteen years was the maximum term for all first offenses above the grade of petty larceny. For a second offense in these crimes, the penalty was increased to imprisonment for life, with hard labor or solitude. Lesser offenses were visited by imprisonment not less than one year, or, for second offenses, up to three years.

An escaped prisoner, if recaptured, must undergo twice the period of imprisonment specified for the original sentence. An escaped prisoner, who on the original commitment had been sentenced to life imprisonment, and who was again convicted of any crime above petty larceny, was to receive the death penalty.

To us of to-day, such long sentences will seem often out of all proportion severe and unjust. But we must realize that they represented the first rupture, in a new republic, with a relatively general use of torture and capital punishment for similar offenses. It was coming to be conceded, in an age that proclaimed all men to be born free and equal, that even the most wicked and despicable had certain elementary rights to life, ultimate liberty, and a mild chance to be happy, and that there rested on the State an actual obligation to amend the criminal as well as to punish him. The State constitutions of New Hampshire and Illinois, for instance, recognized this obligation.

It is important for us to understand what "reformation" implied, in this early period of devoted effort to reform, when possible, the convict. It meant primarily a religious and spiritual conversion within the prison house. This mundane life was but the threshold to either heaven or hell. If criminals were to be saved, impressive, and when necessary stern, means were essential. Far better to simulate by means of a rigid but just prison discipline and environment, for the purpose of redemption, even some of the impending tortures of the next world, than to introduce and tolerate a leniency in prison discipline that would lead to the mutual corruption of prisoners and to the destruction of their souls.

Therefore, it was strongly believed that within these living tombs, where silence and solitude should prevail, and where a stern and unbroken routine should weigh impressively upon the prisoner, he would thus be delivered over to reflection, remorse and perhaps to repentance and ultimate reformation. With such methods of mental and spiritual persuasion could be combined that arduous and persistent, soul-mortifying labor that should teach daily the Biblical injunction that man must earn his bread by the sweat of his brow. In short, whatever punishments might be visited upon the guilty convict would be for his own ultimate good and the salvation of his soul.

It must be remembered that the wickedness and the evil supposed to be lodged in the prisoner were far more keenly sensed, far more unquestioningly believed in, than is the case to-day. There was a sharp cleavage in the public mind between the good and the bad.

There was little sense or theory of "relativity" in morals in those days. If the good citizen was one of the elect, the criminal on the other hand was in imminent danger of becoming one of the damned. If the severe tortures, the mutilation and the deaths of previous days were now to be abandoned as salutary agencies, not only for the protection of society, but for the ultimate well-being of the criminal himself, there must be devised adequate and intimidating substitutes. And for a community that believed inflexibly in the existence of a state in the hereafter of everlasting torture for evil done in this world, and unrepented of, it was surely not difficult to concede and even argue the propriety and necessity of severe punishments in prison for evil done in defiance of law.

Even if revenge was no longer to be the aim of punishment, the prisoner's amendment was not the only thing to be considered. Beccaria had recently written that penalties must not be arbitrary but precise and just, fitting the crime. The human mind strives ever to achieve a just ratio between crime and its punishment. W. S. Gilbert interpolated even in light opera the same striving, for in the Mikado's kingdom:

> "My purpose all sublime
> I shall achieve in time,
> To make the punishment fit the crime,
> The punishment fit the crime!"

So, with the philosophical Beccaria of the late eighteenth century, grievous crimes must be attended by grievous penalties. Above all, the punishments must follow the offense *with certainty*. It was not the severity, but the certainty of the punishment that would reduce crime and deter criminals.

Furthermore, the criminals of the time were not regarded as of a class to warrant much consideration. The public thought of them in terms of the poor wretches or horrible malefactors whom they had seen exhibited in the places of public punishment. Moreover, what was at the time analyzed as the "scum of Europe" was furnishing a high percentage, perhaps a fourth, of the prison population; vagrants and strangers from other States were giving a like fourth. The colored race gave to the earliest prisons a proportion of inmates many times greater than its proportion in the general population of the States. Only with the Revolution had England ceased to send white convicts to America. Slavery was still, of course, an institution in many States.

It is not difficult, therefore, to understand the humanitarian zeal of men like Caleb Lownes and Thomas Eddy. The prison reformers of this early period were constantly dominated by ardent, stern and sombre religious convictions, and their efforts were in the last analysis religious and missionary, rather than social and ethical alone.

On the other hand, close association with prisoners led these thoughtful men to appreciate the powerful influences of social and economic conditions in forming character and in contributing to individual downfall. Gradually, out of the hour of these prison populations, and out of the early hypotheses of total depravity and individual responsibilty, came at last the value realization, at least, of the power of social, industrial and mental factors in leading men into prison.

And so, a quarter century later, in 1824, only a few years before his death, Thomas Eddy wrote that the great error of all governments had been in not affording instruction to the lower class of society, and in inflicting punishments often very disproportionate to offenses.[21] The absolutely arbitrary injustice of the penal code was abhorrent to him, whereby the difference between grand and petty larceny — and of a consequent sentence for years to a State prison, or a far shorter sentence to the Bridewell — depended upon whether there was *less* than $25 or *more* than $25 in the purse that was stolen — the criminal knowing nothing as to the exact amount in the purse, and having the same purpose of theft, whatever the amount might be. So Eddy pleaded for varying sentences, and the practice of wide discretion by the judge.[22]

As early as 1801, in his "Account of the State Prison," Eddy laid down the principle that there were three things to be considered, in the endeavor to attain the end of human punishment, namely, the prevention of crime:

Amendment of the offender;
Deterrence of others from crime;
Reparation to society and to the party injured.

The first aim he regarded as the highest in importance. Justice, not revenge, was the true foundation of the right to punish.

Eddy found three classes of criminals in prison:

Men grown old in profligacy and violence, unfeeling and desperate offenders, who show no signs of contrition, and yield little hope of amendment;
Those who in early life have received a moral and religious training, and though afterwards led by passion and evil example, still retain some sense of virtue;
First offenders.

The most efficacious means of reformation Eddy found in regular labor and exact temperance. One-tenth part of the criminal population Eddy regarded as depraved and hardened, and so about 22 of the most obdurate criminals were separated from the others and worked in separate apartments, from which they could not emerge, and where they were constantly watched by keepers.

Let us return to some details of the early Newgate prison. While Eddy was warden, he published, in 1801, an "Account of the State Prison." At this time, the beginning of the ultimate catastrophe was not yet visible. To the meritorious convicts, the three R's were being taught in the winter, and the educated convicts acted as instructors. To enter the class taught by a certain keeper, an over-stint of work amounting to four shillings in value must have been done during the week. Religious and moral instruction was furnished.

---

[21] Life of Thomas Eddy, p. 82.
[22] Same, p. 87.

The opening of the penitentiary in New York was not followed by any diminution in crime. Rather was there an increase, which Eddy attributed, not to the reduction of severe penalties, but to the rapid growth of New York's population and wealth, with its attendant luxury, and its corruption of manners, and to the great number of indigent and vicious emigrants from Europe and from the West Indies.[23]

From 1797 to 1801 there were received. into the prison 693 convicts:[24]

	Males	Females
Whites	469	44
Colored	145	35
	614	79

Of these, there were 290 "foreigners," the chief countries represented being:

Ireland	117	Germany	18
England	49	Africa	18
West Indies	49		

The so-called foreign population was, therefore, 42 per cent. of the total commitments, and the colored inmates far exceeded the proportionate number of colored population in the State.

In all periods, those engaged in prison administration and in the treatment of the delinquent have sought the causes of crime. Generally, the findings have been limited to certain conspicuous factors, which often have been after all only the results of antecedent conditions, and therefore not the causes themselves. Comprehensive studies of causes we have not found in this period. Eddy attributed to three causes in particular the development of crime (causes which in each instance were only manifestations of the quest of pleasure):

Intoxication.
Horse Racing.
Animal Baiting.

The multiplicity of dram shops and taverns aroused in particular Eddy's ire. He felt that reformation would be a long process, and not reasonably to be expected in less than four or five years. Therefore he held that no pardons should be allowed in less than from four to five years after commitment — and in the case of life prisoners, in not less than seven years.

Thomas Eddy thus early put his finger upon one of the chief causes for the continuance of crime. If crime is to be reduced, its inciting causes must be reduced. We have already spoken, in connection with the Walnut Street Prison, of the effects of the abuse of the pardoning power. In New York, even in the first four years, from 1797 to 1801, 27 of the outgoing population of

---

[23] Account of State Prison, p. 58.
[24] Same, p. 79.

Newgate had been pardoned. The sentences of the convicts during this same period show how inevitable were to become both congestion and the consequent free use of pardons:

Sentences to Newgate Prison, 1797-1801

Life	77	2 years 6 months	4
14 years	6	2 years	65
12 years	1	1 year 6 months	5
10 years	4	1 year 1 day	22
7 years	19	1 year	14
6 years	4	Less than 1 year	3
5 years	22		
4 years	34	Total	344
3 years	44		

In short, life sentences had been imposed on 23 per cent. of those committed to Newgate Prison, a percentage exceeded only by those committed for two years.[25]

The chief crimes during this period, as indicated by the causes of commitment, were:

Grand larceny (over $12½)	260	Burglary	34
Petty larceny	277	Assault and battery	20
Forgery	66	Horse stealing	15

It was in this early period that the prison industries most nearly paid the expenses of the prison. In 1802 the net earnings were given as $21,874; the disbursements for support and clothing, maintenance of keepers, and transportation of convicts to the prison were $22,357. A contract was entered into with an outside manufacturer for the hiring of the labor of a certain number of inmates on boots and shoes, the work to be done within the prison.[26]

A change in the administration of the prison was quick in coming. As early as 1800, the complexion of the board of managers began to change, through the appointment of new members for political reasons, and the sagacious policies of the Quaker members began to be overruled. In 1803 Thomas Eddy found the position of warden intolerable, and resigned.[27]

Of all causes of failure of American prison administration, politics may perhaps be placed first. A prison requires an upright, humane, intelligent and efficient management, and above all, it needs continuity of tenure for able officials. To those who follow this study of American prisons, the noxious influences of politics will become so often apparent as to seem finally almost universal. The demoralization of the prisons through the spoils system occurred repeatedly. Both in Philadelphia and New York, the very beginnings of the prison reform movement were frustrated, within a few years, by the unintelligent, if not deliberately intentional, appointment of unfit managers.

Thus did the prison, which Thomas Eddy had in large measure built, and in which he had been the first warden, pass from his control. The prison had cost in the original appropriation $208,000. New York lost in Eddy's resignation a valuable man,

---
[25] Account of State Prison.
[26] Report of Inspectors for 1803, p. 1.
[27] Life of Thomas Eddy, p. 19.

one who might, under favorable circumstances, have invested the wardenship of a prison with a dignity and standing that might have had permanent effects later on. For we learn, from "The Historical Discourse of John W. Francis," on November 17, 1857, on a half century's personal reminiscences, that Thomas Eddy was a rare soul:

"He was a philanthropist in the fullest sense of the term, free from all sectional bias . . . associated with the Manumission Society, the New York Hospital, the Free School System, the Society for the Reformation of Juvenile Delinquents, and the most prominent individual to project and organize the Bloomingdale Hospital for the Insane.

"His fiscal integrity afforded a captivating illustration of his Christian belief. His early career in merchandise proved disastrous, and embarrassments to himself and friends for years followed. By the simplicity of his habits and a rigid economy, he was again made whole, when he discharged with fidelity every obligation with interest.

"I always thought that by this one act he had mounted at least a rung or two up Jacob's ladder."

Almost from the first, trouble occurred at times in the matter of discipline. In June, 1799, 50 to 60 men revolted and seized their keepers, and not until the guards opened fire on them with ball cartridge — by which several were wounded though none were killed — was the mutiny quelled. In April, 1803, 40 men broke from the prison into the prison yard, and caused a fire. The keepers killed several inmates during this riot. In May, 1804, a still more dangerous riot occurred. The keepers were locked into the north wing of the building, which was then set on fire. A prisoner who repented of his act released the keepers. There was a building loss of $25,000, and many prisoners escaped.

There were losses now from bad debts, and a loss of $11,000 on the labor of prisoners. "More room!" was the inspectors' plea in 1806. The prison was suffering from the indiscriminate herding of prisoners in the Bridewell. In this local institution, which was built on the Common (where now is City Hall Park) in 1775, were confined those convicted of small thefts and petty offenses, and those awaiting trial or conviction. The Bridewell was called "a nursery of criminals for the State prison." It was the jail for New York City.[28]

It was for these prisoners that Eddy urged in 1804 the erection of a new prison, with separate cells for the solitary confinement of each prisoner, for periods not exceeding 30 days for the lesser offenders, and from 60 to 90 days for the more serious offenders. Eddy urged that these inmates of the Bridewell should be kept in perfect solitude, on spare diet, which would be in his opinion a course of treatment severer than confinement for one or two years in the State prison. This plan would also relieve the courts of the necessity of sending convicts to the State prison for less than three years.

Eddy's project was not realized. It was not until 1838 that the Bridewell was torn down — at which time was erected on the site of the Collect Pond on Center street the first "Tombs," so-called

---

[28] Account of State Prison, p. 62.

because of the remarkable Egyptian architecture. In the "Halls of Justice," as the entire building was called, the local jail occupied a part.

Eddy's plan is historically of great interest, because it seems to have been the earliest project, in the North Atlantic States, for a prison that should be operated entirely on the principle of separate confinement without labor. Eddy meant that the punishment should be quick, severe, forbidding, and soon ended. But the city of New York refused to meet the total expense of such a structure, which the State desired to load upon the city, and so the project fell through. When, a score of years later, solitary confinement without labor was tried out in Auburn Prison and at the Western Penitentiary of Pennsylvania, it was found to be cruel and impracticable.

By the year 1808, the pardon evil had obtained large sway at Newgate in New York. Necessity was pleaded as the reason for the regular practice of granting pardons to a sufficient number of convicts to make the total number of discharges equal to the commitments within the same period to the State prison. And this vicious custom continued regularly from this time on.

An outgrowth of this oppressive congestion was the suggestion of the board of inspectors in 1809, for the first time, that a second prison be built, somewhere in the interior of the State. It had been originally intended, by the law of 1796, to provide for two State prisons, of which one was to be located at Albany. But the plan was abandoned, and the entire appropriation made available for the State prison which was erected in Greenwich.

By 1814, citizens of New York had become greatly alarmed, because groups of forty or fifty of the "best" prisoners were being pardoned on the occasion of the semi-annual visits of the judges to the prison, and were let loose at the same time upon the community.[30] The evils arising from the pardoning power, as we have said, lay in the *abuse* and not in the *use* of this means of grace:

"A penitentiary", wrote William Roscoe in 1819[31] concerning the failure of the earliest system of American prison discipline, "where penitence is of no avail, is a solecism; . . .if the principle of pardon were abolished, these establishments would be no longer places of reformation, but places of punishment. The extension of pardon to penitent and reformed criminals is not only an act of strict and unalterable justice, but is essentially necessary to the very nature of a penitentiary."

The commissioners who in 1817 studied the Massachusetts State prison saw also the necessity of a judicious exercise of the pardoning power, and stated that

"if it were understood by the convicts that they could free themselves from confinement only by their industry, and that their return to society would depend wholly upon their own exertions, a new spirit would prevail among them, which would ensure the performance of their assigned tasks."[32]

"The most notorious felons," said the Report of the Society for Preventing Pauperism in 1822,[29] "have again and again been

---
[29] Report of Society for Prevention of Pauperism, p. 16.
[30] Report on Penitentiary System of United States, by Hopkins, p. 94.
[31] Roscoe. Observations, p. 106.
[32] Report of Commissioners to Massachusetts Legislature, 1817.

pardoned from our penitentiaries, while the young and inexperienced culprits, for committing crimes of comparatively petty magnitude, are kept in for years.''

The report indicated that in a certain five years, 740 convicts were pardoned, and only 77 through expiration of sentence. Of 23 convicts convicted of second and third offenses in 1815, 20 had been previously pardoned, and only 3 had been discharged at the expiration of sentence.

Quoting Sir James McIntosh in the British House of Commons about the year 1819, the report said:

"One pardon contributes more to excite the hope of escape than 20 executions to produce the fear of punishment."

At this time, the additional expense of a military guard at the prison should be mentioned. For many years, to keep order and to prevent riots and escapes, in a region considerably outside the city, a captain, two corporals, a drummer and a fifer, and some twenty privates were employed, at an annual expense of about $8,500.[33]

By 1815, the garb of the convicts had been changed, and we find the first mention of stripes. In winter the convict costume consisted of a jacket and trousers of striped woolen, and in summer of striped cotton and linen. Second-termers (those who had already served a term in prison) wore a garb with one side of the jacket and trousers brown; third termers wore a tri-colored cap of blue, red and white with the numeral "3" in front.

To-day the ignominious stripes and the parti-colored or motley uniforms have been in general abolished throughout this country in the State institutions of the north. The additional humiliation of stripes has been abandoned. "Stripes burn into your flesh through the cloth," said a prisoner many years ago to the writer. In the restoration of the self-respect and self-confidence of the prisoner stripes and humiliating uniforms can play no part. The "prison gray" has become a customary shade for the prison uniform, and the writer, sitting some years ago upon a bench on an inspection of Sing Sing, noted that the garb of an inmate who sat next to him at the time, in conversation, was in shade and in general in texture little different from the suit the writer was wearing. Other forces than the conspicuous and deterrent stripes are to-day employed to inhibit men from escape from prisons.

There were, by 1815, three visiting physicians and one surgeon, serving without compensation. They visited in turn once a week or oftener if necessary. There was a resident physician, who had board and lodging.

A custom that later provoked public criticism, and which led undoubtedly to disorder in the prison, was the rewarding, "to a certain" extent, of the prisoners by giving to the especially industrious inmates a pint of "wholesome beer." The inspectors believed that this bonus stimulated to diligence and exertion.[34]

---
[33] The guards performed the ordinary duties of a guard, on the walls, and in rounds.
[34] View of New York State Prison.

There was a chaplain, the Reverend John Stanford, who supplied the desk once a month. On other Sundays clergy of different denominations preached. There was always good deportment in the prison at the services, and many persons in the vicinity of the prison attended worship at the prison. It was also the chaplain's duty to visit the sick weekly.

In 1815 the warden of the prison proposed a noteworthy improvement in the methods of classification. We are especially concerned, in this study, to discover the origins or early development of theories or methods that later proved their efficacy in American prisons. And we find here the first suggestion of grading prisoners along lines that later in the century became epoch-making, and that led directly to the American reformatory system.

The warden — at this time designated as "Agent" — recommended that, as an incentive to industry, good order, and reformation, a classification be made of the convicts, forming them into three or four classes, selected from among the best behaved prisoners, having reference to their terms of service. No pardon, moreover, should be granted save within the first class of prisoners, except in special instances.

"We will suppose", said the Agent, "that there are seventy in the first class, whose terms of sentence are from three to five years. These men shall be informed that on a continuance of good behaviour, one half of their sentence will be remitted, and they will be entitled to their pardon accordingly; assuring them that particularly favorable circumstances may obtain it sooner, subject, however, to degradation by the board of inspectors."

Furthermore, the agent recommended that there should be given a certificate of "liberation by merit" to those convicts who had during their confinement met the approbation of the board of managers. In the agent's opinion, the grading method would be an inducement to reformation and industry, and would obviate the wholesale discharge of convicts twice a year.[35]

It is recognized, to-day, that the proper classification of prisoners is a *sine qua non* of reasonable and constructive treatment of inmates. We spoke, in the opening paragraphs of this study, of the new receiving and classification prison shortly to be opened in place of the old Sing Sing Prison. To-day the prison physician, the psychologist and the psychiatrist are integral parts of the staff of the "progressive" prison and reformatory. Individual treatment of the inmate is regarded as practically as important in prison as in a hospital. To deal with prisoners in the mass is the sign of unenlightened administration. It is well established that in every prison are found a number of groups of inmates, some insane some feebleminded, some psychopathic, some suffering from disease, and some relatively normal. The prison of to-day is becoming a sifter of these groups, classifying them as to conditions and as to treatment.

Yet this recognition of the widely varying individualities in the prison population is of comparatively recent occurrence. The psychologist and the psychiatrist are still rather novel members of

---

[35] View of New York State Prison, p. 71.

the staff of many a prison. The physician, only a few years ago, was still the general authority on all the physical and mental states of the prison population. "Horse sense," an attribute confidently announced by many a prison warden as present in abundance in his own make-up, was the main basis of administrative judgment.

Returning now to our discussion of the Newgate Prison of New York, we find that the prison inspectors' report for 1815 carried some enlightened prerequisites for any recommendation on their part for a prisoner's pardon. A majority of the inspectors should join in every recommendation for pardon, and they should previously inquire:

> Whether the prisoner was convicted by clear and undoubted testimony.
> Whether the circumstances attending the commission of the crime denoted a greater or less degree of depravity.
> Whether the prisoner had already suffered a punishment sufficient to satisfy society, and to afford a reasonable ground to believe that his release would not diminish the dread of future punishment in him, or inspire the hope of impunity in others.
> Whether in prison he had conducted himself with uniform decency, industry, and sobriety, and had never attempted to violate any of the regulations.
> Whether, from what was known of his temper, character and deportment, it was probable that, if restored to society, he would become a peaceable, honest and industrious citizen.[36]

The above-cited recommendations of the agent and the practical prerequisites for pardon laid down by the board of managers were in some respects a remarkable foreshadowing of the indeterminate sentence and of the later grading of prisoners by classes, with eligibility for parole only after the attainment of a certain standing within the institution. Indeed, even the theory of the "ticket of leave," employed in England in connection with transported convicts, and which gave the chief suggestion for our American system of parole, is foreshadowed in the above "liberation by merit."

Meanwhile the pardon evil was becoming intolerable. Of all convicts committed between 1811 and 1816, for a second or third time, two-thirds had been discharged from their former sentence by pardon.[37] In 1816 and 1817, a total of 573 convicts were pardoned.[38] It was no longer the case of an occasional release by grace. It was a constant procession of outgoing convicts as the newcomers arrived. Clearly, the prison system, from any deterrent standpoint, had wholly broken down. Such a situation could not long continue. The whole administration of prisons was rapidly becoming a civic disgrace.

To add to the problem, between 1815 and 1822, the failure of the prison to succeed as a financial undertaking was still more marked. A very intelligent inmate, writing in 1823 under the title "Inside Out"[39] of his several years' imprisonment in this New York

---
[36] Roscoe. Observations, p. 108.
[37] Report of Massachusetts Commissioners on State Prison, 1817.
[38] Report of Agent of the Mount Pleasant State Prison, No. 92, In Senate, New York, 1834.
[39] "Inside Out, or an Interior View of the New York State Prison." By One Who Knows. New York. James Costigan, 1823.

Newgate, drew a graphic picture of the brutality and misery of the place. Among the punishments prevalent were:

The chaining of inmates to the floor, on their backs, for several consecutive days, with diet of bread and water, in solitary confinement;

The "Sunday Cell", about 5 feet in height, and 3½ feet square, in which a man of ordinary stature could neither stand erect nor lie down;

Blocks and chains;

Flogging.

Solitary confinement for slight offenses.

The inmate writer of "Inside Out" inveighed especially against the brutal callousness and coarse ignorance of the keepers and guards.

We meet in the above list of so-called punishments our first example of the inevitable development within the prison of methods of physical discipline, amounting often to torture. We shall meet constantly the narratives of such infliction of pain, for the maintenance of discipline and for the punishment of those who have disobeyed the prison rules. The prison offered an exceptional chance for the infliction of grave corporal punishments and even torture. The place was behind great walls, ever concealing what was going on; the public had little interest in the prison; there was always the easy excuse that the one punished was unruly, or gravely disobedient, or dangerous, or obstinate. The prison authorities were in the earlier years not supervised by any State authority, and had practically free rein to do their will. The warden and the officers could during most of the twenty-four hours do their own will with the prisoners, unbeknown to the board of managers. The prisoner's word was of little or no weight; the word and asseveration of the warden or other officers was far more potent. The prisoner often realized that to complain to a member of the board of managers of treatment received at the hands of the officers was tantamount to additional and far graver punishment later on by the officers complained against. The prisoners were regarded as most dangerous men; they had forfeited by their crimes the same consideration that men "on the outside" might expect.

Moreover, we are in our study in the period when bodily punishments had taken the place of capital punishment for many offenses. Imprisonment alone seemed no adequate punishment to many an officer and guard. When the prisoner was unruly, or participated in some outbreak, there was little ground for leniency, and much ground for drastic, prompt and persistent punishment. Thus did the prison become a place of dread doings, removed from public gaze and public knowledge, a place of oblivion, where all the power rested in a few hands, and where the mind of the prisoner was ever on escape from the wretched, and often horrible, surroundings.

This degeneration of the prison from the high ideals of Caleb Lownes and Thomas Eddy was so far advanced that about 1820 private indignation meetings of influential citizens began to be held in New York City.

"These meetings were private, because a knowledge of the acts of mischief, as taught in these places (the prisons), could not be communicated to any but good citizens."

In 1822 the State government stepped in with an investigation of Newgate and other prisons. Regarding the New York institution, the report of the State committee stated that it was operating "with alarming frequency to increase, diffuse and extend the arts of vice, and a knowledge of the arts and practices of criminality."[40] The causes of the failure of Newgate prison were summarized as follows:

The overwhelming number of convicts.
Their profligate and abandoned character.
The impossibility of making their labor successful.
Pecuniary embarrassment in the affairs of the prison.
Enormous demands on the public treasury, without the intermission of a year.
New and fruitless endeavors to make labor productive.
The fearful progress of the prisoners in corrupting each other.[41]

It will be noted that while the writer, himself a convict, of "Inside Out" lays some of the blame for the situation upon the callousness and cruelty of the officers of the prison, the State committee's report recognizes no such factor in the disintegration of the prison. To them, congestion, idleness, recidivism and debauchery were spelling the breakdown of the first State prison of New York.

Recidivism — that is, the return of a prisoner for a new crime — has always been one of the most frequent phenomena of all prisons. Convicts committing a second crime within the State in which they have committed their first, are naturally sent again to State prison. They become the "second-termers," the "third-termers," the "repeaters," the "habituals" of the prison statistics. The annual reports of the prison inspectors of Newgate cited as early as 1815, many illustrations, of which the following is typical.[42] It happens to be the record of a woman "repeater," but many examples might be culled similarly of men "repeaters":

CHARLOTTE THOMAS, alias MARGARET DEVIRE.
Admitted, January 28, 1797, for grand larceny. Sentence, 4 years. Pardoned in 3 years, 6 months.
Readmitted, April 14, 1801, for petty larceny. Sentence, 2 years.
Readmitted, June, 1803, for petty larceny. Sentence, 3 years.
Readmitted, August 12, 1806. Two indictments for petty larceny. Sentence, 4 years.
Readmitted, June 19, 1813, for grand larceny. Sentence, 3 years, 1 day.

"Such a prison," wrote William Roscoe in 1819,[43] "is no longer a school for reform, but a receptacle and shelter for acknowledged guilt." Roscoe held the remedy to be in an adequate classification and consequent separation of groups of prisoners from each other. "No delinquent," said Roscoe, "should twice be sent to the same penitentiary, but other measures, perhaps transportation for life, should be adopted."

---
[40] Hopkins, p. 96.
[41] Same, p. 93.
[42] Annual Report for 1815.
[43] Observations, p. 99.

"Liberated felons jeered at the State Prison, and denominated it their 'college'. Many committed crimes for the express purpose of getting back to prison again."[44]

We find the Senate committee in New York, four years after similar action in Pennsylvania, making in New York the same radical and fundamental proposal for a prison administered on the basis of solitary confinement, without any employment of prisoners. There should be a renovation of Newgate prison to this end, and a gradation of punishments. Because of the greater consequent severity of the punishments, in solitary confinement and in enforced idleness, it was maintained that the period of imprisonment could be shortened at the time of sentence. Solitude, silence and darkness, with stinted food, should in the opinion of the Senate committee effect the purpose sought.

A further radical recommendation was that all industries be abandoned. The committee maintained that this would actually reduce the expense of the operation of the prison. With the use of the solitary cells, there would be reduced rations, and so the prisoners would need less, because less active.

To such extremes were the intelligent citizens of New York and Philadelphia driven in their penal theories! Both cities came thus to advocate a system of imprisonment that to us of to-day seems little short of deliberate torture. Yet with both groups of reformers, there was unquestioned sincerity, and a belief that even if an evil, it was the least evil that could be devised, and still insure the maintenance of a prison discipline that would both punish and amend.

The Society for the Prevention of Pauperism had, in 1822, indicted the then existing system, or lack of system, in a graphic description, suitable to close this chapter upon New York's first effort to solve the State prison problem:

"Our prisons (referring to penitentiaries in the several States) are communities by themselves. All the characteristics of social intercourse are presented. The members of these little communities are comfortably clothed, comfortably fed, condemned to moderate labor, and easy tasks, permitted to have their hours of ease and recreation, indulged in talking over their exploits in the paths of guilt, suffered to form new schemes for future execution, and to wear away their term of service, under circumstances calculated to deprive it of every salutary effect".

---

[44] Senate Document 92, 1834, p. 5.

CHAPTER VII

NEWGATE OF CONNECTICUT

On the seventh of December, 1775, George Washington, commanding the American forces, addressed a letter to the "Committee of Safety" at Simsbury, Connecticut, as follows:

"CAMBRIDGE, *Dec.* 7, 1775.

GENTLEMEN.— The prisoners which will be delivered you with this, having been tried by a court martial and deemed to be such flagrant and atrocious villians that they cannot by any means be set at large or confined in any place near this camp, were sentenced to Simsbury, in Connecticut. You will, therefore, be pleased to have them secured in your jail, or in such other manner as to you shall seem necessary, so that they cannot possibly make their escape. The charges of their imprisonment will be at the Continental expense.

I am, etc.,
GEORGE WASHINGTON."

This letter sent certain prisoners of war to one of the most terrible and at the same time one of the most picturesque prisons that we meet in our study of early American prisons. In 1707, a company had been formed in the little hill village of Simsbury, Connecticut, about fifty miles north of New Haven, and some miles west of Hartford, to operate a copper mine. In 1705, a vein of ore had been discovered there. As gold was believed to be not far distant, a company to work it had been quickly formed. The company's vicissitudes do not concern us, but after several companies in turn had sought to make money out of Connecticut copper, the mine was abandoned until 1773, when the Colony of Connecticut made of this strange cavernous property, with its several levels of underground galleries, an underground prison. It was dubbed Newgate, perhaps with the hope that the name would be as terrifying as the prototype in London.

From 1775 to 1783, this Newgate was the national prison of the Continental Government, and from 1790 to 1827 the State prison of Connecticut. During the Revolution it was used in part as a prison for Tories. From the first the prison was a scene of violence, stupid management, escapes, assaults, orgies and demoralization. It was the first State prison we have record of in our study in length of use in this period. It was bought in the beginning and "fortified as a prison" for the sum of $375. In 1827, the newly erected State Prison at Wethersfield superseded this notorious underground institution.

Newgate of Connecticut has no comparative value in our study. It seems to have been little, if at all, affected by the new movement in prison administration in Philadelphia or New York. No reformative influences are narrated by its chief chronicler, Richard

Phelps. Taking Phelps' record at its face value, it would be hard to find adjectives sufficiently graphic to describe conditions in this prison. The old mine was forever a makeshift prison.

The entrance to these dungeons, as described by Charles Burr Todd in 1881, is by a perpendicular shaft fifty feet deep, "whose yawning mouth is still covered by the guardhouse standing in the center of the prison yard. To one of its sides is affixed a wooden ladder, down which the visitor must climb to reach the dungeons below."

"At the bottom of the shaft, a flight of stone steps leads down thirty or forty feet farther to a central chamber, which contained the sleeping apartments of the convicts. On one side a narrow passage leads down to a well of pure water, above which an air shaft pierces the sandstone for seventy feet until it reaches the surface and admits a few cheering rays of light into the dungeon. Everywhere else a cimmerian darkness prevails.

These caverns may be briefly described as comprising three parallel galleries in the heart of the mountain, extending 800 feet north and south, and connected by numerous cross passages cut to facilitate communication, while lateral galleries honeycomb the mountain on either side. The lowest depth reached is three hundred feet. The galleries are cut through the solid rock, and are low and narrow, except in the case of the chamber above mentioned. Their floors are covered with a soft adhesive slime, and in some places with water, which drips unceasingly from the roof, and the intense darkness and noxious gases which prevail make their passage difficult, though not impossible. Besides the main shaft there are other means of exit from the dungeons — two air shafts, both of which open in the prison yard, and a level or drain leading from the northeast gallery, and having its outlet without the prison wall."

In 1773, Connecticut passed an act directing that male prisoners not under sentence for capital crimes should be imprisoned in the mines. A keeper, Captain John Viets, was appointed. Burglary, robbery and counterfeiting were punished, the first offense by imprisonment not exceeding ten years, the second offense by imprisonment for life. Punishment which might be inflicted upon the convicts was moderate whipping, not exceeding ten stripes, and putting shackles and fetters upon them; the keeper was also instructed to employ them at labor in the mines.

Wooden buildings were more than once constructed at the mouths of the shafts, only to be burned by the prisoners. When the convict band emerged from their caverns and into daylight in the mornings, their appearance seemed like the "belching from the bottomless pit."

The prison was thus described by Phelps, who saw it in its later days:

"The horrid gloom of this dungeon can be realized only by those who pass along its solitary windings. The impenetrable vastness supporting the awful mass above, impending as if ready to crush one to atoms; the dripping water trickling like tears from its sides; the unearthly echoes responding to the voice, all conspire to strike the beholder with amazement and horror."

John Hinson was the first prisoner formally committed to Newgate on December 2, 1773. On the eighteenth night of his confinement, being the only prisoner, he was drawn up through one of the shafts in a bucket that had been used for hoisting ore, the rescuer of Hinson being one strong-handed Phyllis, serving on one of the neighboring farms. Escapes in similar ways were not infrequent in the earlier years. The prisoners were lodged in huts and cabins, made in the caverns. The most atrocious congestion and commingling of prisoners came to be practiced in time. In a room 21 feet long, 10 feet wide, and less than 7 feet high, 32 men were crowded at night. The prisoners were secured with iron fetters around the ankles. While at work, a chain fastened to a block was locked into these fetters, or around the ankle. No female prisoners were at first sent here, but served their terms in country jails. Later, an act of the Legislature admitted them to Newgate.

During the eight years of the war of the Revolution, Newgate became widely celebrated, because of the housing of prisoners of war.

We read frequently, in this early period, of the dense ignorance and inefficiency of the guards and keepers, not only at the Connecticut Newgate, but at other prisons. Here is a letter from a guard discharged from Newgate in Connecticut:

To the Hon. General Assembly, The humble petishen of Able Davis; whare as at the honorable supene court holden in Hartford in December last I was conficted of mis Deminer on the count of newgate being burnt as I had comand of said gard and was order to bee confind 3 month and pay fourteen pounds for disabaing orders, I cant read riten, but I did all in my power to distingus the flame, but being very much frited and not the faculty to doe as much indistress as I could another time and that is very smaul, what to do I thot it best to let out the prisners that war in the botams as I had just time to get the gates lifted before the hous was in flames, and the gard being frited it twant in my power to scape them. I now pray to the Deflahaned from further in prisment, and the coust of said sute as I hante abel to pay the coust, or give me the liberty of the yard as I am very unwell as your petishner in duty bound will for ever pay.

HARTFORD GAOL, *January 14th*, 1783.

ABEL DAVEIS."

Dodd tells of a desperate outbreak that occurred during the time of the imprisonment of prisoners of war on May 17th, 1781.

"At that time there were thirty desperate men confined in the vaults. The guard in charge of them consisted of a lieutenant, sergeant, corporal and twenty-four privates, several of the latter mere boys, and all lax in their ideas of discipline. The officers were armed with swords and pistols, the privates with muskets and fixed bayonets.

"On the night of the day in question, after the prisoners had been fastened in the dungeons, the wife of a convict named Young appeared and desired to see him, and, as there was nothing suspicious in this, the request was readily granted. Two officers lifted the trap, the rest of the guard being asleep, but no sooner was the heavy door unfastened than it was thrust violently up from beneath, and the whole body of prisoners rushed into the room.

"The two officers were at once struck down, the arms of the privates seized, and, after a sharp tussle, the insurgents became masters of the prison. In the *melee*, six of the guard were wounded — one mortally — and a like number of assailants. After this exploit, the victors proceeded to close the hatches on their former guards and fled to the forests, and, with one or two exceptions, succeeded in escaping.

"This wholesale delivery produced the wildest excitement, and expressions not very complimentary to the management of the prison or to the honesty of the guards were freely bandied about."

It was a motley company, this Newgate crew of convicts. They were allowed to gamble away their daily rations of a pound of meat, a pound of bread, a pint of cider, and potatoes. A near-by tavern offered its commodities to those convicts who possessed money earned through working for themselves or others, after the daily prison stint was done. Flogging, the stocks, heavy irons, hanging by the heels, and other stern survivals of the Colonial period were customary punishments. The compulsory daily work consisted of making nails, barrels, shoes, wagons, and of doing farm and job work, and operating the tread mill, which was a form of punishment quite unusual in America.

Dodd has this of interest to say, regarding the sanitary conditions:

"Other observers have noted the fact, recorded by them, that the confinement was not detrimental to health; indeed, some of the prisoners reached extreme old age while incarcerated there. The circumstance was attributed by some to a medicinal quality of the mineral rock which forms the wall of the cavern; others supposed it to be due to the equable temperature. In 1811, experiments were made to ascertain the mean temperature of the mines, when it was discovered that the mercury ranged eight degrees lower there in the hottest days of summer than in the coldest days of winter, and that the mean temperature was forty-eight degrees."

Edward Augustus Kendall traveled through the northern parts of the United States in 1807 and 1808, and visited the Newgate Prison, of which he wrote:

"When the bell summoned the prisoners to work, they came in irregular numbers, sometimes 2 or 3 together, and sometimes a single one alone; but whenever one or more were about to cross the yard to the smithy, the soldiers were ordered to present, in readiness to fire. The prisoners were heavily ironed, and secured both by handcuffs and fetters; and being therefore unable to walk, could only make their way by a sort of jump or hop. On entering the smithy, some went to the sides of the forges, where collars, dependent by iron chains from the roof, were fastened round their necks, and others were chained in pairs to wheelbarrows. . . . Prisoners in the yard are treated precisely as tigers are treated in a menagerie; and if the minds of men are influenced by education, then the education of a tiger may be expected to make a tiger of the man."[1]

This miserable makeshift of a prison was abandoned in 1827, when the convicts were removed to the new State prison at Wethersfield. A history of cruelty, riots, insurrections, vice and crime — such is the sum total of Newgate's contribution to early American prison history. Receiving those steeped in crime, it degraded them still more. It forced the debauched and the decent, the young and the old, into intimate physical association. It was a plague spot on American prison history, quite comparable with the convict ships of the transportation period of England. As one chronicler well says of it, "the system was well suited to turn men into devils, but it never could have transformed devils into men." It seems not to have been susceptible to the reform wave that affected Philadelphia, New York, and Massachusetts, to which we shall shortly give our attention.

Yet, in Connecticut for twenty years, prior to 1827, it was held, in public opinion, that Newgate was the best prison in the country. The Boston Prison Discipline Society's annual report for 1827 remarks, however, that "there has been a great change in public opinion in the last two years."

---

[1] E. A. Kendall. "Travels Through the Northern Parts of the United States in the Years 1807 and 1808. Vol. I, pp. 206-218.

CHAPTER VIII

THE MASSACHUSETTS STATE PRISON

It was more than ten years after the introduction of the new system at Philadelphia in 1790 before Massachusetts set to work to build a prison, and to adopt in general the new methods tested out in Pennsylvania and New York. The history of the Massachusetts State Prison, in the period that ended approximately with 1829, when another prison building was erected with separate cells for individual prisoners, and when the so-called "Auburn system" of silence, separate cells and associated labor was introduced, is given to us in a number of annual reports of boards of inspectors, descriptions of the prison administration, and in a popular description, compiled from old records by Gideon Haynes.[1] Haynes laid much stress upon the severe disciplinary features of the early years of the prison. The inpsectors' reports stress especially the financial difficulties of the institution. The student gains a very positive impression of stern treatment and of the subordination on the part of the administration of any reformatory influences to the demands that the prison be run economically and even stingily.

Prior to 1785, Massachusetts had no places save county jails for the imprisonment of convicts.[2] In 1785, a prison was built on Castle Island, in Boston Harbor, but because of the insecurity of the prison it was abandoned in less than twenty years. Inmates could escape across the ice to the mainland in the winter, and if good swimmers, could not be deterred from escape in the summer. Charles Bulfinch, in his report to Congress in 1827 on the subject of penitentiaries, stated that on the occasion of Castle Island being ceded to the United States in 1804 by Massachusetts, the Legislature of that State directed that a State prison be built in Charlestown. And so Massachusetts began to build a prison on four acres at Lynde's Point, just across the Charles River from Boston, in Charlestown. The prison was to be "for the reformation as well as the punishment of convicts." It was opened on December 12th, 1805.

The original intention was that the plan of the prison should embrace only solitary cells, 7 by 9 feet. But when built, the prison resembled in general plan and structure Newgate of New York.

---

[1] *Pictures from Prison Life.* An Historical Sketch of the Massachusetts State Prison. Gideon Haynes. Boston, Lee & Shephard, 1869.
Account of the Massachusetts State Prison. By the Board of Visitors. Charlestown, 1806.
Report on the Penitentiary System of the United States. New York, 1822.
Rules and Regulations of the Massachusetts State Prison, 1811. (In Appendix to Account of Massachusetts State Prison.)
Description and Historical Sketch of Massachusetts State Prison. 1816 or 1817.
Report of Committee appointed in 1816 to consider subject of the State Prison of Massachusetts and to inquire into the mode of governing the Penitentiary of Pennsylvania, 1817.
Report of Board of Visitors, 1823.
[2] Pictures, etc., p. 13.

[68]

It was 200 feet long. The central section, 66 feet long and 28 feet wide, contained rooms for the keeper and other officers, as well as a kitchen in the basement, and a chapel and hospital in the upper story. On each end of the main building was a wing, 67 feet long and 44 feet wide, four stories high, containing in the first story 28 cells, 8 feet by 11 feet; the second story, 30 cells of similar size, and in the third and fourth stories a total of 32 rooms, 17 feet by 11 feet.[3]

Like a massive fortress this prison was built, conditioning perhaps in part the growing idea that the prison house should be of monumental proportions. Safety, of course, was constantly suggesting the necessary use of stone and iron. This Massachusetts prison was supposedly fireproof, and it was held to be impossible to undermine it. The outer walls of the prison were four feet thick; the doors of the basement story were of solid wrought iron, weighing from 500 to 600 pounds each. The prison yard, 375 by 260 feet, was surrounded by a stone wall actually five feet thick at the bottom, three feet thick at the top, and fifteen feet high. Truly a bastile!

Naturally, prison buildings, because built for security, are of an enduring construction when once completed and in operation. Therefore, when once a great prison structure has been built, it has lasted long, and often has continued to condition a form of treatment long after a less enduring structure might have been scrapped to give place to new methods. A striking example of this is manifest to-day in the State of New York. The reformatory treatment of the so-called young offender, now committed to Elmira Reformatory, is far different in theory and practice from what it was fifty years ago, when the Reformatory was first designed. The prison-type of cell, the great congregate structures, the relatively restricted area within which the large inmate population is handled, are all obsolete in reformatory designs of the present day. Yet, because of the very large financial outlay of the State as represented in the great congerie of buildings at Elmira, the Reformatory continues to function there, although the treatment would be far more satisfactory, and probably far more conducive to rehabilitation, were the Reformatory upon a wide acreage, with relatively small group-buildings, giving the chance for much more individualized treatment of inmates. The State prisons now used in Massachusetts, Connecticut, New York (Auburn and Sing Sing) and New Jersey were all built nearly a century ago.

The cost of the Massachusetts State Prison, which is the subject of this chapter, is said to have been $170,000.[4]

A board of five managers, called "visitors," was appointed by the Governor and his Council. Their duties were similar to those of the boards in the prisons of New York and Philadelphia. The industrial activities in the workshops (located wholly within the prison yard, 122 feet long by 25 feet wide) were also similar to the earlier prisons heretofore described. Contract labor was used

---
[3] Report of Society for Prevention of Pauperism, p. 19.
[4] Pictures, pp. 13ff.

when possible, the first contract being let in 1807, when William Little engaged the labor of 20 men, to work at a plating and harness business, paying for their total services $40 a week for the first six months, and $50 weekly after that.[6] The chief industrial occupations were the hammering of stone, foundry work, blacksmithing, shoemaking, tailoring, carpentry and paint-shop work.

The dietary for the week was thus laid down by the board of visitors:[5]

Sunday.	1 lb. bread, of cheapest materials; 1 lb. coarse meat, made into broth.
Monday.	1 lb. bread; 1 qt. potatoes.
Tuesday.	1 pt. Indian meal, made into hasty pudding; 1½ gill molasses; I qt. soup made of fox heads and offal.
Wednesday.	Same as Monday.
Thursday.	1 qt. Indian meal made into hasty pudding.
Friday.	Same as Tuesday.
Saturday.	½ lb. bread; 4 oz. salt pork; 1 qt. pea or bean porridge.

From the first, the prison seems to have been a center of severity, outbreaks, and escapes. As early as 1809, a "refractory room" was established in the basement, 25 feet long, grated and otherwise fortified.

"Here there were a suitable number of chains for the legs, and of a proper strength, to be worn by the prisoners confined in this room."

Financial difficulties were present from the first. Many resignations and appointments to the boards of visitors were recorded, which must have seriously interfered with any consistent policy of administration. There was friction with the officials of the State. By 1810, five years after the first prisoner was admitted, the total cost of maintaining the prison had exceeded the receipts by $50,238.[7]

However, in 1811 we read of a secular privilege accorded, apart from school work. The warden was directed by the board of visitors

"to indulge the prisoners on the approaching Thanksgiving in such manner as he shall judge advisable, not exceeding double the expense of their usual fare."

The warden was also instructed to arrange for a Thanksgiving oration by a citizen, T. Austin.

One of the problems that to-day are in the forefront of questions of prison administration is the problem of recreation for prisoners. Indeed, it will be found that much of the honor system is based upon the conferring of recreational privileges in return for the increased responsibility of inmates to conduct themselves properly, work better and not attempt to escape. The visitor to a modern prison is struck forcibly with the "privileges" enjoyed by many if not most of the inmates. These privileges are largely recreational. There are occasionally baseball games that may be played, or attended. There are occasional concerts or movie shows in the

---

[5] Pictures, pp. 13ff.
[6] Pictures, p. 18.
[7] Pictures.

auditorium. There is the free time daily in the yard. There is conversation at meals. One may play musical instruments in the cells at certain times in the day or evening. And so forth. Even the permission to have occasional visitors, or to write or receive letters from outside, or to wear certain articles of clothing furnished from the outside, are all recreational privileges in the larger sense. They alleviate the ordeal of imprisonment, and furnish pleasure to the inmates thereby benefited.

The granting of recreational privileges has been found in these later years to be one of the strongest inducements to good discipline that can be employed. To bring some variety into the monotony of prison life through actual pleasures has been equivalent to putting before the inmate one of the strongest incentives to behave himself.

When shall we find the early prisons affording to the inmate any alleviations, any pleasures? When shall we discover the use of the desire for pleasures on the part of the inmate capitalized, so to speak, by the prison administration? Shall we find that public opinion demands so strongly the punishment and the actual terrorizing of the prisoner, that no admission of alleviating recreations and pleasures is tolerated? Shall we find the early prisons such edifices as fitly to bear above their entrance gates: "Abandon hope, all ye who enter here!"

Throughout our study we have been keen to discover any approaches on the part of wardens to an individualistic treatment of the inmates such as is to-day a marked characteristic of so-called modern wardens. In Massachusetts, as early as 1811 we find record of a punishment in the prison savoring of the old Colonial days in that State. An order of the prison board of visitors recorded that

"a gallows be erected in the prison yard, at an elevation of 20 feet, on which certain prisoners, 7 in number, shall be placed, and sit with a rope around their necks for one hour, once a week, for three successive weeks; that for 60 days they wear an iron collar and chain as the warden shall direct; and that they wear a yellow cap, with asses' ears, for 60 days; and that they eat at a table by themselves; etc., etc. The sentence shall be read in the hall at breakfast, in presence of all the prisoners."[8]

In Massachusetts, as well as in New York, certain elementary efforts to grade the prisoners were made. The garb of the convicts had been, until about 1812, one-half red and one-half blue. Nothing much more ignominious could have been conceived. The second-termers were now garbed in a still more motley fashion, in three-colored garments, distinguished from the clothing of other prisoners by one stripe of red, one of yellow, and one of blue. They ate at separate tables, apart from the other prisoners, had only two warm meals a day, and for the other meal only bread and water, except on Sundays.

Third-termers were dressed in four colors, one stripe of yellow, one of red, one of blue and one of black. It is hard to form a picture of such an inharmonious combination of colors, that must

---

[8] Pictures, p. 24.

have looked like a prismatic nightmare, and have transformed the inmate into a deplorable object. The wearer's humiliation and degradation were deliberately sought as one of the purposes of the prison discipline. Later, undoubtedly the many-colored stripes merged into the stripes of black which became in prisons the conventional pattern, alternating with the white stripes or the absence of color. The third-termers also ate separately, performed the most menial and hardest labor, and were allowed to see their friends only twice a year.

Still worse was the fate of the retaken convict who had escaped. He was compelled to wear an iron ring on the left leg, to which a clog, attached by a chain, was suspended during the entire term of the prisoner.

That the reaction from such extreme severity — to say nothing of the solitary cells that were used for more customary punishment — was such as to fan the prisoners to continued efforts to escape was certain. In 1813 there was an effort to burn the workshops. For this, one of the culprits was chained to a ringbolt for 24 hours. For an attempted escape, George Lynds was compelled to wear an iron jacket for eight days, and to stand in the broad aisle of the chapel with the same on two successive Sundays; to sleep also in solitary confinement for 90 days, and to wear a clog with an iron chain for 82 days afterwards.

The echoes of the earlier public punishments and practices in Colonial times are evident in the above. Standing the culprit in a humiliating position before the gaze of the public was customary, as in the stocks, the pillory, or at the tail of a cart. The public display before church-goers on Sunday of the convicted offender was also a frequent punishment, and the stool of penance directly below the minister's pulpit, and in full view of the congregation, was a well-known punishment. Chains and clogs were paraphernalia of the past. In short, we find in these Massachusetts examples of punishments within the prison a ready adaptation of the older tried-and-true public punishments of the days before State prisons.

In the following year the punishment for a serious assault was as follows: [9]

"That he wear an iron collar round his neck for 90 days and a clog on his left leg for 6 months, and that during this whole time he be chained to his work-bench; that he sleep in solitary confinement for 6 months, and that during that period he receive only bread and water for his supper; that he be brought into the inner yard on the four succeeding Saturdays, between the hours of three and five in the afternoon, and be placed for one hour on an elevation, and a label on his breast with these words: 'For stabbing two fellow prisoners; that no letter pass to or from him, or that any relative or friend visit him during his confinement, or any convict speak to him; and in case, during the performance of any part of the sentence, he be guilty of any misconduct, such parts of the sentence as have been inflicted be considered as null, and he shall be held to suffer the same over again.''

And yet, in the face of such unmitigated severity of treatment, we find the board of visitors announcing in its description of

[9] Pictures.

the prison, in 1815, that the keeper should always have in view the reformation of the prisoner. Among the rules then published were the following:

> Prisoners must not be struck by officers, except in self-defense;
> Keepers must not swear;
> The principal keeper has authority to punish offenders by confinement in their own rooms, or in the solitary cells, and by reduction of food.
> Force is allowed only in self-defense, or when the security of the prison is in danger.
> Ordinary drinking water only is allowed — but such convicts as are employed at hardest labor may be indulged in small beer at the warden's discretion.
> Silence is required of convicts when at work.
> Each officer shall have a gun, a bayonet, 12 cartridges with ball, and the same shall be kept at all times in a safe and convenient place, ready for use. Also a strong and heavy cutlass, to be used as a side arm, shall be worn by the keepers when the prisoners are at work.

Moreover, the board went on record in 1815 as expressing the hope of "promoting the eternal salvation of some individuals, of which every instance is, according to the unerring word of truth, a more important object than the gaining of the whole world." This was a quotation from John Howard. But in the same year, the board of visitors stated their theory of prison discipline:

> "It should be as severe as the principles of humanity will possibly permit. His (the prisoner's) clothes ought to be a means of punishment. He should be cut off from the world, and know nothing of what is happening outside. Whenever a prisoner transgresses, he should be punished until his mind is conquered. Convicts ought to be brought to the situation of clay in the hands of the potter. The guards should consider the prisoner as a volcano, containing lava, which if not kept in subjection, will destroy friends and foe."

This was reformation by terrorism. It was no wonder that the prison was at all times a "volcano, containing lava." The wonder is that reformation could be anticipated under such conditions, which in effect gave over to the executive of the prison almost entire authority to do as he pleased with the inmates. For it was early found possible to charge, in any instance that might be questioned, that the guards and keepers were obliged to act in self-defense.

It was in 1815 that the differentiation of garb for the several classes of prisoners was abolished, and the costume, one-half red and one-half blue, was readopted. Those inmates who had previously been confined in the prison wore a number on their back, indicative of the number of times they had been confined in the prison. In 1816, there occurred an insurrection of the convicts, and 16 men got over the walls; 15 of them were shortly recaptured — undoubtedly to undergo the punishments described above. This outbreak led to the appointment of a military guard, as at Newgate in New York, but after two years it was discontinued.

Up to this time, the earnings of the convicts has been able to meet only the expense of their maintenance. This was, it was said, due in part to the poor physical condition of the inmates on their entrance to the prison. Many prisoners were sent to prison for short terms, or from long distances, and only a small proportion could be used at once in productive employments, even if there had been a sufficiency of suitable labor, which there was not. The long duration of terms of solitary confinement was a financial loss to the prison. Many trades had been experimented with, without result. Shoemaking was practically the only permanently suitable occupation. In this branch, the labor of the convicts was sold at from 40 to 50 cents a day. Inmate labor was let to contractors for whatever purpose the contractors desired. The chief trades in operation, and the number of convicts employed were in 1816 reported to be as follows:

Shoemaking	38	Stone hammering	31
Weaving	31	Tailoring	17
Spike and nail making	26	Brushmaking	12

Oakum picking, a distinctly primitive occupation, was the chief work of those who could be employed at nothing else.

Congestion was increasing, as in Newgate and Walnut street, with similar results. By 1816, 300 convicts were living promiscuously in the Massachusetts State Prison. In some of the rooms four convicts, in others eight, were lodged without any supervision at night. The records of this year show the presence of four inmates under the age of 14 years. A legislative committee in 1817 recommended that because of the intolerable conditions at the prison, it be either abandoned or become a penitentiary house of the type urged by John Howard. Ninety persons were at the time at the prison under commitment for a second, third or fourth time.

This legislative committee held that the State Prison should be reserved for the most serious offenders, whose terms were of three years and more. Women and juveniles should be imprisoned in county jails instead of being sent to the State Prison. The present buildings should be substantially enlarged. In various sections of the State there should be Bridewells for the confinement of lesser offenders.

One of the chief criticisms by the committee against the penitentiary system in this and other States was its expense. It was said that the prisons were not reforming the prisoners, and that they were not supporting themselves. In Pennsylvania, with a population in Walnut Street Prison of 652 prisoners in December, 1816, the year's cost for the maintenance of prisoners was $45,651; the salaries of the officers amounted to $9,569. The value of the prisoners' labor was but $18,809. In short, the net expense of the year was in Philadelphia $36,411.

New York, with a prison population at Newgate of 753, was losing $40,000 a year. The total expense of erecting and supporting the New York State Prison (Newgate) was, up to 1827, $1,237,343.[10] Massachusetts, with an average prison population at Charles Town of about 275, lost in 1816, $13,000. In short, the committee felt that the prison was in no way a success. It did not pay, it did not reform, it did not prevent recidivism, and it was an increasing

---

[10] B. P. D. S., 1827, p. 113.

scandal. There was impending in Massachusetts what during the same period impended and eventuated in Pennsylvania and New York — demoralization, and the movement for a sweeping change in the system.

We meet, however, in this same report, a suggestion of a constructive nature as to the after-care of released prisoners — the first, in point of time, that we have discovered. The Committee suggested that there should be erected outside the walls a wooden building, where might be lodged those discharged convicts who were entirely destitute. They could here secure lodgings and meals from the prison at a cheap rate, and have a chance to occupy themselves at their trade until they could find some other employment.

But this plan, eminently sensible in an era which gave no official thought whatsoever to the prisoner, once he had passed the prison gate, and sent him out with little or no money with which to try to "make good," found deaf ears in the Legislature. It was again an idea broached far before its time.

The commissioners who drafted the above-mentioned report, obviously borrowing the idea from New York, recommended a reclassification of all inmates into three grades, with advancement or degradation at the discretion of the board of visitors. The suggestion was made also that pardons should be conferred only from the first grade. This project was actually worked into law in 1818, but according to Haynes the classification was never judiciously employed, and was finally dropped, a system of severity and degradation being substituted.[11] A labored explanation of this action was given in the report of the board of visitors for 1823. According to them, economy and reformation were *adverse* objects in the establishment of the prison. So the directors had tried a middle course, not sacrificing all hope of amendment among the convicts for a little increase of pecuniary emolument (in the industries), but, on the other hand, not following the illusory prospect of complete reformation by sacrificing to such a theory all regard for economy.

The board said flat-footedly that the system of a three-grade classification was impossible, from the standpoint of reformation, and that it was made solely in the interest of finance, to secure greater earning power for the institution. Thus was a radical and constructive project, which decades afterwards in another form became one of the bases of the American reformatory system, calmly and with complete lack of insight dismissed!

Much of the ingenuity that might have gone into the successful development of such a plan as the above seems to have been given over to the devising of new forms of punishment. In 1822 the feasibility of installing a "treadmill" was considered. This ingenious instrument of English origin operated upon the principle familiar in the dog churn or the squirrel's wheel. The luckless convicts must tread for a specific time daily this "discipline mill."

[11] Pictures.

The power therefrom was to be used in the grinding of corn. When it was found that an average of but one bushel a convict per day would be secured, the plan was dropped, not because it was a hard task for the convict, but for its uneconomical features.

The first record of a recreational feature we find at this period. In a report of the Massachusetts House of Representatives it was stated that inmates in the rooms lodging from 6 to 10 convicts were allowed occasionally the use of musical instruments, with lights in their rooms.

The Prison Discipline Society of Boston showed in 1826 that the prison population was increasing faster, relatively, than the population of the State. Furthermore, with a colored population in the State of less than 7,000, and with only one-seventy-fourth of the population in the State colored, there were 50 colored convicts in the prison, in a total population of 314, or approximately one-sixth. This proportion was similar to the proportions in other States.

The record of escapes and outbreaks continued in similar fashion until 1829, at which time the north wing of the new prison building was constructed by the labor of convicts, and the institution began to operate upon the "Auburn plan." And it was only in this year that the custom ceased of branding, on their discharge, the "repeaters" at the Massachusetts State Prison with the letters M. S. P. upon the arm.[12] Again a survival of the brutal directness of maiming and mutilating punishments of the Colonial period in Massachusetts!

---
[12] Laws of the Commonwealth, 1829.

CHAPTER IX

THE DEVELOPMENT OF THE AUBURN SYSTEM

When in 1910 the International Prison Congress, composed of representatives from all over the world of those who deal most intelligently and scientifically with the problems of crime and abnormal behavior, convened for the first time in the United States, a special train, furnished by the United States Government, conveyed the delegates from over a score of nations to the principal prisons and reformatories of the United States on a tour of inspection and study.

No prison was more eagerly visited than Auburn Prison in the city of like name, in the State of New York. For it was here in the west central part of the Empire State, that during the third decade of the nineteenth century a system of prison administration arose that has for a century wielded an enormous and preponderating influence upon prisons and reformatories throughout this country, and has made its influence constantly felt in other lands. The "silent system" of Auburn Prison is perhaps the best known historical feature of American prison history.

Auburn Prison produced a type of cellblock and of administration that traveled the country over, found numberless imitators, and conditioned prison architecture for nearly a century in this country. The two most recent examples of completed State prisons — in New York, at Great Meadow, and in Minnesota, at Stillwater — are conspicuous examples of the developed "Auburn plan" of cellular architecture, in which the cells are enclosed within a great containing building, the cells being back to back, several tiers in height, and therefore designated as the "inside-cell" type of construction. They are of steel, large, airy, and sanitary, in contrast to the early cramped, dark, half-airless, unsanitary cells of the original Auburn wing. But the relationship is there — and it is against that century-old type of cellblock architecture that during the last decade a spirited fight has been waged in our country for a more individualistic, humaner, more private kind of cell. Of all this we shall speak in detail when we come to a discussion of the celebrated contest between the advocates of the "Auburn system" and the "Pennsylvania system," that developed when the new prisons in New York and Pennsylvania were opened, and when two entirely different forms of construction and administration engaged the active interest and attention of State after State, desperately hunting for some form of prison regime, and architecture that would meet the needs of a commonwealth in despair at the demoralization of an older system, tried and found wholly wanting.

The period of prison administration that we are now entering, the decade from 1820 to 1830, is perhaps as engrossing to the student of prison matters as any period of the nineteenth century. It is the decade in which our prison system develops a second time with striking rapidity, and in which administration becomes organized and standardized for the first time — so definitely standardized, indeed, that a century has hardly sufficed to change many of the methods and habits then instituted. Indeed, American prisons cannot be understood with any clearness unless this particular period is understood. Origins of the majority of even recent prison practices in administration can be traced back to this decade. It is the era that the popular mind has supposed gave birth to the American prison system. Yet, as we shall see, this is the decade in which the insurgent and reactionary movement against the failure of the first prison system found its expression, and in which the pendulum swung to such an opposite extreme that there was fastened upon this country a system replete with severity, regularity, perpetual silence, and the domination by the prison authorities of the inmate's body and spirit.

Within relatively few years of 1816, when the State of New York began the construction at Auburn of the new prison for the western part of the State, the "Auburn system" was already hailed as the long-hoped-for solution of all penological ills. It had the beauty of a finely functioning machine. It had reduced the human beings within the prison to automata. In less than ten years from the date of its origin, it had already become a model. In 1826, the Prison Discipline Society of Boston (a philanthropic organization that had just sprung into existence) asked in its first annual report:[1]

"What could with propriety be done for criminals that is not done at Auburn? Here is exhibited what Europe and America have long been waiting to see, a prison which may be a model of imitation."

In the United States, Sing Sing Prison has enjoyed the perhaps doubtful fame of being the best-known penal institution, and also perhaps the most notorious. But it was Auburn — and the Eastern Penitentiary of Pennsylvania — to which distinguished European visitors, studying prison administration, came in the period between 1830 and 1840. France, England, Prussia and Canada studied our contributions to penology. It was our American institutions that conditioned in large measure the subsequent construction of English and Continental prisons.

And, finally, it was by the working out of poetic justice — if such a term may be used in prison history — in Auburn Prison, where the famous system had had its birth, that Thomas Mott Osborne in 1913 and 1914 gave to many of the stupid and cruel remnants of that original system, handed down through the century and flourishing lustily not ten years ago, their death blow.[3]

Let us therefore approach with especial interest this period of unusual historical import. It was revolt against the appalling failure of an earlier penitentiary system that led to the surprising developments of the new system. Indeed, as de Beaumont and

---

[1] B. P. D. S., 1826, p. 27.
[3] T. M. Osborne. "Within Prison Walls."

de Tocqueville, sagacious and sympathetic critics of our American prison systems in the thirties of the nineteenth century, said, the experiences of Walnut street in Philadelphia and Newgate in New York, and Charlestown in Massachusetts had led, *not to a penitentiary system, but to a bad system of imprisonment*,[2] a system which was

"in general ruinous to the public treasury; it never effected the reformation of the prisoners; every year the legislature of each State voted considerable sums toward the support of the penitentiaries, and the continued return of the same individuals into the prisons proved the inefficiency of the system to which they were submitted."

However, Auburn Prison did not start as an iconoclastic, insurgent institution. It was no deviation, at first, from the conventional construction of the times. That part of it which was built between 1816 and 1819 was put up on traditional lines. It contained 28 rooms, each intended to house from 8 to 12 prisoners. There were, in addition, 61 cells, each destined for one convict, or for two if necessary[4] — a powerful invitation to vice and dishonesty.

The first warden of Auburn was Captain William Brittin, appointed in 1818. His principal keeper — the disciplinarian and general routine manager of the prison — was Captain Elam Lynds. Captain Brittin was a master carpenter, who had been at first employed by the commissioners to build the prison. Captain Lynds we shall find to be the outstanding figure in American prison history during the decade from 1820 to 1830, and one of the men still quoted as a pioneer.

The prison was governed by a board of five inspectors, residing in the village of Auburn, and appointed for two years by the Governor and the Senate. They received no compensation. They appointed the "agent and keeper," the two offices being combined, and designated by us in this study by the generic term: "Warden."

In 1819, the Legislature of New York, on the recommendation of Governor DeWitt Clinton,[6] ordered the erection at Auburn Prison of an additional wing, made up wholly of solitary cells. This northern wing was finished in 1821. The present American prison system grew out of those solitary cells at Auburn Prison. It was this new wing that became the model for American prisons. In 1821, Captain Brittin died, and Captain Lynds, who had been a hatmaker in Auburn,[5] was appointed agent and keeper — a combination really of two functions, and a title that has survived until to-day in New York State prisons.

In the earliest years of the new prison at Auburn, the wages were small, and the dangers great. Captain Brittin, for being both warden and master carpenter, received an annual salary of $1,800, but other wages were as follows:

Deputy Keeper	$450	Chaplain	125
Clerk	450	Surgeon	200
Turnkey	350		

[2] Beaumont and de Tocqueville, p. 22.
[4] B. and T., footnote, p. 4. Also Julius. S. Z., p. 141.
[5] Julius. S. Z., p. 142.
[6] Governor's Message in Journal of New York Assembly, 1819, p. 18.

In 1819, three years after the establishment of the prison, while construction was still going on, the board of inspectors, alarmed at the possibility of outbreaks, recommended the organization in the village of Auburn of an independent company of militia, to be composed of 30 privates and several officers, whose duty it should be to assemble at the first alarm and rush to the prison. Indeed, both Captain Brittin and Captain Lynds had been officers in the recent war with Great Britain.

In 1821, the New York Legislature made mandatory a three-fold grading of inmates at Auburn prison, in an effort to rectify prison abuses. The first class was composed of the most hardened and vicious criminals, who were to be confined to solitary confinement, without any labor whatsoever to distract their minds. The second class, more corrigible, were to alternate between solitary confinement, and labor as a recreation. The third class, being the most hopeful, were to work in association during the day, and to be in seclusion at night.

Here was a new method proposed for classification — one that became in time, so far as the third class of inmates was concerned, a standard for the entire country, with the exception of one prison, the Eastern Penitentiary of Pennsylvania, which adhered to absolute separation of each inmate from the other at all times. No prison prior to the plan proposed for Auburn Prison had worked its inmates during the day in association, and locked them up in separate cells at night. Exactly this combination of day-association and night-separation became the keystone of the Auburn system.

Who the inventor of this method of classification was is lost in doubt. Even in 1832, when de Beaumont and de Tocqueville published their account of their studies of American penal institutions, they could not dispel the obscurity. The noted French visitors asked whether it might not have been Governor De Witt Clinton, or Mr. Cray (one of the board of inspectors), or Captain Brittin, who, according to Gershom Powers (himself a later warden at Auburn) was largely the initiator of the Auburn methods of prison construction and of discipline. Or was it Captain Lynds, to whom public opinion at the time seems to have attributed the system? According to Julius, the Prussian scholar who in 1839 published his study of American social conditions, Cray developed the Auburn system in 1823,[7] after the tragic failure of the system of solitary confinement, which we shall shortly describe.

And who was the inventor of the Auburn type of prison building, which became the standard type of structure for practically all American prison cellblocks for nearly a century? Even to-day, the great new prisons at Great Meadow, New York, and Stillwater, Minnesota, are but the latest developments of the original Auburn type of "interior cellblock"; they have an abundance of light and air, and their cells are of steel and of considerable size, radical improvements in every way upon the catacomb-like pile of masonry

---

[7] Julius. Sittleche Zusbaende. Vol. II, p. 142.

of the original cellblock at Auburn. But the line of descent is direct. Where did the type arise? Was it original with Auburn? Who was the builder, and what were his models?

Gershom Powers wrote thus, in 1828:

"I know not who was justly entitled to the distinguished credit of having discovered the invaluable principle upon which our north wing of cells is constructed. Captain Brittin claimed it during his lifetime, and his friends for him, after his death. Another master builder, now of Montreal, also made the same claim, which was said to have been favored by the opinion of Governor Clinton. Captain Brittin however, was the first who applied the principle practically, and constructed the first block of cells upon the present general plan."

It is noteworthy that no mention is made by Powers of any participation in this plan by Captain Lynds, to whom much of the creation of the Auburn plan and system has been attributed. Doctor Julius, a visitor from Prussia, wrote on his return to Prussia in 1833 that the American reformatory system, "concerning which there has been so much talk in Europe during the last forty years," was, so far as the Auburn system was concerned, undertaken at the prison in Ghent in Flanders in 1791, on the lines laid down by Count Vilain XIV, and was introduced into America in 1820 by the building of the north wing of Auburn Prison.

For the Ghent prison maintained separate confinement of prisoners at night, associated work during the day, and perpetual silence. It is hardly to be doubted that echoes of the Ghent system, described and discussed in many European treatises of the time, reached this country. John Howard had described Ghent as a model prison in structure and administration. Gloucester Prison in England was authorized in 1785, and maintained separation of prisoners day and night. Milbank Prison in London was built in 1812 on a modified Howard plan. Here, solitary confinement was complete. Yet we find Governor Everett of Massachusetts stating in 1836 that there was no evidence that the Ghent plan awoke general attention, or that it was imitated elsewhere than in Europe.

In 1821, in obedience to the Legislature, and, ironically enough, on Christmas Day, eighty of the worst convicts within the new prison, almost half of the total population, were condemned henceforth to silence and to solitude without work, and with no companion save the Bible. Let us recall that three years before in Pennsylvania, the decision had been reached to erect a prison at Pittsburg on the same basis of administration.

The board of inspectors of Auburn Prison pledged their adherence to their "new system" in the following words in 1821 — a profession of penological faith that for deliberate elimination of hope can scarcely be equalled:

"The end and design of the law is the prevention of crimes, through fear of punishment, the reformation of offenders being of minor consideration. . . . Let the most obdurate and guilty felons be immured in solitary cells and dungeons; let them have pure air, wholesome food, comfortable clothing, and medical aid when necessary; cut them off from all intercourse with men; let not the voice or face of a friend ever cheer them; let them walk their gloomy abodes, and commune with their corrupt hearts and guilty consciences in silence, and brood over the horrors of their solitude, and the enormity of their crimes, without the hope of executive pardon."

One has but to ask himself how long, under such unvarying separation from all human contact and feelings, one would retain his faith, and even his sanity? Indeed, this sentence to nothing less than a living death, and to the perpetual horrors of solitude without anything to do, drove irresistibly toward madness. By the end of a year and a half:

"a number of the convicts became insane while in solitude; one was so desperate that he sprang from his cell, when the door was opened, and threw himself from the gallery upon the pavement, which nearly killed him, and he undoubtedly would have destroyed his life instantly, had not an intervening stovepipe broken the force of his fall. Another beat and mangled his head against the walls of his cell until he destroyed one of his eyes."[8]

Such an outcome horrified the State. Governor Yates, who on an official visit to Auburn Prison had been an eye-witness to this alarming physical and mental result of the eighteen months of solitary confinement of these miserable victims of a new theory of punishment ordered the abandonment of the system. By the end of 1823 he had pardoned most of the survivors. But the end of the gruesome story was not yet, for though they had gone out of the prison on the ground that they had had sufficient punishment, the subsequent careers of many of the released men were criminal ones. The terrible effects of constant solitude had not made them honest, but they had been broken. One released inmate committed a burglary on the first night of his release. Twelve of the released men were ultimately reconvicted and returned to Auburn.[9]

Here was a noteworthy and notorious trial of the effects of solitary confinement. Method after method had now been tried in prison administration, and had been found wanting in beneficent results. The humane discipline of the early Quakers at Walnut Street had eventuated in partisan politics, the evils of congestion, and the demoralization of the inmates. The rigors of Newgate in Connecticut had become a scandal in the community. Massachusetts, with severity of treatment and a disregard of reformative methods, had developed a prison that was also a scandal. And now, with the extreme application of solitary confinement without labor, only a year and a half was needed to prove that, literally, madness lay that way. What was now to be the solution?

Nor, were other States more successful in their experiments with solitary confinement. In Virginia, when the Governor ceased to pardon convicts, it was stated that in no case did any convict survive a serious attack of disease. Their only hope in the enduring of their misery had been the ultimate possibility of freedom through a pardon. In the State prison of Maine, at Thomaston, wherein the law provided for the solitary confinement of certain convicts during long periods, the prison physician stated that the majority of such inmates spent more than half their term of confinement in the prison hospital, it being the custom of that prison to take the inmates from the solitary cells to the hospital, in order to restore them sufficiently to be again placed in solitary confinement![10]

---

[8] Gershom Powers. General Description of Auburn Prison, 1826, p. 83.
[9] Powers, p. 83.
[10] B. P. D. S., 1827.

We do not believe it necessary to take time, to-day, to argue the barbarous and futile nature of long-enduring solitary confinement without labor. Only the exceptionally strong-minded or the greatly dulled intelligence might seemingly endure such confinement long.

That way, disease and madness lay. Yet, so violent were the reaction and the indignation against the then prevailing abominations of the older prisons, where inmates congregated in idleness, that eminent citizens like Roberts Vaux of Philadelphia, and a representative senate committee of New York, recommended such absolute separation of the most hardened convicts, not only from each other, but from any chance of employment.[12]

Even Edward Livingston, distinguished jurist and author of the remarkable draft of a penal code and a code of prison discipline for Louisiana in the twenties of the nineteenth century, was a strong advocate of silent and uninterrupted separation of convicts, without work. There was great theorizing in matters of penology at this period. Was it not known that the martyrs and the political intriguers had endured constant solitary confinement for years? To which argument Gershom Powers, warden of Auburn Prison, replied in 1828 that the example of martyrs and patriots who had endured similar conditions successfully was no criterion, because such persons are sustained by devotion to liberty or to religion in a righteous cause, while the criminal has no high moral sanction to lend strength to his struggle for endurance.[11]

In the last analysis, however, the agitation for the establishment of such solitary confinement was caused by the realization that something had to be done to secure a prison system that would work! In the prison at Auburn, prior to the experiment in solitary confinement, conditions had been atrocious. Pardon-brokerage was the steady and profitable business of many persons. In 1821, 41 convicts had been pardoned, and only 9 convicts were discharged by expiration of their sentence. Moreover, the discipline of the prison had become very lax. In 1882, 75 convicts who had been sent away some miles from the prison to work on the "Great Canal" that was then being constructed through the State, all escaped.[14] Therefore the inspectors stated, in all soberness, that in their new effort to make prison life and its punishments terroristic, they were attempting the salvation of the prisoner.

The long-expected was also happening. It was now often being urged that there should be a general return to bloody and grievous corporal punishments, or to a wide extension of the use of capital punishment. Or even to transportation to some distant part of the United States, or to some lone island in the Pacific.[13] The relative leniency of the first prison system, followed by such a discouraging succession of failures of treatment, was already therefore in danger of being superseded by an abhorrent revival of medieval methods of punishment.

---

[11] Letter from Gershom Powers, etc.
[12] Report of New York Senate Comm., 1823.
[13] Report on Penitentiary System, 1822, p. 76ff.
[14] Reports of the Inspectors.

Thomas Eddy, who as we know had been the first warden of the New York State Prison, and who was renowned as a philanthropist, adhered to the then accepted theory of rigorous discipline of convicts. In a document citing the fourth annual report of the London Society for the Improvement of Prison Discipline, he quoted the European authority:

"The committee are of the opinion that severe punishment must form the basis of an effective system of prison discipline. The personal sufferings of the offender must be the first consideration, as well for his own interest as for the sake of example. The Society (of London) recommends a system of hard labor and regular employment, a system in which spare diet and occasional solitary confinement and habits of order and silence are steadily enforced."

It is easy to see from the above how sanction was secured for the unmitigated severities of the Auburn system, which within comparatively few years was found to depend, for its continued success, upon the lash. Furthermore, the London Society argued that the prisoners should not be allowed to share in their earnings, because the hope of recompense would mitigate the severity of their punishment!

"It is as unwarrantable to mitigate the force, and soften the rigour, of that punishment which the laws inflict, as to increase its penalties. It never can be proper that the criminal should quit confinement with emolument derived from conduct, which the discipline of the prison should *compel* him to maintain . . . If prisoners expend a portion of their earnings in food, the efficacy of restricted diet is counteracted, and frequently wholly lost."

In short, there was being evolved, as we shall more clearly see in the pages to come, a system of discipline in which the convict was deprived of any inducements whatsoever to conduct himself properly in prison, save that he might escape actual physical punishments. The prison was to be, in brief, a place of terror. Yet, the London Society conceded that on the discharge of the convict, he might be furnished some relief in cash.

At this psychological moment events occurred, which together undoubtedly went far to determine the course of prison history for the century to follow. The first influence was the report of the Senate Committee of 1822, relative to the reorganization of the State Prison in New York, which we have already discussed in the chapter on Newgate in New York. (Page 43.)

The second influence was the publication of a detailed report by the New York Society for the Prevention of Pauperism in 1822 on the Penitentiary System of the United States. The third factor was the independent and aggressive effort being made within Auburn Prison itself to arrive at a workable system of prison administration.

The New York Society for the Prevention of Pauperism organized 1818 or 1819, was an association of representative citizens in New York city, who had been led into the study of crime and delinquency through their inquiries into the causes of pauperism. This Society played, as we shall see in a later chapter, a very important role in the foundation of the House of Refuge in New

York, the first juvenile reformatory in the United States. We shall now discuss the special report of a committee of this Society published in 1822, and containing a wealth of material gathered from governors, wardens, inspectors, and many other citizens. We have here one of the earliest surveys of a social problem in the field of delinquency by a civic and philanthropic organization.

The report of the committee, after arraigning with cumulative and undeniable facts the prevailing prison conditions, held it imperative that a new system of prison discipline should be established, in which the principal elements should be:

Solitary confinement.
Hard labor.
Moral instruction and discipline.

The committee maintained, in amplification of the above, that the internal structure of existing prisons should be so changed as to provide the largest number of single and separate cells. Solitary confinement of prisoners without labor should be resorted to only for a certain length of time in the case of hardened convicts, or for punishment. *All other prisoners should work in their cells.* For each prisoner there must be provided, therefore, a separate cell. This plan, we would mention here, was the one finally adopted and exemplified in the administration of the Eastern Penitentiary of Pennsylvania in Philadelphia.

Failing the possibility of providing a sufficiency of separate cells, a classification of prisoners along rigid lines should be instituted. Young and old, hardened criminals and novices, should be separated from each other. There should be silence at all times, so far as that could be maintained.

The wholesale granting of pardons should be done away with. Prisoners should not be led to expect reduction of sentence through pardons. Prison officials, especially the keepers and guards, should be more carefully appointed. Much of the corruption within the prison arose from the complicity of officials in the criminals' acts in the institution. Furthermore, the cancer of idleness and sloth should be extirpated by hard labor. Prisoners in the old prisons were loafing, and were contriving crimes in their associated idleness. Hard labor was indispensable in any reform of the prison system.

Nor should the prison be regarded as primarily a financial undertaking or problem. Less attention should be given to making the institution a self-supporting prison, and more attention to enforcing a stern and rigid discipline, for the ultimate benefit and possible reformation of the inmates themselves. While the diet should be suitable, and while undeviating cleanliness should be observed, there should be nothing incident to the prison life that might be either pleasant or inviting! "A penitentiary should be a place where everything conspires to punish the guilty." Extreme but orderly severity should characterize the new prison system.

In the above outline was published for the first time a definite program for prison reform by an organization of citizens banded together for philanthropic purposes. Solitary confinement and hard labor were the two chief elements of the proposed system. Or, in the absence of such possibilities, a reversion to the most severe classifications of the past. One other, and highly important, recommendation was that there should be established a separate correctional institution for juvenile offenders, and that they should no longer be sent to State prison. Within two years the House of Refuge in New York city was established.

Meanwhile, at Auburn Prison, there was being developed a system, after the failure of the solitary system without labor, that was quite different from any then in practice in the United States. By 1823, the so-called "Auburn system" was in full operation. It provided for the separate confinement of each prisoner in silence in his individual cell at night, and for the work of the prisoners in association in silence during the day. The old prisons commingled their inmates day and night in large workrooms and nightrooms. Here at Auburn, there had arisen now a system that grouped the prisoners during the day for maximum industrial production, and separated them absolutely at night for the maximum prevention of contamination or of plotting against the safety of the institution, or for escape.

"Let those prisoners who are not in solitary confinement," said the inspectors, be allowed to work, under a discipline so rigid as to prevent all conversation with each other, and be compelled to perform as much labor as their health and constitutions will permit. Under such a system of punishments the State's prison horrors would be seen, and its terror felt in the community; and if it failed to reform offenders, it would at least drive them from that government, whose laws they had violated, the certain and severe penalty of which they had thus been made to realize."

The board reported as early as 1823, however, that it was not in favor of a grading system. "Prison officials should be relieved of the classification of convicts. Sentences of the courts should be more definite and should be strictly executed." The system of grading was not long followed out at Auburn.

The theory of the "Auburn system" was simplicity itself. Maintain silence at all times, and you remove absolutely from prisoners the chance to corrupt each other. They can do each other no damage by their physical proximity, but, if granted communication with each other, they become a force for evil and an ever-present source of insurrection and riot. If perpetual silence be maintained, there is no reason why prisoners should not work in the shops in association during the day. Prisoners *must* be employed. Prisoners are sent to prison to do hard labor. It is a part of the sentence. The shops are the logical places of employment. Any scheme for employing prisoners separately in their own cells is economically unsound. Prisons should, so far as is compatible with the proper treatment of inmates, be made to pay expenses.

In short, the keystone of the Auburn system was *silence!* This was the new element, introduced to solve the prison problem. And within a year it actually seemed as if a new era in prison administration had come. Hard work during the day had supplanted idleness at Auburn. Hard work was productive, healthy, and taught the inmates the principles of self-support against the time when they should be discharged from prison. Hard work had reformative value. Was it not an edict from on high that man must earn his bread by the sweat of his brow? Had not this very United States been made possible by the hard labor of settlers in a frontier land? Was there any reason why men in prison should not work at least as hard as the honest, God-fearing supporter of a family on the outside?

And the silence that was perpetually required of the convicts seemed admirable. Evil communications corrupt good manners. No longer would there be heard in prison yard or night-room the foul-mouthed recidivists of the Newgate type! Such men were dangerous and wicked criminals, thinking and plotting escapes, riots and the contamination of others. Rob them of their power of communication and you remove from them their deadliest weapon! Discipline was found to be rendered much easier by silence. Captain Basil Hall, a chaplain of the British Royal Navy, visiting Auburn Prison about 1829, admired the unbroken silence, saying that it was as profound as if the workmen had been made of the marble which they were employed in hewing.[15]

The Prison Discipline Society, founded in Boston in 1825, championed the Auburn system from the start. The following graphic picture was given in the first annual report of the Society in 1826 of the daily routine in Auburn Prison:[16]

"The unremitted industry, the entire subordination, and subdued feeling among the convicts, has probably no parallel among any equal number of convicts. In their solitary cells, they spend the night with no other book than the Bible, and at sunrise they proceed in military order, under the eye of the turnkey, in solid columns, with the lock march to the workshops, thence in the same order at the hour of breakfast, to the common hall, where they partake of their wholesome and frugal meal in silence. Not even a whisper might be heard through the whole apartment.

"Convicts are seated in single file, at narrow tables with their backs toward the center, so that there can be no interchange of signs. If one has more food than he wants, he raises his left hand, and if another has less, he raises his right hand, and the waiter changes it. When they have done eating, at the ringing of a bell, of the softest sound, they rise from the table, form in solid columns, and return under the eyes of the turnkeys to the workshops.

"From one end of the shops to the other, it is the testimony of many witnesses that they have passed more than three hundred convicts without seeing one leave his work, or turn his head to gaze at them. There is the most perfect attention to business from morning till night, interrupted only by the time necessary to dine — and never by the fact that the whole body of prisoners have done their tasks and the time is now their own, and they can do as they please.

"At the close of the day, a little before sunset, the work is all laid aside, at once, and the convicts return in military order, to the silent cells where they partake of their frugal meal, which they are permitted to take from the kitchen, where it is furnished for them, as they returned from the shop. After supper, they can, if they choose, read the scriptures, undisturbed, and can reflect in silence on the error of their lives. They must not disturb their fellow prisoners by even a whisper. The feelings which the convicts

---

[15] B. P. D. S., 1828.
[16] Same, 1826, p. 36.

exhibit to their religious teacher are generally subdued feelings. . . . The men attend to their business from the rising to the setting of the sun, and spend the night in solitude.''

De Metz and Blouet, reporting in 1837 their study of American prisons, said of the prisoners at Auburn:

"They march very close together, one hand on the shoulders of the preceding convict, and all turning their head in the direction of the guard. They mark time until commanded to cease.''

A picture familiar to many persons still living, who remember the lockstep customary, until relatively recently, in American prisons.

As late as 1910, the writer of this study, in visiting Auburn Prison, found many of the above methods of daily routine surviving. There was substantial, if not unremitted, industry. There was silence, prevailing throughout the institution. The inmates ate in a gloomy basement messhall, all facing in one direction, as is described in the above excerpt from the report of the Prison Discipline Society of a hundred years ago. The stripes had gone, but the men marched in somber silence to and from their work. Silence prevailed in the cellhouse at night, and the very same structure that had housed the inmates in 1826 was still in active use, with the same wretchedly small cells. At work, the inmates in the shops were still prohibited from lifting their eyes and gazing at the passing visitor. So strong was the power of survival of the methods fastened upon American prisons by the sudden and almost complete domination of the Auburn system!

Yet, the principle of silence has been from time to time challenged during the century that has gone. As early as 1837, in Miss Harriett Martineau's "Society in America," she expressed her strong doubt as to the reasonableness of the silent system.

"Talking is an innocent act, and an unavoidable act. The prisoners ought to talk, and they do. It is surprising to me that any effectual reformation can be looked upon from men who have the prohibition to speak set up before their minds as the chief circumstance and interest of their lives for five, seven, or ten years. How the disordered being is to be rectified, how the prostrated conscience is to be reinstated, while an innocent and necessary act is thus erected into an offense, I leave those who are most versed on moral proportions to decide.''

However, silence has reigned literally in prisons and reformatories, practically into the present day. The writer of this study was fortunate in being able to aid in bringing about the abandonment of the silent system in one of the New York prisons less than ten years ago. The absurdity of preserving the silent system at meals, when on the farm at Great Meadow Prison the men talked freely with each other, as well as in the recreation hours in the prison yard, showed simply the extent to which tradition ruled in a custom that no longer had a ground for existence. And it is, or was until recently at least, to be chronicled regarding a mid-western prison that, conceding something to modern theories, the inmates were permitted to talk on Monday, Wednesday and Friday at table, but were required to keep silence on Tuesday, Thursday and Saturday, or vice versa!

The great success of the Auburn system lay in the fact that it worked! By 1828, so many distinguished visitors from both America and Europe had visited the prison that the warden then in command, Gershom Powers, published a book of general information about the prison.[18] Powers believed absolutely in a repressive institution. The principal duties of the convicts were to obey orders, and to labor diligently in silence. They were not to sing, dance, whistle, run, jump, or do anything that would have the least tendency to disturb or alarm the prison.[17]

Unquestionably the overwhelming silence of the place, and the unswerving order of the inmates, were the two most profound impressions made upon visitors. De Beaumont and de Tocqueville wrote that the silence at night in the great cellblock was that of death:

"We have often during the night trod those monotonous and dumb galleries, where a lamp was always burning; we felt as if we traversed catacombs; there were a thousand living beings, and yet it was a desert solitude."[19]

According to William Crawford,[20] the English visitor in 1832, Auburn Prison occupied a plot of ground forming a square 500 feet in length either way, enclosed by a boundary wall 2,000 feet long, 30 feet high, and 4 feet thick at the base. The power for the prison was had from a small creek on the south. The prison looked to Crawford like a great manufacturing plant. He held the construction of the prison to be defective, because there was no central point where the prison could be in general overseen and inspected.

The total expense of construction of the prison, without including the labor of the convicts, was above $300,000.[21]

The prison buildings formed three sides of the square. The front of the prison was 280 feet long, and each wing was 240 feet long, and 45 feet deep. The keeper's house was four stories high in the middle of the front of the prison. The south wing of the prison was built with passages on one side of the building, and large rooms on the other. Half of this south wing was given over to a dining hall, and chapel made out of the old rooms, for this was the original building at Auburn. In addition, the south wing was rebuilt to allow of a kitchen and the female department.

By 1825, the north wing had been completed. This was five stories high, and was 42 feet in height. The passageway between the walls of the prison building and the cells was 9 feet in width, the cells themselves 7½ feet long, 3.8 feet wide, and 7 feet high. There were 550 cells. The floors were of oak planks on brick arches. The external walls were of stone, 2½ feet thick. The middle wall, between the banks of cells, was two feet thick; the partition walls between the cells one foot thick. In the walls of the building were large grated windows. The doors of the cells were of oak planks,

---

[17] Powers. Report, p. 24.
[18] A General Description of Auburn Prison.
[19] B. and T., p. 32.
[20] Crawford, pp. 24ff.
[21] G. Powers. Report, p. 5.

bound together with iron; the upper part was of iron grating. The gallery just outside the cells, above the ground floor cells, was three feet wide.

The convicts slept in hammocks in the cells made of imported canvas, stretched by cords, and hung by the corners on hooks, rather loosely, or stretched tightly on long narrow wooden frames, which lay flat at night, and were turned up edgewise during the day. The hammocks were discarded within a few years from the beginning of the new system of Auburn Prison, because they occasioned pain in the breast and limbs.

There was a so-called ventilator in the cell, with a pipe 2½ inches in diameter, with a flue to the roof. The ventilation was defective. The air pipes allowed conversation between the cells, which defeated the basis of the Auburn plan of silence. The heating of the cells was said by Crawford not to be in general difficult. There were stoves in the area outside the tiers of cells.

There were new cells in the south wing erected in 1822, 220 in all in this building. This made a total of 770 cells at Auburn Prison. In the new cells there were set iron-grated doors from top to bottom. By a curious arrangement, the doors were set into the recess of the cells almost two feet. The workshops were in the rear of the prison. The entire length of range of the workshops was nearly 2,000 feet. The passageway, whereby the visitors and guards could supervise or see the prisoners at work, was introduced in 1828, and was 2 feet 6 inches wide. The convicts did not face each other when at work.

There were two reservoirs in the yard, in one of which the prisoners could bathe in summer.

The usual dress of the convicts consisted of vest and trousers, striped, made of cotton and wool, and made in prison. The cap was of the same material. The shirt was of cotton. The prisoners wore knitted woolen socks, and leather shoes. The annual expense of clothing the prisoners was $5.87. The contract price for the prisoner's food was 5 1-40th cents per day. There was fresh beef once a week. The following typical meals were cited by Crawford:

Breakfast: Cold meat, bread, cold hominy, hot potato, pint of rye coffee, sweetened with molasses.
Dinner: Meat, soup from broth thickened with Indian meal, bread, potato.

According to Powers, the rations per man per day were as follows: [22]

10 oz. pork or 16 oz. beef. ⎫
10 oz. wheat flour. ⎬ Daily.
12 oz. Indian meal. ⎪
½ gill molasses. ⎭

2 qts. rye. ⎫
4 qts. vinegar. ⎪
2½ bushels potatoes. ⎬ Per 100 rations.
4 qts. salt. ⎪
1½ oz. pepper. ⎭

---

[22] Powers. Report, p. 43.

Salt pork and salt beef was furnished alternately each three days, and fresh beef once each week.

In the morning there was cold meat, bread, slice of cold hominy and hot potatoes. Also a pint of hot rye coffee, sweetened with molasses. For dinner meat, soup made from the broth, thickened with Indian meal, hot potatoes, and cold water to drink.

The prison was governed by a board of inspectors, who were appointed for two years. They received no compensation. They had the power of removing the warden (called "Agent"), deputy keeper and all subordinates. The salary of the agent was $1,250, and he was bonded for $25,000. The deputy keeper was the "principal keeper" of to-day. There were 20 assistant keepers and 10 guards, including a sergeant. The prison at this time would have a population of 770 if full.[23]

The construction of the prison was such that the entire interior central yard could be surveyed at a glance. Visitors were not permitted to pass through the shops, but the wall in the rear of the shops was so constructed as to afford space for a narrow passageway, made light by numerous small orifices, through which not only keepers, but the many visitors could survey the convicts at work, without the knowledge of the latter. Each visitor paid twenty-five cents as admission fee, and the total income from this source in Auburn in 1830 was $1,524. The visiting of prisons by the public was possible to all, according to de Beaumont and de Tocqueville.[24]

As early as 1822, the board of inspectors of Auburn had raised the price of admission for visitors from 12½ cents to 25 cents, on the novel ground that visitors might thereby be discouraged from attending in such numbers; the visitors were acquiring the idea, from the appearance of the prison, that prison life was not so hard and severe as was commonly thought! On the other hand, *all* visitors should not be excluded, for then the public would regard the prison as a Bastile or inquisition!

Said de Beaumont and de Tocqueville:

"These establishments in the United States are considered as belonging to all. The prisons are open to every one who chooses to inspect them, except in the Penitentiary at Philadelphia, where it is not permitted to see the prisoners, because the visits of the public would be in direct contradiction to the principle of absolute solitude, which forms the foundation of the system."[24]

The Auburn System demanded absolute separation of the prisoner from the world. No communication with or from friends or relatives was allowed the convicts save under most exceptional circumstances, but the family of the prisoner might, on inquiry, learn of the inmate's condition, and might also, like other visitors, walk along the passageway behind the walls of the shop and see the prisoner at work, though unobserved by him.[29] The news of the outside world was practically shut off, and the inmate was consigned to a practical oblivion.[27]

---
[23] Crawford. p. 26.
[24] B. and T., p. 30.
[27] Gershom Powers. Report, p. 17.
[29] Same, p. 34.

Hard labor, under this new system, became a fetish. Hard work was the rule of life outside the prison. If the prison could be made less costly by the labor of the prisoner, hard work should be the rule inside the prison. All of the prisoner's time was held to belong to the State.[25] If society had the right to take away his liberty, it had also the right to control his labor. The prisoners must work all the time during working hours. There was no over-stint — no task, after the regular day's assignment of work was done, at which they might earn a small bonus for themselves. Such perquisites were deemed highly demoralizing factors in the old prisons, the means of the bribery of officers, of gambling, and of the purchase of small luxuries. So here at Auburn, work must go on unremittingly, and without any compensation to the prisoner. Those soft-hearted persons who would make a prison anything but most rigorous were condemned as follows:

"Led too far by their theories, their sympathies seem to be all on the side of the convicts; and the comforts and conveniences that they would place in the way of the criminal, to induce him to reform, are so great, as to render his situation incomparably more pleasant and gratifying than that of many honest persons in the community who have never violated the laws."[26]

In order effectively to block any chance for the convict to have converse even within the prison with other persons, it was provided that

"no assistant keeper shall hold commonplace conversation with convicts, or allow them to speak to him on any subject, except on necessary business."[28]

There is in this protest of those who rebelled at alleviating and reformative influences in prison a constantly recurring comment and criticism of mild prison methods. The situation has always been clearly seen, but the solution has been difficult. The trouble has always arisen from the fact that the prison has, in the minds of different members of the public, different functions. If it is simply to punish, then punishments grievous and even torturing in their nature are admissible, according to the degree of punishment regarded as necessary and within the law. If the prison is primarily a money-earning institution, then the hard labor of the prisoners is the most important consideration, and all else must be subordinated to that achievement. If the prison is to reform, then it must be determined what are the elements making for reform, and they must be applied in proper balance. If to reform a prisoner it is necessary to educate him, the time given to education must be taken out of time that might be given to labor. If reform is to come through the application of humane principles of treatment, then punishments must yield to other methods, when possible. It is, in short, the clash of the several prominent "interests" of the prison program that has ever and again confused the prison problem.

But, as in the new system of Auburn Prison, there appear at times champions of a reformatory treatment who adhere to a belief

---

[25] B. P. D. S., 1833.
[26] Wharton-Shaler-King. Report.
[28] Same, p. 20.

in most rigorous methods as the surest reformative influences. Reformation by horror, constant hard labor, and by the breaking of the spirit, was the Auburn method. And the Boston Prison Discipline Society, progressive in its day, held that prisoners should defray by the fruits of their own labor in prison their expenses of food and clothing, medical care, moral and religious instruction, if possible the salaries of the officers and guards, and also the expenses of their own conviction and transportation.[30]

If, then, there were no inducements in the form of privileges at Auburn Prison that might be earned by the prisoners for work performed, there must obviously be some compelling force to secure such an output of product, and such obedience to the rigorous and unremitting rule of silence. *This force was the constantly impending punishment, and its frequent application.* It was frankly conceded by the administration that the system could not be maintained without prompt, severe and effective punishment. Pages upon pages were written in the early years of Auburn to justify the use of the "stripes," as flogging was called. The practice of the United States Navy was cited as proof that flogging was recognized and conceded to be necessary. The subordinate officers of the prison, who had authority to inflict corporal punishment, were justified by Powers, the warden, who said that they stood legally in the same relation to the convicts as the master stood to the apprentice, or as the schoolmaster to his scholar.[32] Decisions of judges from the bench upheld the actions of keepers who flogged.

Judge Walworth of Cayuga County, in which Auburn is located, said in 1826 in charging a jury:

"Confinement, with labor merely, has no terror for the guilty. . . . It is through bodily suffering alone that the proper effect upon the prisoner is produced, and thence the necessity of a rigid enforcement of the prison discipline upon every convict by the actual infliction of bodily suffering, if he will not otherwise submit to the rules."[31]

Edward Livingston, analyzing this opinion in his Introductory Report to the Code of Reform and Prison Discipline, stated his abhorrence of the illegal and arbitrary use of the lash by subordinates, and pointed out that so wide and illogical was the power of the keepers, that they flogged because a convict spoke to his neighbor, and flogged the convict if he denied having spoken to his neighbor.[33]

The board of inspectors of the prison held that inferior officers should be invested with power to punish. "The danger of abuse," they maintained, "is an evil much less than the relaxation of discipline produced by want of authority." It is worth noting that an earlier legal obligation of the inspectors to be present at such punishments was claimed to be so frequently inconvenient, and *to cause them such painful feelings*,[34] that they asked to be absolved from this duty, which was granted.

---
[30] B. P. D. S., 1827.
[31] B. and T., p. 159.
[32] Gershom Powers. Report, p. 23.
[33] P. 519.
[34] Beaumont and de Tocqueville, p. 43.

In short, the door was thrown wide open to the practically indiscriminate use of corporal punishment, upon the judgment of the inferior officer.

Punishments were inflicted with a rawhide whip, applied to the back in such a manner as (according to the rules) not to expose the head, face or eyes, or in any way put the convict's health or limbs in danger. This being a "high and delicate trust," the keepers were admonished to exercise the prerogative with humanity and discretion! In aggravated cases, a cat, made of six strands of small twine, was applied to the back of the convict. Whipping the convict for violation of rules seemed to Powers to produce less personal suffering to the convict than any other punishment that could be devised.[35] It was prompt; it was dreaded by the convict; it was soon over. The convict could then return to work, and little time was lost in the shop. The certainty of immediate punishment for an offense committed was held to be an important point in its favor.

Powers even claimed that the Auburn system of corporal punishment produced an excellent frame of mind in the prisoners:[36]

"A single unarmed keeper who may be in the shop with 50 or 60 convicts armed with deadly weapons, the implements of their trade, will order one of the most desperate of them to come before him for some offense as a father would call upon a rebellious son, or a teacher his disorderly scholar, and punish him in the presence of the other convicts. The delinquent almost uniformly receives his punishment submissively, and returns quietly to his labor. No rising or mutiny is ever occasioned, but, on the contrary, in the few cases where a delinquent has resisted, and attempted violence upon his keeper, the other convicts have never failed to rush instantly to his relief and protection. . . . Nearly six hundred men, possessed of the best possible means of defense and escape, restrained only by wooden gates, which are constantly opening, are kept in perfect security and control by a few unarmed keepers and two guards armed with muskets."

"Obey orders!" was the rule of prison life imposed constantly upon the convicts. It was unsafe ever to transgress a rule in the shops.[37] The entire system depended upon instant obedience to authority. There was to be no argument as to the circumstances of any individual case. A convict's word was never taken even against another convict, and much less against an officer.[38]

Yet the "watch" itself was not wholly trusted. Julius tells of the method of checking up the night-watch:

"There is in the wall, which separates each of the divisions from the other, a little window, through which the watchmen, of whom one goes on beat and one rests, must pass every half hour a leather ball, which thus in two hours has made the rounds. Only by an understanding among all night watchmen can this plan fail."

It was inevitable that with the development of this policy of severe and frequent corporal punishments, hostile criticism should soon develop against the new methods of the prison. Between 1825 and 1845, two controversial questions became the chief problems of both Auburn and Mount Pleasant (Sing Sing) prisons,

---

[35] Gershom Powers. Report, p. 23.
[36] Powers. Letter to Hon. Edward Livingston, pp. 22, 23.
[37] Gershom Powers. p. 13.
[38] Same, p. 25.

namely, prison punishments and prison labor. The first of these problems, in the early years of Auburn, we are now considering.

Perhaps we shall understand much better the course of prison discipline at Auburn Prison if we seek to understand Captain Lynds, who was twice warden at Auburn, twice warden at Mount Pleasant Prison (Sing Sing), and seemingly almost continually under public criticism for his severe methods of disciplining convicts. Captain Lynds' ideal was a prison that functioned with high industrial efficiency. Captain Lynds did not believe in the permanent reformability of adult convicts.[39] Silence was in his opinion indispensable to such a prison, not for reformation, but to prevent plots, riots and escapes. Any violation of rules must be punished at once. Deferred corporal punishment lost much of its force. Couched in present-day language, his first order to his keepers would have been: "Never let the convict start anything! Get him first!"

When Lynds was for the second time warden at Auburn, a disturbance in a certain tier of cells was reported to him. He ordered that some fifteen to twenty-five convicts be taken out, and that all of them be flogged. Among them he held that the right man would be found!

Lynds became the leading authority of his time in prison management, and he was commonly reputed to be the founder of the Auburn system. He was its most consistent and rigorous exponent. He resigned several times from a prison wardenship because of irreconcilable differences between himself and his superiors. In general, he dominated the inspectors. Their penal philosophy, expressed in annual reports, was mainly his own. His principles and theories undoubtedly also affected legislative committees, directed to investigate prison conditions.

As early as 1824, within a year of the definite establishment of the Auburn system, Captain Lynds' administration was already under fire. Punishments had been made very severe "because every other system had failed." [40] Although a school was maintained on Sunday for the younger convicts, it was given up shortly, because Lynds emphasized the increased danger to society of the educated convict! In 1824, a special commission, appointed by the Legislature with Samuel M. Hopkins as chairman, was directed to investigate the Auburn methods. Unquestionably the commission's report reflected Lynds' dogmatic and tenacious principles, in reporting that the State could not and ought not to undertake at the public's expense the moral reformation of convicts.[41] So excellent was the Auburn system in their eyes that they even advocated its adoption in the disorganized prison in New York city. These commissioners were shortly directed by the Legislature to build a projected new prison at Mount Pleasant, to supersede the one at Greenwich. That they should engage Captain Lynds for that task was natural. He was the ablest man in sight.

---

[39] Beaumont and de Tocqueville.
[40] New York Assembly Journal, 1823, p. 29.
[41] New York Assembly Journal, 1825, p. 108.

But Auburn continued to be under fire under Captain Gershom Powers — whose words relative to the value and excellence of capital punishment we have recently quoted. Startling stories, circulated in the village of Auburn by discharged officers and others, of brutal beatings at the prison by insane male convicts, and of the death of a female convict induced by blows, made a second investigation unavoidable. Again were sent as an investigating committee, Messrs. Hopkins, Allen and Tibbits, now the builders of Mount Pleasant Prison. Their bias, sincere in all probability, was unmistakable. The testimony of no convict was admissible. Should such evidence be admitted, any keeper could at any time be put on trial at the pleasure of a convict, with no loss to the convict, but with ruinous expense to the defendant.[42] Keepers could thus be always in partial subservience to convicts, through fear of what they might testify.

The commission's report supported emphatically the Auburn system of punishments. Rewards to prisoners were inadmissible, because the convict was condemned to punishment. Personal punishments alone could govern desperate convicts; without prompt correction, at the discretion of the assistant keepers, the whole structure of the system would fall.[43] The report of the committee would to-day be dubbed a whitewash. Most obvious cases of flogging of feebleminded and insane convicts were justified, condoned or explained away. That a dangerous convict, after repeated flogging, finally settled down to do women's work was held to be a general justification of the system. The sum total was that, according to the commissioners, in a little more than four years under Captain Lynds, six cases of punishment deserved special attention, of which two were abuse, while under his successor, a Mr. Goodell, a mild-mannered and good-natured man, there were twenty-one conspicuous cases of punishment, of which twelve were abuses.

The sudden and brief appearance of this Mr. Goodell as warden of Auburn Prison following Captain Lynds is more than usually interesting. This warden started out with deliberate humaneness of treatment. The commissioners, reporting upon his term of office, contemptuously attacked his theories as "grounded upon the good qualities of convicted felons,"[44] which led him to seek, by kindness and confidence, to inspire the convicts with a spirit of willing and generous obedience. The results were said to be a serious relaxation of discipline, and an insolence and decrease of work on the part of the prisoners. No less than six vicious attacks on keepers occurred in Goodell's administration, and which in a year was terminated by his own fatal illness. What might have ultimately been accomplished by Goodell can be only a matter of conjecture. The incident is of especial importance, in the history of prison administration, as being the earliest recorded effort to soften the rigors of the Auburn system at the institution itself.

---

[42] New York Senate Journal, 1827. No. 50, Appendix A, p. 2.
[43] New York Senate Journal, 1827. No. 50, Appendix A, p. 8.
[44] Op. Cit., p. 30.

Even at this time, there was sounded by Edward Livingston, the eminent framer of the Code of Reform and Penal Discipline for the State of Louisiana, a most cogent and prophetic warning against the perpetuation of the system of severity of punishments — a warning which, however, was not heeded: [45]

"A superficial view of this subject has led to the belief that the great secret of penal legislation is, to annex a penalty of sufficient severity to every offense; and, accordingly, all the variety of pains that the body of man could suffer, infamy and death, have figured as sanctions in the codes of all nations; but although these have been in a train of experiment for thousands of years, under every variety that Government, manners and religion can give, they have never produced the expected effect. The reason is to be found in the insurgent spirit with which man was endowed by his beneficent creator to answer the best ends of his nature.

The same feeling that, elevated, refined and applied to the noblest purpose animates the patriot to resist civil tyranny, and the martyr to defy the flames; when it is perverted, and made the incentive to vice and crime, goads on the convict to arraign the justice of his sentence, to rebel against those who execute it, and to counteract its effects with an obstinacy in exact proportion to the severity of the punishment. . . . Few instances can be found in which any series of constrained acts have produced the habit of continuing them after the force was removed."

Yet it is easy to misjudge and to overestimate the severity of the disciplinary features of Auburn Prison. The rules were indeed rigid and the punishments speedy and harsh; that the keepers were equipped with legal power sufficient to guarantee their legal and political "safety" in inflicting punishments is evidenced in the following section from a law passed in 1819, wherein it is provided that if a prisoner in a State prison refuse to comply with the rules of the institution,

"It is hereby declared to be the duty of the respective keepers under the direction of the inspectors to inflict corporal punishment on such prisoners by whipping not to exceed 39 lashes at any time, or to confine them in solitary cells on bread and water, or to put them in irons or stocks. . . ."

In 1828 the revised statutes gave further range of action to the officers of the prison, by providing that, in case of violence on the part of convicts, or attempts to escape,

"officers of the prison shall use all suitable means to defend themselves, enforce the observance of discipline, to secure the persons of the offenders and to prevent any such attempt at escape."

As Klein observes, in "Prison Methods in New York State," this is an even more generous blanket license for the imposition of punishment than that contained in the law of 1796, for it was exceedingly simple for officials to consider any movement on the part of the prisoner as violence, attempted violence or attempted escape.

Miss Harriet Martineau, in her "Retrospect of Western Travel," published in New York in 1838, says of the punishments then observed in the women's quarters in Auburn Prison:

"The arrangements for the women were extremely bad. The gabble of tongues in the one room (in which the women prisoners were confined) was enough to paralyze any matron. There was an engine in sight which made

---
[45] Op. Cit., p. 16.

me doubt the evidence of my own eyes; stocks, of a terrible construction; a chair, with a fastening for the head and all the limbs. Any lunatic asylum ought to be ashamed of such an instrument. The governor (i. e., warden) liked it no better than we. He pleaded that it was only means of keeping his refractory prisoners quiet with only one room to put them in. . . . The first principle in the management of the guilty seems to me to be to treat them as men and women. . . . Their humanity is the principal thing about them; their guilt is a temporary state. The insane are first men, and secondarily diseased men.

"The women, all in the attic story of the south wing, were in Power's time under the supervision of the steward keeper of the kitchen. They were employed mainly in picking wool, in knitting, and in spooling, although to very little advantage, as no means of coercion could very well be adopted, according to Warden Powers, nor any restraint be put upon their conversation with each other, because they were left alone, except once a day, when the steward keeper went with three of his kitchen convicts, taking the rations of the women, and the other supplies, and ordered out the work that they had done. They were visited by the physician when sick, and sometimes by the chaplain."

Nevertheless there is abundant testimony, even from prison chaplains, that the well-behaved prisoners suffered little punishment.[46] Never had the Reverend Jared Curtis

"heard a convict complain that more was exacted of him than was reasonable, or that his rations were not good, and in sufficient quantity. . . . A large portion of the convicts are better fed and clothed, and are in all respects more comfortable than when they enjoyed their liberty and were preying upon the community."

Even the most tender-hearted and humane philanthropists could not refrain from feeling at times that the lash was necessary. It was an age in which the use of the rod was far more customary than to-day. "Spare the rod and spoil the child" is an adage enjoying the strength of long-time sanction. Even some twenty years after the establishment of the Auburn system, Dorothea Dix herself, in 1845, sanctioned reluctantly the use of the "cat" as a last resort:

"Those who at present urge the abandonment of all modes of maintaining discipline except the language of persuasion must be either reckless of consequences, or ignorant of human nature as manifested by a considerable portion of ignorant, long-abased convicts. Those who discover (i. e., show) few traits above the lowest of the brute creation can no more, at first, be influenced to obey rules and general order by mild influence and words, than the tiger or hyena can be brought to tameness by an expressive word or gentle regard. . . . I am certain I could never subdue my instinctive horror and disgust of punishment by the lash. . . . I could never order, witness or permit its application, but I am forced, with unspeakable reluctance, to concede that I believe it may sometimes be the only mode, under the Auburn system, by which an insurrectionary spirit can be conquered. It should not be inflicted during the first moments of excitement . . . (and) not until reasonable and mild measures have been persevered in, and proved to be unavailing. . . ."

We have found, then, as pillars of the Auburn system, the factors of silence, separation, hard labor and severe corporal punishments. What, on the other hand, did the new system offer of reformative value?

Much, according to its sponsors, in addition to the above-mentioned features, all of which were held to be reformative in themselves.

---

[46] New York Senate Journal, 1827. No. 50, Appendix A, p. 8.

Sunday, at Auburn Prison, was a day without work by the convicts. After the usual breakfast in the messhall, they were marched back to their cells, where, except for the period of church service, they were allowed for the rest of the day to be on their beds, until the bell rang in the evening for undressing.[47] Recall the not very remote New England Sunday, vivid memory of my own boyhood for instance, when any active pleasure on Sunday was regarded as quite contrary to the purposes of the Lord's Day! No games were played by "properly" brought up youngsters, thirty years or more ago in New England, and to hear band music or to go skating on Sunday was quite outside the correct observance of the day.

Therefore, it is readily understood that, a hundred years ago, in the Auburn prison, there would be nothing approaching active movement in the prison population on Sunday. Imagine the long Sunday, passed in cells of less than 200 cubic feet of space, without reading matter, save the one Book always present, which, however good, would at times pall. No visitor, no friend, no chance to have intercourse with even a fellow-inmate, no hope of any change on the morrow, or next week, or next month, except for those soon to go out of the prison. No exercise, no chance to bathe in the sun, or breathe the fine country air. No slightest chance to gratify the instincts of sociability, of play, of ambition, of anything! Sunday differed from any other day only in being a day of no work, and a day when for those who elected to do so, church might be attended, within the prison, of course.

Such convicts, choosing church, remained in their seats in the messhall at the close of breakfast, and were taken by two keepers into the chapel, where they were taught by some twenty young men from the local theological seminary in the village, who volunteered their services.[48]

The resident chaplain had general supervision over the Sunday school. Any conversation whatsoever between the young citizen-teachers and the convicts on any subject other than the lessons was rigorously forbidden. The Sunday school privilege was eagerly embraced by about a fourth of the prison population. It was absolutely the only alleviation of the entire week! One prisoner pleaded for any form of punishment other than that of being deprived of his Sunday school.[50] To De Metz and Blouet, the prisoners stated at Auburn that Sunday was the hardest of the week to endure, because of passing the day in a narrow cell.[49] In addition to Bible study, and religious instruction, convicts were taught reading, writing and arithmetic.. As early as 1822, it was seen that the Auburn prison population was highly illiterate. More than three-fourths of the population could barely read and write, and not one in ten possessed any high degree of intelligence.[51]

---

[47] Powers. Report, p. 34.
[48] Powers, p. 34.
[49] De Metz and Blouet, p. 13.
[50] B. P. D. S., 1827, p. 93.
[51] Report of Inspectors, 1822.

The chaplain was regarded as the only officer of the prison whose work was clearly reformative. The "agent and keeper" (the two titles of the executive officer of the prison) was the business manager of the institution. Reformation was not his duty. Frequently he doubted if it could be achieved. The principal keeper was the general disciplinarian and was also the captain of the prison staff of keepers and guards. These officials were not concerned with the saving of the prisoners' souls, but with the security of their bodies, and the protection of the citizens from their depredations. They had the routine tasks of keeping order, preventing escapes, maintaining industry and punishing for violations of rules. The physician's task did not extend beyond the intermittent and relatively cursory care of the sick. And so the chaplain — tolerated rather than actively favored by the administration — must be the prisoners' guide back to rectitude and honesty.

Hence the insistence by Warden Powers, who for his time was clearly an enlightened warden, that there should be a resident chaplain, giving his whole time to his work. This was, of course, a considerable innovation. This service of the chaplain, Reverend Jared Curtis, was at first partially contributed by the Boston Prison Discipline Society, which from 1825 on furnished and paid his salary. It was not surprising that a philanthropic society of another State should maintain a chaplain at Auburn. That prison, for a time, was the only typical prison exemplifying the new system. The Boston Society started out by being not local or even State-wide in its interests, but national, and it early made through its representative, Louis Dwight, frequent and valuable visits to many American institutions, the results of which appeared year after year in the annual reports of the Prison Discipline Society, and furnish to us to-day the most cogent and most accessible source of our information of this period.

Warden Powers felt, in 1828, that the State itself ought to appoint such an officer as the chaplain. The duties of the chaplain should be to have the special supervision of the religious instruction of the convicts, visiting and conversing with them in their cells, imploring a blessing at their tables before they sat down to eat, and praying with them after they went to their cells at night, and before they lay down to sleep.[52] Everything that the chaplain did, however, must conform to the rules of the prison.

To-day the progressive and socially-minded chaplain is, in a modern State prison or reformatory, one of the most influential and most necessary officers. There are a thousand and one intimate needs of the prisoners. The Sunday service is but a small, though important, part of the chaplain's weekly work. He it is who in particular furnishes the link between the inmate and his family outside. He advises with the prisoners, often teaches, often prays with them, not infrequently becomes the intimate sharer of the inmate's secrets. The chaplain is at the bedside of the sick, and is the solace, so far as there can be solace, of the man about to pay the

---

[52] Gershom Powers, p. 54.

extreme penalty, and he walks with him to the chair or to the gallows. The chaplain's work is never done — and his strength among the inmate population depends almost entirely upon his own personality and his own conception of his high duty and privilege.

In an outline by the warden of Mount Pleasant Prison, Robert Wiltse, in 1834, the following duties and obligations of the chaplain were outlined, which applied in all probability to Auburn Prison also, and represented the attitude of the time toward the activity of the chaplain within the prison:

The chaplain was to conform strictly to all the rules of the prison. He was to furnish the convicts with no intelligence save what his profession required him to give. He was to give no hope or promise of pardon, or of attempting to procure a pardon.

He was to have free access to the convicts save when they were in the shops at labor. He was to make the convict feel the necessity of amendment, and of strict obedience. He was to convince, if possible, the convict of the justice of his sentence.

Turning back to the period of the wardenship of Gershom Powers, we find how absolutely divorced from the task of individual counsel and co-operation with the inmate was the position of warden at that time. Powers, by his own statement, regarded his duties toward the inmate of such distant nature that not until the discharge of the convict from the prison did he invite him into his office and there, *for the first time,* "enter into a free and friendly conversation with him," endeavoring "by desultory course of inquiry" to arrive at a knowledge of his former history; how he was "bred up;" what means of literary, moral and religious instruction he had enjoyed, etc. The prisoner was also asked in detail as to the effects of his confinement; in what respect he had endured the most suffering, how he had been treated, and in what business he was now to engage. After the convict had stated that of all the impulses and of the temptations of prison, the craving to talk with his fellow-man was the greatest, and that he often did not know the names of his fellow convicts who had worked for months at his side, the convict was given the customary three dollars allowed by law, and he was dismissed — of course, with admonition and advice! [53]

Powers believed that it was wise to postpone this interview until the last moment of the convict's prison term, because

"during the period of their confinement, the convicts have so many motives for concealment, that the same reliance could not be placed on the statements they might make." [54]

Wardens of the present day, reading of this early method of Gershom Powers, and thinking on their own present methods of dealing with their individual inmates, will, many of them, ponder at the wide difference between the present and the past. For it is by far the most common custom of wardens to hold frequent interviews with the inmates, and in particular to grant to inmates the privilege of an interview upon a request placed in the designated

---
[53] Powers. Report, p. 50.
[54] Powers, p. 49.

box in the prison yard or building, and accessible to all prisoners. Indeed, I have seen in prison after prison during the last ten years, a really striking knowledge and intimate interest on the part of wardens as to their inmates' desires and affairs. The many big-hearted wardens who in recent years have often made bold experiments with the honor system have recognized that one of their chief functions in their prisons has been to know their inmates not simply officially but personally, and with sympathy and interest in their affairs. They have recognized the high value of such a relationship in inducing reformation and a sense of responsibility.

Have we not, even already in this study, seen emerge from the gray background of these prisons that pass before our eyes the figures of outstanding personalities? Have we not been, perhaps unconsciously, seeking to understand the prison by interpreting the man who was the warden, or who built the institution, or whose penal philosophy led to some result which we have noted. Have we not already seen pass before us the spirit of William Penn, of William Bradford, of Caleb Lownes, of Thomas Eddy? And, in the times of great demoralization, and of failure, have we not marked the absence of any outstanding personality? Where were the men to combat the debacle in the Massachusetts State Prison, or at Newgate in Connecticut?

But with the rise of the new system at Auburn, we find looming up successively, as contributors to an organization that was for its time the most successful in the country, the figures of Captain Brittin, of Elam Lynds, and of Gershom Powers. We shall see the dominance of Lynds at Mount Pleasant Prison mark that institution with specific characteristics. Throughout this study we shall in reality be noting the close correlation of the dominant personality with the note-worthy product, in some form, within the prison.

Indeed, I have recently written, apropos of the spirit manifested in a modern prison:

"No warden in any prison can conceal the 'spirit of the prison' from the trained observer. A warden can attempt to camouflage his institution by expatiating upon the high polish of the floors, the excellent cleanliness of the nooks and crannies, the fine light bread, the precision of administration — and those are necessary parts of a prison regime, but not the soul of it. The warden can seek by hale and hearty joviality, or by an assumption of learning, or confidential communications, or apparent solicitude for his 'boys' or for 'penology' and the like, to conceal other conditions of dubious nature.

"But he cannot camouflage the way the inmates react to him, look at him, get ready for him as he approaches — and these things are tell-tale barometers of an institution. This Raiford project (i. e., the State Prison Farm of Florida, which the writer had just visited, and which had inspired the article) could hardly last over night, with the present very few paid employes if something beside the law did not hold it together. Even the powerhouse, the electric plant, the mechanical heart of the institution is run wholly by inmates. At any instant, of an evening, the lights could all be cut off, the power shut down. The few cars or teams could be commandeered without too much difficulty. So something must hold Raiford together, for throughout the institution, during the day, there are no guns. The gangs working under inmate overseers are not dominated by shotguns or rifles.

"The something that makes Raiford go is probably a combination of good spirit, the sense of a square deal, a traditional submission to authority, and a fear of the extremely heavy penalties for attempted escape. . . . The spirit of an institution is the finest asset — or the greatest liability — that can be presented to the State by the institution. Industry, product, buildings, discipline, are, of course, essentials. But the intangible thing, the spirit of the place, the thing that underlies the daily life of the place, underlies honor systems, attempts at self-government and the like — that is the conditioning factor in reclamation and rehabilitation, the cement that holds the hghly dynamic mass from flying off centrifugally, when guns and guards are lacking, and the portals yawn with temptations to escape."

So, in this earlier era, we begin to think of prisons as Captain Lynds' prison (Sing Sing), or Gershom Powers' prison (Auburn), or a little later Samuel Wood's prison (Eastern Penitentiary of Pennsylvania), and Amos Pilsbury's prison (the Connecticut State Prison at Wethersfield).

Hopkins wrote:[55]

"Many at Auburn prison are often moved to tears under the preaching of an eloquent and able minister there. . . . I have also heard them sobbing in great numbers, at a few words spoken to them in public by Mr. Powers, in which he alluded to the situation and feelings of their friends. . . . We must avoid extremes in judging of them. They are not the innocent victims of unjust laws; but neither are they all demons. They are men, though greatly fallen."

For, despite the apparently paradoxical attitude of mind toward the establishment of friendly relations with the prisoners during the terms of the incarceration, Powers appeared to be sincerely interested in at least establishing the fact that Auburn Prison was a reformative institution. He tried hard to learn, by letters sent out to postmasters, district attorneys and others, something about the subsequent career of convicts discharged from his prison. In his edition of 1828, he stated that of 160 prisoners released, 112 were described by correspondence as being subsequent to their prison careers decidedly steady and industrious, and of relatively good character; 12 as somewhat reformed; 2 as not much improved; 4 of whom nothing was known; 2 as deranged, and 20 as decidedly bad.[56] At this time, 29 prisoners at Auburn had been previously confined therein. Powers deduced therefrom that his statistics

"warranted the increased exertions of the legislators and of all who feel an interest in the moral improvement and reformation of this degraded and unhappy class of our fellow beings."[57]

This is an early effort to prove results statistically, and cannot be accepted as conclusive. There is no indication that the entire prison population that had been discharged had been studied. Furthermore, it has been found, even in these modern days, that the information gathered through correspondence is frequently inaccurate or too general to be wholly trustworthy. In the early days of Auburn Prison, when postal service was primitive and dilatory, it could hardly be expected that such information would be full or to the point. Moreover, the statistics as gathered show

---
[55] De Metz and Blouet, p. 346.
[56] B. P. D. S., 1828.
[57] Powers, p. 71.

that some sixty-five to seventy per cent. of the released inmates, as included in the total number studied, were "behaving themselves." But these former inmates had been but a short time out of prison. The test of reformation is not by any means the first six months, or the first year out of prison, but a period of at least several years. The chief fallacy still existing in the majority of the reports of institutions maintaining parole lies in the assumption that any released inmate who passes successfully through the period of parole — six months or a year, or even more — is "reformed." Few correctional institutions, even to-day, in the United States have statistics showing the subsequent record of released inmates extending beyond the conclusion of the period of parole.

We turn now, briefly, to the industrial phases of the earliest history of Auburn Prison. It was in the years from 1828 on, that Warden Powers and his successors could record the financial success of the prison as an industrial plant. The Boston Prison Discipline Society held in its first annual report that prisoners should practically defray the expenses of maintenance of the prison. By 1828, the earnings of Auburn for the fiscal year had come to within $1,000 of the total disbursements, which were $35,504. Warden Powers maintained that

"the most sanguine economist never dreamed of making public prisoners pay for their support, and also for prisons to confine them."

But he added in the same year that he believed no further appropriation would ever be necessary for the support of the convicts in the prison, unless in case of some unforeseen calamity.[58]

The distribution of labor and the earnings at Auburn Prison in the year ending October 31, 1827, were as follows:

	No. of Convicts	Average Daily Earnings per man	Total Earnings for month
Cooper Shop	106	$0.27	$770
Tool Shop	25	.37	246
Shoemaker's Shop	69	.33	551
Tailor's Shop	57	.23	282
Weaver's Shop	104	.25	485
Blacksmith's Shop	34	.48	335
Turner's Shop	16	.30	123

In addition, there were working on October 31, 1828, 90 others, besides 14 females, at building, and as cooks, washers, woodsawers, scrubbers, waiters, etc.

At the time of Power's wardenship, the complicated problems of the competition of prison labor with free labor had already arisen, as well as the equally perplexing problem of contract labor — the letting of the labor of the prisoners to private firms or individuals. The prison, through its products, was influencing the "open market," and was arousing the ire of the "free mechanics," as the laboring man and the artisan of the day were called. Within a few

[58] B. P. D. S., 1828, p. 164. Gershom Powers. Report, p. 48.

years after the establishment of Auburn Prison upon a basis that from the standpoint of the administration was industrially "sound," Auburn Prison was to become the storm center of a violent agitation against prison-made products and the contracting of the labor of prisoners.

Discussion of this very important development must be deferred to Chapter twelve. We can, however, make a rapid survey of the prison labor laws of the State of New York up to the period we now leave, for discussion of other prisons and States.

The law of 1796, applying then, of course, to the newly planned State prison that was built in Greenwich, provided that

"it shall and may be lawful for the inspectors of each of the said prisons either by themselves or by an agent or agents to be by them from time to time appointed, to purchase such . . . tools, implements, raw or other materials on which to employ the convicts . . . and shall cause to be kept regular accounts of all the articles so to be purchased and of the avails arising from the sales of any articles manufactured by the convicts in such prisons . . . and to carry the residue to the credit of the State.

We have seen in Chapter 6 the early undertakings of the prison at Greenwich. The first labor opposition appeared about 1801, and came from boot and shoemakers, resulting in an amendment to the law, and requiring that boots and shoes made by convicts should be branded with the words "State Prison." Some three years later, a further law prohibited the employment of more than one-eighth of the convicts in the State Prison in the making of boots and shoes, excluding from this number those who had learned their trade before commitment.

In 1819, the prison authorities were empowered by law to employ convicts

"upon any of the public avenues, roads, streets or other works in the city of New York, and also on other public works in the counties of Richmond and Kings (now Staten Island and Brooklyn).

A further law authorized, in 1820, "the purchase of marble quarries to be operated by convict labor from the New York Prison." In 1817 a law had been passed permitting the employment of prisoners on canals to be constructed under the canal commissioners of the State.

In 1817, there had been a radical effort made, through law, to do away with the manufacturing by the State of prison-made products on its own account. In that year, a law prohibited

"the purchase of any materials to be wrought or worked up for sale by the convicts confined in the State Prison on account of the State after October 31, 1817."

The law furthermore directed that convicts were to be

"solely employed in manufacturing and making up such material as may be brought to the State Prison by or for individuals or convicts to whom such materials may belong, to be manufactured at fixed prices for labor bestowed upon them, to be paid by the owners of the goods to the agent of the said prison for the use of the State."

This is an early form of the system known as "piece-price," whereby the State acts as the manufacturer of the goods, but does not undertake to market them, or to procure the raw materials in the first place. This plan did not work successfully, and in the following year, 1818, the prison was by law permitted to continue the earlier system of manufacturing on its own account and selling its products in the open market, a system known later as the "State-account" system.

In 1821, contract labor was authorized by law, whereby the labor of prisoners might be leased to outside firms or "contractors" at a daily rate per capita, specified in the contract. Such work in the majority of cases in our American prisons has been done within the prison walls, and where the actual physical presence of prisoners has been contracted for, as in the turpentine groves of Florida or on railroad construction, the method of contracting has been known as the "lease system."

The commission that was appointed in 1824 to examine into the subjects of prison and prison management reported that

"the largest source of income is from the labor of convicts done for account of individuals, and on raw materials and articles brought into, and worked up in the prison workshops and charged to the employers or contractors by the piece."

Prison labor, presumably with emphasis on the piece-price system, had thus far been profitable at Auburn Prison. But under the statutes of 1828, the year of Gershom Power's revised account of Auburn Prison, contract labor was introduced as a permanent policy of the State prisons of New York. The law of 1828 provided that

"whenever the inspectors of either prison shall so direct, it shall be the duty of the agent of such prison to make contracts from time to time for the labor of convicts confined therein, or of any of the said convicts with such persons and upon such terms as may be deemed by the said agent most beneficial to the State . . . it shall be the duty of the agents to use their best efforts to defray all the expenses of the said prisons by the labor of their prisoners."

We turn now, at this period of the more stable utilization of contract labor in the prisons of New York, to a study of the early years of the most noted prison upon the American continent, the State prison erected from 1825 on in the village of Sing Sing on the banks of the Hudson.

CHAPTER X

THE EARLY YEARS OF MOUNT PLEASANT PRISON (SING SING)

On an April evening in 1920, the writer of this study, accompanied by a song-leader who had done service in the army during the war, and an accompanist who had played and sung, up and down the trenches in France, went up to Sing Sing Prison from New York to aid in conducting the first "community sing" in that century-old institution. The song-leader, after his remarkable experience of that evening, was dubbed the "man who put the 'sing' in Sing Sing."

To the writer, sitting in the extreme rear of the great room that serves as auditorium and chapel, watching in the semi-darkness (as the slides were thrown on the screen with the words of the popular songs), and seeing over a thousand men sitting there, singing lustily, resonantly, with fine volume and with surprising accuracy of tone and appreciation, the mental pictures of the origin in 1825 of this Bastile on the Hudson recurred with almost poignant vividness. Here in A. D. 1920, were convicts, assembled together without guards, singing the same songs that the men of the army had sung in France, in going into battle, and in the training camps of this country. Here was an essentially normal process — singing in common — and here were a thousand men on honor, conducting themselves without the presence of prison officials, enjoying the unusual treat of singing human songs in a human, co-operative way! Murderers, burglars, robbers, embezzlers — all sorts and kinds of criminals — sang of home, and of mother, and of the simple virtues, sang of love, and hope, and joy, of country and of God!

The meeting was being conducted by the Mutual Welfare League, a self-governing organization of the prisoners that was founded in 1914 by Thomas Mott Osborne, when he became warden of Sing Sing Prison. The man who introduced the song leader and the accompanist that evening was a convicted murderer. The inmate guards were of all degrees of crime. During the day and the evening, the officials of the Mutual Welfare League controlled, within such limits as the warden designated, the social side of the inmates' prison life.

Yes, through the span of a century, fundamental changes have come over the prisons of the country! Sing Sing, as we said at the beginning of this study, is shortly to become the most noteworthy example in the world of the receiving and distributing prison. But when, in 1824, the Legislative commission, consisting of Stephen Allen, Samuel M. Hopkins and George Tibbits, were appointed to visit both Auburn and Greenwich Prisons, their sole purpose was to report on their relative merits, and to plan for some institution that would solve the notorious problems of the old prison in Greenwich.

This commission, reporting in 1825, adhered with conviction to the merits of the new system at Auburn. They had been profoundly impressed with the talents, integrity and system of discipline inaugurated there by Elam Lynds, the Auburn warden.[1] Undoubtedly, the commingling and the idleness at the Greenwich prison accentuated by contrast the impressiveness of Warden Lynds' new methods. The commission gave also special study to the economic responsibilities of a prison. Prisoners should not only *not* be idle, but they should meet so far as possible the cost of maintaining the prison. According to the commissioners,[2] the kind of work fitted for a State prison should embody the following properties:

It should be of a kind for which there is a great demand.
The material should be cheap.
The trade should be one that is easily learned.
It should be a business that cannot be so conducted by machinery as to reduce the wages too greatly.
The trade should be one at which hard labor can be enforced, and also be made profitable.

The commissioners advised the abandonment of the State prison at Greenwich, because it was of unfit construction, and incapable of maintaining profitable industries. Casting their business gaze toward other States, they saw both the State prisons of New Hampshire and Massachusetts carrying on a profitable industry in stonecutting. Where could a quarry or quarries be secured near New York? Either at Marble Hill, near New York (just beyond the extreme north end of the island of Manhattan) or in the village of Sing Sing. Why should stone cutting be the determining industrial factor in the establishment and location of the new prison?

Because:[3]

The raw material would require only the labor of convicts in its preparation.
The demand for the article as a building material was bound to increase.
A prison located on the Hudson River, near New York, would make the expense of transportation by water to the place of demand slight. There would also be demand for the stone from outside the State.
The quarries under consideration by the commission would not come in competition with others, since they were the nearest ones to New York city.
Such quarries would furnish hard and constant labor to the convicts — thus meeting the requirements of their sentences.
In this business, the manual labor would not be likely to be displaced later by machinery.
Furthermore, the prisoners could build their own prison from the materials at hand; the stone prison thus constructed would be both fireproof and impregnable. Repairs on a stone prison would be much less costly.

These arguments impressed the Legislature, as did also the estimate of a probable cost of only $62,671 for building a prison of 800 individual cells — this sum to include maintenance of 100 working convicts the first year of construction, and of 200 such convicts in the next two years. The old prison in New York might be sold

---
[1] Report of Select Comm. of New York Senate, 1831, p. 2.
[2] Assembly Journal, 1825, p. 112.
[3] Op. Cit. (Assembly Journal), p. 132.

for $50,000, and if the $40,000 of repairs necessary to the old prison were added thereto, the State would gain financially by the erection of a new prison elsewhere.

The commissioners carried the day, and were also appointed a commission to locate and build the prison that was to become the best known — at times the most notorious — in the world. An option was secured at Mount Pleasant, in the town of Sing Sing, of a tract of 130 acres, called the Silver Mine Farm, and belonging to John Fleetwood Marsh. On this land, rising steeply from the Hudson to a height of some 170 feet, and 33 miles from New York, a silver mine had been extensively worked before and up to the War of the Revolution.[4] It was reported that silver ore in considerable quantities had been taken out. More recently, several tons of copper ore had been extracted.

The State appropriated $70,000 in March, 1825, with which to build the new prison. Mr. Marsh's farm and a small adjacent parcel were bought for $20,100. Captain Lynds was engaged to build the new prison — on his guarantee that he could successfully meet the wholly new problem of constructing a great prison by the labor of desperate convicts, lodged not in a walled prison, but literally in the fields.

The undertaking was daring, but Lynds was filled with confidence. He picked his hundred convicts from Auburn Prison, instead of from the near-by prison in New York, because the Auburn prisoners were more familiar not only with cutting and laying stone, but also with his swift and heavy hand.

In the spring of 1825, the convicts were taken from Auburn Prison to the canal, seven miles away, whence they were brought in two canal boats to the Hudson River, and thence in freight steamers to Sing Sing, where they arrived on May 14th. Each man made the journey with shackles on one leg. On the same day they erected a temporary barracks,[5] and soon afterwards a cookhouse, and a blacksmith's and carpenter's shop. They proceeded at once to the leveling of the broken and precipitous side hill for a prison site. From the outset this task proved slower and more arduous than had been anticipated. The convicts were guarded by officers with guns, and from the first a rigid discipline of obedience and silence was enforced.

We must make no mistake about the methods pursued in maintaining this system of out-door employment of convicts at Mount Pleasant Prison. This was no forerunner of a system of outdoor convict labor on an honor basis. Riots and escapes were prevented only by absolute obedience to the commands of labor and silence. Guards had full authority to inflict "stripes" without even reporting such floggings to their superior officers.

"Why are these nine hundred malefactors less strong than the thirty individuals who command them? Because the keepers communicate freely with each other, act in concert, and have all the power of association; whilst the convicts, separated from each other by silence, have, in spite of their

---

[4] Senate Journal, 1829, p. 304.
[5] Senate Document 92, 1834, p. 7.

numerical force, all the weakness of isolation. Suppose for an instant, the prisoners obtain the least facility of communication; the order is immediately the reverse; the union of their intellects, effected by their spoken word, has taught them their strength; and the first infraction of the law of silence destroys the whole discipline."[6]

Clearly, then, the sanction for silence, as an integral part of the Auburn system, rested on the necessity of preventing disorder, riots and escapes, as well as on the importance of preserving the individual prisoner from the contaminating influence of his associates. The warden of the period was probably far less worried about the possibilities of still further demoralizing his inmate population by mutual opportunities for conversation than he was about the chances of the development of plots through mutual communication. The same principle of perpetual silence, therefore, which appealed to the philanthropist for its preventive and reformative value, was pleasing to the prison official as a disciplinary and precautionary measure.

By the coming of cold weather, 60 cells had been built of the 800 proposed. The prison was to be a single building, 476 feet long, 44 feet wide, and four tiers high. The plan of the cellblock was to be almost identical with that of Auburn. The cells were placed back to back. Their dimensions were depth 7 feet, width 3 feet 3 inches, height 6 feet 7 inches. These cells are used to-day, nearly a century after they were built, and are intolerably small, often very damp, and altogether unfit for human habitation. They will be abandoned with the completion of the new receiving and classification prison.

Two reasons conditioned the location of the prison at the water's edge. First, the importance of having the workshops at tidewater, in order to facilitate the delivery of the stone with the minimum of cartage. Secondly, for reasons of health,[7] by which was meant probably the importance of securing easy drainage facilities. This latter reason is the more surprising because in later days, one of the chief criticisms of Sing Sing Prison was its dampness and consequent unhealthiness. When William Crawford, the English visitor, went through the prison in 1832 he found the prison cells deficient in ventilation, they had a close and offensive smell, probably owing to the low situation in which the building stands, and which prevents as good a circulation of air as might be obtained on a higher spot. The floor is damp in wet weather."[8] In 1845, for instance, only twenty years after the beginning of the construction of the prison, Dorothea Dix wrote that the location of the prison rendered the cells damp, and even the fires in the stoves in the corridors failed to correct this condition.

Within six months of commencing work on the prison, in 1825, the convicts were already being housed two in a cell. The campaign, nearly a century later, for the permanent abolition of Sing Sing, was based largely upon the pernicious "doubling up" of prisoners in these viciously small cells, in a great, damp bastile-like

[6] B. & T., p. 26.
[7] New York Senate Journal, 1827, p. 62.
[8] Crawford, p. 29.

structure. Here, at the very outset of this prison's history, the same practice was begun, with the inevitable excuse of "lack of room." Obviously, it broke down temporarily the Auburn system of separation and silence, the cardinal principles of the new method, just as in our own time the doubling up of prisoners, two in a cell, has broken down morality, health, and lessened the possibility of reformation.

We find reference, at this time, to what and how much the convicts in 1825 ate, and how they were fed. A certain Ebenezer Wilson secured the contract for feeding the prisons, at 8¼ cents a day per capita, on the following dietary — the meat being salt, not fresh:

1 lb. prime beef, or ¾ lb. prime pork.
12 oz. rye flour.
6 oz. Indian meal.
¾ gill molasses.

And for every hundred rations:

3 bushels potatoes.
4 qts. rye for rye coffee.
2 qts. vinegar.
2 oz. pepper.

During the first year, so alert were the guards that there was but one escape, and this convict was retaken. There were three deaths, and "some sickness." A hospital was lacking.

A year later, $63,503 of the original appropriation of $70,000 had been expended, but only 170 feet of the cellhouse had been erected. Work was delayed by the great amount of excavating and leveling. The maximum of 200 convicts, that had been planned for the second year could not be employed for lack of quarters. The simple expedient of housing convicts under such circumstances in temporary shacks was evidently not deemed longer feasible, although it had been done the year before. Convicts transferred from the State prison at Greenwich had proved poor workers, and also refractory. Lynds always maintained that the prisoner must go through a process that we would to-day call "breaking," before he became a useful and docile convict. These men from the old State prison did not fall into the Lynds' system of discipline. On December 1st, there were 169 convicts at the prison, of whom 158 were quarrying, cutting stone or excavating.

An incident of 1826 throws a side light on the curious sense of what was felt to be a privilege granted by the then commissioners. The Legislature raised the question why the iron grated doors in the Mount Pleasant Prison should be hung flush with the corridor, instead of nearly two feet back, at the inner end of the recess of the cell door as at Auburn. The commissioners solemnly assured the Legislature that they had done this partly in order that the prisoner, when pacing up and down within his cell, might extend his walk from 2½ to 3 steps!

Another year, 1827, saw 428 cells completed, and 372 cells yet to be built. The commissioners were delighted with the site. "A more healthy situation could not have been selected."[9] The Reverend Gerrish Barrett was appointed chaplain, his salary of $200 being paid partly by the commissioners and partly by the Boston Prison Discipline Society. An interesting light upon the methods of this early prison chaplain is thrown by the report of the Prison Discipline Society of 1829, showing the manner in which Gerrish Barrett taught a certain illiterate convict at Sing Sing. The statement was made in schedule form:

February 22d, 1829.	Began the first verse of Genesis and learned 4 letters.
February 23d.	Learned 5 letters more.
February 24th.	Could say all the letters in the first line.
February 25th.	Knew all the letters in the first verse.
February 26th.	Knew all the letters in 2 verses.
February 27th.	Spelled all the words of one syllable in the first verse.
February 28th.	Partially learned the words: ''created'' and ''heaven.''
March 1st.	Besides learning ''created'' and ''heaven'' more perfectly, spelled the word ''beginning'' correctly.
March 2d.	Read the first verse in the Bible for the first time.
March 3d.	Read the first line of the second verse.
March 4th.	Read all the second verse.
March 5th.	Read correctly the third verse.
March 6th.	The fourth verse.
March 8th.	Five verses.
March 10th.	Six verses.
March 18th.	Read with ease to the sixteenth verse.
March 19th.	To the twentieth verse.
March 22d.	To the twenty-third verse.
March 29th.	Read correctly the first chapter of Genesis.

Tabulating his activity as chaplain, he stated that during a period of 18 weeks, 770 chapters containing 19,328 verses had been recited by the convicts. Forty-two entire books had been committed to memory; one man in 17 weeks committed 49 chapters, or 1605 verses, another 1,296 verses.

There were 235 convicts at work on December 31st, 1827. In April, 1828, the Legislature authorized the removal of all the convicts from the New York State Prison, and ordered that, since there were no quarters for female convicts at Mount Pleasant, the commissioners should contract for their custody by the city of New York.

The State was becoming solicitous as to the proper care of its female prisoners. Governor DeWitt Clinton in 1828 recommended that there be established somewhere in the State a separate penitentiary for women prisoners. Although in the prisons at Auburn and New York there were not over 50 women, their condition was deplorable. They were not separated from each other, they had little work to do, and were mainly if not wholly in charge of male officers. One woman in Auburn Prison had become pregnant while in prison, and had also been severely flogged. The Mount Pleasant prison commissioners were instructed in 1828 to present plans to the Legislature for a woman's prison.

By May, 1828, all the male prisoners had been moved to the new prison, which was already becoming popularly known as Sing Sing,

---

[9] Senate Journal, 1828, p. 44.

from the name of the village. The city of New York bought in this year the abandoned prison in Greenwich for $100,000 — apparently a good bargain for the State. By October, the main building at Mount Pleasant was finished.

The prison was 482 feet long, 44 feet wide, and 32 feet high. In this same year, the warden started to build an "appurtenant building" to the south, at right angles, and toward the river, to be 81 feet long, 40 feet wide, and two stories high, for kitchen and hospital. Later, a second similar building was added, containing a chapel seating 900. The prison was taking on the proportions of a hollow square, with a proposed prison yard 480 feet long by 300 wide. The yard was made entirely of filled-in land — which became a most serious cause of the later dampness at Sing Sing.

At the end of 1828 there were at Mount Pleasant Prison 513 convicts. In 1828 the commissioners began to make contracts to cut stone for public corporations. Contracts were entered into with the city of New York for stone-cutting and blacksmith work for the local penitentiary; for stone for the court house in Troy; cut stone for the State House in New Haven; cut stone for the City Hall in Albany; coping stone for Fort Adams in Rhode Island; and for an iron steamboiler to be sent to "Mexico in South America."

Workshops were planned for the north side of the prison yard, to take the place of an otherwise necessary wall, and on the west side there was constructed during this year and 1830 a wharf approximately 600 feet long by 30 feet in width. The prison was thus practically completed, and the Legislature had appointed the commissioners a board of inspectors for the year 1830 when suddenly serious charges of cruelty and maladministration were brought against Captain Lynds by Samuel M. Hopkins, one of the commissioners.

The situation that arose was sensational. Captain Lynds was at the height of his prison career. He had achieved what had seemed impossible, in building the greatest and newest prison in the United States without an enclosing wall, and wholly by the labor of desperate convicts. He was popularly held to be the founder of the Auburn system. He was undoubtedly its most rigid and uncompromising adherent. His prisons at Auburn and Sing Sing had been ruled with an iron hand. He had succeeded, conspicuously, as a prison administrator. And now he was publicly charged, before the Legislature, by Mr. Hopkins with, among other things:

Ordering prisoners not to complain, under pain of punishment, of want of food.
Keeping prisoners on short rations.
Tolerating maladministration of office by an assistant keeper who received presents from the food contractor.
Charging for extra rations without warrant.
Bad faith and evasiveness.
Accepting lower grade beef than was contracted for.
Cruelty and bad temper.
Doubtful pecuniary transactions.
Unwarranted discharge of a faithful employe.
Unwarranted breach of good relations with the chaplain.

Without doubt, Mr. Hopkins believed his charges to be tenable. He claimed to have been deceived in Lynds, and he recognized that in now making frank confession of his error, he was exposing himself to severe and mortifying remarks from the enemies of the rigid system he had championed. Hopkins' declaration of his position in 1830 deserves extended quotation, for it foreshadows the inevitable ultimate breakdown of the Auburn system in its original rigor:

"That system of prison government which originated chiefly in this State, and which is known as the Auburn System, begins to prevail extensively in the United States, and attracts great attention in all civilized countries. This system consists chiefly in a discipline which is very strict and summary. To produce such strictness there must be absolute command.

"To insure to the principal keeper the means of safety and strictly governing such dangerous subjects, he must, it is thought, have the appointment of his assistants. We have, therefore, in the midst of a free country, a despot executing his commands through officers entirely dependent upon his will. It is, then, a despotism, in comparison with which the government of a camp, or a ship of war, is mild and free.

"The life and limbs of the convicts; their treatment in sickness; their starvation or other sufferings; their moral treatment and hopes of amendment, all depend upon the will of the absolute dictator. We who are commissioners, have strenuously advocated this system, as unavoidably necessary. It has been supported against a vast array of opinion, and against the authority of great names, both in this and other countries; and the Legislature has, in milder terms, adopted it.

"But we never advocated such a despotism except in connection with a most effectual plan of inspection and control; with moral discipline also; with religious teaching, by a devoted and attentive chaplain; and the whole plan implies, and so our reports state, that the principal should be a man of humanity, morality and integrity. All this is attainable. Without it I have never supposed that the system can be, or ought to be, endured in a free country, or in any country. . . .

"The eyes of mankind are on us. Other nations are waiting with anxiety to see the issues of this experiment."

Here is the first outspoken and illuminating rebellion against the already famous Auburn system. It is the revelation of the "inside" by one on the inside, not a diatribe against a system by one who is on the outside, a disgruntled prison official, a newspaper correspondent, or a legislator stirring up a sensation. Yet a "select" committee of the Senate, after conducting an extended investigation in 1830, exonerated Captain Lynds and his subordinate. They found the several charges either ungrounded, or due to misconstruction on the part of Hopkins. They condoned the system of legalized cruelty and not infrequent torture that were a keystone of the Auburn system.

With the findings in detail of the select committee we can be little concerned. We need not regard their action as a deliberate whitewash. They may well have been in earnest. But there stand out from this investigation several points of permanent truth. The government of the prison *was* despotic, and *had* to be so under the Auburn system. There was only one way to success under that system, and that was by the complete acquiescence of the inmate in the rigors of the system. Lynds achieved his results through the iron hand.[10] He did not believe it to be even the free citizen's duty to go beyond law and order. He was not a man of vision, but of dogged action. Successful despots need imagination, and so Lynds kept getting into trouble, in pursuit of his methods.

Commissioner Hopkins had had many years of experience to draw on in arriving at his conclusions. He had himself conducted two investigations at Auburn Prison. He had himself condoned the Auburn system in official reports — and he had learned much since, especially the way in which novices in investigating prison conditions and prison administration can be misled.

However, the salient fact of Hopkins' statement was that the warden, if a despot, could control to an amazing extent the testimony of his subordinates in any public investigation. Subordinate officers, on the witness stand, become surprisingly like the three Chinese monkeys, who hear not, see not, and speak not. Their jobs and their salaries depended upon holding their place in the warden's estimation, and in the early days, before the advent of the civil service, the subordinate officer, if hired by the warden, was naturally his creature, unless he was of most independent temperament. Moreover, the position of guard and keeper was one paying little, and narratives of prison life in the nineteenth century are filled with assertions of the illiteracy and ignorance and stupidity, not to say cruelty, of the under officers of many a prison.

If we seek further reasons for the failure of most investigations, we find that the testimony of the convict himself is discredited, so that the bulk of testimony before a committee is one-sided. In many instances, moreover, the single-mindedness of the investigating committee can be questioned. There is the natural desire to suppress, if possible, the development of a public scandal in a State institution. Politics plays an important part in the application of the "soft-pedal." When glaring offenses of administration are evident, political pressure is only too frequent to "go easy" with the offender, on the ground that "he thought he was doing his duty." And so forth.

We have cited instances still only too familiar in the effort of commissions and organizations, at times, to arrive at the truth regarding the conduct of penal and correctional institutions. And if this condition is not rare to-day, what must it have been in the early years of American prisons, when there was as yet no organized public opinion in the form of societies or groups, demanding that the truth be known! The Boston Prison Discipline Society, strong in its activities from its organization in 1825, was an ardent champion of the Auburn system, and had committed itself so thoroughly to the methods employed that it became strikingly one-sided, through the years, in its persistent adherence to the system. What chance had Hopkins, with no similar organization in New York — where the Prison Association of New York was not founded until 1844 — to make headway against a prison administration that *did* produce results, in dominating the inmates, in reducing mate-

---

[10] Lynds complained to Dr. Julius that he could not get keepers of sufficient ruthlessness. S. Z., p. 201.

rially the prison expenses, and in giving the public a respite from the tales of horror and demoralization that emanated from the old prison in New York city?

And so, with the exoneration of Captain Lynds; with the passing of Hopkins and his fellow building commissioners; with the completion of the cellhouse and the wharf; with the creation of a prison yard; with the appointment of three new inspectors; and with the reappointment of Captain Lynds as warden, the first period of Mount Pleasant Prison's history is at an end.

Yet, before we leave this initial stage of the history of Mount Pleasant, we can record, as stimulated by the study of the earliest years of Mount Pleasant Prison, some noteworthy and radical suggestions of Captain Basil Hall, of the Royal Navy, who traveled in the United States during 1827 and 1828.[11] He visited Mount Pleasant Prison, and was a graphic observer. He pictured the fearful monotony of the daily life of the convict. "The convicts who are sentenced to confinement in the State prisons of America are chiefly such as in England would be executed or banished."

From Captain Hall has come the earliest suggestion we have traced of the plan of reduction of sentence served in prison — an actual proposal to establish a commutation system of the kind that later became customary, although not within the period covered by this study. Captain Hall's proposal therefore had all the virtues of a radical and highly constructive plan — and like other similarly advanced plans, found no hearing from the "practical" prison administrators of the day.

"Why, if disobedience be punished, should not obedience be rewarded? And how easy it would be to give the convicts a direct and immediate interest in conforming to the rules of the place! Suppose a prisoner were sentenced to several years' confinement; then, if he behave well for a week together, let one day be struck off his term of confinement; if he continue to deport himself correctly for a month, let his term of detention be shortened a fortnight; and if he shall go steadily on for six months, then let half a year be struck off his whole period; and so on, according to any ratio that may be found suitable.

". . . It must surely be the wish of society in general to let a prisoner out as soon as possible, consistently with a certain salutary effect on himself and on others. It has always seemed to me, that by the process of giving the convict a constant, personal interest in behaving well during his confinement, not only might the seeds of virtue be sown, but the ground put in good order for their future growth. . . . If the plan I suggest were adopted, the evils of uncertainty (of sentence) which are great would fall entirely to the prisoner's share, not to that of the public, from being made contingent upon their own conduct. . . . Of course, the pardoning power would need to be tied up more strictly than it is, and imperatively limited by law."

To-day, in the prisons of the United States, will be found printed commutation tables, resembling logarithmic charts, indicating for the assistance of the clerks of the prisons the exact "time off" from the sentences that the inmates may earn through good conduct and other activities. The dream of Captain Hall has come true, long since, and to-day even the commutation tables are disappearing gradually in favor of the exercise of the indeterminate sentence.

---

[11] Basil Hall. "Travels in North America in the Years 1827-28," pp. 36-44.

But at the time of Captain Hall's travels and the publication of his narrative, his proposal found no echo in practice. The vicious pardoning of prisoners continued, forming the only inducement to inmates to conduct themselves properly within the walls. Instead of the erection of an honest and sympathetic system of rewards for good conduct, in a commutation system, the States continued to maintain the arbitrary, unfair, and often reprehensible method of the exercise of grace, through the chief magistrate of the State, the governor. Like the proposals of Doctor Rush, the dreams of Thomas Eddy, the hopes of Louis Dwight for a farm whereon prisoners could recover their normal habits after a term in prison, the futile efforts of Warden Goodell at Auburn for a few brief months to maintain a prison system by loving-kindness, and the more successful undertaking of Reverend Mr. Wells at the House of Reformation in Boston to conduct a boys' reform school on a basis of practical interest, participation in administration, and an abundance of wholesome recreation, so did Captain Hall find his proposals far ahead of his time. And to-day, the historian, able now to chronicle the unquestioned success of all these once proposed methods, as exemplified by noteworthy "going concerns" of the present day, pauses, and dreams of what might have happened, that would have changed the course of prison history, had Rush, and Eddy, and Hall, and Lieber, and Wells, the "theorists," been understood — and followed.

CHAPTER XI

THE WESTERN AND THE EASTERN PENITENTIARIES OF PENNSYLVANIA

It is a coincidence that on the afternoon when I type this chapter of the study of early American prison customs, one of the earliest "customs," namely, a prison mutiny, is announced in the press as occurring in the very prison that we are about to consider — The Western Penitentiary of Pennsylvania. A hundred and three years after the authorization of the prison by the Pennsylvania Legislature, Pittsburg police and other armed forces are keeping a throng of inmates at bay, within the prison yard, where burning shop buildings rise behind the wild prisoners.

Prison riots are not frequent to-day. The ordinary humane methods of progressive prison wardens have made such an occurrence a rarity. Hardly a serious riot has occurred in Eastern prisons in the last ten years. But in the early days of American prisons, we have seen that they were frequent. And it was to make impossible the mingling of the prisoners, and the consequent plotting, that both the Auburn system of "silence," and the Pennsylvania system of "separation" were invented and put into effect during the third decade of the nineteenth century.

In 1818, the State of Pennsylvania took the radical step of authorizing a prison, with entire separation of each prisoner from the other in a separate cell, and absolute separation of the prisoner from any work. The difference between the Auburn system and the Pennsylvania system was the difference between association with silence and separation. The Auburn system ultimately spread throughout the United States, but had practically no structural influence in Europe. The Pennsylvania system, on the other hand, after being imitated in New Jersey and Rhode Island in the State prisons there, was soon abandoned in the United States, except in the State of its origin. On the other hand, the Pennsylvania system became the standard in many parts of Europe.

Around the comparative merits of the two systems was waged for several generations the greatest contest ever developed in prison reform. Acrimonious and often misleading statements and arguments were a part of the battle, which was conducted from headquarters, respectively, in Boston and Philadelphia, the homes of the Boston Prison Discipline Society and the Pennsylvania Society for Alleviating the Miseries of Public Prisons. Europe as well as the United States debated the two competing systems, in conferences national and international. Even to-day, the European system of prison architecture differs radically from the American, and now, after nearly a century, the architectural principle of the "outside cell," or the cell with the window to the outer air, as distinguished from the "inside cell," or the cell with the door furnishing the only light from a corridor between the cell and the outside wall of the cellhouse, is beginning to be adopted once more in American prison architecture, a vindication of the Pennsylvania principle.

Yet the two systems were more alike, from the beginning, than they were different from each other. They were similar in holding to the fundamental principle that prisoners *under no circumstances should communicate with each other.* The two systems held, furthermore, that *prisoners should be separate from each other in individual cells at night.*

The basic difference between the Auburn system and the Pennsylvania system was, that whereas the Pennsylvania system extended the principle of the separation of convicts from each other to *cover every minute of the twenty-four hours,* or in other words, to provide for the perpetual separation of inmates from each other, the Auburn system brought the convicts together during the day in workshops and in the messhall, but under enforced perpetual silence. The Pennsylvania system became popularly known as the "separate system," and the Auburn system as the "silent system."

The Pennsylvania Law of 1818 provided for the erection in Pittsburg of a penitentiary, which should be so constructed as to provide cells for the separate confinement of prisoners. So intense was the feeling that a clear departure should be made from all previous pernicious methods, that the new prison reform movement in Pennsylvania advocated, and successfully, that in the prison to be constructed at Pittsburg there should be absolute deprivation of work, as well as enforced perpetual solitude. The new prison was to abandon all theory of classification — which was the chief contribution of the Walnut Street Prison of 1790 — and instead was to provide a solitary cell for each prisoner's constant use. In short, each cell was thereby to become a miniature prison in itself, and classification was therefore unnecessary.[1]

Three years later, in 1821, a similar law provided for the erection, likewise on the principle of solitary confinement, of a prison for 250 prisoners in Philadelphia.[2] The State was thus embarked seriously upon an experiment heretofore untried in this country, and which would be decisive. No reasonable expense was to be spared to make these prisons adequate and suitable.

By 1826 the Pittsburg prison was finished, and 20 prisoners were admitted. It had cost $165,346, and provided a total of 190 individual cells,[3] at a cost per cell of $978.95. The prison was built in an unusual form, that of a semi-circle. The cells,

"forming the circumference of the circle, were built in a double range, being placed back to back, as at Auburn, but in the form of a circle, the diameter of which was 320 feet; part of the cells facing the boundary wall, and the other part fronting the large internal area. . . . The cells were each about 9 feet long and 7 feet wide. . . . In the front of each cell was a small yard, 6 feet wide, having a doorway in front."

---

[1] B. and T., p. 5.
[2] Richard Vaux. Sketch, p. 33.
[3] Report of Shaler-Wharton-King, p. 36.

By 1827, this Western Penitentiary, as it was called, was in operation, with a few persons confined therein. Each prisoner was shut up, night and day, in a cell, but without any employment. The cells moreover, had been built so small that the maintenance of any trade was impossible that required any equipment. On the other hand, the architect had failed to build a sound-proof prison, and the prisoners were able to talk with each other from cell to cell through gratings.[4] In short, the worst possible results had been achieved. The prisoners could *not* work, but they *could* by conversation mutually contaminate each other.[5] The State had sunk nearly $200,000 in a prison that was worse than useless, on the basis of the adopted system.

The board of managers of this Pittsburg prison reported as early as 1828 to the Legislature that it was hardly practicable, with the present plan of the penitentiary, to carry into effect complete solitary confinement, without keeping the prisoners constantly immured in their respective cells.[6] The board held this to be so inimical to health that they were therefore allowing the prisoners to exercise before the cells of the other prisoners in the corridors.[7] One of the inspectors even urged the establishment of workhouses, where the prisoners might work in association as at Auburn.

By 1833, the board had bluntly recommended that the prison should be either sold or demolished, and in the same year the Legislature passed an act authorizing the demolition of the cells within the walls of the Western Penitentiary, and the construction of cells similar to those that had meanwhile been built at the Eastern Penitentiary in Philadelphia.[9] The Pittsburg prison was by its construction suitable neither for separate confinement nor for labor. This prison had no significance in the prison reform movement, save to point out a glaring and very expensive mistake in penological principles.

Meanwhile, attention was being fastened upon the plans for a new prison in Philadelphia. This institution was to be capable of holding 250 prisoners "on the principle of the solitary confinement of the convicts."[8] Eleven citizens were appointed a commission to secure a site and build a prison thereon. No provision was made in the law as to the employment or non-employment of convicts. Plans presented by the architect, John Haviland, were selected in competition in 1821. Haviland was an English architect who had taken up residence in Philadelphia.[10] A site for the prison was chosen, at "Cherry Hill," several miles from the city, of about ten acres.

In this new prison we find the first effort — and a most impressive effort — on the part of a State to erect a massive, imposing and even monumental edifice. It was easy, of course, to pass in

---

[4] B. and T.
[5] B. P. D. S. Reports of 1828, p. 193.
[6] B. P. D. S., 1830, p. 364.
[7] B. P. D. S. Reports of 1828, p. 193.
[8] R. Vaux, p. 33.
[9] Fourth Report. Inspectors of E. P., 1832, p. 22.
[10] Julius. d. am. Besserungs Systeme, p. 5.

thought from the stronghold-type to the fortress and monumental type. The aim of the building commissioners was to give to this new prison an unusual degree of solidity, durability and grave impressiveness. Like the other prisons we have described, at Auburn and Sing Sing, the Eastern Penitentiary has endured unto our day, and is still in use. It was, at the time of its building, the most extensive edifice in the United States.[11]

A certain George Smith wrote in 1829, of this prison:

"The Penitentiary is the only edifice in the country calculated to convey to our citizens the external appearance of those magnificent and picturesque castles of the middle ages, which contribute to embellish the scenery of Europe."

The front entrance was called the most imposing in the United States. The cornerstone of the prison was laid on May 22, 1823, by Roberts Vaux, one of the commissioners, and a man who wrote much of prison reform in his period. It was the earliest example of the utilization of an American prison as a subject for ponderous and elaborate architecture.

Although the building was thus initiated in 1823, only three of the wings had been completed by 1825, and these contained but 114 cells.[12] The prison was not occupied until 1829. The intervening period was one of serious and prolonged deliberation as to the proper methods of administration and discipline to be introduced into the new prison. The opinion was by no means universal that the separate confinement of prisoners at all times, and particularly without employment, was a sound principle.

Auburn Prison was beginning to be heard from. In the old Walnut Street Prison there had been but a few cells devoted to solitary confinement. The new prison in Philadelphia was to confine *all* prisoners thus — and at this date the sentiment was strongly held that no employment of the prisoners during their incarceration would be admissible. The following arguments, summarized by the writer, were urged in favor of the extreme plan of solitary confinement without work.[13] It should be remembered that the experience of Auburn Prison with solitary confinement without work in 1822 and 1823 was not well known at this time in Philadelphia:

Solitary confinement without labor would effectively separate the prisoners from each other, and therefore from their mutually corrupting influences. No remedy could be otherwise found for the radical evils of association, other than close, strict, solitary confinement, night and day, without labor.

Solitary confinement, without labor, is the severest kind of punishment to the individual convict. Man craves social intercourse. Isolation is a bitter penalty — also a vigorous and constant warning to potential criminals.

Solitary confinement without labor operates directly and forcibly upon the mind. If all external sources of excitement are removed, reflection, remorse and perhaps reformation will ensue.

The term of imprisonment could be shortened, because the end in view — repentance and reformation — could be attained in a shorter time. The punishment, moreover, being severer, the term of imprisonment should be shortened.

---

[11] Description of the Penitentiary. G. W. Smith, 1829, in R. Vaux, p. 56. Notices on the Original, etc.
[12] Julius. Sittleche Zusbaende, Vol. II, page 128.
[13] Shaler-Wharton-King, p. 17ff.

These early arguments were violently opposed by the newly-formed Boston Prison Discipline Society, the New England militant champion of the Auburn system.[14] Although the Society's headquarters were in Boston the range of interest of the members, and particularly of its tireless secretary, Rev. Louis Dwight, covered the entire country, wherever prisons were being contemplated, built or operated. The harrowing experiences of Auburn Prison with solitary confinement without labor came gradually to make a deep impression upon the Philadelphians.

Auburn Prison was, moreover, already also emphasizing the great economic value of keeping prisoners at work productively. And so, after 100 cells had been built in the new prison at Philadelphia, the work was halted, and a commission of the Legislature was created in 1826, consisting of Charles Shaler, Edward King, and T. I. Wharton, to report as soon as possible on the best system of prison discipline that might be adopted.

On December 20th, 1827, the commission, after disposing in their report of capital punishment, mutilations, brandings, whippings, transportation, banishment and simple imprisonment (with the inevitable consequent commingling of prisoners) as out of the question in a sound prison discipline, came out flat-footedly in opposition to the hitherto accepted principle, being tried in Pittsburg, of separate imprisonment without labor. Said the commission:[15]

> Solitary confinement *with* labor is just as effective as solitary confinement *without* labor in preventing the communication of prisoners with each other.
>
> Solitary confinement *without* labor is not at all an equitable punishment. To some prisoners it would be a fearful penalty, to others far less a punishment.
>
> Solitary confinement *without* labor will produce no more serious or valuable reflections on the mind of the convict than when broken by regular intervals of work.
>
> Solitary confinement *without* labor would be a total expense to the State instead of a system bringing a return to the State from the labor of the convict.
>
> Solitary confinment *without* labor produces bodily infirmities, disease and insanity — as shown by the experience of Auburn Prison.
>
> Solitary confinement *without* labor renders the convict unable to pursue an honest calling after his discharge from prison, because of his total idleness within prison walls.

The Legislative commission then proceeded to analyze the project in general of solitary imprisonment *with* labor. The advantages were found to be the following:[16]

> The entire separation of the convicts from any society.
> The acquisition by the convict of habits of industry.
> The contribution by the convict through his industry to the expense of maintaining the prison.

Moreover, a considerable variety of occupations could be provided, such as weaving, cobbling, tailoring; and for the more extensive occupations, such as required large space, separate

---

[14] B. P. D. S., 1827, p. 91.
[15] Shaler-Wharton-King, p. 27ff.
[16] Shaler-Wharton-King, p. 48ff.

individual workshops were possible. Exercise could be also obtained in the small individual yards, directly behind the cells on the ground floor.

But the commission went still further. They even ventured to disagree with the great bulk of public opinion in Philadelphia favorable to the above-mentioned system. They found serious disadvantages in the above projects. The variety of occupations that were possible in separate confinement was necessarily limited, as was also the supply of light or air in the cells. Sedentary occupations were detrimental to health. The impossibility of a sufficient profit from the labor of prisoners under such circumstances was emphasized. Moreover, there could be only occasional observation of prisoners by officials. Discipline of convicts who refused to labor would be difficult, it was said.

And in conclusion, therefore, the commission recommended that in the prison yard of the new prison there be erected, for the purposes of completing the Eastern Penitentiary, a building on the style of Mount Pleasant Prison, or of Wethersfield in Connecticut, with 800 cells, and also that workshops be erected for the joint labor of convicts. The said prison should be supplementary to the cellblocks already erected.

In recommending these features, the commission's attitude was heretical, from the standpoint of the Philadelphia group of reformers, and the recommendations were lost in the sand. The prison, when finally completed, was practically on the original plan, as adopted by the commission appointed to build the prison.

This issue as to the relative value of the several systems: Pittsburgh, Auburn, Philadelphia, was a very intense one among the prison reform forces of the time, as is evidenced by the following quotation from a letter written by William Roscoe, in his old age, to Dr. Hosack, an American friend of Thomas Eddy in New York:[18]

"The relinquishment of it (*i. e.*, the principle of labor) for the Bastile system of solitary confinement would have grieved me more than I can express; but, thank God, my dread of that is over; and I shall now die in peace, convinced that the time will arrive when my own country (England) will follow the example."

Which was a true prophecy.

Let us now become acquainted with the extraordinarily carefully worked-out plan of the new penitentiary, unique in the United States, but clearly showing English influences. No other prison of this kind survives at all intact in the United States to-day. One can, however, still visit the Eastern Penitentiary and find the main architectural scheme of the prison well preserved. It is a notable historical monument.

The prison was located about two and a half miles from the city of Philadelphia, and about one-half mile east of the Schuylkill River.[17] The yard wall, of stone, 30 feet high, 12 feet thick at the bottom and tapering to 2¾ feet in thickness at the top, enclosed

---

[17] Description mainly from B. P D. S. Report for 1827.
[18] Life of Thomas Eddy, p. 324.

approximately twelve acres. This wall, including the keeper's house (a part of the south wall) cost about $200,000, which would be a most noteworthy expenditure for such purposes even in these days.

The facade of the prison was 670 feet in length. In the center of the yard was a rotunda or "observatory," from which seven cellblocks diverged, like the rays of a star — an architectural device that gave rise to the term — Radial Plan. The cells, 11 feet 9 inches long, by 7 feet 6 inches wide,[19] were arranged in two rows, in each of the seven cellblocks, and they faced a central corridor, which extended from the rotunda to the end of each cellblock.

A curious architectural development was the individual "exercising yard," 8 by 20 feet,[20] connected on the outside of the building with each cell. The walls surrounding these exercising yards were 11 feet 6 inches high.[21] An opening from the cell to the yard enabled the prisoner to go out into the yard for exercise at specified times. There was no door into the cell from the central corridor of the cellblock, but there was a small orifice opening from the cell into the corridor, through which the guard in the corridor might observe the prisoner, and deliver to him his food.

In the construction, in later years, of the four last wings, doors were provided from the cells into the central corridor. There was an outer door of wood, with a small, funnel-shaped observation hole in the door. The inner door was of iron grating, with a small opening in the upper half, through which food could be passed into the cell, as well as laundry, labor material, and the like.[23]

When the inmate was let out into the yard, he could be watched by the guard, either from the wall, or by opening the door of the yard. The entrance to the cell from the yard was secured by double doors, one of grated iron, and the other of plank. In the second story of the cellblock, where obviously no yards were possible, the prisoner was allowed an extra cell.[22] Each cell in the prison was used for dwelling purposes, was furnished with a bedstead, clothes rail, seat, shelf, tin cup, wash basin, victuals pan, looking glass, combs, scrubbing brush, broom, straw mattress, one sheet, one blanket and one coverlid. There was a toilet and water spigot in every cell.

When De Metz and Blouet visited the Eastern Penitentiary late in the thirties, they found that

"most prisoners prefer the upper cells to the lower ones with courts, because the lower cells are cold and damp and never receive any sun, because shielded by high walls. The stronger convicts like the lower cells because there is more chance for exercise. The cells are very hot in summer and damp in other seasons. High walls prevent circulation of air. The prison officials thought to give up the courts, but their elimination would have incited to attempts at escape underneath the walls."[24]

---

[19] R. Vaux, Sketch, p. 62.
[20] R. Vaux, Sketch, p. 24.
[21] R. Vaux, Sketch, p. 62.
[22] R. Vaux, Sketch, p. 62.
[23] Julius. S. Z., p. 180.
[24] De Metz and Blouet, p. 56.

The waterclosets were primitive, and permitted conversation between prisoners in adjacent cells, by means of the pipes, but only during the ten to fifteen minutes a day while the pipes were being flushed. To guard against such conversation, serious penalties were inflicted upon inmates thus transgressing, and a force of guards were stationed in the central corridors of the wings to spy upon the prisoners during this process.[25]

For ventilation, there were several holes, about three inches in diameter, near the floor of the cell, passing through the wall to the exercise yard. There were also several flues. The method of heating was by hot air. The prisoners were fed in their cells. Every part of the building was so constructed that it should never be necessary to remove the prisoner from his cell and exercising yard, except when sick. No chapel and no schoolrooms were provided, and no places for labor except the cells.

It is clear from the above description that the architectural features of the Eastern Penitentiary were worked out with much deliberation and system. Consequently, it is of special interest to trace the origin of this general plan of construction, particularly in view of the remarkable influence it had in the following decades upon the construction of prisons in European countries.

It has been quite generally assumed that the design of the Eastern Penitentiary was original with John Haviland, the architect. But we must first of all remember that Haviland was from England, and but recently settled in Philadelphia.[27] The supposed "American" origin of the Pennsylvania plan is unquestionably an error. As early as 1820, the London Society for the Improvement of Prison Discipline had sent to the Philadelphia Society for Alleviating the Miseries of Public Prisons a book of architectural plans of prisons that the London Society had recently published.[26] The London Society's proposed plan for a county jail for four hundred persons embodied a clear-cut radial scheme of six wings, and a central "hub" or rotunda. The similarity of the Haviland plan to this and to other types of English local prisons is far too great to be a coincidence. Haviland's plan was a clear case of borrowing an idea.

The radial type, indeed, had appeared in England in the case of the Ipswich County Jail as early as 1790.[28] Haviland developed the radial plan, especially by the creation of the central building as an observatory, and by the addition of exercise yards attached to each ground floor cell. But the Eastern Penitentiary is a developed imitation of earlier English prison plans.

Furthermore, William Crawford, who visited the United States in 1832 as an official representative of the British Government, claimed that the main principles of the system installed at the Eastern Penitentiary were in force as early as 1794, approximately, in the Gloucester, England, penitentiary. With some trifling differ-

---

[25] Julius. Sittleche Zusbaende, Vol. II, p. 180.
[26] London Society for Prison Discipline. Report of the Committee for 1820, p. 36. Rules for Gaols. 1821. p. 45ff.
[27] Julius. d. amk. B. S., p. 4.
[28] On the Form and Construction of Prisons, London, 1826.

ences in its arrangements, the Eastern Penitentiary seemed to Crawford to be but a counterpart of the Bridewell at Glasgow, Scotland, a prison put into operation by 1824.[29]

However, great the similarity was in the matter of methods of administration at Gloucester or Glasgow, the direct line of descent of the Pennsylvania system is easy to trace on American soil, without attributing preponderating influence to the British Isles. As early as 1788, the Philadelphia Prison Society stated that, on the whole, they were unanimously of the opinion that solitary confinement and hard labor, with total abstention from spirituous liquors, would "prove the most effective means of reforming these unhappy creatures.[32]

In 1827, the estimated cost of the prison, when it should be completed, was $500,000 for 250 prisoners, or $2,000 per prisoner, an enormous sum even for the present day, and one which at the time brought down severe criticism upon the prison. The New England prison reform group did not fail to seize the chance to contrast this huge expenditure with the expenditure for Wethersfield, the Connecticut State Prison (which is another prison still in use to-day). This prison was erected in 1827 for approximately $35,000 for 136 prisoners,[30] an average per capita expenditure of nearly $258.00.

For several years, the completion of the Eastern Penitentiary was held up, because of the vigorous attacks upon the general plan of structure and administration. The Boston Society annually raised its voice in loud protests. At what amazing per capita cost was this prison being built! How would it be possible to exclude the possibilities of communication between prisoners? Look at Pittsburgh's failure! How nasty to make of each cell a water closet! What folly not to realize that a prison should make as much as possible from the labor of prisoners toward the maintenance of the institution! Was not Auburn Prison practically paying all its expenses? Gershom Powers, the Auburn warden, dilated upon many structural disadvantages of the plan.[31] The Shaler-King-Wharton report above referred to had deterred for a time the Legislature from making appropriations for the completion of the buildings, but in the end the building commission carried the day.

While the erection of the new prison was being thus delayed, conditions of lawlessness in and about Philadelphia were becoming most serious — reminiscent, indeed, of similar terrifying conditions prior to the establishment of the Walnut Street Prison in 1790 as a penitentiary. In the report of the board of inspectors of the Eastern Penitentiary for 1836, it was stated, in retrospect, that, immediately prior to the opening of the new prison in 1829:

"it was no novelty to hear of combinations of rogues for the purpose of housebreaking, counterfeiting, robbery in the public streets, and violence of

---
[29] Crawford, p. 13.
[30] B. P. D. S., Vol. I, p. 124.
[31] G. S. General Description, etc., pp. 86ff.
[32] Report of Joint Committee of Leg. of Pa., relative to E. P. of Pa., Harrisburg, 1835, p. 20.

all kinds. It was no uncommon thing for the magistracy and other officers to form 'possies' to visit the haunts of vice and the purlieus of wretchedness to ferret out felons. Seldom was there a conviction above the grade of petty larceny but disclosed a chain of complicated villiany involving the committal of two or three more.

"Our court calendar exhibited an array of crime at each time, startling to the philanthropist and arguing a deplorable state of society. . . . An auxiliary police was of necessity at times established by volunteers from the citizens who patrolled the streets to secure their sleeping brethren from the insidious assaults of the incendiary and burglar.''

The first inmate was received by the Eastern Penitentiary on October 25th, 1829. From the above description, it is clear that the institution opened very much on the defensive. During 1829, a board of inspectors had been appointed, to take over the management of the institution. The chairman of the board was Charles S. Coxe, a judge of the district court of Philadelphia. Other members were Josiah Randall, a prominent lawyer of the same city; Roberts Vaux, a philanthropist of means, whose name and that of his son, Richard Vaux, were for many decades associated with prison reform; John Swift, a lawyer, and Daniel H. Miller, a merchant and State senator.[32] The board appointed as warden Samuel R. Wood, a Quaker; he was a manufacturer, and had visited European prisons. He had been one of the building commissioners,[33] and was called a "practical" man. Dr. Franklin Bache, who later became noted for the comprehensive and valuable statistics he furnished regarding the health of the prisoners, and who was a great grandson of Benjamin Franklin,[34] was appointed prison physician.

In 1829, a supplementary law was passed, providing that separate confinement of prisoners, *with* labor, should be the discipline of the prison. Uniform rules were adopted by the Legislature for both the Western and the Eastern Penitentiaries. Among these rules were the following:

The warden should be appointed semi-annually.
The inspectors should serve without pay, and should visit the Penitentiary at least twice a week.
There should be an unpaid chaplain. (This provision of "no salary" worked to the great disadvantage of the institution for many years.)
The inspectors on their visits should speak to the prisoners apart from any of the officials of the prison.
The warden must reside in the prison, and must visit each prisoner at least once a day.
He should appoint the under-keepers, called overseers, and must not absent himself from the prison over night without the written permission of the inspectors.
Keepers were obligated to inspect the condition of the prisoners at least three times a day.
The physician must visit every prisoner at least twice each week, and oftener if necessary. He must also examine each prisoner on reception.
In addition to the permission given to certain State officials to visit the prison and prisoners, the same permission was given to the Acting Committee for the Philadelphia Society for Alleviating the Miseries of Public Prisons.

---
[32] R. Vaux. Sketch, p. 83.
[33] Second Annual Report of Board of Inspectors.
[34] De Metz and Blouet, p. 32.
Doctor Bache before serving as physician in the Eastern Penitentiary had been in a similar capacity in the Walnut Street Prison for 12 years.

The same curious custom of a final interview by the warden with the prisoner which was customary at Auburn Prison, was made mandatory by the rules and regulations at Philadelphia. After the interview, the convict was to receive four dollars from the State "whereby the temptation to commit offenses against society, before employment can be obtained, may be obviated."

To what extent four dollars would stand between a released prisoner and another crime, were it impossible for him to find immediate employment, is a question not hard to answer. The State of New York was giving to the released convict only three dollars. In neither Auburn nor the Eastern Penitentiary was there any chance for the prisoner to earn any money toward his own support when he should emerge from prison. Here again, one has to wonder at the wretchedly false economy and poor psychology that would send a convict out, almost literally stripped of all means to make an honest living, and cursed with the stigma of a prison sentence.

Yet the thing happens to-day, in the State of New York. The ten dollars which is given to the convict on release amounts to no more than the three dollars of a century ago. The clothes he receives are generally shed at the first pawnbrokers, if possible. They have the prison pattern and the uncouth cut. The man who during the period of incarceration has been earning the bitterly ironical sum of one and one-half cents a day, which may be diminished by punishments, is still typical, upon his release, of the folly of discharging the convict so poorly equipped with money as to make the very presence of money in the possession of others a temptation to crime. It is only in States where a system of labor prevails that secures for the prisoner some chance to earn, if not a wage, at least some money for overtime work, that the prisoner is freed in part from this grave condition on his release from prison.

Returning to the Eastern Penitentiary, we find that although the sponsors of the plan of constant separation of prisoners, with labor, were positive that the new prison would be

"'an apparatus for the expeditious, certain and economical eradication of vice, and the production of reformation.'"[35]

Richard Vaux, writing in 1872 an historical treatment of the Eastern Penitentiary, stated[36] that when the prison was ready for the reception of the first inmate, in 1829, little was known as to the effect of the solitary discipline on the prisoners.

Said Vaux:

"Indeed, the discipline itself was a theory. For many years following, it was not possible to do more than supervise the administration and put it into working order. It required some time to settle what were the consequences of the discipline. . . . To finish all the buildings, suffer the more serious criticisms of the management, and harmonize almost irreconcilable opinions, if not feelings, among those who were first connected with

---

[35] G. W. Smith in Vaux, p. 58.
[36] p. 85.

the administration of the Penitentiary, distracted the minds of those who were charged with the government of the institution. . . . From 1829 to 1835, the attention of the inspectors was not wholly concentrated on the workings of the system. . . . The period from 1829 to 1849 was one of experiment and experience. From 1849 to 1870 one of development and progress.''

The seventh and last wing of the prison, on the original plan of Haviland, was not finished until 1836, when the institution offered a total of 586 cells.[37]

---
[37] Julius. Sittleche Zusbaende, Vol. II, p. 129.

CHAPTER XII

THE EARLY DEVELOPMENT OF PRISON LABOR IN NEW YORK

Within ten years from the time when the Auburn system was established, in 1823, there developed out of the much-praised "perfection" of the system itself an unexpected and highly complicated problem. For just when Auburn Prison began to boast exultantly that it had ceased to be a financial burden to the State, and that its annual earnings were beginning to exceed its annual disbursements, the "mechanics" of the State became violently aroused to the threatening competition of convict labor with "free labor."

Moreover, the Mount Pleasant Prison at Sing Sing became also, as early as 1831, six years after its founding, a target of bitter criticism from mechanics in New York City, who claimed that the prison was making contracts to sell marble at prices far below those possible in the open market. The prison was furnishing to a museum in New York marble for $500 that would cost from $7,000 to $8,000 in the open market.[1] This led to one of the first of the almost innumerable petitions to the Legislature from mechanics during the next decade for relief from this growing and menacing evil.

Labor was becoming at Auburn and Mount Pleasant prisons a source of profit to the State, through the letting of the prisoners' labor to contractors. Auburn Prison was, by 1825, a great smooth-running industrial machine — when suddenly two highly disturbing lines of attack upon the system developed. Hostile criticism was leveled at the alleged barbarous punishments necessary under the Auburn system. The second line of attack was from the outraged mechanics of the State, who saw their industrial life threatened with ruin through the convict competition. These two controversial questions became the chief problems of prison administration in the State of New York between 1825 and 1845, the period we are now to consider.

We have already alluded, in Chapter Ten, to the early investigation, in 1826, by the special commission of which Samuel M. Hopkins was chairman of Auburn Prison's alleged cruelty to inmates. Having dismissed as practically ungrounded the accusations of brutality, the commissioners addressed themselves to the system of labor at the prison. Endorsing the principle of letting out the labor of prisoners within the prison to contractors, they mildly criticised the prison authorities for having let contracts without previous adequate public announcement. Obviously, verbal announcement "around Auburn" was not a sure and impartial way to advertise for bids. That favoritism could thereby benefit chosen friends or business acquaintances was clear.

---

[1] Assembly Document No. 279, 1831.

Moreover, the commissioners found the contracts bringing in altogether too little money. We read between the lines the significance of the facts that the tailors earned for the prison an average of but 15 cents a day, the coopers from 15 to 22 cents, the shoemakers 25 cents, and the weavers from 10 to 15 cents. Both Captain Lynds and Captain Powers favored the letting of contracts without general bidding. They held the dangers of intercourse between irresponsible contractors and prisoners to be so great as to make it imperative that the warden should have broad liberty to choose responsible contractors.

It was at this period (1828) that Auburn Prison announced its confidence that no further appropriations would be needed from the State for maintenance.[2] This was a tremendously powerful argument for the continuation, intact, of the new system. (And this kind of an argument is to-day, in 1921, a powerful argument for the retention of contract labor in prisons.) Other States were making money from systematic prison labor. Hard and steady employment seemed likely at last to banish the nightmare of heavy annual State expenditures for maintenance and upkeep. Moses C. Pillsbury had become warden of the New Hampshire State Prison in 1818. The loss to the State in the previous year had been $4,325. From 1822 to 1826 the net proceeds (chiefly from stone cutting) had been, after defraying every expense, $7,596.[7] Massachusetts State Prison announced a profit of $9,151 in 1825 and $8,819 in 1826. Even the female department of the Maryland State Prison, under the able Mrs. Rachel Perijo as matron, changed its balance from an average annual deficit, before she came, in 1822, of $1,099 to an average annual surplus of $492.[3] Such reports were in striking contrast to the annual expense of the Walnut Street Prison of about $30,000, and to the continuing deficit of the State Prison in New York city, that had since 1797 cost the State a total of $1,237,343.[5] Massachusetts had expended more than $300,000 for State prison maintenance.[4]

Old Newgate in Connecticut had cost that State since 1791 more than $200,000,[8] but now, within six months of the establishment of the new State prison at Wethersfield in 1827 (see Chapter Seven), the net earnings of 97 convicts for the State were $1,017, over all expenses of management and support.[6] And Captain Lynds, the warden at Mount Pleasant, said in this same year that he would ask no greater privilege from the State, when the prison at Sing Sing should be completed, than to receive the earnings of convicts, above every expense for food, medical attendance, moral instruction, keeping, etc., and that he would enter into a bond for $100,000 to release the State from all further charges for current expenses, in consideration of receiving the proceeds of the labor of the convicts.[9]

---
[2] B. P. D. S. 1828, p. 164 — G. Powers. Report, p. 48.
[3] B. P. D. S. 1826, p. 34.
[4] B. P. D. S. 1828, p. 161.
[5] B. P. D. S. 1827, p. 113.
[6] B. P. D. S. 1828, p. 163.
[7] B. P. D. S. 1827, p. 35.
[8] B. P. D. S. 1828, p. 161.
[9] B. P. D. S. 1828, p. 164.

In short, convicts were practically for the first time being turned not only into assets for the State, but into a profitable business for certain firms or individuals on the outside who contracted for the labor of the convicts, and made "good money." It looked like a good bargain "all around." The prison philanthropists, like the Boston Prison Discipline Society, were maintaining that economy was concomitant with moral improvement in a prison administration, thereby tacitly putting the stamp of approval on the making of money in a prison. The public, wearied with alleged visionary schemes of reformation, was glad to have a burden lifted from the taxpayers of the times. The rigid discipline of Auburn and Sing Sing prisons appealed to the public, which had heard much about the bad management and the high cost of the prisons of the past, and also of the debauchery and demoralization attendant apparently upon the existence of prisons. The cheap cost of construction of the new type of prison, as at Sing Sing and at Wethersfield, by the labor of prisoners, was a further appealing argument. It must have appeared to the thoughtful minds of the period that at last the secret of efficient prison management had been revealed.

We can therefore readily understand why the new prison system sprang into popularity, why severe punishments were in the main tolerated, or why excuses were found for their continuance, and why the emphasis of the Auburn system shifted increasingly from producing reformation to producing profits for the State. The prison system was now appealing to the State where the State was most easily influenced — in its pocketbook. Penal servitude was becoming a profitable business to the State, and the general feeling that prisoners should be severely disciplined was being gratified at the same time — and justified.

We are analyzing these formative years in some detail because it was in just these years that there was being firmly moulded the system of prison discipline that became the American standard for generations. American life and standards of to-day are well understood only as one knows the history of our people. That special phase of American institutional life represented by our prisons, with their remarkable and often intolerably stupid and unjust practices, cannot be understood except as we survey the past. Powerful economic and moral forces have in the past conditioned and traditionalized our penal institutions. Administrative habits of yesterday and even of to-day, strong and dominant with the force of long usage, are but the acquired characteristics of the periods of the past. The era that we are now surveying was primarily one in which such methods and principles became fixed. Historically, therefore, the period from approximately 1820 to 1840 is of exceptional significance in the development of American prison customs.

The net earnings of certain prisons continued to be conspicuous during the next few years. Wethersfield in 1828 earned $3,229 above every expense;[12] Maryland's penitentiary at Baltimore registered net earnings of $9,804. In 1829, Wethersfield earned $5,068 over all expenses; Auburn nearly $6,000. By the end of March, 1832, Wethersfield showed net earnings for four and one-half years of $25,853; the deficit of old Newgate for the same period would have been $51,103,[10] showing a net gain for the Connecticut Prison for this period of $76,956. From 1828 to 1833 Auburn Prison netted over $25,000.[11]

It was against such impressive financial arguments that, early in the thirties, those mechanics of the State of New York who were affected by the specific prison industries began vehemently to protest. That which a special committee of the Legislature in 1833 called a "magnificent result that could not have been dreamed of a few years before."[13] and as emanating from the exalted spirit of free governments — namely, self-support of prisons through instruction and persuasion of prisoners — the mechanics who were stone-cutters, coopers, or weavers were already condemning as a "tyrannical State monopoly."

A factor that made the industrial situation still more intense was the failure of the Sing Sing quarries to produce the anticipated high grade of marble. Moreover, to a Legislative committee in 1832, the ignominy and humiliation attached to teams of convicts, pulling blocks of stones like weary dumb brutes, and harnessed to carts, seemed so great as to demand the installation of other occupations than quarrying. The labor of prisoners should be hired out to contractors, as at Auburn, Charlestown, and Wethersfield. The inspectors at Mount Pleasant Prison had ordered the warden not to make such contracts, because they *believed* that any profit accruing therefrom should go to the State, and not into the pockets of contractors.

With this opinion the Legislative committee begged to differ.[14] Even the Reverend Louis Dwight, secretary of the Boston Prison Discipline Society, lent his endorsement to the proposal to let the labor of prisoners out to contractors. On the basis of Wethersfield, said the committee, Mount Pleasant should be netting $70,000 a year! And then the committee of the Legislature made a subtle suggestion. Whatever profits accrued ought, in order to stifle criticism, to be added to the common school fund — an act that would render in the course of a generation the State prisons a matter of trifling necessity, because of the increased education of the young.[15]

The convict-labor storm was gathering rapidly over the prisons. To the Legislature of 1834 came petitions from groups of mechanics in sixteen counties, stating that the labor of the convicts was being sold at reduced prices to the contractors, and was thus, by the

---
[10] B. P. D. S. Vol. 1, p. 550.
[11] B. P. D. S. Vol. 1, p. 808.
[12] B. P. D. S. 1829, p. 255.
[13] Assembly Journal, 1833, 199, p. 7.
[14] Op. Cit., p. 13.
[15] Op. Cit., p. 15.

ability of the contractors thus to undersell in the open market the products of prison labor, affecting injuriously the mechanical industry of the State.[16]

A Legislative committee took the matter under consideration. It reported that it was advantageous to the contracor to be able to count upon a dependable number of men. The labor problem ought easily to be self-regulative. The mechanics ought themselves to bid for the contracts; the State ought to demand high prices for the labor of the convicts. It was hard, anyway, to compete through convict labor with the mechanical industry of the country. The State maintained no monopoly. Convicts were offered to all bidders, and sold to the highest bidder. If one bidder was cleverer than the other, that was no cause for complaint. Markets were not overstocked because of the output of prison-made products. An addition of 1,000 convicts a year would produce no permanent effects upon the prices or wages in that market.[17]

Moreover, did the mechanics claim that convicts should not be permitted to learn industrial trades in prison, on the ground that after leaving prison such convicts, in their newly-learned trades, might be employed in shops with honest journeymen and apprentices, whose morals they might corrupt? Did not the mechanics realize that discharged convicts *must go somewhere?* Must *do something?* Think of the fine reformative effects of the industrial training within the prison! There was no monopoly in prison labor, if the different contracts were let to the different persons, who were the highest bidders. There was a sufficient demand for all products represented by prison labor, and the limited output of the prisons could not affect the markets or wages. The State must lessen its public burdens by a wise use of the convict, who was the slave of the State. The Auburn system was now the model of the world, and no change ought to be hazarded.

The arguments of the Legislative committee contained certain fallacies which the mechanics were not slow in replying to. The contract labor question would not down, by the simple application of a Legislative report. The Assembly appointed a "select committee," which reported in 1834 that the mechanics had charged fraud and favoritism in the letting of contracts. Convicts, said the mechanics, should not be so employed that the products of their labor would bear heavily on any *special* trade. They were confined in prison for the benefit of all the citizens, and so they should be supported by the means of all. In this argument the mechanics were working toward the oft-proved fact, in later days, that although the sum total of prison labor is but an infinitesimal part of the total labor forces of the country, nevertheless, when convict labor is applied mainly to specific and relatively few trades, it does produce a material effect upon those trades, lowering the prices and affecting the number of workers in free labor that can find work in such trades. In short, although 1,000 convicts, working in a State where 500,000 other persons may be working, is a

---

[16] Senate Document, 1834, 14, p. 1.
[17] Op. Cit., p. 3.

negligible number, 1,000 convicts working at a trade at which only 2,000 or 5,000 or 10,000 persons are working on the outside may condition to a preponderating degree the market and the prices of the trade in question.

Moreover, the mechanics in 1834 assailed bitterly the theory of the reformation of convicts. They maintained that every indulgence to a convict beyond a mere wholesome supply of his natural wants was detracting by just so much from the efficiency of his punishment.[18] The supposed feeling of humanity had degenerated into a morbid sensibility that would consult the interest and wellbeing of the criminal at the expense of the community, against whose rights he had offended.

The mechanics continued their argument by asking that the effect be considered that the example of punishment under such an attitude of mind would have on society. The convict gets the idea that there is public sympathy for him outside the walls; he believes himself a martyr, the object of public attention and pity. When he returns to society, he believes himself entitled to all its privileges, fit to associate with respectable citizens, and with no feeling of public infamy or degradation. Then, if society rejects his claim, he reverts to crime. This will be almost inevitable, because no man who has been subjected to infamous punishment as a convict can be expected to become a useful citizen. Therefore, the system is wrong in so far as it is based on the theory of reformation.[19]

A second serious objection, said the mechanics, was that honest citizens would not associate with the discharged convict. Men are known by the company they keep. Two hundred rogues a year would be going into the trades. Rogues draw honest men down to their standards. The great majority of discharged convicts were under thirty years of age. They would accumulate in the mechanical trades. They would not leave the State for greater opportunities, because other States would be adopting the system of New York. The influx of discharged convicts into the mechanical trades would cause the journeymen in these trades to be regarded with suspicion. People would fear to have discharged convicts in their vicinity. Masters would, unaware, be taking discharged convicts into their own homes, among their own wives and daughters. Other journeymen would be quitting the employer who hired a discharged convict. Robbers, ravishers, false swearers and thieves ought not to be benefited to the injury of those honest persons who had a claim on the laws for protection. Rogues are no legitimate part of the community.

Moreover, the prisons, in meeting their expenses by contract labor, taxed the labor and industry of the mechanics, and exempted other classes from contribution, argued the mechanics. It would be more just to punish the convict by idleness, or by unproductive labor, and maintain them by general taxation. The State sold their labor cheaply; the contractors thereby manufactured cheaply and

[18] Assembly Document, 1834, 353, p. 3.
[19] Assembly Document, 1834, 353, p. 5

undersold the honest mechanic. The contractor would practically monopolize any particular branch, by throwing an oversupply into the market, which act would crowd out all except those with much capital.

From the standpoint to-day, the arguments of the mechanics, from their own personal standpoint, will be conceded to be cogent. The "reformed" convict does go back into society. He does mingle with the "honest" workmen. At that time, before the organized labor union methods of identification, it *was* hard to tell whether the journeyman might be a convict or not. The released convict did compete with free labor. In the prison, as we have already said, a relatively slight output in a few industries would disturb the price equilibrium of that industry. The choice of a few industries for convict labor purposes did unduly compete with outside production, and other industries went scot-free of such competition. The mechanics certainly had a grievance.

But, on the other hand, the State did not, of course, want to give up a thing that was working so well from the administrative standpoint. So we feel in the reply of the Legislative committee a distinct side-stepping and an ignoring of uncomfortable truths. The committee maintained that the direct effect of competition was not so great as had been stated. It was said by the committee to be a mere trifle in proportion to the whole manufacturing industry — which was true, but did not meet the point of the special competition alleged by the mechanics. The committee said that, moreover, if labor was thus obtained at low rates, and mechanics were thereby forced to work more cheaply, the community in general would be benefited in securing both labor and products more cheaply — another fallacious economic doctrine.

Nevertheless, the committee stated that it felt the justice of much of the mechanics' criticism — a feeling accelerated no doubt by upwards of 200,000 signatures attached to the memorials of protest. Some modification of the system was advisable, no doubt. The most important objection was the teaching of mechanical trades to the convicts. Certain branches of trade ought to be designated that would not come into competition with trades followed in the United States — trades in which the mechanics of other States or of foreign countries sent large quantities of manufactured articles into the State of New York. Furthermore, the convicts might be employed on roads and other public works, in the stone quarries at Sing Sing, and in preparing stone for public buildings and works.

The committee went on to report that there was the possibility of the transportation of convicts to some region remote from civilized settlements. Further suggestions were that those convicted for a term less than three years might serve their sentence in county jails, and that infamous corporal punishment might for certain offenses be inflicted instead of imprisonment. The appointment of three commissioners was recommended, with authority to remedy the evils and to report to the next Legislature, that of 1835, a plan of State prison industries, and use of labor.

We can readily picture to ourselves the keen interest with which the makers of those 200,000 signatures upon the petitions of mechanics against convict labor awaited the report of the Legislative committee, which report appeared in 1835,[20] and found that in some articles, and to some extent, the complaints of the mechanics were well grounded, and ought to be relieved. That the trade was degraded by the entrance therein of convicts the commission would not admit, but it did hold that the mechanics were thereby exposed and should be protected.

The crux of the problem was, obviously, the question of finding some proper and satisfactory employment for the convicts. What could they do, with the least competition with the petitioners? The bodily health and the sanity of the convicts required work. Labor was salutary, and diminished crime. Idleness and the association of convicts with each other was absolutely inadmissible, and would always lead to depravity and vice. Solitary confinement without labor had been proved impossible, both at Auburn and Philadelphia. Transportation was an expensive failure. Banishment meant turning prisoners loose on other States, which would, of course, retaliate. Employment of convicts on public works was no solution, for citizens (mechanics) were employed thereon as well as in mechanical pursuits. The work was, moreover, temporary.

To the commissioners the solution lay in placing limits on the number of convicts employed in any one prison industry. Convicts should be mainly employed in those branches supplied chiefly by importation from foreign countries. Publicity should be given to the time and place of letting contracts. To search out new trades, the commission might even send an agent to Europe. Such trades being once established, the commission believed the convicts on discharge would no longer seek employment in shops of citizen mechanics. Convicts having no regular calling should be taught an occupation in which they could start, on a small scale, when they emerged from prison. The manufacture of silk was urged as a novel and profitable industry.

It is not hard to see that the commissioners made a poor figure both in their report and in their recommendations. Intentionally or not, they failed to weigh justly the obvious grievances of the mechanics, who were getting more and more pinched by the competition of the prisons. More petitions had been presented to the Legislature on the subject of contract labor than had ever before been presented on any subject.[21] No doubt, the Senator and the Assemblyman of that day lived politically with his ear as close to the ground as at present. And he heard about a public convention of mechanics, attended by 99 delegates from sixteen counties, held at Utica on August 20-21, 1834, to protest against the "war of the State upon the property and the rights of the honest and industrious mechanics," as the Geneva mechanics put it.[22] Auburn

---
[20] Assembly Document, 1835, p. 135.
[21] Assembly Document, 1840, 276, p. 5.
[22] Assembly Document, 1834, 352.

mechanics inveighed against the favoritism manifest in letting and reletting the contracts of the prison. Albany mechanics showed that 100 dozen large combs, that cost $58 to make in Albany, cost only $15.50 in the prisons. The New York city coopers represented that nearly as many coopers were employed at Mount Pleasant as in New York itself.

More and more it seemed apparent that the mechanics had the facts, and the commissions of the Legislature had the defensive theories.

"Would men of wealth (asked the mechanics' convention),[23] like to have the ex-convict, on his return to society, mingle in the drawing room with *their* sons, and *their* daughters? And perchance improve his condition by marriage with an heiress of their fortunes? Would the lawyer, the divine, the merchant, desire this close association that would be forced upon the honest mechanic? An affirmative answer to such questions would be revolting to the moral sense of the community."[25]

And so the convention resolved that, should their petitions fail, they would cause the ballot boxes to speak a language that would not be misunderstood. They would form associations in each county, and also hold annual meetings of protest and propaganda. The "Mechanics' Magazine," a trade journal, pledged itself never to abandon the cause of doing away with the State prison monopoly. One hundred thousand copies of the proceedings of the convention were printed.[24]

So strong was the pressure on the Legislature of 1835 that a law was enacted which promised material alleviation to the mechanics, and which we summarize:

No mechanical trade should hereafter be taught to convicts, except for the making of articles chiefly imported from abroad. Artisans might be employed from abroad as teachers.

No contract for a longer period than six months should be made by the warden, without the consent of the prison inspectors. Due public notice should be given of contracts soon to be let. No contracts should be made for a period of more than five years.

In branches of industry supplied chiefly by domestic labor (as contrasted with foreign products) the number of convicts to be employed should be limited to the number of convicts *who had learned a trade before coming to the prison.*

Existing contracts should be fulfilled, but contractors should be urged, if possible, to abandon them.

The silk industry (growing and weaving) should be introduced.

We have italicized the words in the third paragraph above: "*who had learned a trade before coming to the prison,*" because this clause proved in practice to be a peculiarly useful and barefaced "joker" for the prison authorities during the next half decade. While the intent of the law was probably to limit the number of convicts in *any* trade in prison only to those who already had practiced that trade, the wardens of Auburn and Sing Sing prisons read the law literally, and turned into trades all those who claimed to have followed *any* trade before coming to prison.

---

[23] Proceedings of the State Convention of Mechanics, 1834, p. 6.
[24] Assembly Document, 1840, 276, p. 6.
[25] State Convention of Mechanics. New York Mechanics' Magazine, p. 6.

The silk industry never proved popular or feasible. A few mulberry trees were planted, but the prison industries went diligently on. The wardens were unable to persuade the contractors to give up their lucrative contracts. Warden Levi Lewis of Auburn felt a great pity for the contractors, who had gone into the business with reluctance, as an experiment, and had taught the business to the convicts.[26] Why should the contractors now suffer unfairly and unjustly through general public letting of contracts? Moreover, while such competition might bring higher bids, the warden also worried lest some contractors might bid more than they could afford, thus bringing on a subsequent failure. If such contractors were prosecuted, they would appeal to the sympathy of the Legislature. Any litigation in such an event would seriously demoralize the steady industrial activity of the inmates.

On their part, the mechanics had not come forward with any clear-cut proposals as to substitutes for the present system.[27] They knew that they were detrimentally affected by the system, but they could not bring forward any counter-proposals that would match up in attractiveness to the present conditions of industrial activity within the prisons. They talked vaguely about solitary confinement without labor, or transportation, both manifestly impossible, and both involving the expenditure by the State of considerable sums without any economic return. Furthermore, both transportation and imprisonment without labor had an unsavory history that could be adduced against them. The petitioners should remember, said one committee of the Legislature, that while they, the mechanics in certain trades were complaining, most of the citizens were not at all worried about the situation.

So the arguments were tossed heatedly back and forth. Stress continued to be laid by the mechanics on the inadequacy of the prison punishments. A legislator, friendly to the cause of the mechanics, stated in a minority report in 1835 that a detention in prison was hardly dreaded any longer, and that there were many honest mechanics who would be willing to exchange positions with the convicts.

We might parenthetically remark that the same argument has been one of the stock phrases of those who in these more modern times find fault with lenient and so-called progressive prison administration, but we have yet to find any earnest effort of the so-called honest workman to make his way into prison. Many a workman who has suddenly been discovered to be dishonest has found his way there, but the universal experience has been that he desires to have his prison term cut just as short as possible.

The minority member whom we have mentioned above had to suggest, however, as substitutes for the obviously lucrative contract system only the theoretical proposition of transportation to some remote part of the world, or the discredited solitary confinement

---

[26] Assembly Document, 1835, 135, pp. 27-28.
[27] Op. Cit., p. 330.

without labor. And so the contract system went on, practically unimpeded by the new law, and in defiance of the mechanics. Some of the chief contracts in operation were the following:

MT. PLEASANT PRISON

Nature of Contract	No. of convicts	Date made	No. of yrs. of contract	Contract price per man per day
Copper nail boots and cap fronts	50 to 100	1833	5	$.35
Boots and shoes	80	1833	7	.35
Coopers	150	1832	7	Piece price
Locksmiths	30	1833	5	Piece price
Saddlery, etc	40	1833	5	.37½
Tailoring	30	1833	3	.31¼
Blacksmith and locksmith	60	1833	5	.40
Hat finishing	30	1833	5	.40

AUBURN PRISON

Nature of Contract	No. of convicts	Date of contract	Duration of contract	Contract price per man per day
Coopering	50	1832	3	$.28
Carpenters' and joiners' tools	45	1829	10	.30
Boots and shoes	All in that trade	1832	3	Piece price
Weaving cotton bed ticking	85	1827	10	.25 or .15
Tailoring	35	1833	6	Piece price
Brass clocks	15 to 25	1833	1	.20 to .30

For several years, from 1835 until 1840, there was a lull in the controversy. For a time, the new law was apparently given a chance to work. But in March, 1840, there came a strong recrudescence of the mechanics' campaign. A public meeting "in the matter of teaching mechanical trades to State prison convicts" was held in New York city. Again the old and well-grounded arguments of opposition were advanced. The bill of 1835, it was claimed, was passed to blind the eyes of the mechanics.[28] The chief aim of the State was to make as much money as possible. All talk of convicts being reformed through learning trades was a pretence. In reality, the system had utterly failed to produce reform. That the arguments of the mechanics were based on sporadic statements of well-known persons, and not on any careful statistical proof, made the facts seem no less strong or convincing to the mechanics.

Had the law of 1835 been made a joke? Most decidedly! Did not Mr. Wiltse, the warden of Mount Pleasant, report in 1840 that in the last two years the prison had made $111,773 over all expenses? "A more unequal, unjust and destructive system could not have been devised, nor could more disreputable and dishonest

[28] Assembly Document, 1840, 276, p. 6.

means have been construed to perpetuate it," said the mechanics. The meeting again urged solitary confinement, but this time *with* labor. The Philadelphia system was warmly endorsed. The Auburn and Mount Pleasant prisons should be built over by the labor convicts to provide large cells for solitary labor. Many of the present contracts made since 1835, were probably illegal.

The customary senate Legislative committee made its report. The mulberry trees had not flourished and were not favored at Auburn. The committee praised Captain Lynds (who was now for the second time warden of Auburn), and the inspectors for their efficiency in letting contracts on favorable terms, as shown by the following comparative statement:

Trades	Former rates per day	New rates per day	Trades	Former rates per day	New rates per day
Machine shop	36¼	37½	Shoe	31¼	40
Tailor	32	52	Cabinet	32 7-10	42
Carpet	24	32	Cooper	35	37½
Comb	32	35	Tool	30	37½
Cotton weaving	18	20	Stone	44	50
Hames	31 9-10	35			

At Mount Pleasant Prison, of 767 convicts, 543 were working in nearly a dozen different contract occupations.[29] Mr. Wiltse frankly acknowledged his interpretation of the law of 1835 to be that he could put a convict, who professed a trade, at any trade within the prison. If the mechanics should gain the day and abolish contract labor in Auburn and Mount Pleasant, the annual appropriations by the State would have to be not less than $120,000.

Senator Henry Livingston of this same committee made a minority report, stating that the law of 1835 was almost wholly useless as a relief to the honest mechanics.[30] The revenue to be obtained from convict labor was the primary consideration, and led to "the grossest irregularity and the most revolting inhumanity in the government of the prison."[31] There was under Captain Lynds at Auburn a want of humanity in the treatment of convicts suspected of insanity. It was generally assumed that such convicts were feigning, even in the absence of all possible motive. Lynds had told several of his keepers that six blows with a cat were simply an aggravation; that he must have keepers who could not count six! For a trifling offense a convict had been stripped naked and whipped from 50 to 500 blows — the said convict being also subject to fits![32] The treatment of deranged convicts was revolting, beatings continuing until the body of the insane inmate was cut from shoulder to heels. And no record of this punishment had been entered on the prison books!

But Mr. Livingston, in his turn, did not give constructive suggestions as to how contract labor might be reasonably abolished.

[29] New York Senate Document, 1840, 37, p. 48.
[30] Op. Cit., p. 7.
[31] Senate Document, 1840, 37, p. 5.
[32] Op. Cit., p. 9.

He did recommend the wholesale removal of the present brutal officers. And, in truth, Captain Lynds and Mr. Wiltse both severed their connections in this year with Auburn and Mount Pleasant respectively.

A committee of the Assembly in 1840 was cheerfully frank in recognizing the injustices of contract labor to the mechanics. The law of 1835 was being evaded in that while the *entire* trade was no longer being taught to novices, *piece work* had been developed, and, for instance, twelve different processes in making barrels were now carried on, each process attended to by a different convict. Not one of these convicts was alleged to become a cooper or to learn a trade.[33] The committee declared that the whole system of the letting-out of contracts should be abandoned as soon as it could be legally done. But beyond recommending also that stone-cutting for the State be the principal occupation at Mount Pleasant, the report was not constructive.

The subsequent report of the Legislative committee of the Assembly, for 1841,[34] must have been highly exasperating to the mechanics. Based upon an *a priori* opinion and dogmatic assertions, and devoid of impartial or statistical study, it was a thorough whitewash of the prevailing prison methods. The alleged competition between the regular mechanic and the prison convict was said to be essentially without foundation. The amount of convict labor was comparatively trifling, and the quality inferior. Not so many convicts were thus employed as was commonly supposed. No satisfactory reason had as yet been brought forward why the present system should be discontinued. Convicts were not taught a full trade, anyway, but only a part of a trade. Mechanics could not be degraded by association with convicts. To grant the mechanics' petition for abolition of contract labor would mean enormous expense accruing to the State. And so forth; the repetition of the now time-worn arguments.

An Assemblyman, George Weir of New York, had introduced a bill[35] (which was referred to this committee) providing that no contract should hereafter be made for the labor of prisoners; that no mechanical trade or business should be thereafter taught to prisoners, and that no machinery should thereafter be used that was driven by horse, steam or water power. Solitary confinement without labor should prevail. These propositions the committee bluntly disapproved, on the basis of the arguments of previous years. But the committee went further, and announced that there had been no evasion of the law of 1835. Everything was alleged to be serene in the prisons, and even the prisoners were said to approve of the system of discipline and labor. The committee turned down as entirely impracticable a suggestion that prisoners might be paid a portion of their earnings, the same to go to their families.[36] Such an innovation would involve complicated bookkeeping, would interfere with discipline, and besides exciting jealousy and strife would

[33] Assembly Document 339, 1840, p. 8.
[34] Assembly Document (1841), 186.
[35] Op. Cit., p. 14.
[36] Op. Cit., p. 28.

introduce deception and fraud, and be also unprofitable to the State. "But we shall not dwell further on the subject," said the committee, in abruptly dismissing the subject, thus ending in a wholesale fashion the very suggestion which in a measure would have solved some of the problems of prison discipline. In these more modern times, one of the chief arguments for the perpetuation of the contract system in those States where it still exists, is, that it does give the prisoner a chance to earn by overtime work something to be sent to his dependents outside the prison walls.

In this same year, 1841, the mechanics met again in an indignant State convention at Albany on September 1st with Assemblyman Weir in the chair. The mechanics still refused to formulate an alternative plan, claiming that that was the Legislature's business. In truth, the mechanics were in difficulty. They could not convincingly argue that industrial education was harmful to the convict; they could not convincingly assert that compulsory and solitary idleness would be beneficial to the convict — and in refusing to offer a substitute plan for the lucrative convict labor system, they clearly side-stepped a responsibility that was at least partly theirs. In short, they wanted all competition abolished, and did not care primarily what happened to the convicts or to the State.

So the mechanics had to argue that the convicts should not be taught trades, because the very filling of those trades by discharged convicts would make it harder and harder for them to obtain employment in the said trades.[37] Stress was laid on the non-reformative nature of the present prison system, said to be proved by the fact that one-third of those convicts admitted to the prison had trades. The educated convict was, therefore, more dangerous to society than the untaught convict! The mechanics ridiculed the "State Universities of Sing Sing and of Auburn." Had not the alleged reformers, anyway, abandoned the reform principle in abandoning the complete teaching of a trade, and in substituting a single operation for each laboring convict? Again the mechanics threatened to use their votes, representing one-fourth of the total population of the State, to defeat the chief executive and the hostile Legislature.

And, in truth, the mechanics had their legislative inning in 1842, for Mr. Weir was in this year appointed the chairman of the Assembly's committee on State prisons. The report of that committee arraigned most unmercifully the contract labor system that had been so laboriously whitewashed by the same committee the year before. The possibility of making the prison an agent of industrial reformation was denied.[38]

"To look for a decrease of crime until governments shall cease the system of benefitting the few by the plunder and deprivations of the many is impossible."

High crimes were said by the report to be incited not by the poor but by the rich, the "moneyed rogues." One of the chief

[37] Proceedings of the State Convention of Mechanics, 1841, p. 8.
[38] Assembly Document (1842), 65, p. 3.

causes of crime was alleged to be the dishonesty of the banking system, and the explosion of banks from one end of the country to the other.

Silence, said this insurgent prison committee, contained no reformative principle; it contributed to discipline, and it swelled the quantity of production to the contractor. Reformation must take place not inside but outside the prison, through favorable circumstances, steady employment, good wages, and the enjoyment, by those who labor, of equal station with respectable men. Teaching trades in prison was like dipping out the ocean with a bucket. Moreover, the committee failed to find that the articles of confederation of the State afforded privileges to criminals; there was no specification contained therein that they should be instructed in agriculture or the mechanic arts. Criminals had sacrificed all the advantages of citizenship; they were placed in prison for punishment; they should be supported not by competing with the honest mechanics, but by a general tax. The agents (wardens) of Mount Pleasant and of Auburn were found by the committee to have broken high-handedly the laws themselves in perpetuating and renewing contracts.

But when it came to putting forward a constructive substitute for the existing conditions, the committee, despite its bitter diatribe, and despite the general arraignment of the prisons, offered relatively moderate recommendations. Convicts should be employed so far as practicable in the manufacture of articles necessary for their own consumption, and for the inmates of the State Lunatic Asylum at Utica. The quarrying at Mount Pleasant Prison should be carried on more extensively. Silk should continue to be manufactured at Auburn. And the State should, if possible, go into the business of mining and smelting of metal ores.

There are two phases of the above-mentioned report that should be noted in their relation to modern prison methods. The committee disparaged the prison as a reformative agent, and by indirection placed the chief field of reformation in society itself. The committee, turning the attention of the Legislature from a consideration of prisons to society itself, urged better living conditions, the square deal for labor, and steady employment. There was in the committee's report the suggestion of the palliative results of prison methods.

To-day the old adage that an ounce of prevention is worth a pound of cure is so generally accepted in the correctional treatment of crime and delinquency that it hardly needs to be stressed here. The prison is recognized as the last institution in the series of corrective and reformative efforts of society to deal with the delinquent. The further back toward childhood and early adolescence one goes to-day in the treatment of delinquency, the more popular, and also the more efficacious, is the treatment. Moreover, it is quite as generally recognized, also, that the general improvement of industrial and social conditions has a fundamental relation to crime and delinquency and that it is far better to improve a community than it is to improve a prison. But it is also recognized that we still have prisons with us, and that a part of the imprisonment of industrial and social conditions of society relates specifically to the improvement of prisons, for prisons are one of the still necessary institutions of society.

The second noteworthy point in the report of the above-mentioned committee was the suggestion that to the largest extent possible the inmates produce the articles that they themselves could consume, and that could be consumed by the State Lunatic Asylum at Utica. Herein we find an early suggestion of the prison labor system that later was developed to a greater extent in New York than in any other State, namely, the "State-Use System," the basic principle of which is the prohibition of the sale of prison-made goods in any open market, and, on the other hand, the manufacture by the prisons of goods for the use of the institutions and departments of the State and its political divisions, such as the counties, the cities and the villages. In short, the theory of the State-use system is that there should be, by the prisons, the least possible competition by prison labor with free labor and that therefore no industries should be carried on in the prison for the supplying of the open market in the State in which the prison is located, or any other State. But, since the State seeks thus to minimize any competition of prison labor with free labor, organized labor must recognize on the other hand that the State and its political divisions furnish themselves a market which free labor *can* supply, but which to the greatest possible extent must in fairness be left for prison labor to supply, since prisoners must labor, for obvious reasons, and there must be somewhere an outlet for their product.

The State-use system is not, to-day, a popular system in the States of the Union. Only New York and New Jersey, Ohio and Illinois have adopted the system, wholly or in large part. The system is not yet concomitant with self-support of prisons through the labor of prisoners. New York State has yearly deficits of large amounts for the maintenance of its prisons, and no method by the State-use system has yet been put into practice that has even approached a solution of the problem of maintenance of prisons by the labor of the inmates. On the other hand, there is left, through the State-use system, a considerable part of the day for the academic and vocational education of the inmates, and for their recreation.

Turning our attention again to the report of the Assembly committee of 1842, we find in the same Legislature the mechanics winning a partial victory, because a law was passed providing that convicts should work in prison at trades already learned by them — and not at new trades. Any contracts made in violation of the law of 1835 were to be annulled. A commissioner, Ransom Cook, was appointed by this same law to examine lands in relation to possible mining or smelting operations.

In short, out of the agitation of the mechanics throughout a decade, there had come, not the abolition of prison labor, but its restriction, and the movement also to found a new State prison in New York, where mining and smelting should be the chief industry. Within a year, in 1843, the annual earnings of Auburn Prison had fallen off from $57,722 to $49,652. The prison was earning $1,000 a month less than in the previous year. Unless the existing contracts were legalized, an appropriation of approximately $25,000 would have to be asked for, in order to carry out the law of 1842.

In 1844 a new State prison was established by law, to be located north of a line drawn east and west of the city of Albany. Only the manufacture of iron should be undertaken in this prison. No contracts should be made by this prison for the labor of prisoners. So far as practicable, the prison should be built by the labor of prisoners.

CHAPTER XIII

OTHER EARLY PRISONS IN NEW ENGLAND

MAINE

The State prison of Maine contributed nothing to the early prison movement except a "horrible example." The prison was established at Thomaston, 80 miles northeast of Portland, in 1823, three years after Maine had been set apart from Massachusetts as a separate State. Prior to that, convicts from this section of New England had been sent, often at great expense, and with considerable difficulty of transportation, to the Massachusetts State Prison at Charlestown.

The prison at Thomaston was the second in the United States to be built on the Auburn plan. It was located at the side of a supposedly inexhaustible quarry.[2] The 48 cells, later increased to 71, were literally pits, set back to back, designed for solitary confinement. They were but one story high, and sunk below the surface of the ground.[1] They had no doors or passageway, and were entered *from the top* through an aperture two feet square, secured by an iron grating.

A more gruesome and unhealthy prison abode could hardly be imagined. By means of a ladder the convicts descended into these "rooms of indescribable gloom." The ladder was then withdrawn. The cells were 8 feet 9 inches long, 4 feet 6 inches wide, and 9 feet 8 inches high. A small orifice, 8 inches long by 1½ inches wide, built on a slant, admitted air but practically no light. The cells, supposed to be heated from a flue in the floor, were so desperately cold that in the formidable Maine winters not infrequently two prisoners would be placed in a cell together to keep each other warm. In the winter the prisoners had to stay in bed constantly from sunset to sunrise to keep warm, a process vicious and debilitating to mind and body. There were no lights in the cells.[4] The governor of Maine, pleading in 1839 for a modern prison building, stated that the then existing prison building at Thomaston seemed to have been constructed with a view of inflicting the greatest punishment in the shortest time and at the least expense.

To these terrible cells the courts, from 1823 to 1827, when the law was amended, sentenced convicts with the provision that all or a portion of the sentence should be spent in solitary confinement without labor, and on bread and water. This accumulation of barbarous penalties brought speedily its inevitable horrors. One man, sentenced to 70 days, hung himself after four days; another man, condemned to 60 days, committed suicide after 24 days.[7]

---

[1] Crawford. App., p. 88, from whom the details of following description.
[2] B. P. D. S., 1827, p. 98.
[4] Crawford. App.
[7] Crawford, p. 15.

Many prisoners had to be repeatedly taken from solitary confinement to the hospital in order to be restored to a condition that would permit them to be again returned to the same torture!

The prisoners were placed in their cells one hour before night each week day. They remained in their cells all day on the Sabbath, except, for one and one-half hours.[6]

Insanity and disease were the inevitable corollaries of this treatment, which itself seems to have been the echo of the campaign in New York and Pennsylvania in the twenties. With the abandonment of solitary confinement in Maine in 1827[5] under such conditions, it was still reserved for punishment of infractions within the prison. These terrible conditions were used as material by the Boston Prison Discipline Society in its campaigns against solitary confinement without labor.

Stone-cutting was the main occupation at this prison. There were also blacksmiths, wagon-makers, joiners, shoemakers, and tailors.[3] The few women convicts worked in the washhouse under a matron. There was little difficulty in disposing of the manufactured articles, which were manufactured and sold by the prison, no contractors being employed.

The pits were the worst part of the prison life. The necessity of placing at times two men in a cell broke the rigors of the undiluted Auburn system. Discipline was consequently lax. Friends might visit the convicts. To this was added the almost inevitably demoralizing feature of those prisons in which salaries were small. There were frequent cases of untrustworthiness of the guards, who, receiving less than $200 a year, were generally unfit to be placed in authority over others. Liquor and cards found their way to the prisoners.

The following salaries were paid in 1827:

Warden	$700	Chaplain	$100
Keeper	200	Inspectors	206
Clerk	200	and $91 to each of the officers for board.[10]	
Overseer	180		
Physician	100		

The prison was a constant expense to the State, although annual financial statements often showed apparent earnings over expenses from the labor of convicts, who received no "overstint" compensation, but only a suit of clothes and from $2 to $5 when discharged. The governor stated in 1837 that the prison had cost the State since 1823 a total of $123,489 (mainly, however, for buildings), in addition to the sums arising from the labor of convicts.[9]

It is a striking thing that, despite the pits, the health record was regarded as good. The average death rate was not over two per cent. Women and children were not sent to this prison, but to county jails,[8] until in 1830 a separate building was built for the women.

---

[3] Crawford. App.
[5] B. P. D. S., 1827, p. 89.
[6] B. P. D. S., 1831, p. 612.
[8] B. P. D. S., 1827, p. 101.
[9] B. P. D. S., 1837, p. 121.
[10] B. P. D. S., 1827, p. 98.

After having considered in 1836 the possibility of relocating the State prison at Hallowell, just south of Augusta, the Legislature decided in 1839 on a reconstruction of the prison at Thomaston. The Auburn plan for the prison had been advocated by a legislative commission, in preference to the Pennsylvania plan, on the ground that it was less expensive to build, fully as easy to administer, and, while less expensive to maintain, quite as popular among the authorities on prison discipline, as well as quite reformative! The new prison was to contain 136 cells in a building 140 feet long, 44 feet wide and 25½ feet high. The prison was built by 1845. The 108 cells, 7 feet by 7 feet by 4 feet, were more than adequate for the population, which had averaged about 80.[11] The new prison cost but $13,177. And in 1845, for the first time, the labor of a portion of the convicts was contracted for shoemaking, at 40 cents a day for trained men, and 30 cents a day for new hands.

The prison during the first twenty years of its existence gave some attention to religious instruction, and maintained a Sabbath School. The inspectors of the prison seem to have been highly unsympathetic to any of the efforts at moral and religious instruction. The law required the chaplain to make daily visits to the prison for the purpose of conversing with the convicts; but, reported the inspectors, "the effect of such visits is to afford opportunity for such as are inclined, to spend a part of their time in idleness and deception, while their sentence requires constant labor." The board of inspectors considered it useless to compel the prisoners to attend Sunday School. The prison was reported by Dorothea Dix in 1845 to be deficient in the means of general moral instruction.

NEW HAMPSHIRE

New Hampshire made a real contribution to prison management and progress in this country. From New Hampshire came the Pilsburys. First, Moses C. Pilsbury, warden from 1818 to 1826 of the State Prison, which had been erected in Concord, the capital of the State, in 1812. The son of Moses Pilsbury was Amos, who became warden of the Connecticut State Prison at Wethersfield. The son of Amos was Louis, who became in 1877 superintendent of State prisons in New York.

Moses Pilsbury, while warden at Concord, New Hampshire, was held in high esteem as an administrator. Always at his post, he was unceasingly vigilant, did the duties of contractor, keeper and clerk, was prompt and efficient when correction was necessary, humane in principle, tender in sickness, without cessation in the instruction of prisoners, and religious in temperament.[15] Moreover, he won special praise for converting the deficit of the prison into a surplus, the institution having earned for the State from $1,000 to $5,000 a year from 1822.[14] Moses Pilsbury was the first and earliest

---
[11] B. P. D. S., 1845, p. 506.
[14] B. P. D. S., 1826, p. 32.
[15] B. P. D. S., 1826, p. 36.

of the enlightened wardens of what might be called the second period of American prisons, that began roughly with the establishment of Auburn Prison in 1816.

The prison at Concord was originally of the old Walnut Street type, built in 1812, with large night-rooms, lodging from two to six convicts.[13] The area of the prison was greatly restricted, the enclosing wall being but 260 feet long by 200 deep.[12] The prison building was 70 feet long, 36 feet wide, 3 stories high, and contained 36 cells. No quarry or navigable water adjoined the prison. From a quarry two miles distant, rough granite was brought to the prison, which, when prepared for market, was carried to the Merrimac River, that flowed through Concord, and thence by boat and canal to the Boston market. In the earlier years the chief employment was stone-cutting.[19]

The satisfactory discipline of the prison was achieved by Warden Pilsbury through constant vigilance. He was an ardent believer in separate confinement. Plots, he said, were hatched in night-rooms,[16] and he had frequently overhead whole histories of villainy in listening to the conversations of convicts at night.[20] Pilsbury condemned the practice of paying assistant keepers and guards so little that frequent changes occurred, and that men of proper character were difficult to obtain. Improper familiarity between keepers and convicts inevitably developed.[17]

New Hampshire's prison was small, inexpensive and rural. The total salary list in 1826 was but $1,565, of which the warden received $800. The expense for food, clothing and bedding for the same year was only $1,366 for 70 prisoners. The mortality was less than two per cent. Besides the stone-cutting, the prisoners worked as smiths, coopers, weavers, tailors, painters, and at general work around the yard. Crawford found the prisoners rising at 4:30 in summer, and working until 7, when they had one hour for breakfast. They then worked until 12, when dinner occurred. They had their meals in their cells. They returned finally to their cells at 7 in the evening. Lights were placed in front of the cells in winter.

The daily rations of the prisoners, without variation, were: 14 ounces of salted beef, 1¼ pounds of rye and Indian bread, and a sufficient quantity of potatoes, and porridge or beans or peas for supper.[18]

In 1827 Mr. Pilsbury was called to the wardenship of the new Connecticut Prison at Wethersfield, in spite of the bonus of $200 which had been for a number of years appropriated him by the New Hampshire Legislature. Successive wardens did not reach his administrative ability, and Crawford found marked laxity in the management.

---

[12] Crawford. App., p. 78.
[13] B. P. D. S., 1826, p. 25.
[16] B. P. D. S., 1826, p. 25.
[17] B. P. D. S., 1827, p. 55.
[18] B. P. D. S., 827, p. 143.
[19] B. P. D. S., 1826, p. 101.
[20] Same, p. 25.

The diminishing population of the prison, from 1828 on, was a cause of wonder. A State with nearly 300,000 inhabitants had only 48 convicts in its State prison in 1828. For several years the average was not over 60; less than one-half the number in the Vermont State prison, and about one-third as many as at Wethersfield.[21]

Two of the principal causes were said to be the debtor laws and the pauper laws.[22] There were few debtors in the county prisons in training for careers of crime, and the New Hampshire almshouses were not sustained, as in other States, by a heavy State tax for the support of foreign paupers. Moreover, the laws of New Hampshire provided shorter penalties for crimes that elsewhere were visited with severe sentences.

The Constitution itself of New Hampshire declared:

"A multitude of sanguinary punishments is impolitic and unjust, the true design of all punishments being to reform, and not to exterminate, mankind."[25]

In 1832 a new cell building of three stories was erected at the prison, on the Auburn plan, with 120 cells, each 6 feet 10 inches long, 3 feet 4 inches wide, and 6 feet 6 inches high.[23] At this period the relaxed discipline was similar to that of the State prison of Maine. The prison population was not considered a vicious one. Crawford found corporal punishment forbidden by the law of the State, and solitary confinement the only severe punishment, up to 30 days. This punishment was not used over once a month. The total population on May 31, 1832, was only 89, and but 14 convicts were admitted, and but 16 discharged during the fiscal year. Their sentences ranged as follows:[24]

Life	5	8 years	3
13 years	1	7 years	11
12 years	2	6 years	8
11 years	1	5 years	32
10 years	7	Under 5 years	19

By far the largest proportion of the 407 admitted since the opening of the prison in 1812 had been convicted of stealing. The chief offenses were:

Stealing	248	Forgery	22
Horse stealing	46	Making counterfeit notes or money	10
Passing counterfeit money	23		

Only two persons had been executed in 25 years. There had been since the opening of the prison but 7 persons committed for manslaughter. The population had been almost entirely American-born, 371 out of 407, England furnishing 11 and Ireland 16. Of the 407, 220 had been between 20 and 30 years of age, and 56 under 20. About 25 per cent. of the prisoners had been discharged by pardon. At the time of Crawford's visit there was only one woman prisoner.[26]

---

[21] B. P. D. S., 1831, p. 436.
[22] Crawford. App., p. 78.
[23] Crawford, p. 80.
[24] B. P. D. S., 1831, p. 436.
[25] Bradford Enquiry, p. 6.
[26] Crawford, p. 81ff.

By 1835 it was announced that, except for a few years, the prison had been a heavy burden to the State. Since, therefore, it was likely to continue to be so in the future, the board of inspectors contracted for the labor of the prisoners in such a manner as if possible to meet all expenses.[29] The contractors were to pay all the expenses of the prison, including the salary of the officers. The then warden denounced this proposition, because of the inevitable clash of the interests of the prison and of the contractors.[26]

In 1837 the affairs of the prison were unsatisfactory, and there was much complaint in the public press. The next year the earnings did not meet the expenses. The "elder Pilsbury," Moses, was called back to the wardenship. He designated the contract system as the worst of all systems, destroying all the good contemplated by the friends of prison discipline.[27] In 1840 Pilsbury requested the Legislature not to consider him again a candidate for the wardenship. He said:[30]

"The contract system cuts off all hope of the reformation of the prisoner."

There was a single contractor now, who received all the earnings, and supported the institution.[31] Moral instruction was given, at this period, to the prisoners by a chaplain appointed by law, who also taught the prisoners. There was a small prison library. Citizens were admitted to the Sunday services in the prison — an unusual custom.

VERMONT

Vermont and Maine were States so relatively remote, in the early days of the Republic, from the progressive influences in prison management that it is not surprising that little development of modern methods or constructive principles emanated from their prisons. In 1809 Vermont built its first State prison at Windsor on the west bank of the Connecticut. In a plot 280 feet long and 200 feet deep were the keeper's house and the cellhouse, the latter structure being 84 feet long, 36 feet wide, and containing 35 cells,[33] each of which, according to the then customary plan, was designed to hold from two to six persons.[32] When the Auburn system began to influence New England, Vermont erected in 1831 an additional cellblock, on the Auburn plan, with 136 individual cells, 7 feet long, 3 feet 6 inches wide, and 6 feet 9 inches high, with wooden doors, in which a nine-inch aperture was constructed for the admission of air and light. It can readily be seen that this provision was deplorably insufficient, and must have rendered the cells almost dark, and badly deficient in air.

Vermont's early prison history did not affect materially the course of American prison discipline. Representatives of other States seemingly did not visit Vermont, or seek to learn from her.

---

[26] B. P. D. S., 1836 and 1837.
[27] B. P. D. S.,1838, p. 219.
[29] B. P. D. S., Vol. I, p. 874.
[30] Same, Vol. II, p. 445.
[31] Same, Vol. II, p. 333.
[32] Crawford App. p. 84.
[33] Reynolds, p. 10.

Her methods were economical, not to say frugal. The superintendent of the prison, who filled the roles of contractor, clerk and agent, received annually but $850; the keepers and guards received annually only $130, and the physician $100.[34] Crawford, the English official visitor to our prisons in the thirties, found in 1832 the cells dirty and offensively close — as was natural — and the discipline lax. Corporal punishment by flogging was prohibited by law, the dark cell and restricted diet being used as severe measures.[32]

The prison's chief industry was weaving. For several years after its establishment, the prison cost the State from $5,000 to $7,000 a year. Then, for a long period, it made both ends meet. Later, in 1838, all labor of convicts was leased to a contractor, who in turn guaranteed to meet all the expenses of the prison. Nevertheless, in 1845 the prison cost $2,000 more than its income. The average number of prisoners during the twenties was approximately 100.

Crawford found in 1832 only one woman prisoner in the population of 119. She sewed constantly. The male convicts worked at dyeing yarn, weaving, spinning, tailoring, shoemaking, blacksmithing and as wheelwrights. Each convict had a stint to do and received compensation for overwork. Snuff and tobacco were allowed the well-behaved prisoner in moderate quantities. Letters could be sent to and from friends. Visitors were admitted with frequency. The prisoners wore party-colored clothes, half green and half scarlet.[35]

We have a variant from the dry official reports of this prison in the shape of a collection of "Recollections of Windsor Prison," by one John Reynolds, a long-time inmate of the prison, who was discharged about 1830, and who gave a vivid and apparently relatively dispassionate account of the life in the institution in his time. Reynolds was an educated man, thoughtful, and gifted in expression. It is to be expected that the autobiography of a prison inmate will be colored, and one-sided, but on the other hand, so is the official report. The released inmate seeks ordinarily to produce an account highly colored and spectacular; the official report seeks to eliminate color, so far as possible, and it seeks the opposite of the spectacular. The inmate's report is a case of special pleading, and often largely a narrative of abuses and injustices; the official report is a case also of special pleading — to the Legislature, and to the public — and is the opposite of the inmate's report, for it does not narrate abuses, and portrays no injustices to prisoners, so far as its own deliberate management is concerned.

Between the emotional and subjective report of the released inmate and the cold but subjective report of the administrative body of the prison lies frequently the truth. In the case of John Reynolds, we have a man who was sufficiently logical and intellectual not to distort and rejoice in unreliability. Plunged into this

---
[32] Crawford. App., p. 84.
[34] B. P. D. S., 1827, p. 103.
[35] Reynolds, p. 15.

prison maelstrom of human wreckage, the outstanding features of the prison life were to him the State's inhumanity and stupidity, as represented by the acts of officers and keepers. The very prison building was an example. The coldest part of the prison in the winter had not a spark of fire in any of the halls.

"Many a time," he wrote, "have I made large balls by scraping the frost with my hand from the stone sides of my cell!"[36] In the solitary confinement cells, in winter, the wretched prisoner had to keep walking to keep from freezing to death![37] One small piece of bread, and a pail of water each twenty-four hours were his portion; a single blanket his defense against the bitter Vermont cold. With wholly inadequate nourishment he fought for life by pacing the dark cell. Of a certain young Dean the author tells, who with frozen ears and shivering limbs, exhausted by the very exercise necessary to prevent freezing, was dying in solitary confinement for want of sleep.[38]

It was a serious problem, not confined to Vermont or Maine alone, that all the American prisons in the northern States faced in the winter time. There was great difficulty in procuring an equal or an adequate amount of heat. Miss Dorothea Dix, writing in 1845, said that she knew of no prison where, as yet, the officers were fully satisfied with the area stoves. Some cells were hot and stifling, some cold and uncomfortable.

This narrative of Reynolds teems with graphic and heartrending tales of the extreme sufferings of prisoners. The insane were flogged for feigning insanity. Instruments of torture were: the block and chain, a log of wood, from 30 to 60 pounds in weight, to which a long chain was fastened. The other end was around the prisoner's ankle. He carried it wherever he went. Sometimes he had to wear it for months. Also the iron jacket, a frame of iron that confined the arms "down and back." A person wearing this jacket could not lie down with any comfort. The sick were considered as criminal in their sickness, and many died before they could convince their keepers that they were sick. Sick persons were allowed no food, but a dish of crust coffee and a piece of bread, once in 24 hours. Often they were given an emetic, or blistered. Reynolds wrote that the physicians were in the main honorable men, but were given no authority. Ministers neglected the prison, and men who had been as long as six months in the hospital died without a visit from a clergyman. Twenty years after the founding of the prison, no Bible class or Sunday School had as yet been introduced, for the keepers "had hatred of the holiness and the purity of the Gospel." Ultimately, through the publicity of a letter smuggled out of prison, the needs of the prisoners were made known, and a chaplain appointed. Reynolds held that "you cannot do anything to a prisoner until you convince him of your real friendship for him."

---

[36] Reynolds. Recollection of Windsor Prison, p. 11.
[37] Same, p. 36.
[38] Same, p. 66.

What was the attitude of the prisoners toward religion and its doctrines? Those whom Reynolds knew held almost universally to the "endless punishment school."[39] All were agreed that the means of grace were confined to this life, and that if a man died in sin, his doom in misery was fixed forever. Reynolds found both high motives and appallingly base characters within the same prison group. Though the number of sincere and hopeful Christians was very small, there was not one man among them in whose mind the pulse of virtuous principles was not still beating.

It was natural, therefore, that this sensitive and well-educated prisoner, Reynolds, should declaim in utmost bitterness against the keepers. By laws, made for a humane government of the prison, were trampled under foot by every keeper and guard, from the highest to the lowest. The longer a keeper stayed at Windsor, the more brutal he became. "Hence prisons," said the author, "grow worse as they grow older. They all had their origin in a merciful design . . . they gradually sink down into the gloom of unalleviated despotism," The stripling keeper, at eight dollars a month, imagines himself something and descends to every arbitrary manner. How can prisoners reform when they see their officers, who are supposed to have special reference to the good and moral reformation of prisoners, act thus?

Were the prisoners incapable of being reached through kindness? It was told by Reynolds, as an example of the generous-heartedness of the inmates, that a woman whose husband was an inmate came with her two children a distance of 300 miles to see him. She had spent her money and had already suffered on the road. As soon as this was known, the prisoners made up a purse of $14 and gave it to her, and also cloth to dress her two children. Husbands and sons, working in prison shops, were particularly careful to keep their earnings, and at convenient times to send them to their parents and families.

The author maintained that if any good was to be effected in the reformation of prisoners, they must be treated with kindness and respect.

"You may *snarl* them into sin, and tread them down to *hell,* but you must love them into *repentance,* and support them up the ascent to *heaven.*"

There was no danger of any prisons, by humane treatment, ever becoming so mild as to be a desirable residence for any one.

"Take the purest apartment in heaven and confine a seraph there, and the simple fact that he is a prisoner would make his home a hell. The devil himself would prefer liberty, in the world of woe, to imprisonment even in paradise; freedom with damnation, to salvation with restraint. . . . Our prisons are such scenes of cruelty and such schools of crime because Christian churches and Christian individuals are destitute of the practical good-will and the expansive benevolence of the Gospel of Christ."

It is impossible not to feel that through Reynolds' account of life in Windsor Prison we get a lightning flash into basic truths about the prison systems of the time. It is the minimum, in most

---
[39] Reynolds, p. 111.

instances, that the student can draw from annual reports, and even from Legislative documents, regarding the punishment and cruelty sides of prison administration. It needs a Reynolds, or an anonymous writer, fearing for his very safety even after prison, to induct us into the actual horrors of the time.

We cannot pass over the statement of Reynolds that imprisonment itself is the central fact of prison life. "Better freedom with damnation, than salvation with restraint." [40] He has thus graphically phrased almost a century before the weaker and more frequent repetition of the same emotion to-day, what is pointed out in the contention of many reformers of to-day that it is not the punishments in prison that count most, but the fact of the impossibility of being free and one's own master. Freedom is craved without cessation. It is maintained that the chief punishment is inflicted upon the criminal when he is shut up within prison walls, and that extra punishments are not needed for the prevention of crime, or the reformation of the offender.

Reynolds felt bitterly toward the Boston Prison Discipline Society which, by championing the Auburn system, and by condoning thereby the severe practices of that method, as well as flogging, seemed to him to torture the prisoner while it could, and then threw him out, unprotected, unhelped, and friendless, on the scorn of mankind, to pursue from necessity his old course, and be sent back again. So, after his discharge from Windsor, Reynolds endeavored to found the "Prison Missionary Society" in New England, which

"aimed to treat the prisoner as a human being, and to effect his reformation by the mild means of the Gospel . . . and to go with him when set free and to prevent him from being compelled to sin again by giving him clothes, money and employment, and elevating him to the dignity of a citizen and the respect of mankind." [41]

However, for lack of financial support the plan of Reynolds fell through, and was soon of necessity abandoned. His motives were such as to-day would have the highest moral support, although it is still a fact that charitable organizations or individuals devoted to the succor of the released prisoner are not among those most readily or spontaneously supported. Moreover, his protests against the Boston Prison Discipline Society were in part well grounded. The Boston organization was a militant society for prison reform, not for the individual succor of released prisoners. We do not find in its records that it functioned as a relief society. There was already great need of the after-care that Reynolds, knowing from personal experience the vital dearth of such effort, urged be given. But he was before his time! Since his day, many men have come out of prison, to become missionaries in the field of the succor of the convict.

---

[40] Reynolds, p. 207.
[41] Same, p. 144.

Because of his own experience, and because of what prison did to all inmates, Reynolds inveighed with intensity against the prison system.

"Windsor prison is called a penitentiary; as properly might hell be called heaven. The spirit of the penitentiary systems finds no place there to lay its head. Not the reformation of the convict is sought but their warnings; and they are treated just as an intelligent but heartless slaveholder would treat his negroes—made to work as long as they can earn their living, and then cursed with freedom that they may die at their own expense."[42]

---

[42] Reynolds, p. 130.
Recollections of Windsor Prison: containing Sketches of its History and Discipline; with Appropriate Strictures, and Moral and Religious Reflections, by John Reynolds, Boston. Published by A. Wright, 1834.

CHAPTER XIV

THE MASSACHUSETTS STATE PRISON
1826-1846

"The State prison at Charlestown resembles a great manual labor school," wrote F. C. Gray in 1847;[1] "the shops are not equalled, except in such great establishments as Lowell." Looking backward from this prosperous conclusion of the period we are about to consider, we find that ten years before the statement of Gray, in 1837, Governor Everett of Massachusetts had said, at the annual meeting of the Prison Discipline Society of Boston that

> "this, then, is the glory of the modern prison discipline; an awful waste of life, of human blood, has been prevented; the tortures of the former modes of punishment are disused; the aggravated corruption, which badly managed prisons unavoidably produced, is succeeded by a purifying moral influence, and in numerous well-attested cases, character has been retrieved."[2]

In 1838, the Boston Society stated that it was not aware of any penitentiary that had a better system of moral and religious instruction than the State Prison of Massachusetts.[3]

And it is true that in the years from 1829 on, Massachusetts made an earnest effort to work out, on the basis of the Auburn system, a plan of prison administration that would embody both efficiency and humanity. Her history during this period is of special interest. It will be remembered that the first twenty years of the Massachusetts State Prison had been years marked with cruelty and demoralization after the earliest years. Now, with the erection of a new prison building in 1829, and the introduction of the Auburn system, a remarkable change for the better quickly followed, and conditions, which at the old prison had demanded marked improvement, or the abandonment of the penitentiary, were now substantially changed.

The old conditions had obtained as late as 1827, when a representative of the Boston Society found forty convicts scattered in different "apartments," without keeper or inspector for the whole. Similar license was tolerated in the hospital. The keeper could not approach the cells at night without the giving of warning by moving heavy doors.[4]

Recidivism was unchecked.[5] A typical recidivist was one Henry Wood, from Acton, Massachusetts, who had the following record:

Life sentence for burglary. December 11, 1800. Pardoned, November, 1811. Six months' sentence for theft, May, 1812. Discharged, November, 1812.

---
[1] Gray. Prison Discipline in America, p. 47.
[2] B. P. D. S., 1837, p. 177.
[3] B. P. D. S., 1838, p. 221.
[4] B. P. D. S., 1827, p. 59.
[5] Ibid., p. 60.

Sentenced to three years for theft, December, 1814. Discharged, December, 1817.
Life sentence for theft, November, 1818. Discharged, October, 1824.
Sentenced to seven years for larceny, May, 1825. Now (1827) at head of cook room, with ten young convicts associated with him at night.

A general search of the old prison, in 1825, had disclosed in the prisoners' cells counterfeit bills already altered or in process of alteration; also between 20 and 30 copper-plate dies, prepared and neatly engraved; also a large iron or steel press.[6] In short, the manufacture of counterfeit money within the prison! A keeper was detected furnishing, three times in succession, bills to be altered by the prisoners. The counterfeiting of bank bills was a frequent and lucrative crime; the annual report of the Boston Society in 1827 carried a list of 237 counterfeits of bank bills then current in 18 States and Canada.

A great variety of skeleton keys had been taken in a similar search of convicts' rooms and persons, under the old regime. The prison was a veritable training school, in depravity. A Boston merchant, Marshall Prince, who had lost the key of his iron private chest, tried in vain among Boston locksmiths to get it open. But when he carried it to the State prison, "it was opened before he had scarcely time to look about him."[7] Not only did unnatural crime flourish, but the prison was again and again the scene of riots, insurrections and other dangerous manifestations.

So terrific were the well-known evils in the prison that in 1828 the Boston Society exclaimed that a "holy God, for twenty years, has been a witness (to the conditions), and we tremble for ourselves, as citizens of the State, lest we shall be found partakers in the guilt of the existence and unnecessary continuance of such an evil."[8]

One of the most disturbing features of the situation was the so-called "overstint," or bonus, granted by the contractor for overtime work as a stimulus to convicts. Such overstints totalled about $6,000 a year, and were used by the convicts in ways antagonistic to the efforts of the prison authorities to maintain order, discipline and control. Despite the ruling of the inspectors that the overstint might be used only for the families of prisoners, or be kept until the prisoners' release, and despite the strict prohibition to sell, bargain, or give any part of the overstint from or to one another, in practice the convicts sometimes even employed it in hiring legal counsel and other persons to obtain pardons for them, and sometimes in employing lawyers to obtain or prevent the passage of criminal or penal laws, which the convicts liked or disliked.

On such occasions a purse was made up by the prisoners. Sometimes the fund was used to corrupt the small officers of the prison, to obtain indulgences or to effect an escape. The most common use of the overstint was to procure luxuries such as tea, coffee, tobacco, milk, crackers, fresh fish, butter, cheese, cider and apples. These articles materially supplemented the legal dietary of coarse beef

[6] B. P. D. S., 1827, p. 62.
[7] Ibid., p. 63.
[8] B. P. D. S., 1828, p. 157.

or pork, rye and Indian meal, molasses, salt fish and lard,[9] and defeated the announced purposes of a monotonous and coarse diet as a punishment and deterrent.

Naturally, in such a prison, petty "perquisites" flourished among the keepers, who took stores, stock and the labor of convicts in their own departments at very low price. The abuse extended to the taking of leather, iron and the like. Officers had shoes, clothes and farm utensils made up by prisoners out of prison stock for their own use; they had their wood sawed and carted by convicts, and took provisions for themselves and their families. The commissary officer, though paid a set salary, obtained from $400 to $500 a year in addition to his business. An overseer in the stone department received $354 as salary, but made also $3,000, and also had an income from contracts. The lesser officers received five per cent. commission on the proceeds from fees of visitors, and were allowed 150 pounds of pork for tending the swine. These and many other "emoluments" had been sanctioned by the board of inspectors, but had no legal sanction. The whole situation, in short, was demoralizing, and was heightened by a division of authority between the board of inspectors and the warden, and consequent friction that developed into animosity,[10] and that led in 1828 to an administrative organization, whereby the warden became the dominant executive authority.

The State was consequently forced into a radical reorganization of the prison. The Prison Discipline Society furnished an architectural plan on the basis of the Auburn structure, and urged the adoption of constant silence and the separation of prisoners at night.[11] The Legislature of 1826 authorized the erection of a building of unhammered stone, for the separate confinement of 300 convicts. In the same year a very constructive law was passed, giving to the city of Boston authority to discontinue sending juvenile delinquents to State prison, and to commit them instead to the House of Correction at South Boston.

The new State prison building received the first prisoners in October, 1829. It was 200 feet long, 48 feet wide, with a corridor 9 feet wide (and opened to the ceiling) surrounding the cellblock, which was four tiers high, each tier containing 38 cells, or 304 in all. Each cell was 7 feet long, 7 feet high and 3 feet 6 inches wide. The doors were of wrought iron, with iron gratings in the upper part, fastened by a lever lock. In short, a prison building of the Auburn type.[12] The new prison was a ponderous edifice, and contained about 11,000 tons of granite, 20 tons of cast iron, and 45 tons of wrought iron.

Opposite each cell, in the outer wall, nine feet away, was a little window, similar to the small windows at Sing Sing prison, built on the theory of contributing light to the individual cells through the grated doors of the cells. The light must have been deplorably

---

[9] B. P. D. S., 1828, p. 183.
[10] B. P. D. S., 1828, p. 183.
[11] B. P. D. S., 1826, p. 43.
[12] Haynes, p. 48.

scanty, for the Boston Society within a few years began to advocate for American prisons, the insertion of long wide windows into the outside walls of such cell-houses. To-day the long wide windows are a regular part of this type of construction, and the light of the sun floods into the corridors of the cellblock.

The new prison, including a chapel for 320 convicts and kitchen, cost about $86,000.[13] The size of the prison yard at this time was 500 by 240 feet. The State had bought five acres outside the walls for a wharf and a garden.[14]

The revolution in prison discipline thus brought about came without riots or bloodshed. By 1831, there was high praise for the prison in Governor Lincoln's message to the Legislature. Convicts were now separated at night, and there was silence, order, industry, respectful and cheerful obedience, harmony, mildness and authority among the officers.[15] The official and Legislative reports for the next decade and a half bring records of almost uninterrupted administrative serenity at the prison, and of a gradual socialization in the mental attitude of warden, chaplain and physician. Corporal punishment was employed with relative infrequency at the prison. In the six years from 1829 to 1834, the official statements showed a yearly average of 64 different persons thus punished, out of an average population of 260 persons, with a total average of 451 blows.[16]

Following the introduction of the Auburn system, there was for some years a notable decrease both in commitments and recommitments, a phenomenon occurring also under similar conditions in other States, and seeming to show the deterrent influence, although only for a few years, of a new and rigorous penal system. In 1816, 1817, and 1818, when the old prison was operating, the yearly commitments had been between 130 and 165. But in 1831, with the Auburn system in operation, there were but 71 commitments, a smaller number than, with one exception, had occurred in any year from 1807 to 1827.[17]

Through the period that we are now considering, the moral and religious instruction at the prison was a prominent feature. The Reverend Jared Curtis, who had been "loaned" in the early twenties to Auburn Prison by the Boston Society as chaplain, returned to New England to become the resident chaplain at Charlestown. In 1829 a Sabbath School was organized, teaching not only the Bible but the three R's. We shall see how out of the use of the Sunday School and of the chaplain there developed not alone at the Massachusetts prison, but elsewhere the simpler and more elementary conceptions of the social treatment, so to speak, of the inmates. The chaplains teach not only the Sunday lesson, but the A. B. C's and some arithmetic and penmanship. The idea of a secular school gradually evolves. In time we shall find in this same prison the idea of a gathering of the men, to be instructed in ethical

---
[13] Haynes, p. 51.
[14] Laws of Commonwealth, etc., 1829.
[15] B. P. D. S., 1831, p. 449.
[16] Julius. Sittleche Zusbaende, Vol. II, p. 200.
[17] B. P. D. S., 1832, p. 557.

subjects apart from the Sunday lesson or sermon. As the conception grows of the convicts' *similarity* to other men, instead of the dissimilarity, the sense of obligation increases on the part of the State to give to the convict what he had lacked on the outside, culminating in the seventies in the elaborate reformatory system that had its origin at Elmira.

At Massachusetts, by the end of the third decade of the nineteenth century, a morning and evening daily assembly in the chapel had been instituted, with prayer and the reading of the scriptures. A definite chapel was built as a part of the new prison, wherein on the Sabbath about 50 young convicts were instructed. By 1831, from 130 to 140 residents of Charlestown, of different religious denominations, had been found willing to engage alternately, from ten to twenty at a time, as teachers in the prison Sunday School.[18] A general public interest was being aroused.

On Saturday afternoon, the convicts who sang well were gathered for practice, preparatory to the divine service on Sunday.[20]

De Metz and Blouet found, in connection with the Massachusetts prison, that it was very hard to get suitable Sunday School teachers, who would limit themselves to a discussion of the lesson. They were inclined to talk on foreign matters, and they caused consequent confusion among the prisoners. The Wethersfield Sunday School had to be closed on this account.[21]

We find, in 1832, the chaplain issuing in the annual report of the board of inspectors some social statistics regarding the prisoners. This is noteworthy, not because of the intrinsic value of the collated facts, but because they are *published* facts, gathered with the evident design of knowing more about the men in prison. The prison is emerging from the period when the inmates were treated as so many human beings consigned to oblivion and requiring no study. It is an effort, in a simple way, to understand the problem of the inmate. It is the birth, in Massachusetts, of the statistical method, applied to prisoners with the sanction of the board of inspectors, and the warden.

The chaplain had examined verbally 256 inmates. Of his figures we reprint the following:[19]

Total examined	256
Of these, colored, including Indians	48
Born outside the United States	48
Did not know alphabet when they came to prison	20
Could read only in easy lessons for children	21
Could not write	64
Accustomed to ardent spirits before 16 years of age	127
Intemperance led to crime	156
Intemperate habits when admitted to prison	167
One or both parents intemperate	50
Guilty of theft before 16 years old	45
Brought up without regular trade or employment	82
Left parents without consent before age of 21	68
Lived in habitual neglect of the Sabbath	182

[18] B. P. D. S., 1831, p. 451.
[19] Same, p. 543.
[20] Laws of the Commonwealth, 1829.
[21] De Metz and Blouet, p. 22.

The statistical methods of Curtis were primitive, and his goal in the publication of the figures very obvious. He took his facts in large part undoubtedly from the lips of the inmates, a poor statistical method when accuracy is required. He probably colored the reports of the inmates with his own strong bent of mind. Moreover, he was obviously convinced that the youth who lived in habitual neglect of the Sabbath, was idle, ran away from home without his parents' consent, and stole before he was sixteen, and drank, would get into State prison. It is no disparagement to his figures that we surmise his strong propensities to prove a point. Much later than Curtis have we found figures equally general and perhaps equally "predisposed."

In 1833, the Sunday School had developed an attendance of about 150, the warden and the deputy warden attending alternately, and the chaplain acting as superintendent. The prison report of this year asserted that several discharged prisoners had reformed during the last three or four years, and a large number had become industrious and worthy men.[22] It would seem that "reformation" meant in the period under discussion a religious conversion, and that those who had become industrious and worthy alone had not been considered "reformed."

The presence of insane persons in the convict population was not only disturbing to the discipline, but was a piteous spectacle. In the absence of a State asylum for the insane, the courts were forced to commit the criminal "lunatics" to prison, or to the county jails and houses of correction. Emphatic agitation by Governor Lincoln led in 1830 to the establishment of the State Lunatic Asylum at Worcester. The horrible condition of the miserable and ignored insane in the county prisons of Massachusetts was almost beyond belief. Of the first 164 individuals transferred to Worcester, considerably more than half came from the jails and houses of correction, and about one-third of the whole number had suffered jail confinement for periods of from ten to thirty-two years.[25]

Strangely enough, the law of 1830 permitting the transfer of the insane, though applying to county and local prisons, did not extend to the State prison. Warden, physician and chaplain urged the extension of the law to permit the removal of idiots and lunatics from the State prison:

"The prison affords no means of relieving these unhappy prisoners. They cannot be safely employed in labor, and they are not subjects of discipline, so they are necessarily confined in solitude, aggravating the disease. In this prison the insane are forgotten by the public, and sequestered from the humanity of their friends and kindred, and doomed to spend years in hopeless misery."[23]

In 1844 the board of inspectors announced that a penitentiary was doubtless a very fit place to punish crime, but not to cure a malady of body or mind.[24] In the same year an act was at last passed by the Legislature permitting the transfer of insane convicts to Worcester. This was a merciful provision. Insane prisoners, in

[22] B. P. D. S., 1833, p. 628.
[23] Senate Document 17, 1843.
[24] Senate Document 5, 1844.
[25] Senate Document 10, 1834.

an institution operating on the contract plan, were apt to be regarded as simulating insanity in order to avoid the strenuous labor of the shops. Appalling testimony of the flogging of insane persons came frequently to light in the official investigations of prisons administered on the Auburn plan, in Massachusetts among other States. Dorothea Dix cited an instance — typical undoubtedly of many similar instances — but without naming the institution, in which a prisoner who declared himself unable to work was repeatedly flogged, as the rules of the prison required. Ultimately the shrieks and tortures of the wretched man compelled the guards to suspend the floggings. He was subsequently found to be insane and was removed to an asylum.[26]

The above efforts of Massachusetts to eliminate one class of inmates — the mentally unbalanced — from the prison population is of especial interest at the present day, because of the introduction, mainly within the last decade, of the intensive studies of the psychologist and the psychiatrist into penal institutions. The most obvious forms of insanity were recognized eighty years ago in the Massachusetts prison. But the subtler forms of mental irresponsibility are but now being brought to light, and to-day it is generally held among the scientific colleagues of the warden — the psychologist and the psychiatrist, and also the prison physician — that there are three or four well-marked classes of mental cases in the prison population, each of which needs to be carefully studied to determine the degree of responsibility, and also the best disposition of the case.

In addition, therefore, to the clearly insane, the prison of to-day shows the presence of a considerable number of feeble-minded persons, some of whom are so distinctly non-improvable as to warrant their removal to asylums for the feebleminded, and their treatment wholly from the standpoint of their mental condition. In addition, the prison contains a third group, the so-called psychopathics, those who are eccentric, odd, "cranky," "nutty," and in general so constituted that they cannot long conform to the routine of prison life, but become again and again the "bad actors" of the prison population. They cannot generally be adjudged insane, and therefore are not subject to removal to a hospital for the insane. They remain in the prison population, and are intermittent disturbers of the prison discipline and daily life. The solution for this class will be probably found in their segregation in a separate part of the prison, or in a separate prison. The feebleminded of custodial condition will be also segregated, as in the case of the recently established institution in New York State, at Napanoch, where a former reformatory has been converted by law into an institution for the care of the delinquent feebleminded.

The determination of mental states is a scientific and complicated process, beyond the elementary tests that determine the most obvious cases of insanity or feeblemindedness. Therefore, it can be readily seen that Massachusetts in the early forties of the last

---
[26] Dix. Remarks, p. 41.

century was undoubtedly segregating only the most obvious cases of insanity, and that many a case that should have been treated wholly from the standpoint of mental conditions remained in the prison to be dealt with as responsible.

The State Prison authorities in Massachusetts were concerned far more than were those of other States about the lot of the discharged prisoner. While New York and Philadelphia were heatedly controversial regarding the relative value of the two State prison systems they were developing — while New York was engaged in a constant economic battle with the "mechanics" in the matter of prison labor, and was exploiting the prisoner for the sake of the balance sheet, and while Philadelphia was keeping the inmate of the Eastern Penitentiary absolutely secluded from the approach of any other inmate, the Massachusetts authorities were acquiring the social sense prison administration. They were seeing that the discharged prisoner was a problem as serious as — and perhaps a more serious problem than — the inmate who came to the prison for the first time. The glaring folly of turning a released prisoner loose without help or funds — except for the trivial few dollars that were customary — and expect him in some way or other, to become honest and God-fearing and to refrain henceforth from crime, was beginning to sink into the official minds of Massachusetts. Something had to be done for the "man coming out." We saw, in our study of the Vermont prison, how a single ex-convict, Reynolds, sought to make Vermont understand the point and failed. Massachusetts ultimately did better.

As early as 1816 a committee of the Legislature had recommended that a wooden building should be erected outside the walls of the State prison as a "home" for discharged prisoners. The Legislature took no action, and the project died. Again, in 1829, the question was raised in the Legislature, and the board of inspectors were asked to give their opinion as to the feasibility of such an asylum for the employment of discharged prisoners, with wages in proportion to earnings, until the discharged man should find other honest employment, thus giving an opportunity to those sincerely desirous of reforming.

By a curious process of reasoning, the inspectors advised emphatically against the project.[27] In the first place, it hadn't been done anywhere else. They conceded that it was harder for discharged inmates to find work than for anyone else, and they stated that the extent of the mischief caused by the inability of discharged prisoners to secure employment could not be accurately determined. However, there were serious objections to herding discharged prisoners together. Such an asylum would become a school of crime, and a center of criminal associations, where those seeking criminals could always find them.

Therefore, such an asylum would simply be what the State prison was before the Auburn system was introduced, a center of promiscuous and debauching association. But if the asylum should

---

[27] Senate Document 2, 1830.

be conducted *on* the Auburn plan, with solitary confinement at night, and vigilant inspection by day, to limit and prevent corruption, then it would be exceedingly doubtful if any convict would voluntarily enter such an establishment. So the inspectors, having reasoned clear around the circle, suggested the greater feasibility of allowing prisoners to remain in the State Prison itself for a time after discharge, at a fixed stipend, because the inspectors saw no difference between the State Prison, as conducted, and the kind of an asylum that their own imaginations had developed.

We find no record that this proposed asylum was established, beyond the statement of Francis C. Gray,[28] probably referring to this movement, that the plan was put on trial and was abandoned after a few years. Despite his statement, we are led to believe that he was in error, for even the reports of the Prison Discipline Society bring no mention of the undertaking, which would have been the first of its kind in this country of which we have learned.

However, by a law of 1845, a new and unusual official effort — which still exists in 1921 — was made by Massachusetts to render easier the lot of the man leaving prison. A "State Agent" was appointed

"to counsel such discharged prisoners as may seek his aid and take such measures to procure employment for such of them as may desire it, by corresponding with persons in agricultural and mechanical pursuits, and with benevolent individuals and associations."[29]

Close on the heels of this entirely new principle of State aid, a voluntary association was formed in Boston, called the "Boston Society in Aid of Discharged Convicts," which co-operated with the State Agent, and indeed appointed him also the agent of the private society, thus enabling him to fill both the State position and the private position. He visited prisoners prior to their release, found work very successfully for them, secured or supplied board and lodging for them in respectable families until work was secured, and in general created in the American system of prison discipline a new and highly important branch. It was even in the previous year, 1844, that the Prison Association of New York was founded, which also established immediately as a part of its work the relief of discharged prisoners. Therefore, in these two leading States, at this date, a new and vitally important work was officially taken up by two new organizations and an official agent of the State in the case of Massachusetts. The responsibility of society for the assistance of the inmate subsequent to his prison term was at last recognized officially, by both the State and the community. Gray cited one respectable cabinet maker who had employed in the last twelve years some fifty discharged prisoners and had never discharged one of them for bad conduct. Only two or three left of their own accord.

Shall we not anticipate that in an intellectual center like Boston there should early develop something like a prison library? The

---

[28] Prison Discipline in America, p. 56.
[29] Gray. Prison Discipline in America, p. 57.

enormous amount of time spent by the prisoner by himself in his own cell naturally led to the idea that he should be profitably employed, and since he did not live in association, and had no human companion, the book early suggested itself. Indeed, one complaint against the "over-stint" of the twenties had been that prisoners sometimes used the money for the purchase of "infidel books."[30] By the end of the period we are now studying (1845) the prison library was being maintained by an appropriation of $100 a year from the earnings of the convicts, though it was not supported *by* the convicts. Books of a religious or moral nature might be taken out and returned by the prisoners weekly. Many of the convicts owned their own books; just as many of them owned musical instruments, which books and instruments were purchased for them by the warden from their own money. Those who chose, could pass one hour on Saturday afternoon in the chapel in the practice of music. The convicts had, in all, about five hours a day for reading and writing in their own cells, including the time allotted to them for their meals.[31]

The library had been initiated by a donation of $50, given by the mother of a life prisoner to her son, that he might have proper reading. The books purchased with this sum he used for a while, and then placed them in general circulation, for his fellow-prisoners. Prisoners added their own books to the library, and a gift of $50 came from a New York friend. The prisoners were furnished from the outside with temperance and religious papers and tracts.[32]

To-day the prison library is one of the essentials of a well-conducted prison. Indeed, the "turn-over" in the books in many a prison exceeds, it is said, the circulation in many a public library. Books are a solace to the prisoner, the extent of which cannot be measured. And we note also in the Massachusetts "program" of the social development of the prison the permission for an hour of instrumental practice on Saturday afternoon. Herein lay the germ of the development of the prison orchestra, which has finally come to pass in many prisons. At the church service on Sunday there was music, both vocal and instrumental.

Two other developments, just at the close of this period, distinguish significantly the Massachusetts State Prison as the leader in humanitarian work during this period. There were, when Gray wrote in 1847,[33] more than 100 small gardens in the Massachusetts prison yard, each the property of the prisoner who cultivated the few square feet of earth, bounded by refuse boards. Therein the convicts were permitted to grow tomatoes, lettuce, cucumbers, onions and other vegetables for their own use, and the convicts were even allowed to leave the shops for a few minutes in order to attend to their gardens. Needless to say, they were privileged to eat individually what they raised individually.

---
[30] B. P. D. S., 1829, p. 245.
[31] Gray. Prison Discipline in America, p. 53.
[32] Dix. Remarks, p. 53.
[33] Gray. Prison Discipline in America, p. 51.

All this was a breaking down of the original severities of the Auburn system. Where so many possible contacts of the prisoners with each other existed, there could not fail to be association. Indeed, in no prison has it ever been possible, apparently, to keep the inmates from communicating to some extent with each other. In the rigid Auburn system, the prisoners nevertheless talked, even though it might be almost literally by ventriloquism. In the Eastern Penitentiary of Pennsylvania they conversed through the sewer pipes when the closets were being flushed. Here in Massachusetts they evidently gave the prisoners some chance to associate and to exchange ideas, for a huge stride in progressive and humane management was taken by the Massachusetts authorities when they not only allowed gardens, but actually instituted a debating society — around the early forties.

In the prison gardens lay the germ of one of the strongest principles of modern penology, namely, the reclamation of the inmate through the creation in him of an abiding interest and pleasure in producing honest values, and in returning to the soil. Nature has an exceptional effect upon many prisoners. Contact with the animals of the farm is a potent, if often temporary, influence for good. The broad fields, the crops, the forestation, the work on the highways, all bring the inmate out into nature, and during the process, it is generally found that disciplinary problems are fewer, and that the prisoner's own character is strengthened in responsibility and in his relations to his fellows. Throughout the entire period that we have been considering, from 1776 on, the latent forces within the prisoner have almost uniformly failed to be understood. He has been tortured, disciplined, driven to work, condemned to silence, forced into a regime where a year was but a succession of uniformly monotonous days, deprived of friends, and stripped of hope. An outcast in prison, he has emerged from prison into a state of at least partial outlawry and almost total ostracism, deprived of citizenship and shunned of honest men. He has been *driven* to work, and commanded in every detail of his prison life. He has been required to be the passive agent of the State, and that prison has been best disciplined where the prisoner has received orders and has obeyed them implicitly. The keystone of the Auburn system has been seen to be silence and obedience, under almost certain infliction of grievous punishment in case of disobedience. The system itself has been proved to be the antidote to the kind of lewd and vicious self-expression among the inmates that flourished in the old promiscuous prisons.

In 1843, the warden suggested, and the inspectors approved of the proposition, that as an encouragement to the prisoners, he be allowed to give, with the approval of the inspectors, one or two days in each month off the sentence, in case of good conduct. We do not find that this was carried out.[35]

If we ask ourselves why it was not obvious to the early administrators that rewards were the most effective methods of securing

---
[35] Senate Document 17, 1843.

diligence in work and readiness to obey, we have to note that even Dorothea Dix wrote, in 1845, that

"some persons advocate the system of rewards in prison for a term of good conduct or for special diligence. Any supposed advantage from this plan would be overbalanced by increased difficulties of discipline. Jealousies and quarrels would arise; the judgment of the ward-officer would be at fault, and insubordination would follow. Complex rules, like complex machinery, are often out of order."[34]

The quotation is interesting, because it acknowledges that the administrative equipment of the prison was not such as to be relied upon for the exercise of fair and careful judgment. The "honor system," even in primitive form, could not as yet be set up, because the honor system depends upon fairness of judgment in the subordinate officials of a prison. The statement of Dorothea Dix was not that the inmates could not be dealt with as individuals, but that the prison was not equipped with officers to perform that task. Furthermore, there was the assumption that unless all inmates were treated alike, there would be grievous disciplinary troubles. The whole reformatory system, introduced with the establishment of Elmira Reformatory in the seventies, was the direct protest against the theory of the mass-treament of the individuals that make up the prison population. One of the fundamental distinctions between the State prisons and the reformatories, for years, was that the prison was the seat of mass-treatment of inmates, and the reformatories the seat of a progressively intelligent treatment of the individual prisoner.

In 1843, Warden Lincoln, who for eleven years had managed most acceptably the prison, was assassinated by an insane convict. His place was filled by Chas. Robinson, promoted from deputy-warden. It was under this latter warden that certain humanities of prison life began to flourish. Robinson wrote, in his first report:

"I have long looked upon a man as a man, whether he be the occupant of a palace or a prison. The more he has erred or strayed, the more he is to be pitied. . . . If I have erred at all, I should prefer to err on the side of kindness, clemency and humanity. . . . With the exception of three cases, the government of the prison has been administered without corporal punishment. The shower bath (installed a few years before) has not been used. . . . There is no sane convict that cannot be reached by sincere and persevering affection. Men may be governed by severity, but not reformed. . . . It requires more time to govern by appeal to the affection, to reason and to conscience."[36]

It was not surprising that in accordance with this remarkably modern attitude, there should have developed another innovation in American prison life — a society among the convicts for moral improvement and for mutual aid. The warden was president of the society, and any convict might belong to it by giving a formal promise to lead an orderly and virtuous life, and by taking in addition a pledge of total abstinence from liquor. The society met once a fortnight and some previously determined question

---

[34] Dix. Remarks, p. 12.
[36] Senate Document 5, 1844.

was discussed at each meeting. A committee of the conference was appointed to promote the objects of the society, the said committee consisting of the warden, chaplain (who was vice-president), the clerk (who was secretary) and six convicts, who were chosen by a majority of the members, and approved by the warden as president. About three-fourths of the total population of the convicts belonged to the society, which was founded because the convict was seen to be much like other persons, and not an incarnate demon.

Said Gray, in 1847:[37]

"All such intercourse among them as does not tend to corrupt them, to produce disorder, or to interrupt their labor — if in the presence of an officer — is humanizing and beneficial. If people say this is not the Auburn system, then let us call it the 'John Howard system.' We've come back to him!"

It certainly was *not* the Auburn system. It was penological heresy of the most insurgent sort. This Massachusetts system admitted through the "Society for Improvement and Mutual Aid" the convict to a place, however slight, in the administration of the institution, for it gave him a chance to express an opinion, before the prison community, on moral and ethical questions, whereby, at least indirectly, the ethical standards of the institutions themselves would be affected. It gave the convict, moreover, a sense of being a member of a community, a fellow-being not only with his convict associates, but with the officers themselves. It made the prison no longer simply a walled enclosure, within which certain desperate humans endured a wholly unnatural and non-social existence. This society restored to him the power and the pleasure of normal speech, where silence had been the first of the prison commandments. The society recognized in him an individual, sentient, sensitive man, with the ability and the right of independent thought.

In truth, this society, more than any other phenomenon of the Massachusetts prison, proclaimed the fact that the Auburn system did not compass all wisdom in prison discipline. Whether the society ultimately failed or succeeded, the first great step had been thus taken in Massachusetts toward establishing inmate interest and inmate participation in the principles and the methods of administration of the institution. And, with a prophetic voice, Gray designated the prison as an "asylum and moral hospital for guilt," which, he said, some of the benevolent believed that it should be.[38]

Sunday Schools had already developed in American prisons, but such gatherings had been composed of small groups of convicts, in classes *taught* by citizens, and held to certain well-defined religious and elementary educational lines. Undoubtedly the Sunday School was the first step toward a larger grouping of prisoners — but the distance between small, segregated classes in Sunday School and a body embracing three-fourths of the population, for

---

[37] Gray. Prison Discipline in America, p. 52.
[38] Gray. Prison Discipline in America, p. 63.

the discussion of ethical questions, was considerable. Sunday Schools were but a slight departure from the cardinal principle of constant isolation of the prisoners. The mutual benefit society, on the other hand, announced by its very existence that mental intercourse among prisoners, if decent and supervised, was beneficial. In short, the complete integrity of the Auburn and the Pennsylvania systems was challenged by this convict society — and it was a noteworthy phenomenon in the progress of American prison administration.

To-day, associations of and among convicts are a part of the program of most progressive American prisons, ranging from religious associations of not especially close structure to the Mutual Welfare League, which in its original form at Auburn and Sing Sing Prisons was a democracy among the prisoners, functioning through various committees and representative groups. It is no longer surprising to find the convicts maintaining certain group organizations. It is recognized that Americans are prone to "join" things, and many prisons have taken advantage of this trait to permit, for the good of the prison administration, the inmates to maintain certain organizations.

It is also worthy of note that from 1838 on, the convicts were allowed a distinct "Sunday suit," the Massachusetts State Prison being perhaps the only prison in the United States to give to its inmates this physical mark of recognition of the Lord's Day.[40] George Combe, the Scottish phrenologist, visiting the prison in 1838, found the customary prison costume to be of coarse woolen cloth, with the left side blue and the right side red.[39]

In our chapter on the State Prison of New Jersey we shall speak of this noteworthy Scotch phrenologist and social philosopher in detail. When he visited the Massachusetts prison, he found that the prisoners appeared like tradesmen in a well-regulated factory. He examined the heads of eight or nine criminals, and found the animal organs large in proportion to those of moral sentiments and intellect, but not so much so as the average of criminals he had examined in Britain.

Spurzheim in 1832 found — so the story goes — in this prison a head so well developed in moral and intellectual qualities that he couldn't conceive how the man came to be under sentence for a crime. Afterwards it was discovered that he was not guilty![42]

Yet the gradual introduction of these much more lenient methods of dealing with the inmates was not without comment, even from the friends of humane administration. Dorothea Dix visited the prison several times during this period, and found the discipline "lax in the extreme."[41] "Since the prison rules have been modified," she wrote, "or dispensed with, as time advances the difficulty

---
[39] Combe. Notes on the United States, p. 182.
[40] B. P. D. S., 1838, p. 221.
[41] Dix. Remarks, etc., p. 19.
[42] Notes, etc.

of preserving order and assuring obedience has increased." She published the following comparative table, indicating the growing frequency of punishment:

	Stripes (i. e., flogging)	Days solitary
April, 1844	1	6½
April, 1845	4	18½
May, 1844	15	5
May, 1845	12	18
June, 1844	12	5
June, 1845	16	37

A typical month may be cited to show the causes of punishments inflicted:

	Cases	Stripes	Days solitary
June, 1845.			
Refusing to work	3		3
Making a noise while in his cell	6		6
Idleness and gross insolence	1		4
Quarreling with a fellow convict	3		6
Gross insolence to an officer	4	3	6
Disobedience of orders	1		1
Gross insolence to an officer and disobedience	2	5	3
Refusal to labor and hiding his tools	1		4
Insolence, disobedience and idleness	1	8	
Insolence, and having prohibited articles	1		1½
Fighting with a fellow convict	1		2
Gross laziness and inattention to work	1		1

Dorothea Dix continued:

"The system of indulgence often works well for a few months, and possibly for a year or two. . . . But I have never known any prison in which discipline is much dispensed with, which has not fallen into confusion, and in which it could be found that the good of the convicts has eventually either morally or physically been promoted. Rules must be established and enforced. . . . I respect the feeling which has prompted the wish to dispense with forms and the appearance of restraint, and some close rules, . . . but I am, from a four years' observation of jails and penitentiaries, obliged to allow, that greater restraints are necessary in all these than our wishes, putting aside reasoning and consequences, would determine. . . . It is with convicts as with children; unseasonable indulgence indiscreetly granted, leads to mischief, which we may deplore but cannot repair."

It would be difficult to find in any present-day writings of students of American penology a more cogent statement and warning as to the dangers of the too hasty or comprehensive efforts at the "democratization" or communizing of the prison population, or of the over-trustful nature that sees in a prison population only, or largely, the place in which to experiment with advanced forms of social relationships. The honor system, too liberally installed; the mutual welfare league movement, too hurriedly superimposed upon a bewildered population, by nature looking for "cinches" and "easy berths," can be to-day still diagnosed by the careful yet comprehensive analysis of Dorothea Dix, written as a result of an extended investigation, over a half century ago. Favors within prison walls have to be given with great discretion; the establishment of new "rights" for the inmates has to be accompanied with patient and repeated interpretation to the inmates. An administration that is lenient and inclined to be idealistic gets easily the reputation of being "soft" and "easy," while the administration that closes down on privileges and seeks to revert to ancient methods can no longer, on the other hand, be regarded by the inmates as proceeding in a usual or reasonable manner. Hence, the prison administration finds itself between the two extremes, and most prison wardens, who seek to think the situation through, determine to be fair and square with the inmates, granting increased privileges only gradually, and being suspicious of comprehensive or wholesale plans for more freedom within the prison, basing their opinions upon what they know of the past, plus their own hesitation in establishing, where it is not absolutely necessary, a condition that once granted cannot be easily withdrawn.

According to Dorothea Dix, there was no prison between Canada and the Carolinas and Tennessee where so much freedom was enjoyed as at Charlestown.

We turn, finally in this chapter, to the industrial and financial aspect of the prison administration. Other American prisons, like Auburn and Wethersfield, featured their industrial successes during this period. Massachusetts made no such consistent record of success. Stone-cutting was for years the chief industry.[43] From 1814 to 1824, under the old-fashioned system, the total net expense of maintaining the prison had been $78,328.44. For the prison, the State had paid out from 1805 to 1828 more than $300,000.[44] There followed then several exceptional years of activity in stone-cutting. But in the entire period from 1828 to 1846, the total net earnings of the prison above all expenses amounted to but $9,522.84. In short, it just paid expenses, salaries, food, clothing, bedding, and the bounties to discharged convicts being paid out of gross earnings.[45]

The prison was, however, a busy institution. The total gross earnings from 1832 to 1846, inclusive, amounted to $516,461.96, the average annual per capita sum earned by each prisoner *for the prison* being $121.42.[46] Under the Auburn system, introduced with the new prison building, no overstint was allowed.[47] On his discharge, the prisoner received five dollars and a suit of clothes.[48] Combe wrote in his diary in 1838 that the prisoners appeared like tradesmen in a well-regulated factory.

[43] B. P. D. S., 1826, p. 16.
[44] B. P. D. S., 1828, p. 164.
[45] Gray. P. D. in App. No. 1.
[46] Gray, p. 77.
[47] B. P. D. S., 1832, p. 539.
[48] B. P. D. S., 1833, p. 637.

The following were the chief occupations at the beginning of the period we have been discussing:

Total population, September 30, 1826, 313:

On Contract.		For the Prison.	
Stone-cutters	105	Weavers	10
Lumpers, transporting stone	21	Tailors	13
Cabinet makers	35	New building	34
Brush makers	26	Washers and waiters	10
Whitesmiths and tinsmiths	6	In hospital	10
Shoemakers	3	Blacksmiths	5
Copperplate printers	1	Cobblers	5
Coopers	7	Oakum pickers	8
		Cooks	9
		Barbers	3
		In cells	2

The proceeds of the labor, in the stone department, of about one-third of the number of inmates on the prison were more than sufficient to cover the cost of provisions, clothing, bedding and salaries of officers.[49]

To facilitate the stone industry, a lock-gate was built in the northwest part of the prison yard, through which boats laden with stone could pass from the bay. In this basin, prisoners were permitted to bathe in the summer, once each week, for ten minutes at a time.[50]

[49] B. P. D. S., 1827, p. 109.
[50] Haynes, p. 51.

CHAPTER XV

CONNECTICUT

With the building of the new State prison at Wethersfield in 1826 and 1827, and with the appointment of Moses C. Pilsbury, formerly warden of the New Hampshire State Prison, as warden, Connecticut entered upon a period of prison administration that in less than twenty years brought to it the reputation of being the "pattern prison of the Auburn plan."[1] The new prison was opened on October 1, 1827.[4]

The contrast with Old Newgate's history and reputation was striking. Just as Old Newgate at Simsbury had been a State scandal and a constant financial burden, so now Wethersfield grew to be the pride of the State and far more than a self-supporting institution. The new Connecticut prison first imitated Auburn, and then passed it in the race for supremacy among American prisons. In the increasingly heated discussions of the relative merits of the Auburn and Pennsylvania systems, Wethersfield became ultimately the mainstay of the Auburn supporters. Its fame traveled even to Europe, and ardent philosophical analyses were there made of the principles of prison discipline, especially by the French and the Germans.

Wethersfield produced large and constructive results, satisfying almost completely the demands of the period for a successful prison. It had been economically built, the 136 cells on the Auburn plan having been erected for approximately $30,000, as well as a keeper's house, hospital, offices, and a department for female convicts who were under charge of a matron, Mrs. Griswold.[5] Later buildings, including workshops, were built by the labor of the convicts with equal economy. The cells in the new prison building were 7 feet long, 3 feet 6 inches wide and 7 feet high. The building was four stories in height,[2] 177 feet long, 48 feet wide and 36 feet high.[3]

Wethersfield's success was primarily due to the two Pilsburys, Moses C. and Amos (born in Londonderry, N. H., in 1805), who were wardens from the start in 1827 until 1845, Moses resigning because of ill health in 1830 and his son succeeding him. Moses Pilsbury, a native of Newberry, Massachusetts, had been a lieutenant in the War of 1812, and was a self-made man. He was made warden of the New Hampshire prison in 1818. Many years later he was called the "founder and head of improvements in our prisons, at least in the New England States."[6]

---

[1] Report of Directors, 1844.
[2] Dix. Remarks, p. 44.
[3] B. P. D. S., 1827, p. 110.
[4] Minutes of Testimony, taken before John Q. Wilson, etc., Hartford, 1834.
[5] Same, p. 3.
[6] Biographical Sketch of Amos Pilsbury (p. 2) Albany. Joel Munsell, printer, 1849.

"This accomplished disciplinarian, whose mere look was sufficient to quell the fiercest of these hardened creatures with whom he had to deal, was a man of medium stature, calm and gentle in aspect and demeanor, full of tenderness and human sympathy."[7]

Moses Pilsbury's reputation was made largely in Concord, where he maintained the State prison of New Hampshire on a paying basis, both before and after his service in Connecticut. He was said to be the first warden who made a prison more than self-supporting, and who read the Bible daily to the prisoners assembled. He died in Derry, N. H., in 1848, aged 70.

Amos Pilsbury, when but nineteen years of age, was appointed watchman and guard at the New Hampshire State Prison in 1824, and became deputy warden the following year. With his father he went to Connecticut in 1827, holding the position of deputy warden in Wethersfield also. In 1830 he was appointed warden.

Two dominant characteristics were prominent in Amos Pilsbury's long wardenship. He created a remarkably lucrative prison for Connecticut, and he established and developed a clear-cut system of prison discipline. The two Pilsburys achieved the reputation of being the best prison keepers in the world.[8] Of the two, Amos became far better known, his career in Wethersfield being succeeded by similar service in the Albany penitentiary.

We find in Amos Pilsbury the first noted professional prison warden, with a system that for the time was enlightened and constructive. Captain Lynds of Sing Sing and Auburn was in the business of running a prison, but we do not gain from him a penal philosophy. Moreover, Lynds was a man of cruelty, and of limited vision. Pilsbury was the first to exemplify through a relatively long period of administrative activity that wardens are made, and not simply born of political will or favor. He was a salient and dominant figure at a time when prison administration was developing into a profession, and prison discipline into a system. He was thus described, in 1840, by a writer in the Philadelphia Courier, who claimed to have studied as many penitentiaries as any man of his age:

"Captain Pilsbury has the true system of management. It is the mild system, that which appeals to the better instead of the worst feelings of human nature. He seldom punishes, but when he does he takes special pains to show the criminal that he regards him as an unfortunate human being, not as a brute. Here is the mistake made in other penitentiaries."[9]

Of "Captain" Pilsbury, as he was called, there exist several stories. A certain desperate convict named Scott was serving a term of fifteen years at Wethersfield. He at one time cut off one hand to avoid work, but was immediately attended to and in an hour was turning a large crank with the other hand. Pilsbury wrote in 1835:[10]

"Convicts cannot be managed as they should be unless they know for a certainty that punishment will be inflicted for the violation of the rules of the prison. The State prison is designed to be a place of punishment."

---

[7] Op. Cit., p. 8.
[8] Sketch of American Prisons (Year 1860), p. 16.
[9] Biographical Sketch of Amos Pilsbury, p. 9.
[10] Report of Directors, p. 16.

Crawford in 1832 found Wethersfield not using corporal punishment, yet discipline was well enforced. The penalties were solitary confinement in a darkened cell, and reduction in diet. The prison was said to be extremely well managed, and great attention seemed to be paid to the moral and religious instruction of prisoners.

Yet, firm as Pilsbury was with the prisoners, he gave evidences of believing also in the sense of honor in at least some prisoners. A committee of inquiry reported, in 1835, that when both the Pilsburys were at Wethersfield, the male convicts who were in their employ, probably as domestic servants, were permitted to go out of the prison and about the town of Wethersfield.

"On one or more instances the convicts, to the number of three or four, at a time, were sent with a guard to Hartford in a boat. . . . It might be to show the extent of moral restraint, which these wardens had the tact to impose upon their prisoners. Let the cause be what it may, the Committee report it as an error which has not often been, and probably never will again be, repeated."[11]

The story is exceedingly interesting to the student, for it is the earliest instance we have found in the new system of anything approaching the "trusty" system of dealing with specific prisoners, picked for their apparent trustworthiness. It became ultimately customary in the State prisons to trust a few picked inmates, to give them positions of a certain diminished responsibility to enable them to enjoy certain favors not granted the other inmates. Out of the trusty system grew finally the honor system, in which the trust is spread by the warden over larger groups, and in which the self-respect and the self-expression of the inmate is given a much larger field.

In the case of the inmates taken by the guard in a boat to Hartford several miles away, there may have been even little of the trusty element, for a guard accompanied them. But it is recorded, as above stated, that inmates were allowed to go about the town of Wethersfield. And this young warden had courage and confidence, as is illustrated by the following anecdote.[12]

"Captain Pilsbury on one occasion was told that a prisoner who had been recently committed had sworn to kill him and that he had actually sharpened his razor for that purpose. Without hesitancy he sent for the man to come to his office.

" 'I wish you to shave me,' said the warden, and seating himself added, 'Here is all the apparatus.' The man pleaded want of skill. 'Never mind,' said the warden, 'you are not intractable, and you will soon learn, and I intend you to perform my toilet duties daily.'

"The man with trembling hands went to work; he performed the shaving poorly, for he was wholly disarmed and was trembling more from fear, blended with growing confidence in the warden, than for the continuance of his fell purpose to take his life.

"When asked the next day why he did not cut his throat while he was shaving him, as he said he would, he exclaimed: ' May God forgive me, but I did intend to kill you if I could have found an opportunity, but now my hatred is broken down!' "[15]

---
[11] Report of Committee on State Prisons, 1833, p. 17.
[12] Biographical Sketch, p. 9.
[15] Biographical Sketch, p. 10.

Several variants of this story are worth recording, as evidencing other angles of this noteworthy early illustration of the application, on the one side, of the trusty system, and on the other of plain "grit" and confidence on the part of the prison warden. Miss Martineau, in her "Society in America,"[16] places on the warden's lips the words: "I have been told that you meant to murder me, but I thought I might trust you." "God bless you, sir, you may!" replied the regenerated man. The chronicler of the Philadelphia Courier states that neither version was quite correct, but that the warden, hearing from prisoners that they were afraid to be shaved by the desperate criminal, who was the same Scott that afterwards cut off his hand, took his seat in the barber's chair, with the outcome as above told. And within the last few months the writer of this study has heard a very similar story attributed to a former warden and a barber in Sing Sing Prison.

The board of directors in 1831 indicated the policy of the prison administration:[14]

"Corporal punishment is rare, but mistaken kindness is bad for a certain class of convicts. The comfort of the convicts should not be so studied as to render the prison a desirable residence. When this becomes the case, our criminal code becomes a bounty law for crime." . . . "The Legislature never intended that the appetites of the convicts should be consulted in the variety of the food provided for them."

Miss Martineau's book records graphically several other stories of the humanness and administrative sagacity of Pilsbury. It is stated that a certain incorrigible negro was permitted to be on the "range" of cells, on agreement that the warden and the negro would trust each other. Finally, however, the warden had to take him to a solitary cell, because he did not live up to his pledge to behave. On the way to the cell, Pilsbury said to the negro:

"Do you think you been fair with me?"

The negro burst into tears, and Pilsbury, believing in the negro's remorse, gave him again the free range of the cellhouse. He reformed entirely.

An inmate of the prison sought to escape, and sprained his ankle in his unsuccessful attempt. Pilsbury did not chide him, but actually in the middle of the night arose and made the prisoner's ankle comfortable with the warden's own pillow. Again reformation was reported to have ensued.

To the writer of this study, Mrs. Butler, daughter of Zebulon R. Brockway, said in July, 1921, that when she was younger, it was a byword in the Brockway family that when a certain fixed and intense look came over Mr. Brockway or one of the others in the family, it was "the Pilsbury eye."

It is hardly too much to say that Wethersfield, under Amos Pilsbury, was the training school and standardizer of the system of prison discipline that flourished in American prisons throughout the nineteenth century, and out of which developed the American reformatory system. The connection is direct and clear. It was

---

[14] B. P. D. S., 1831, p. 520.
[16] Martineau. Society in America, Vol. II, p. 282.

not from Auburn and Sing Sing that the lessons came, but from Wethersfield, and from Amos Pilsbury, who engaged Zebulon R. Brockway as a clerk in Wethersfield Prison in 1848. Brockway went with Pilsbury to the Albany Penitentiary from 1851 to 1853. Brockway has written in his autobiography: "Fifty Years of Prison Service,"[13] that the Pilsbury system of prison management, exemplified first at Wethersfield, as related to the economies and discipline, constituted a sound and invaluable basis for building the "Ideal Prison system for a State," an article which Mr. Brockway read at the first National Prison Congress at Cincinnati in 1870, a basis which Mr. Brockway also naturally built upon when, six years later, he became the first superintendent of the New York State Reformatory at Elmira.

Mr. Brockway wrote:

"The stringent discipline maintained by the Pilsburys is necessary for the desirable institutional and individual prison economies; reformatory disciplinary training devoid of some friction is by that sign shown to be fallacious."

One day, Mr. Pilsbury, accompanied by the board of directors of the prison, entered the shoeshop, the discipline of which had been demoralized during Mr. Pilsbury's absence, while he was suspended on charges, from which he was later absolved. The prisoners arose from their seats, armed with their shoe knives, and demanded that Mr. Pilsbury leave the shop. This he refused to do, telling the prisoners that though at that moment he had no authority over them, he would not leave until they had returned to their work. "His bold attitude and strong personality so dominated them that one by one the men, including their leader and spokesman, resumed their seats and their work," wrote Mr. Brockway,[17] who adds that shortly after this event, Mr. Pilsbury, on a visit to Sing Sing, discovered the instrument known as the cat-o'-nine tails, which he brought back to Wethersfield, applied to the first disturber on the following morning, and restored thereby as if by magic good order, industrial efficiency and salutary discipline. The cat was rarely used afterwards.

The charges against the administration of Mr. Pilsbury were investigated by a Legislative Committee in 1832, and were typical of similar allegations against prison executives rising from time to time in other States. Briefly, it was claimed that the accounts were not kept according to law; that the prisoners were not getting enough food; that for several weeks they were furnished with bad water; that they suffered from cold and bad air; that the sick were treated with great cruelty; that the by-laws were disregarded; that there were depredations upon public property; that the prisoners were illegally punished, and that prisoners were permitted to leave the prison.

In general, the charges were either "not proved" or "explained." However, as cited above, there were instances in which

[13] Fifty Years of Prison Service, p. 34.
[17] Fifty Years of Prison Service, p. 29.

the convicts had been used outside the prison. A novel comment of the Committee follows:

"The Committee is persuaded that the convict, when once in his cell, enjoys as much of warmth and purity (of air) as are to be found in the well-filled tenement of a crowded city, and at no time does he suffer more hardship than an ordinary seaman on a voyage."[18]

When Mr. Pilsbury was reappointed by a new board of directors, in 1833, the board reported that the prisoners had sought to dictate the appointment of a new warden. They presented a mandatory petition to the new directors — and there had been a virtual mutiny in the shoe shop. They had threatened that if certain officers were appointed, they would kill them. The directors, in their report, stated that this condition came directly from the letting down of unrelenting and firm discipline during the brief wardenship of a Mr. Montague after the suspension of Mr. Pilsbury. Under Montague the prisoners talked, arranged plans, and the underkeepers traded with the convicts. There was compensation for overwork; food, fruit and delicacies were bought, and there were numerous newspapers in the cells. Montague was removed by the new directors and Pilsbury reappointed.

"Prison management by the Pilsburys always held predominant the aim and the inspiration of the economies. Profitable employment of prisoners, so that the cost of supporting prisons should be defrayed out of the products of their labor, was a tenet instilled by Moses Pilsbury, made remarkably effective by Amos Pilsbury at Wetherfield and Albany, and afterwards by his son Louis D. Pilsbury in his management of the State prisons of New York."[21]

What were Amos Pilsbury's conclusions, toward the close of his first score of years of prison service, as to the reformative value of the system of prison discipline that he had espoused? Not optimistic. He wrote:

"After an experience of twenty years, I am constrained to say that the effect in general has not been to reform those who in early life have been disposed to crime, even when the best opportunities have been afforded to them for reformation."[19]

Dorothea Dix wrote in 1845:

"We claim too much of our prisons, on whichever system established.[20] We too often judge convicts by false standards. We promise, through all reformed prison systems, too much, even under the most favorable modes of administering them. It is not easy to correct a trivial, inconvenient habit, for a short time indulged; shall a whole life of wrong and mistake be amended by a few years of imprisonment?"

Thus we find her condemning in considerable measure the leniency of the Massachusetts system, which was based upon a belief in this capacity for good reactions by the convict to very humane treatment, and also condoning the ineffectiveness of all systems in general, on the ground that too much is expected of the prison as a reformative institution. She has, we found, excused flogging when

---
[18] Report of Comm., p. 11.
[19] Dix. Remarks, p. 18.
[20] Dix. Remarks, p. 67.
[21] Fifty Years of Prison Service, p. 30.

necessary. We cite quotations from her because she was unusually enlightened, and yet unable to develop a clear penal philosophy. How much less might the wardens of the period, harassed by a thousand cares, solve the increasingly complex prison problems?

Let us turn to a study of the industrial effectiveness of Wethersfield. Old Newgate, prior to the establishment of Wethersfield, had been for years an average expense to the State of $5,680. For the first six months of the new prison, ending March 30th, 1828, there was already a surplus of $1,017 over all costs of management and support, including the salaries of the officers.[22] By 1831, the prison industries had earned a surplus of $17,139,[23] and if there was included the annual expense that would have been incurred had Old Newgate been continued instead of Wethersfield, the State had already saved over $41,000, or enough to more than pay for the construction of the new prison. By 1843, the earnings by the prison industries, over and above all expenses of the prison, had amounted to over $107,000, which from time to time had been turned back into the State treasury.[26]

The women prisoners had been placed by 1831 in separate cells. In that year the prison chaplain, Gerrish Barrett, wrote:[25]

"I suppose the female department here is the best arranged of any in the world. Formerly, when they were all in one room, the noise they made might be heard at a distance; and hair, torn from each others' heads, might be seen strewed about the floor. Now, they are lodged in separate cells, more than support themselves by their labor, and are much changed for the better as to their outward appearance."

What it cost to run a prison was shown in the balance sheet for 1831:

Income.		Expenditures.	
Smith	$818 96	Provisions	$3,190 60
Coopers	852 19	Clothing and bedding	719 89
Shoe	4,003 28	Wages, subsistence, fuel, etc.	3,037 89
Nail	527 84	Hospital	293 78
Carpenters	2,408 52		
Tailors	19 02		
Chair	4,247 94		
Females	45 47		
Interest	13 84		
Charged for laborers	594 15		
Visitors	634 97		
		Total expenditures	$7,342 16
Total	15,166 18	Balance gain	$7,824 02

Out of this capacity for earning a handsome surplus came to Amos Pilsbury two constructive ideas, namely, the subsidizing, from the surplus earnings of the prisoners, of the erection or improvement of county jails, and the erection of a State asylum for the insane. County jails in Connecticut, as in other States, were places of promiscuous association and idleness. They possessed the

[22] B. P. D. S., 1828, p. 15.
[23] B. P. D. S., Vol. II, 1840.
[25] B. P. D. S., 1831, p. 470.
[26] B. P. D. S., 1843, p. 55.

worst attributes of the old type of State prisons, like Newgate in New York. Moreover, they received the lesser offenders, and were literally the feeders for the State prison.

There was continued concern in the board of directors, undoubtedly stimulated thereto by the warden, as to the reformability of the convicts, and also as to the possibilities of the prevention of crime if approached early enough in life. The directors in 1836 found little hope of reformation in the State prison convicts. They cited numerous facts confirming this opinion from other States. Reformation, they held, came best through preventive education:

"Mere confinement will not do it; their minds must be improved, new desires must be created, new impulses awakened, and they must be made to realize that there are other joys than the sensual."

Hartford County had built in 1837 a very modern county jail, embodying the architectural and disciplinary features of Wethersfield. Only as the county jails inculcated the tested principles of prison discipline into their own administration could the army of recruits to the prison be reduced. In 1840, Mr. Pilsbury proposed to the General Assembly of Connecticut that the warden be authorized to pay $1,000 to each county in Connecticut that would undertake to build a county jail on the plan of Hartford County's institution.[24] This measure, carried in the General Assembly, was designated by the Boston Prison Discipline Society as probably the most important measure that had ever been adopted in the country for the improvement of county prisons. The directors of the State prison were to judge as to whether the county prison had been constructed in accordance with the terms of the law. In 1841, the warden was authorized to pay to Hartford, New Haven and New London counties the bounties of $1,000 each. The warden now went further, and urged that the surplus earnings, to the extent of from $3,000 to $5,000 a year, be appropriated to the erection of an asylum for the insane poor.[27]

There were at this time at least six insane convicts at the prison.

As early as 1834 the board of directors had reported:

"There are, and ever have been, in the prison a class of convicts that either from partial derangement, or deficiency of intellect, or turbulence, pretending to be insane, cannot at all times be kept quiet; these sometimes in the night season make a noise, and by the cry of fire or some other alarm, greatly agitate the prisoners around them and disturb the whole establishment. The directors suggest a separate block of cells for these, and for the useless and broken-down prisoners."

The warden estimated that the insane poor in the State were at least in the proportion of one to every thousand of the population. The most dangerous of this group found their way into the State and county prisons, into cells or chains, for purposes of safe keeping. Pilsbury wrote in 1841:[28]

"They are unfit subjects of punishment, whether their own good or the good of the criminal is considered, to say nothing of humanity and public justice."

---
[24] B. P. D. S., p. 831, p. 467.
[27] B. P. D. S., 1841, p. 52.
[28] Report of Directors, 1841, Warden's Report, p. 7.

A number of States had already made provision for the insane poor and criminal, but none had done so by the earnings of the criminal population. Connecticut's delay in this provision would be less regretted if it should provide such institutional care without taxing the State treasury of the people.

In 1844, the directors reported that the subsidizing of county jails had caused great improvement at Hartford, New Haven and Windham, but that in a number of counties the gift of $1,000 was not sufficient to encourage counties to undertake the very considerable expenditures necessary to the erection of a new county jail. Therefore, it would be well to distribute the surplus earnings of the prison to each and every county:

"Then the State will have not only the pattern prison on the Auburn plan, but also a modern county jail in every county of the State." [29]

On the other hand, it is clear that Pilsbury had not arrived at the point, in his penal philsosphy, of giving to the prisoners a share of their own earnings. It is a significant statement of Brockway,[30] that Amos Pilsbury, in his sick room at Albany, just before his death, expressed with deep feeling his regret that he ever paid into the public treasury the earnings of prisoners instead of using such surplus funds for the prisoners' benefit. But, in the height of the Wethersfield operations, thirty years before, the intellectual or social welfare of the prisoners still counted little as against the financial advantages accruing to the State.

We have from the prison chaplain, Gerrish Barrett, in 1831, a picture of the intellectual capacity of the inmates at that time: [33]

"No convict now in this prison received a liberal education. Very few have come under Sabbath School instruction. 76 are unable to write; 106 out of 141 fail of spelling many words of 1 or 2 syllables. 30 cannot read; 60 out of 150 were separated from parents before they were 10 years old, and 36 others before 15 years old."

The age of the prison population seems to have been in these years strikingly young on the average. In 1829, it was reported that of the 134 prisoners, 102 were under 30, and 24 were short of 20 years.

"We need some provision for correction and reformation of juvenile offenders, and punishment of minor offenses. Such offenses now go unpunished often because of lack of proper punishments."

In 1835 there were further findings of Brewer:

"Few prisoners in early life had good examples or proper instruction. One-half the whole number were deprived of homes before they were ten years old. Accounts of villainy in newspapers stimulate some to crime — also the liking for notoriety.

"Lazy habits, roving dispositions, violent shocks of mind, such as love of gambling, are frequent preludes to their careers. The hardened convicts have not had their stubborn wills subdued in boyhood.

"There is a close connection between crime and the absence of moral pledges and domestic links. About half the convicts have no parents alive. 138 of the 200 never married. Of 62 married, half were not living with their

---
[29] Report of Directors, 1844.
[30] Fifty Years of Prison Life, p. 33.
[33] B. P. D. S., 1831, p. 475.

wives at the time of committing crime. Three-fourths of the convicts have been intemperate. Ignorance and crime are closely connected. No temperate and industrious follower of a trade, or similarly constituted head of a family or owner of real estate, was found among the 200 convicts. Not one of the 200 received a collegiate or classical education. Only 17 out of the 200 could write or cipher as far as the single rule of three.'' [34]

In 1841, Josiah Brewer, the resident chaplain, asked rather timidly if there were not too much attention paid to pecuniary advantages, and not enough to intellectual help in the prison discipline. And Dorothea Dix wrote in 1845 that ''the chief defect in Wethersfield is the too little time given to moral instruction, and too little time to the prisoners for reading and self-improvement.[31]

A committee of inquiry in 1842 found a life of deadly monotony the prisoner's portion:

"The voluntary laborer works for himself, and has holidays for recreation. The prisoner works for others. His variety is from cell to work bench and from work bench to cell. His relaxation for six days is to march across the same yard, work at the same bench, return to the same cell, to eat his meals from the same kit, sit on the same stool, and lie in the same bunk. He rises and lies down, goes in and goes out, moves and stands still, begins work and quits work, always under authority, never from free choice, except a choice of evils." [32]

In this year, the chaplain became more insistent. He wanted a school for the younger criminals in prison, one-fourth of the entire prison population was under 21 years of age; some of them were just entering their teens! The chaplain won his case from the directors. In 1843 the directors extolled the unusual efforts they had made to instruct the younger convicts. There was now a Bible and reading class of 30 inmates under the age of 21 on Sunday taught by the warden, chaplain and clerk.

Two of the chaplains at Wethersfield, Gerrish Barrett and Josiah Brewer, possessed analytical, constructive, and deeply religious minds. Particularly was Gerrish Barrett a lover of character analysis. He has left some very interesting and graphic studies of prisoners in the long-forgotten chaplain's annual reports of Wethersfield. Some of his observations follow: [35]

Men sleep more, dream more, have stronger craving for food and *time past* seems to be shorter, and *time to come* longer in prison than when at liberty.

It is always found that open acts of crime are preceded by smaller and secret offenses; and seldom is one convicted of crime whose life had been regular till he was 18 or 20 years old.

Some in prison make singular development of the social principle. They can hardly be prevailed upon to kill, or even to frighten, the rats and mice that happen to come into their cells. They are pleased with their company, love to look at their bright eyes, and see them jump about the cell. By a peculiar noise which they make, they call them to the mouth of the ventilators, and there divide their food with them. Yet these same men have so little true benevolence that if at liberty they would probably not respect the property, if they did the person, of their fellow man.

Some pass their lonely hours in singing to themselves without audible sound. They can judge of the measure, harmony and melody of a piece of

[31] Dix. Remarks, p. 22.
[32] Report of Comm. on State Prisons, 1842, p. 41.
[34] B. P. D. S., 1835, p. 876.
[35] B. P. D. S., 1837, p. 128.

music, and highly relish its performance, by merely causing imaginary sounds to pass through their minds. They lie awake at night, enjoying sweet sounds of silent melody.

Much the greater portion of convicts are not only ignorant but extremely grovelling and sensual. Their prevailing sentiments are the sexual, and these are extremely gross. They spend hours in the silence and solitude of their cells, forming in their minds pictures of these acts of sin. . . .

It may be predicted with considerable certainty what course of conduct a convict will pursue after leaving prison, if it can be ascertained what were his prevailing thoughts and feelings while in prison.

A bad man, if left to himself, is not likely to grow better.

As a spider weaves its web from its own bowels, so will many criminals weave schemes of future villainy from the prevailing and most agreeable exercises of their own souls.

Convicts are men, and differ in moral character like other men. Some give good evidence of being reformed, some doubtful evidence, and some, most miserable, seem to have wandered beyond the precincts of hope. Reformation takes place in different degrees.

The number discharged from the prison since its beginning does not vary greatly from 400. Of that number I should think I had heard from about one-quarter, exclusive of those who have made themselves notorious by a repetition of their criminal offenses. Excepting those last named, I do not know of more than three or four whose conduct is not represented as being better than it was before their imprisonment.

It is curious to observe what strong terms of reprobation convicts, once lovers of rum, often, when sober and in solitude, heap upon rumsellers.

These are refreshingly sagacious and careful observations, made at a time when there was still very little published regarding the convict as an individual. These commentaries were the forerunner of the later studies by chaplains of the habits and characteristics of the prison populations. The chaplains were not medical men, and we shall find that the physicians, like Doctor Franklin Bache in the Eastern Penitentiary of Pennsylvania, contributed more scientific studies of the inmates. But the chaplain was close to the men, and sensed more than did the warden and the other officers the intensely human side of the inmate's life and aspirations. It is from the chaplains and the physicians and the prison reform organizations, in this period, that we derive most of the still elementary interpretation of the psychology of the inmate population. The wardens and the boards of inspectors seem to have been too busy with the administrative details to regard the prison problem as fundamentally one of human beings rather than of machinery, industry, and efficiency.

Gerrish Barrett left Wethersfield in 1839, to become a traveling agent of the Boston Prison Discipline Society. He was one of the earliest acute observers of the physical and mental reactions of inmates to confinement. His successor, Josiah Brewer, who secured the educational classes for juveniles, was but three years at the prison.

Not until 1841 do we find the "mechanics" of Connecticut sufficiently stirred by the competition of prison-made goods in the open market to cause the Legislature to investigate. So similar are the items of the petitions of the mechanics to those that had for some years found their way into the New York Legislature, that the stimulus is easily traced. The mechanics claimed that the prison-made goods interfered with business, and caused industrial prostration in some cases; that the prisons were entirely supported by certain classes of mechanical trades, as a result of this successful competition; that there should be a law against the continuation or introduction of any business that was carried on elsewhere in the State, except in articles for the consumption of the prison or of other State institutions. An exception might be made in the case of articles, nine-tenths of which were supplied by foreign importation. Furthermore, no convict should be henceforth leased to any individual or company. No keeper or other individual should be interested in any contract. No steam engine or other power for propelling machinery should be introduced into the prison. All goods manufactured in prison should be marked or labelled as from the institution.

The Legislative committee's analysis showed, of a population of 196 convicts, employments as follows:

On Contracts.

Shoemaking, at 37½ cents	25	
Chairmaking, varnishing and finishing, at 35 to 40 cents	35	
Rule making, at 40 cents	12	
Table cutlery, at 45 cents	25	
	97	97

For the State.

Chair seat frames	12	
Knotting, splitting and shaving cane	20	
Chair seating	50	
Making palm leaf hats (women)	5	
Making cigars (men)		2
	89	89
		186

A great variety of trades had been introduced and discontinued at various times, such as:

Wagon making.	Brittania spoons.	Chisels.
Nail making.	Hammers.	Screw plate.
Clock carving.	Cooperage.	Rifles and rifle pistols.
Shovels and forks.	Tailoring.	Carriage springs.
Whips.	Spectacles.	Sledges.

The Legislative committee agreed with the mechanics that in certain industries the injury was serious. Shoe making did not seem to injure seriously, but chair making and rule making worked great hardship. Table cutlery was largely a foreign product, and was admissible in the prison.

The first introduction into the prison of a mechanical trade, reported the committee, resulted for some time afterward in a greater injury than was commonly supposed. Without the interferences of prison labor, private enterprise adjusts itself to supply and demand. Prison labor causes the withdrawal of private business in some cases, which leads to the withdrawal of capital, the interruption of profits, and loss of wages and skill to the workmen. The changes of trades in prison lead to a dislocation of the equilibrium of production and to injury to those in the trades.

The amount of injury depends upon the extent and proportion of the interference. When a small number of workmen can supply a trade, the interference of prison labor is very serious. The absolute amount of injury will be greater than the oversupply caused by the prison operations. Ten per cent. of excess of a commodity will reduce prices much more than ten per cent. Therefore, if the prison industries cause an oversupply, the mechanics and others lose more than the State gains.

These facts were not earlier discovered, because the industrial system in the prisons is of modern date. Nor was it so effective as it now was, went on the committee's report, and machinery had not been introduced to such an extent. Employers do not protest so long as their business is reasonably profitable, but only when the competition becomes keen, and profits fail. People at large must·also be informed and be convinced, before a grievance will be redressed. These were all reasons why the matter had not come earlier to a head.

The committee found that the frequent changes in industries at the prison had been injurious to mechanics, and of no benefit to the State or to the convicts, and should not be allowed. Many suitable articles of foreign make might be produced at the prisons. The committee did not specify the particular articles to be made. That was a matter for the warden and the directors to determine. Chair making and rule making should be discontinued. Trades in the prisons should be limited to those that would not interfere seriously with the mechanics. No mechanical trade should be introduced henceforth into the prison except for the manufacturing of articles, the chief supply of which should be imported from abroad. So far as possible the prison should make articles for the prison and other State institutions; prisoners might be employed at trades that they had learned and practiced before coming to prison.

The committee did not favor the contract system, which afforded a chance for favoritism on the part of the warden, and collusion between the contractor and the overseers, in order to get more work out of the prisoners. Overseers might easily have a secret interest in the contract, or receive perquisites. On the other hand, the contractors took the burden off the shoulders of the State. Contractors had to furnish stock and sell the product. They lessened the amount of State capital invested, lessened the bother and hazards of purchases, sales and debts, and also decreased the labor and responsibility of the warden.

The committee recommended that hereafter the contracts should not be made for the labor of the prisoners, but for the purchase by the contractors of the finished work of the prisoners. Also, that ample notice of all pending contracts should be given.

Dorothea Dix, analyzing this prison in 1845, found the institution, for all its excellent system, aiming not merely to make the prison support itself, which in her opinion all prisons should do, but to render also convict labor, and the *exhibition* of the convicts to the public, a source of profit to the State.[36] This custom prevailed in all the prisons of the Auburn type in the Northern States, as indicated by the following typical facts:

Visitors' fees at Auburn prison in 1842 were $1,692.75, in 1845, $1,942.75. In two years, this indicates visits of 14,542 persons at 25 cents per person.

Visitors to Sing Sing prison in 1843 paid $311.75, and in 1844, $236.62, making 2,194 visitors.

Income from visitors for two years at Charlestown, Massachusetts State prison, $1,487.75, or 5,951 persons.

Visitors' fees in 1843 and 1844 at Wethersfield, a total of $548.12½ cents, indicating at least 2,192 visitors.

At Windsor, Vermont, in one year, 796 visitors.

At the New Hampshire State prison, in one year, 500 visitors.

At the Ohio State prison, in Columbus, in 1844, receipts of $1,038 from visitors.[37]

The prisons have always been made, in a way, show places, and the fee of a shilling or "two bits," imposed upon the curiosity seeker, was probably partly for the purpose of keeping the attendance of visitors down. Victor Hugo once said that there is nothing so interesting as what is going on behind a high wall when it cannot be seen, and the attraction of the mysterious prison has always been great for many people. In modern days, the imposing of an admission fee has largely been abandoned, on the theory that convicts should not be exhibited as so and so many animals or curiosities. Here and there, however, the custom still exists.

[36] Dix. Remarks, p. 51.
[37] Dix. Remarks, p. 43.

CHAPTER XVI

NEW JERSEY

"A mere burlesque of a prison!" was the description given in 1829 by a witness to a Legislative committee, in describing the old State penitentiary at Lamberton, New Jersey, one and one-half miles south of Trenton. The prison had been established in 1798 upon that site, for the sole reason that "the land had been given by somebody."[2] Like other American prisons of the period, it was greatly influenced by the Walnut Street Prison of Philadelphia, and contained large cell-rooms.

In time, buildings for shops and other purposes had been added, scattered about the yard without unity or design.[1] All the evils of promiscuous association, characteristic of other prisons of the first period, had become notorious at the New Jersey prison, according to the above report. There was hardly a semblance of discipline at Lamberton. From the front windows of the kitchen, prisoners passed and repassed articles to people in the street; discharged prisoners could approach unobserved the various parts of the prison, and throw articles over the walls. Released convicts had even broken into the prison at night, and the authorities were fearful of a jail delivery through an organized body of men recently released from prison.[3]

There was so little discipline that convicts would leave their work in the shops and go into the yard. The greatest familiarity prevailed between certain keepers and certain convicts. There was smuggling and trading between them. A certain desperate group of prisoners was called the "Stanch Gang."

"They will lie, and swear to it; they will steal provision, and carry it off; they will lurk in the kitchen and steal other men's provision; they will threaten each others' lives; they will make dirks; they will make their own cards. They have rules by which they are bound to each other; one rule is that if a man tells anything, they will fall afoul of him, and beat him. Men who tell on others are called 'snitch.'" (The word "Snitch" is a term still current as a verb — to tell tales, to give information about.)[4]

In the cells, under this first system, there was abundant conversation. Supervision was lax, and the construction of the prison made the approach of the keeper audible at a distance. One prisoner made a complete ladder in his cell, with which to scale the walls. The news of the outside world percolated quickly into the institution. Riots were frequent, and hard to subdue. Convicts to the number of 108 had escaped since the founding of the prison in 1798 — more than one-twelfth of all admissions, a number without

---
[1] Report of Joint Comm. Votes of Assembly, 1830, p. 411.
[2] B. P. D. S., 1830, p. 420.
[3] Report of Joint Comm., p. 414.
[4] Report of Joint Comm. Votes of Assembly, 1830, p. 411.

parallel.[5] One keeper had been stabbed, two prisoners shot, and one killed. Fifty-five of the runaways had never been recaptured.

Punishments in the first period were severe. Solitary confinement with bread and water was much used, sometimes for from 20 to 30 days at a time. Sufferings of convicts thus punished were intense, and the convicts had to spend almost an equal time in the hospital, in recuperating. Chains were much used; men sometimes were chained at work, and sometimes to a "fifty-six." One lad of from 12 to 14 years was seen by the committee in 1829 wearing a neck yoke; his arms extended from 18 to 20 inches from his head, to prevent his getting through the gates. A convict had been found in one cell in solitary confinemnet for three days with nothing but water.[6] The committee found that ten prisoners were said to have died from severe punishment in their cells.

The prison had never, up to the time of the committee's report, paid its own expenses from the labor of convicts.[7] From 1800 to 1829, the total loss to the State caused by the prison had been $164,963, a sum equal to one-third of all the taxes raised in the State for all purposes during that period (Votes of the Assembly, 55 Gen. Ass., 1830-31), an average of $5,304 a year. Of the total number of prisoners committed, 1,206 in all, there had been, so far as known, 90 recommitments and a few reformations.

An interesting "budget" of daily expenses of the prison, *per capita,* showed the following:

	Cents.	Mills.
Clothing	4	8
Incidental	2	9
Total excl. salaries	9	3
Officers	9	4
Total *per capita per diem*	18	7

The balance sheet of the prison, compared with that of Wethersfield, for the year 1829, was cited to show the loss sustained by the State of New Jersey from its prison in one year:

New Jersey. Average, 90 Prisoners.		Connecticut.	
Expenses	$6,199 00	Expenses	$5,876 13
Earnings	3,427 98	Earnings	9,105 54
Deficit	$2,771 02	Surplus	$3,229 41

In the "twenties" of the nineteenth century, the penitentiary had undertaken to confine a certain number of convicts in solitary confinement, without labor, during their entire sentence of 18 months or two years. The test was not a rigid one, as that of Auburn Prison in 1822 and 1823. At Lamberton, the prisoners in solitary confinement were largely unsupervised and conversed

---
[5] Reports of Joint Comm. Votes of Assembly, 1830, p. 415.
[6] Votes of Assembly, 1830-31, p. 94.
[7] Report of Joint Comm., p. 422.

freely.[8] Although their diet was restricted to half that allowed to men in the shops, this simply reduced the passions.[9] This procedure, which began in 1825, had no value as a test of solitary confinement, although it was cited later as such by opponents of the so-called "separate system."

The convicts were engaged in thirteen different industries, of which the chief were shoemaking, weaving, and sawing stone.[10] The administrative methods, the experiences with the several industries, and the various methods employed in dealing with the inmates, resembled very markedly the experiences of the Walnut Street Prison, even to the almost literal copying of the rules and regulations, and of the laws founding the earlier institution.

Members of an auxiliary of the Boston Prison Discipline Society, located at Princeton, a few miles distant, visited the prison every Sunday, according to a report of the year 1828, and conducted religious services. One or more of the members visited the prisoners in solitary confinement. By the Legislature of 1829 a permanent chaplain was authorized, and an appropriation of $150 granted — a sum that the Boston Prison Discipline Society had for two years allotted for this purpose.

The joint committee of the Legislature, stating that the only solution was a new prison, recommended the establishment of a modern penitentiary on the type of Auburn or Wethersfield. Obviously, the conditions at the old prison were scandalous. In 1831, there was a striking increase in the number of admissions. The severities of the Eastern Penitentiary on the south, and of Auburn, Sing Sing and Wethersfield on the north, were believed to be driving convicts into New Jersey as the safest place in which to ply their trades. One-third of the commitments in 1832 were of convicts from other States than New Jersey. The Lamberton prison had no terrors for such persons.[11]

In 1833, a joint Legislative committee, declaring that the prison was an incongruous pile, without order or arrangement, and heaped together from time to time, recommended the immediate building of a new prison, not however on the Auburn plan, but modeled on the new Eastern Penitentiary of Pennsylvania, less than 30 miles away. For the first time, a State other than Pennsylvania was thereby adhering to the principle of the constant separation of prisoners. The committee based its decision on its belief that solitude was the most powerful agent in working out individual reformation. Collective labor and instruction, as practiced at Auburn, interrupted and to some extent paralyzed individual efforts at reformation. The association of convicts was fraught with evil consequences. New Jersey should adopt a system that would ensure that no convict should be seen by another. The Pennsylvania discipline was understood to be mild, the severest

---

[8] B. P. D. S., 1827, p. 59.
[9] B. P. D. S., 1826, p. 14.
[10] B. P. D. S., 1827, p. 120.
[11] B. P. D. S., 1831, p. 493; 1832, p. 572.

punishment inflicted being the deprivation of labor in the cell. Solitary labor and confinement were salutary, and deterred from crime; the terror caused in the community by the prison would materially reduce crime within the State.[12]

As to the argument that the prison would be very expensive to construct and maintain on the Pennsylvania plan, the committee stated that labor and profit were, anyway, simply a means, dictated by the wisest benevolence, for the health of the convict's moral and physical powers. The best good of the convict and that of the society he had offended were the high purposes aimed at in prison discipline; and should the labor and profit be even lost, it would bear no comparison to the good to be obtained. However, a convict should in six months earn his maintenance, as had been shown in Philadelphia. The Governor of New Jersey assured the Legislature that as soon as the prison was fully organized, the entire expenses would be paid from the proceeds of the prison.[13]

Therefore, in February, 1833, the Legislature authorized the erection of a new penitentiary, to hold 150 prisoners, in separate confinement at hard labor, and appropriated $130,000 toward the building of the same.[14] John Haviland, who had designed the Eastern Penitentiary, was appointed architect. Ground was selected contiguous to the then existing prison, in the form of a parallelogram, 500 feet by 300 feet. Haviland's design included a central administration building for the dwelling houses and offices of the warden. In the rear of this building there was to be a semi-circular observatory, 55 feet in diameter, from which five wings should radiate, like the fingers of an outspread hand. The wings would contain solitary cells, and were to be two stories high. The cells, on each side of a central corridor 14 feet wide, were 12 feet long by 8 feet wide, equipped as in the Eastern Penitentiary, each cell having its own running water and its water closet. The cells were closed from the corridor by double doors, the interior door being of wood sheathed with iron. In the door there was a small hole for observation from the corridor.[15]

There were, however, to be no exercising yards connecting with the cells. Herein lay a vital and surprising defect, one that ultimately led to the breakdown of the system. The prisoners never, while the system was operating, according to the letter of the law were brought out into the sunlight — and serious mental and physical results arose therefrom. No explanation was given at the time of planning the prison as to the reason for the omission of the exercising yards, but it was probably due to economy.[17]

Haviland's estimate of the cost of the prison was as follows:

External wall	$14,000
Front building, including laundry, culinary, bathing, storeroom, keeper's chambers, observatory, reservoir, belfry	15,000
Culverts, sinks, pipes, covered ways, cooking apparatus, warming and raising water into reservoir	13,000

[12] B. P. D. S., 1833, p. 698.
[13] Same, p. 699.
[14] Crawford, App. 50.
[15] De Metz and Blouet, p. 66.
[17] Crawford, App., p. 49.

A Block, 50 cells	$18,000
B Block, 75 cells	27,000
C Block, 50 cells	18,000
D Block, 75 cells	27,000
E Block, 50 cells	18,000
	$150,000

The estimated per capita cost was but $500 a cell, a noteworthy reduction as compared with that of the Eastern Penitentiary. Governor Peter D. Vroom, Jr., in 1834, doubted not that when the prison was completed, it would be the most perfect in design and execution in the United States. He held that it was not even desirable that the new prison should be a source of profit to the State. If it paid expenses the State would be satisfied.[16]

In the report of the Boston Prison Discipline Society for 1833 is the record of an annual meeting of the Prison Instruction Society in New Jersey, held at the State House in Trenton in January, 1833. Most of the Legislature attended the meeting. The chief objects of the society were:

"To extend to the convicts in the prisons of this State the benefits of the Sabbath school system of instruction, and also to furnish them with preaching. In connection with the foregoing objects, provision shall also be made for inquiring into the relative efficiency of different modes of prison discipline, and of different modes of instruction."

The New Jersey Howard Society was also established in 1833, "to attack the barbarous practice of imprisoning debtors, and to urge better provision for the care of the insane and the reformation of delinquent minors."[18]

By 1837, the new prison had been made ready for occupancy, at a cost of $193,012.[19] Haviland's estimate was thus overreached by far, because only two of the five wings had been built. Blouet reported that there were, when he visited in 1835 the prison, 192 cells, and that the total costs of construction had been approximately $200,000 or over $1,000 a cell.[20] Of course, with the addition of the unbuilt wings, the per capita cost would be lowered.

The old State prison was converted into a State arsenal. For the first time in this year the prison supported itself, except in the payment of salaries to the officers, a regular burden upon the State treasury. There was very uncommonly good health in the new penitentiary, one death only being recorded in 14 months, ending September 30th, 1837.[22]

In the new prison there was no chapel and no chaplain. Volunteers from the clergy of Trenton and vicinity held occasional services. Members of the Society of Friends occasionally visited the prisoners in their cells. Not until approximately 1845 were arrangements made for providing a teacher, uniting the offices of

[16] Votes of Ass., 1834, p. 15.
[18] B. P. D. S., 1834, p. 85.
[19] Governor's Message, January, 1837.
[20] De Metz et Blouet, p. 66.
[22] B. P. D. S., 1837.

moral instructor and school master. At this time, also, a suitable and fairly large library was given by several interested citizens of Jersey City and Newark.[21]

The cells were very comfortable, according to one of the visitors in 1838, well ventilated and free from odor. Joseph A. Yard, a pious Methodist, was appointed warden.[23] The prisoners testified to the humanity of their treatment, but a visitor, reporting to the Boston Prison Discipline Society, stated that he believed that the health of the prisoners and in some instances their minds was being injuriously affected, because of the confinement in a small room.

The character of the population of the prison at this time appears from the Keeper Yard's statement of 1837,[24] which shows that of 135 prisoners in confinement:

12 could read, write and cipher, and had studied geography and grammar.
25 could read, write and cipher.
24 could read and write.
30 could read only.
13 could spell.
18 knew the alphabet.
13 did not know the alphabet.

Of the prison population, 51, or between one-third and one-half, were colored. The chief causes of conviction were burglary, grand larceny, and assault and battery. Of the types of criminals in prison, Dorothea Dix wrote:

"Enlightened transgressors, and men of considerable intellectual capacity, rarely are found in prison. They are too adroit, too cunning, to permit themselves to be ensnared by the emissaries of the law. Feeble minds, too infirm of purpose to keep in the straight path, too incapable of reasoning out their truest good and best interest, and many of constitutionally depraved propensities, chiefly fill . . . our penitentiaries."[25]

The experiences of the prison were closely watched, to discover the effects of constant solitary confinement without open-air exercise upon the prisoners. For the year 1838, the prison physician, Dr. James B. Coleman, stated that there had not been as much disease as might have been anticipated. There was a peculiar tendency of the prisoners to scrofula. There had been five deaths from diseases brought into the prison by the inmates, but aggravated perhaps by confinement. The deaths of four were caused by abscesses in the lungs. In all cases, reported the physician, the lymphatic glands were obstructed to a degree seldom seen in outside practice.[26]

The board of directors had failed, according to their report, to discover the injurious effects upon prisoners that the physician had mentioned. The prisoners presented a pale and rather unhealthy appearance which the board believed was a consequence of living entirely in the shade, and not an effect of disease. The inspectors also asked if the terms of imprisonment might not be abridged because of the severity of punishment.[27]

---

[21] Dix. Remarks, p. 58.
[23] Same, p. 233.
[24] Votes of Assembly, 1837-38, p. 442.
[25] Dix. Remarks, p. 64.
[26] Votes of Ass., 1838-39, p. 43.
[27] Votes of Ass., 1838-39, pp. 71-73.

In another year, the physician was more definite. Sunlight and air were essential to health. Post-mortem examinations had proved the effects that might have been anticipated. Every year of a prisoner's confinement in the cells would show a decline of the physical powers. The enervating influences of cellular confinement had been felt, although the general health was good. It is noteworthy, however, that in this year 37 persons were pardoned.

The convicts who had been transferred from the old prison, where a large part of their day had been spent outside of their cells, had not shown the effects of constant cellular confinement for the first two years, but had now become debilitated, and languid. Said the physician:

"In the prison the physician will see minds that, subject to the common perceptions of out-of-door life, would be as astute as others, indulge in the amusements of the child, wasting their time, after the daily task is over, upon toys; engaged in no thought that is not immediately associated with the things about them; incapable of abstract reflection, or, if showing any evidence of the higher operations of the faculties, it is more the wandering of a visionary, than the operation of a well-balanced mind.

"Among the prisoners there are many cases of insanity. Almost all the cases that have occurred in prison can be traced to onanism. Among the prisoners there are many who exhibit a child-like simplicity, which shows them to be less acute than when they entered. In all who have been more than a year in the prison, some of these effects have been observed. Now they are managed under the most favorable circumstances the nature of their confinement permits. . . . Were another course pursued, and the superintendent (warden) possessed of no sympathy for the convict, in less than a year the New Jersey prison would be a bedlam.

"If there be more disease in solitary confinement, it is of a peculiar character, slow in its work and important in its effects upon the mind. It is for others to determine whether the old discipline, hardening the vicious in the crimes, while it preserves the body in its full vigor, so that at the expiration of the sentence the convict may go forth a more accomplished rogue than when he entered the penitentiary, is to be preferred to another which, while it subdues the evil passions, almost paralyzes them for want of exercise, leaves the individual, if still a rogue, one that may be easily detected."[28]

Despite the findings of the physician, the board of inspectors maintained that under any circumstances the system was far superior to the former conditions at the prison. The inspectors doubted, however, whether many went out of the prison with good moral stamina, it was so easy under this system to be good in the prison.

In 1840 there were reported few known changes for the better among the convicts. No prison, the inspectors concluded, was a school for perfect reformation. The board upheld the system of separate confinement, but maintained that under any management, the prison could not produce the unnatural results, in the way of reformations, that had frequently been claimed by the system's advocates.[29] Many of the sentences were far too long, in view of the severity of constant separate confinement; ten years would be a terrible punishment, hardly to be endured. There were twelve deranged prisoners in the institution, who should have been sent to a lunatic asylum.

---
[28] Votes of Assembly, 1839-40.
[29] Votes of Assembly, 1840-41, p. 215.

The physician reported only two deaths during the year, both however from the effects of solitary confinement. The effects of such confinement were now well determined:

Diminished force of the organs generally.
Particularly a weakening of the muscular fibre.
Obstruction of the lymphatic glands.
Vitiated nervous action.
The mind suffers and the power is weakened.

In 1840 the system of separate confinement broke down at the New Jersey Prison. The physcian was clearly a disbeliever in its beneficent results; the board of inspectors was not convinced of its potency. Therefore, the principle of constant solitary confinement was abandoned when sickness required. A convict was placed in the cell of the sufferer. Inroads on health were causing constant complaints among the prisoners. Applications for pardon were made with frequency on that ground. Some prisoners were indeed pardoned who died shortly after leaving prison.[30]

The cells were often conductive to sickness; there was much trouble with the heating and ventilating system, and this was rectified only after experiments conducted during several years. In winter, many of the cells were so cold as to interfere materially with the prisoner's labor.

We would pause here, for a moment, to emphasize the serious inadequacy of proper ventilation in the early American prisons, particularly in those on the Auburn plan of construction. After the convicts had been for several hours in their cells at night, the air became insufferably impure. The absence of any forced ventilation from the individual cells, the excessive smallness of the cells, the closed windows of the cellhouses in winter, the coal stoves in the corridors, and the emanations from the inadequately bathed prisoners made a condition that often must have been almost intolerable. The Eastern Penitentiary was better equipped, in so far as the cell windows or cell doors were concerned, for pure air could be admitted from the exercise yards to the individual cells. The Trenton prison, being without exercise yards, must have experienced troublesome ventilation problems.[31]

In 1843, the introduction of convicts into the cells of other inmates was extended.

"To prevent the evils of solitary confinement, and especially an abuse common to this system of punishment, other convicts have been put in the cells, and the evils in many cases remedied. Cases of derangement have been prevented by this course. Those suffering from want of air have been turned into the yard for a few hours a day. More pains have been taken to ventilate the cells."

The physician reported that another cause of better health was the rigid exaction of labor from each prisoner able to work. For "despondency," he was liberal in prescribing tobacco. The number

---

[30] Votes of Ass. 1840-41, p. 219.
[31] Dix. Remarks, p. 37.

of insane became less. Expiration of terms, and the use of pardons, had relieved the institution of some of its problems:

"The more rigidly the plan of solitary confinement is carried out, the more the spirit of the law is observed, the more the effects are visible in the health of the convicts. A little more intercourse with each other, and a little more air in the yard, has in almost every case shown a corresponding rise in the health of the individual. That an opinion to the contrary should have been advocated at this time, when the animal functions are so well understood, seems like a determination to disregard science in the support of a mistaken but favored policy." [32]

The reference to the "animal functions" by the physician of the Trenton prison is a quotation from a noted phrenologist of this period, George Combe, who, born in 1788 in Edinburgh, was one of the forerunners of the anthropological school of the Italians, in so far as he attempted to determine traits and tendencies through the contemplation and analysis of physical stigmata, especially of the face and head. Doctor Combe delivered in Edinburgh a course of lectures on "Moral Philosophy," which, collected in book form, presented a discussion of the proper treatment of criminals that was most remarkable for constructive thinking and lucidity, antedating in some of its propositions any American published program of suggestions that we have found.

Combe traveled extensively through the Eastern and Central portion of the United States in 1838. Of the solitary system of the Eastern Penitentiary he said:

"The system of entire solitude weakens the whole nervous system. It withdraws external excitement from the animal propensities, but operates in the same manner on the organs of the moral and intellectual faculties. Social life is to these powers what an organ field is to the muscles; it is their theatre of action, and without action there can be no vigor. Solitude, even when combined with labor and the use of books, and an occasional visit from a religious instructor, leaves the moral faculties still in a passive state, and without the means of rigorous and active exercise.

"The discipline of the Eastern Penitentiary reduces the tone of the whole nervous system to the level which is in harmony with solitude. The passions are weakened and subdued, but so are all the moral and intellectual powers. The susceptibility of the nervous system is increased, because all organs become susceptible in proportion to their feebleness. A weak eye is pained by light which is agreeable to a sound one.

"Hence it may be quite true that religious admonitions will be deeply felt by prisoners living in solitude more than by those enjoying society; just as such instruction, when addressed to a patient recovering from a severe and debilitating illness, makes a more vivid impression than when delivered to the same individual in health. But the appearance of reformation founded on such impressions is deceitful. When the sentence has expired, the convict will return to society with all his mental powers, animal, moral and intellectual, increased in susceptibility but lowered in strength. The excitements that will then assail him will have their influence doubled by operating on an enfeebled system.

"Convicts, after long confinement in solitude, shudder to encounter the turmoil of the world; they become excited as the day of liberation approaches, and feel bewildered when set at liberty. In short, this system is not founded on, or in harmony with, a sound knowledge of the physiology of the brain, although it appeared to me to be well administered. . . . There are advantages that go far to compensate the evils of solitude, but none to remove them." [33]

[32] Votes of Assembly, 1841-42, p. 191.
[33] Votes of Assembly, 1841-42, p. 191.

We find in George Combe an astute student of humanity, in an age when phrenology occupied a respectable position among the "sciences," a precursor of the psychologists and the psychiatrist of to-day, evolving some theories of prison discipline far in advance of the practice of the time. Combe certainly should not be overlooked, in our tracing backward to discover the birth and development of the theory of the indeterminate sentence, and of the theory that incorrigible criminals should be permanently detained in custody. For, as early as 1839, Combe had arrived at the belief that

"the necessity for an asylum for convicts, intermediate between the prison and society, while the present system of treatment is pursued, is obvious. . . . All American prisons that I have seen are lamentably deficient in arrangements for exercising the moral and intellectual faculties of their inmates. During the hours of labor, no advance can be made. After the hours of labor, he is locked in his cell in solitude, and I doubt much if he can read, for want of light; but assuming that he can, reading is a very imperfect means of strengthening the moral powers. They must be exercised, trained and habituated to action.

"There should be a teacher of high moral and intellectual power for every eight to ten convicts. These teachers should go to work on the convicts after the close of labor. In proportion as the prisoners give proof of moral and intellectual advancement, they should be indulged with the liberty of social converse and action for a certain time each week-day, and on Sunday, in the presence of the teacher; and in these conversations or evening parties, they should be trained to the use of their highest powers and trained to restrain their propensities. Every indication of over-active propensity should be visited by a restriction of liberty and enjoyment. . . . These advantages should be increased in exact proportion to the advancement of the convicts in morality and understanding.

"By such means, if any, would the convicts be prepared to enter society . . . so trained as to give them a chance of resisting temptation, and continuing in the paths of virtue. . . . In no country has the idea yet been carried into effect, that in order to produce moral fruits, it is necessary to put into action moral influences, great and powerful in proportion to the barrenness of the soil from which they are expected to spring"[34]

The deep significance of the above passage is, that there is therein clearly recommended a most modern principle in the treatment of the prisoner, namely, the growth toward reformation and reclamation through the opportunity for self-expression within prison walls. It was Mr. Osborne who made current the expression: "Only through freedom can the prisoner become fit for freedom," and the Mutual Welfare League, despite its failures, did at Auburn and Sing Sing prisons manifest the truth of the theory that not only the individual treatment of the prisoner by the prison authorities, but the self-expression of the individual prisoner, are essential parts of a modern prison program. And here was Combe, in an age that extolled a Lynds, and a Pilsbury, who were mainly repressionists, proclaiming that such a system was fundamentally unsound. Surely, an interesting phenomenon — one rising before its time, and failing to prevail, because the world had not caught up to it.

---

[34] Combe. Notes on United States, Vol. II, p. 18.

Other passages from Combe's works are equally prophetic, as in the following foreshadowing of a system of indeterminate sentence and parole:

"How should we treat criminals? (He is here speaking of a class that to-day we should call perhaps moral imbeciles.) They should be placed in penitentiaries, and be prevented from abusing their faculties, yet be humanely treated, and permitted to enjoy comfort and as much liberty as they could sustain, without injuring themselves or their fellowmen. . . . If by long restraint and moral training and instruction they should ever become capable of self-guidance, they should be viewed as patients who have recovered, and be liberated, on the understanding that if they should relapse into immoral habits they should be restored to their places in the asylum." [35]

Phrenologists have long proclaimed that the great cause of the incorrigibility of criminals is the active predominance of the organ of the animal propensities over those of the moral and intellectual faculties, and that this class of persons is really composed of moral patients, who should be restrained but not otherwise punished, during life. [36]

In view of social protection, any individual who has been convicted of infringing the criminal law, should be handed over, as a moral patient, to the managers of a well-regulated penitentiary, to be confined in it, not until he shall have endured a certain amount of suffering, equal in magnitude to what is supposed to be a fair revenge for his offense, but until such change shall have been effected in his mental condition as may afford society a reasonable guarantee that he will not commit fresh crimes when he is set at liberty. This course of treatment would be humanity itself to the offender, compared with the present system, while it would unspeakably benefit society. It would convert our prisons from houses of retribution and corruption into schools of reform. It would require, however, an entire change in the principles in which they are conducted. [37]

There is far greater humanity in a sentence for a first offense that shall reform the culprit, although the offense itself may be small, and the confinement long, than in one decreeing punishment for a few days only, proportional solely to the amount of the crime. [38]

There is something almost uncanny in finding the above sporadic utterances of Combe appearing suddenly in a period far removed still from the development in this country of the indeterminate sentence for adults. Such propositions as above quoted, if presented to-day with emphasis before many a convention of women's clubs or even before specialized workers in delinquency, would be heartily applauded, and regarded as timely and progressive. Yet Combe affected apparently not at all the general course of prison treatment in our country. He was undoubtedly regarded as an example, in that day, of the "high-brow" of today, who often enunciates a perfectly sound theory, one ultimately to be proved by usage, only to be ignored in his time because practical men say that it "simply can't be done." When what is often meant is, that the "high-brow" couldn't do it, and they won't try.

Here and there in this country, sporadic statements were being made, indicating an advanced conception of the social possibilities

---
[35] Combe. Moral Philosophy. Ed. 1863, p. 202.
[36] Notes on United States, p. 9.
[37] Moral Philosophy, p. 222.
[38] Same, p. 224.

of a prison. Doctor Charles Caldwell stated in a course of lectures on "Physical Education" in Lexington, Kentucky in 1833, that

"When established on correct principles, and skillfully administered, penitentiaries and houses of correction are moral hospitals, where criminal propensities are treated as diseases, consisting in unsound conditions of the brain."

But Combe went even farther than has been quoted by us hitherto. He advocated practically a straight-out treatment of the criminal by a kind of indeterminate sentence, administered by a form of court. In a chapter of his "Moral Philosophy," entitled "On the Treatment of Crime," he wrote:

"If the principle which I advocate shall ever be adopted, the sentence of the criminal judge, on conviction of a crime, would simply be one finding that the individual had committed a certain offense, and was not fit to live in society; and, therefore, granting warrant for his transmission to a penitentiary, to be there confined, instructed and employed, until liberated in due course of law.

"The process of liberation would then become one of the greatest importance. There should be official inspectors of penitentiaries, invested with some of the powers of a court, sitting at regular intervals, and proceeding according to fixed rules. They should be authorized to receive applications for liberation at all their sessions, and to grant the prayer of them on being satisfied that such a thorough change had been effected in the mental condition of the prisoner, that he might safely be permitted to resume his place in society.

"Until this conviction was produced upon examination of his disposition, of his attainments in knowledge, of his acquired skill in some useful employment, of his habits of industry, and, in short, of his general qualifications to provide for his own support, to restrain his animal propensities from committing abuses, and to act the part of a useful citizen, he should be retained as an inmate of a penitentiary.

"Perhaps some individuals, whose dispositions appeared favorable to reformation, might be liberated at an earlier period on sufficient security, under bond, given by responsible relatives or friends, for the discharge of the same duties toward them in private which the officers of the penitentiary would discharge in public. For example, if a youth were to commit such an offense as would subject him, according to the present system of criminal legislation, to two or three months' confinement in Bridewell, he might be handed over to individuals of undoubted good character and substance, under a bond that they should be answerable for his proper education, employment and reformation; and fulfillment of the obligation should be very rigidly enforced.

"The principle of revenge being disavowed and abandoned, there could be no harm in following any mode of treatment, whether private or public, that should be adequate to the accomplishment of the other two objects of criminal legislation — the protection of society and the reformation of the offender.

"To prevent abuses of this practice, the public authorities should carefully ascertain that the natural qualities of the offender admitted of adequate improvement by private treatment; and, secondly, that private discipline was actually administered. If any offender, liberated on bond, should ever reappear as a criminal, the penalty should be inexorably enforced, and the culprit should never again be liberated, except upon a verdict finding that his reformation had been completed by a proper system of training in a penitentiary."

The above paragraphs by Combe were presented to students of American prison management in a volume entitled: "Rationale of Crime," with notes and illustrations by Mrs. E. W. Farnham, the matron of Mount Pleasant Prison, in 1846. In short, the theory of the indeterminate sentence, of parole, and subsequent retreatment of the offending person on "parole," or rather, its proposed equivalent of the time, were all thus spread before the American students of prison matters in 1846 — but it was thirty years before the opening of Elmira Reformatory, and in the State prisons of the time no change resulted from this presentation, by an enlightened "prison woman," of a really great penological thinker of his time. Even the phraseology of Combe often brings to us the very phrases to-day in common use, and many a parole board, now sitting in State prison or reformatory, would listen to the repetition of Combe's theorizing, not knowing its origin, and pronounce the proposition: "Exactly what is now being done by us!"

We turn from Combe to a study of the industries under the new system at the new prison of New Jersey. The prison, after a few years, made a very creditable industrial showing. By 1841, the governor could report the prison out of debt, with a small surplus. The yearly deficits or surplus earnings were as follows:

Years	Earnings	Expenses	Deficit	Surplus
1825–1829	$97,995	$77,347		*$20,648
1836–1839			†$5,194	
1840			*512	
1841				*1,272
1842				*4,278
1843				*2,969
1844				*4,709

* Exclusive of salaries.
† Inclusive of salaries.

The greatly increased productivity of the prison was due in part at least to the policy of keeping the prisoners, for purposes of both health and industry, steadily employed in their cells. In 1844, the principal keeper reported that

"under our system no great degree of health can be maintained without regular employment. This, with proper attention to cleanliness, wholesome diet and judicious treatment, appears to be all that is necessary, except in a few isolated cases, to ensure general good health."[39]

The activities of the prison industries appear from the keeper's statement in 1844:

Earnings.		Expenses.	
Weaving	$2,441 75	Furniture	$929 14
Cordwaining	2,261 57	Provisions	4,183 46
Chair making	5,105 08	Hospital	176 79
Sundries	757 10	Fuel	1,432 08
		Incidentals	857 31
		Interest	16 92
			7,595 70
	$10,056 50	Net gain	$2,969 90

Salaries, as well as expenses of repairs and improvements, were paid not out of the earnings of the prison, but from the State

[39] Council, 1844, p. 29.

treasury. So far as possible, the prison aimed to employ the prisoners at contract labor, but opposed the entrance of the contractor, through his agents, into the prison.

A picture of the prison population is given in the report of the inspectors for 1844:

Length of Sentences.

Life	1	7 years	2	2 years	30
20 years	1	6 years	3	1 yr. 6 mos.	12
15 years	3	5 years	24	1 yr. 3 mos.	1
14 years	1	4 years	13	1 year	19
12 years	1	3 years	23	9 months	1
10 years	9	2 yrs. 6 mos.	6	6 months	1
8 years	3				

Year Received into Prison.

1837	2 prisoners	1841	9 prisoners
1838	1 prisoner	1842	19 prisoners
1839	3 prisoners	1843	58 prisoners
1840	6 prisoners	1844	61 prisoners

The above statistical statement, showing no prisoner at the prison who had been admitted more than eight years previously, indicates clearly the custom of pardoning prisoners by the end of from six to eight years, even if such prisoners had been committed for very long terms, or even for life. Harriet Martineau, a very observant traveler in the United States in the "thirties," stated that every one of the prisoners whom she conversed with in the Eastern Penitentiary was in anxious expectation of a pardon.

"A sentence to life imprisonment is generally understood to mean imprisonment for a shorter term than if 10 to 7 years had been named."[40]

The subjoined table shows additional significant statistics of the same period of the New Jersey Prison:

Convictions.		Ages.		Race.	
First	131	10-20	22	White	98
Second	21	20-30	74		
Third	6	30-40	38	Colored.	
Fourth	1	40-50	16	Male	59
		50-60	7	Female	2
		60-70	2		

The above figures are to be taken with many grains of salt, as to their accuracy. The statements of convicts as to age, previous convictions, habits and the like, have always been fairly unreliable. The statements are colored by various motives and in general, as can be readily understood, the convict is not prone to confess earlier convictions. Therefore, the first column, as to previous convictions, is hardly to be regarded as accurate. The probabilities are that the number of first convictions, in New Jersey or in other States, was much smaller than was given.

Apparently the attitude of the board of inspectors and of the warden, at the end of the period we have now under consideration, was humane and benevolent. The inspectors recommended shorter sentences, fully executed, and they vigorously opposed the practice

---

[40] Society in America, Vol. II, p. 288.

of granting pardons. Punishment, they maintained, must be certain in order to be effective. The warden (known as the "Keeper" or "Principal Keeper") stated that no human being could ever be reformed by brutal treatment. An over-stint was put into operation. Men in the past, claimed the keeper, had been wronged out of their earnings. He laid emphasis upon the greater importance in the prison of moral reformation than of great profits.[41]

The attitude of the inspectors toward some payment to the prisoners for their work, even though in the form of a bonus for extra work, was indicative of a changing sentiment in this period among enlightened prison reformers. In earlier decades, the prison executives had opposed the "over-stint" because of its application by prisoners to contraband articles and to the corruption of officers. But in time it became clear that within the prison as well as outside of it there must be a potent economic or moral stimulus. This insight led Dorothea Dix to write in 1845 of American prisons:[42]

"The best mode of aiding convicts is, so to apportion their tasks in prison as to give to the industrious the opportunity of earning a sum for themselves by 'overwork.' A man usually values that most for which he has labored; he uses that most frugally which he has toiled hour by hour and day by day to acquire. I believe every convict will be disposed to make a better use of the money he earns than of that he receives gratuitously. . . . Indulged habits of dependence create habits of indolence, and indolence opens the portals to . . . vice and crime."

It was homely and, to our minds of to-day, self-evident truths that the prison executives and prison reformers were learning in these formative years of the Auburn and the Pennsylvania systems. They were new to them, and were dilated upon in the cogent and expressive language of the day.

For those prisoners who had proved worthy in the prison, the inspectors recommended the passage of a law restoring citizenship rights, which had been forfeited upon conviction. A library was installed by means of a State appropriation of $100, and the books, of religious, historical and miscellaneous nature, were distributed regularly to the prisoners during the year.

[41] Reports of Inspectors and Keeper, 1844.
[42] Dix. Remarks, p. 11.

CHAPTER XVII

MARYLAND

When the Englishman, Crawford, visited the Maryland State Penitentiary in 1832, he wrote that it was remarkable for nothing more than the profits arising from its manufacture.[1] And, in truth, the Baltimore institution developed in the period between 1832 and 1837 into a very productive factory, ultimately possessing shops that the French official visitor, Blouet, described as the best he had seen in any American prison.[2] Directors and officials were chosen because of the industrial capacity. "Product" was almost the sole ambition of the administration. The older prisoners taught the newcomers the prescribed trades. The Boston Prison Discipline Society early cited the Maryland Penitentiary as the most productive in the country[3]— a high compliment in a period when prisons that failed to be self-supporting were regarded as partial failures.

As in the case of the earliest State prisons in other Eastern States, the State prison of Maryland was organized almost entirely on the basis and methods of the humane Walnut Street Prison. The high reputation of the Pennsylvania institution led the Maryland Legislature in 1804 to provide for the erection of a State prison. In 1809 a further law established in detail the government of the prison, modeled on the daily routine of Walnut Street.[4] Prisoners were, for instance, to be kept in solitary confinement for from one-half to one-twentieth of their sentence. As in Philadelphia, they were to labor every day in the year, save Sunday and Christmas Day, or when under punishment, the hours being 8 in November, December and January, 9 in February and October, and 10 during the rest of the year. Even the separate labor account for each prisoner, initiated in the Philadelphia prison, was embodied in the Maryland law. Prisoners suffering from "any acute or dangerous distemper" at time of discharge might be held until sufficiently cured. On admission, the prisoner was to be washed, cleaned, and segregated until regarded as fit to be received among the other prisoners. In short, the enlightened principles of the first reform movement were copied in Maryland law.

Nevertheless, the Baltimore prison appears only infrequently in its early history to have striven for the reformation of its inmates. Crawford found that the prisoners were liable to be flogged for a breach of the regulations, and at the pleasure of the underkeepers, as at Auburn, without requiring previous notice to the warden.[5] Imprisonment, said Crawford, was very far from

---
[1] Crawford, p. 22.
[2] De Metz and Blouet, p. 24.
[3] B. P. D. S., 1829, p. 264.
[4] Acts of Ass., etc., respecting the Penitentiary of Maryland, 1819, p. 5.
[5] Crawford, p. 22.

[204]

having any tendency to diminish crime. Blouet found that prisoners who had not completed their tasks at the end of the day were severely punished, and could not enjoy any earnings through "over-stint," until they should have caught up, through such over-stints, with their regularly assigned daily tasks. However, on Christmas Day the slate was wiped clean for those who had fallen behind in their industry, and a new account was opened.[6]

As an intensive manufacturing center, in which any real welfare of prisoners was subordinated to profits, the Maryland penitentiary had a varied career in the early decades of the nineteenth century. The prison was opened in 1812 [8] in the city of Baltimore, three-fourths of a mile from the center of the city,[7] with a wall-enclosed area of about four acres, and at a cost of $196,000. In the opening month, 51 convicts were removed to the penitentiary from the public roads, to serve the remainder of their sentence therein.[8] Like other prison buildings of this period, this prison, 156 feet long and 36 feet wide, contained large night-rooms, 36 in number, holding from 7 to 10 inmates each.

In time, the same demoralization developed out of these promiscuous dormitories that led in the other States to the downfall of the first penitentiary system. A female department with 6 rooms occupied the southern end of the second story of the prison, and 9 solitary cells, for punishment purposes, were in the northern end of the third story. These were the conditions found when the Boston Prison Discipline Society began to issue its annual reports on American prisons in 1826.

By January, 1825, the convict population numbered 307, of which 62 were females; of the 245 males, 93 were colored, and almost all the women prisoners were negroes. Sentences ranged from 3 months to 21 years.[9] The principal industry of the male prisoners was weaving, carried on by the State, and not by contractors. The sun-to-sun labor of the prisoners on week days was broken on the Sabbath by religious instruction by Methodist clergymen, morning and evening, and by a Sabbath School that taught also the three R's.

A very human touch entered into the industrial history of the institution when, in 1822, Mrs. Perijo was appointed matron of the female department [10]— a section of the prison heretofore, as in other prisons, in charge of a male keeper. Mrs. Perijo was, in her way, an Elizabeth Fry, for she dominated the vicious and debauched women prisoners by kindness and common sense, turned an average annual deficit of $1,099 into an average surplus of $492, and in addition organized educational classes in the three R's, besides teaching the women simple industries and completely changing the discipline and morale of her department. She is the first prison matron of whom we have found record, and like the early penitentiary system in Philadelphia, she also set the standard high from the outset.

[6] De Metz and Blouet, p. 24.
[7] B. P. D. S., 1827, p. 120.
[8] Crawford, App. 94.
[9] B. P. D. S., 1827, p. 120.
[10] B. P. D., S., 1836, p. 34.

The prison was distinctly a going concern in 1828, in which year the earnings exceeded the expenses by $9,804, not including $3,522 repaid on account of loans.[12] During the five previous years the earnings had been large, and the penitentiary in 1829 had an active capital of $76,927, principally earnings. In 1828, the female department, under Mrs. Perijo, had earned $1,355 net.

In 1829, affected by the strong influences of the Auburn system, and by the obvious failure of the prevailing system to maintain discipline, and to be anything but a nursery of crime,[11] the State erected a new prison building, containing 320 separate cells. It is significant that this building, though constructed on the "arcade plan" (with a central corridor), and with cells facing the corridor (instead of being placed back to back, as at Auburn), drew the high praise of the Boston Prison Discipline Society,[12] which shows that the support by that society of the Auburn system was a support of Auburn *methods* especially of silence, separation at night and association at labor during the day, rather than an advocacy necessarily of the so-called inside cellblock which has in tradition become inseparable from the so-called Auburn system itself. In short, the vehement objections by the Boston Society to the Pennsylvania system were not to rooms abutting on a central corridor, but to rooms in which the prisoners not only slept but worked in solitude.

An interesting observation of Dorothea Dix was, relative to this new cellblock, that she much preferred the method of architecture which ranged the cells against the walls instead of throwing them into the center.

"I greatly prefer this arrangement, affording as it does advantages of light and air, unknown in ranges of center cells, so inconvenient and tomb-like in construction as all those are."[13]

The new cellhouse, 5 stories high, contained a central passage 15 feet wide, open from the first floor to the roof. Galleries fronted each row of cells above the first floor. The cells were 6 feet 6 inches in length, 3 feet 7 inches wide, and 7 feet high.[14] In each cell a glazed window, 3 feet high and 4 inches in breadth on the outer surface, broadening to 12 inches on the inner surface of the external wall of the cell, gave light and air. The cells had iron-grated doors — which led to difficulties, because of ready verbal communication between prisoners on opposite sides of the corridors.

Although much nearer topographically to Philadelphia than to Auburn, Maryland adopted the Auburn system, because a committee of the board of directors of the penitentiary had reported, after visiting several prisons in Pennsylvania and New York in 1828, that the Pennsylvania system was expensive in construction, presented difficulties in the supply of food and exercise, and fur-

---

[11] Jol. House of Delegates, 1822, p. 139.
[12] B. P. D. S., 1829, p. 264, 304, 324.
[13] Dix. Remarks, p. 47.
[14] Crawford. App., p. 94.

nished no mental occupation (this latter opinion being based on the earlier plan of solitary confinement without labor at the Eastern Penitentiary.)[15]

With the advent of the new building, the Auburn system was put into operation, but far less rigidly than in the parent institution. Indeed, an educational development of significance occurred, in the establishment of a general system of instruction of all convicts. All parts of the Sabbath Day not devoted to religious interests were devoted to secular study. From this mental occupation throughout the Sabbath resulted, according to the report of the prison board,[16] "the entire destruction of the improper indulgences and corrupt association, to which exemption from labor on Sunday afforded them more opportunity than on any other day." On week days also, the convicts were allowed to read and study, "after performing an amount of labor commensurate with the cost of their support."

The board reported as follows:

> "Convicts are not only capable of intellectual culture, but they gladly resort to the means of instruction . . . which incites to greater industry. Since the institution of our school, there has been less vice and immorality, and the aspect of the prisoners has been greatly improved. . . . We are confident that the only plan for effectuating the design of penal law is to blend productive labor with useful education."

This was an extremely modern statement for the period, and indeed, the Maryland penitentiary seemingly led the way in the extent of the scholastic education given to the inmates, among the prisons of the period.[17] This educational project lasted for several years. In 1833, there were 211 convicts in the Sabbath School who had originally been unable to read or write,[18] instructed by 10 volunteer teachers from the city. The colored convicts were especially appreciative of the school.

Crawford found in 1832 that the disciplinary measures of the prison were relatively rigorous. The lock-step was used in marching the prisoners in mass; there was the customary requirement of silence, and all heads must face in the same direction. Flogging was allowed as a punishment. The prisoners were shaved on one side of the head, which the Boston Prison Discipline Society reported in 1838 was "revolting," and not found in any other prison. The hair was thus half-shaven, until three weeks before the prisoner was to be discharged.

Nevertheless, the prisoners were able to communicate with each other, and sometimes the males with the females. Punishments were solitary confinement, or whipping, or both. Ordinarily five lashes, there could be given as many as 13, or 13 repeatedly. Solitary confinement was seldom for more than 10 or 12 days. The prisoners were never chained, shackled or fettered except for attempts to escape. Then a small yoke was worn about the neck.

---
[15] Report of Committee appointed by Board of Directors of Maryland Penitentiary, 1828, p. 8.
[16] B. P. D. S., 1831, p. 504.
[17] B. P. D. S., p. 504.
[18] B. P. D. S., 1833, p. 620.

The prison garb was of black and white alternate stripes, the material cotton and wool. The stripes were about one inch wide.

The prison had a hospital, a room 45 feet square, with cast-iron beds, and a small room used for cooking. The physician visited the prison nearly every morning. Two convicts acted as nurses. The convalescent patients could take the air, and exercise in the long corridor. Each new patient was vaccinated, and if the smallpox scare developed, the whole prison population. Insane patients were not removed to a hospital outside the prison. If they had not recovered by the expiration of their sentences, they might be retained at the prison.

Meanwhile, through the thirties, the industrial condition of the prison fluctuated seriously. In 1837 and 1838 there was a general derangement and prostration of the trade of the country.[19] The expenses over earnings of the prison were $16,934. Under the old law of 1817, an agent or storekeeper had been appointed to market the goods manufactured by the penitentiary through a store rented in Baltimore. It was ultimately found that it was impossible to compete with the commission merchants of the city on even terms, and so the prison was forced to sell to these same commission merchants at a discount exceeding the expense of rent of the store, and of the salaries of the agent and his assistant. In 1835 or thereabouts, the store was abandoned; the direct sales to commission merchants continued.[20]

However, discontent among the "mechanics" was brewing, and 1,300 citizens of Baltimore petitioned the House of Delegates in 1838 for the abolition of the penitentiary system, so far as it conflicted with the interest of mechanics.[21] In 1842, the directors of the penitentiary sent a special committee to study the industrial methods and problems of other Eastern prisons. The committee reported that the branches then conducted in the Maryland penitentiary did not conflict with the interests of local mechanics, while on the other hand nearly paying expenses. Vigorously opposing any introduction of the contract labor system into the Baltimore prison, the committee said, speaking of the labor troubles in New York:

"In this manner the State of New York has unguardedly created a privileged class in the community, and thereby established a principle particularly odious and intolerable to the mind and feelings of the people. . . . Articles furnished to the market (by the Maryland penitentiary) should be restricted to those classes that belong to the widest range of trade. In the main the articles produced are work of a kind not usually engaged in by citizens of the State."[22]

The end of the period we have been considering found, therefore, the prison in a serious industrial condition. Its earlier prosperous days were no more. From 1822 to 1839 it had operated so successfully that it had received no State aid, save appropriations for the salaries of officers, which were defrayed until 1828. From then on,

---

[19] B. P. D. S., 1839, p. 356.
[20] Report of Select Committee on the Penitentiary, 1836, p. 5.
[21] Jol. House of Delegates, 1836, p. 195.
[22] Report of Committee on Prison Manufactures, 1842, p. 13.

until 1838, the penitentiary met all its expenses of $69,215. It manufactured almost exclusively cotton and woolen cloth, which had a constant sale, with large profits. The mercantile crisis in 1837 brought serious depreciation in prices, and since then there had continued to be a gradual price depreciation, particularly in articles manufactured by hand-looms.

On the other hand, it was now, in 1842, apparently impracticable to further develop other branches in the penitentiary. Losses since 1838 had totalled $46,000. There was a diminution in the number of convicts being committed to the prison — and the "honest mechanic" was objecting impressively to the competition of prison-made goods in the open market.[23]

---

[23] Report of the Committee on Manufactures, 1842, pp. 4-5.

CHAPTER XVIII

VIRGINIA

That the State of Virginia, the "Mother of Presidents," should have built her State prison mainly according to plans furnished by Thomas Jefferson, when he was ambassador to France, is an interesting penological fact. Jefferson learned, while in Paris, of the novel plans of a French architect for a "well-contrived edifice on the solitary plan."[3] The drawings that Jefferson procured being too large, he redrew them on a smaller scale, and sent the plans to Virginia to those directors who had been commissioned by the Legislature to build the State Capitol and to devise a State prison plan.[1]

Thomas Jefferson had become sincerely interested, as early as 1776, in the reform of the criminal laws of Virginia. In a committee of the Legislature of that year, the drafting of a new criminal code fell to him. The committee agreed that the death penalty should be abolished except for treason and murder, and that for other felonies there should be established hard labor on the public works, and in some cases the *lex talionis*. "How this revolting principle came to obtain our approbation I do not remember," wrote Jefferson.

In 1785, the proposed code almost passed the House of Delegates, being beaten by only a solitary vote, the public rage against horse thievery killing the bill.

"In America the inhabitants let their horses go at large in the enclosed lands, which are so extensive as to maintain them together. It is easy, therefore, to steal them and easy to escape. Therefore the laws are obliged to oppose these temptations with a heavier degree of punishment. For this reason the stealing of a horse is punished more severely than stealing the same value in any other form."[2]

In 1796, the Legislature resumed the subject of a revision of criminal law and prison discipline, revised the penal laws after the model of Pennsylvania, and adopted solitary instead of public labor, as well as establishing a gradation in the duration of confinement.[4] The prison, begun in 1796 in Richmond, received its first prisoners in 1800. Its construction was unlike that of any other prison in this country. It was located on a high hill, about one mile south-west of the State House, and about two miles west of the James River.[5]

The cells were arranged in a brick building in the form of a crescent, two stories above the basement.[5] The cells were 12 feet

---

[1] Writings of Thomas Jefferson, Vol. 1, p. 58.
[2] Writings of Thomas Jefferson, Vol. 4, p. 158.
[3] Pettigrove, in " Correction and Prevention. Vol. II, p. 30.
[4] Writings of Thomas Jefferson, Vol. I, p. 64. (Edition edited by P. L. Ford. Putman's.)
[5] B. P. D. S., 1827, p. 128.

[210]

long, 6½ feet wide, and 9 feet high, with arched ceilings.[6] It is fair to infer from the size of the cells that it was originally intended, as Jefferson indicated, that each prisoner should labor in solitude in his cell. Not only did this *not* occur, but within five years of the opening of the prison, three or four prisoners were already being lodged together, and the evils of conspiracies, immorality, and mutual teaching of crime were already flourishing.[7]

Not until after 1823, when a disastrous fire caused necessary renovations to the prison building, were separate cells in sufficient numbers provided. In 1823, a Legislative committee reported that it was surprising that so few of the convicts died, when one reflected that they were almost totally deprived of healthy air, and literally crowded together at night in close and small rooms.[8] A year later, the directors reported that the Virginia penitentiary was so constructed as to permit unrestrained intercourse among the prisoners day and night. "It was both a prison and a workshop, in which the convicts worked in groups and slept in clusters."[9]

The Virginia "Jail and Penitentiary House" was both in location and construction a monumental blunder, which resulted in not only permanent and serious difficulties of administration, but in disease and death to the inmates. Established with high hopes of reformatory influences,[10] the prison was so located as to be later the center of an obnoxious, if not noxious atmosphere. The prison was thus described by a new and horrified superintendent, C. S. Morgan, in 1832:[11]

"The penitentiary is situated on an eminence between two rivers, that come together and empty into a canal, on the margin of the James River, into which all the filth of the prison and the western part of the city of Richmond is carried and deposited. This deposit increases annually, and is less than 200 yards from the prison buildings, and the river less than 400 yards. During the summer the water remains stagnant and full of putrid matter. The whole mass constantly casts off offensive miasma, wafted throughout the prison. . . . How could the Legislature devise a scheme of punishment more dreadful to the human mind, or less qualified to reform the moral condition of the offender?"

Morgan found over a dozen cells or dungeons designed for solitary confinement; these cells were dark, damp and underground. He found — a custom descending from the initial law of 1798 — that the inmates served a considerable portion of their sentences in such solitary confinement. The prison itself was so damp at times that moisture coagulated upon the walls,[12] and there was no method of heating any of the cells. Prisoners' feet had been frozen while in solitary confinement in the cells. These cells had been pronounced by Superintendent Morgan's predecessor, Superintendent Samuel L. Parsons, a Quaker originally from Philadelphia, imminently dangerous to health and sometimes to life. There were, according to Parsons, comparatively few prisoners whose constitu-

---

[6] Crawford. App.
[7] Jol. House of Delegates, 1805, p. 90.
[8] Jol. House of Delegates, 1823, Report of Penitentiary Comm.
[9] Jol. House of Delegates, 1823-24, Report of Directors, p. 31.
[10] Preamble to Amendment to Penal Laws, 1798.
[11] Report of Superintendent, Jol. House of Delegates, 1832-33, Document 1.
[12] B. P. D. S., 1827, p. 168.

tions were not injured by them. The ordinary cells in the first and second story were light and airy, but not warmed, and were exposed on two sides to the cold. Before the alterations of 1824, even these cells had been dark and close. To equip the prison with a heating system always seemed a prohibitive expense.

The design of the prison made the proper inspection by keepers almost impossible. The cell doors were of wood, preventing inspection at night. Yet prisoners could always communicate with each other. In winter, since both ends of the cell were exposed to the air, there was no convenient place for a sentinel to pass the night near the cells.[14] In 1824, for the first time, a wall was built around the prison, some 20 feet high, to prevent escapes. This resulted in a most serious interruption to the circulation of air throughout the buildings. In 1834, it was said by Superintendent Morgan that

"whether the prison be viewed as a mere engine of torture for offenses committed, or whether of terror to prevent crime, or whether it be viewed as a school to reform felons, or a manufacturing establishment to extract from the vicious the means to defray the expenses of their own punishment, humanity and the public interest alike demand a thorough examination and removal of the causes of misery, disease and mortality."[13]

Throughout its early history, the Virginia penitentiary had therefore a large death rate, which sometimes became appalling. Imprisonment within the limits of 100 yards square, and the causes above mentioned, had brought to the prison by Morgan's time a prevalence of disease that caused each prisoner, on the average, to be incarcerated in the hospital several times a year. The following was the death record from 1800 to 1832:

Period	Prisoners received	Prisoners died	Per cent died
1800–1810	450	22	5
1810–1820	603	58	10
1821–1830	625	163	26
1831–1832	88	68	77

The appalling climax was reached in 1832, when 39 prisoners were received and 47 prisoners died. It was, however, in this year that the cholera raged in the prison, with 147 cases, of which 27 terminated fatally.

Morgan knocked great windows into the outside walls, built a respectable hospital, and succeeded in getting the Legislature materially to lessen the periods of solitary confinement. The results were as follows:[15]

	Proportion of Deaths to Population.
1800 to 1824, at which time the high outer wall was built	1 to 10.5
1825 to 1833, during which the high wall stood	1 to 3.7
1834 to 1839	1 to 12.7

[13] Jol. House of Delegates, 1832-33, Document 1.
[14] B. P. D. S., 1827, p. 129.
[15] Jol. House of Delegates, 1838-1839, Document 1, Superintendent's Report.

There were, of course, other serious factors contributing to the high death rate of this institution. The inhumanly long periods of solitary confinement played a leading role in this tragedy. The law of 1796 provided — as did the Pennsylvania law — that each convict should pass not more than one-half nor less than one-twelfth of his sentence in solitary confinement. Whereas other States in general did not put this law into very serious effect, Virginia adhered to it with horrible fidelity, particularly during the long superintendency of Mr. Parsons. By law, the first six months were passed in a dark, labor-less inactivity. As the number of admissions grew, literal obedience to the solitary confinement section of the law became difficult. In 1815, Superintendent Parsons, recently appointed, advocated the abrogation of the law, because it could not be carried into effect, there being then only 6 solitary cells available.[16] The law, however, was not amended, and in 1824 Mr. Parsons stated that the lives of most of these prisoners, doomed to 6 months of uninterrupted and dark solitary confinement, were in imminent danger.[17] The solitary confinement law was nevertheless rigidly enforced.

At this time there was coupled therewith, as a severe depressant of hope in the prisoner's breast, an equally rigid enforcement of the law prohibiting the Governor from granting pardons. The hope of pardon had been in the earliest days of the Virginia institution an instrument leading to good conduct and a fair degree of health. We have already seen, in States like New York and Pennsylvania, to what an excessively liberal extent the chief executives of the States had exercised their demoralizing prerogative of pardon. Prison lost its terror and justice her power, in the eyes of the public, when criminals so easily regained their liberty. Therefore, in spite of the obvious tendency of the hope of pardon to stimulate the prisoner to good work[18] and good conduct, the power of pardon was through many years exercised with far too great liberality,[19] and in 1823 the Executive was deprived of the power of pardon.

In 1825, Superintendent Parsons traced the high mortality of the prison partly to the mental despair of the prisoner, cut off from hope of mercy, and doomed to serve the entire period of his sentence, *with* the required solitary confinement, but without the hope of executive clemency. Mr. Parsons reported:

"Whenever a convict sentenced for life has been seriously attacked by disease, he has sunk under it. There has not been a single instance where a convict, whose sentence was for life, ever recovered from indisposition. . . . Nothing has presented itself more destructive to the health and constitution of the convict than the six months' close and uninterrupted solitary confinement upon first reception. . . ."[20]

Parsons recommended the shortening of the period of solitary confinement on reception and the repetition of three months of solitary confinement immediately preceding the convict's discharge.

[16] Jol. House of Delegates, 1816, App.
[17] Jol. House of Delegates, 1824-25, Governor's Message, App. 5.
[18] Jol. House of Delegates, Governor's Message, 1807.
[19] Jol. House of Delegates, 1822-23. Report of Pen. Comm.
[20] Jol. House of Delegates, 1825-26, App., Superintendent's Report, p. 5.

The prison physician stated that the low diet (bread and water) in solitary confinement during six months produced scurvy and debilitated the system so that a prisoner hardly ever recovered from its effects. Apparently to offset the high death rate, he recommended that the sixth months' solitary confinement be at the close of the convict's term! Should the prisoner die afterwards, he would no longer be in prison!

In 1826 the Legislature lessened the initial period of solitary confinement to three months, and added a three months' period at the conclusion of the convict's term, which should be the bitter "crack of the whip," that would warn the convict never to commit crime again. In 1832, the Legislative committee advocated the entire abandonment of solitary confinement at the end of the prisoner's sentence. There was no substantial benefit from it. It was injurious to health. It obliterated habits of industry acquired in prison, and abstracted the best time and labor of the convicts.[21]

In 1833, the law was amended to provide that the amount of time passed, by sentence, in solitary confinement should not exceed one-twelfth of the entire sentence, and should not exceed one month at any time.[22] Morgan, the new superintendent, was opposed to solitary confinement at all, save for punishment for violation of prison rules. Each convict was now placed in solitary confinement for one week in each six months, and for an entire month during the last year of his term.[23] This reduced the total number of days of solitary confinement in 1835 to 2,719, as against 3,695 in the previous year.[24] In 1838, the Governor urged further decrease of such punishment, and in some cases its entire abolition. By 1840, the solitary confinement record for the year totalled only 399 days, about a tenth of what it was in 1834.[25]

We have presented in really gruesome detail the above only too gradual mitigation of solitary confinement in Virginia because it illustrates more graphically than we have found in any other State not only the cruelty, horror and danger to life of the practice, but also its futility. When prisoners were decreasingly subject to long periods of such treatment — and when the prison was ultimately "aired out"— health increased, and the annual mortality rate went down. But, at its lowest rate, the Virginia penitentiary still occupied a notorious place among American prisons. Superintendent Parsons claimed in 1829 that the high death rate in the Virginia penitentiary was due in recent years to ill health because of the cessation of pardons.[26] However, a comparison of the Virginia prison and the Connecticut State Prison at Wethersfield destroys the superintendent's argument, for in Connecticut also there was no exercise of executive clemency, and the pardonings of the Legislature were very infrequent.

---

[21] Jol. House of Delegates, 1832-33, Document 30.
[22] Jol. House of Delegates, 1833-34, Governor's Message, Document 1, p. 128.
[23] Jol. House of Delegates, 1834-35, Document 7.
[24] Jol. House of Delegates, 1835-36, Document 7.
[25] Jol. House of Delegates, 1840-41, Document 9.
[26] Jol. House of Delegates, 1828-29, App., p. 6.

Indeed, it is very difficult to find in the entire course of the administration of the Virginia penitentiary during the period from 1800 to 1844 any evidence of an enduring humanitarian effort to reform, or even to deal with prisoners according to the best principles of penal justice of the period. During the entire span of the 44 years under our study, there was no chaplain, nor were there any fairly regularly conducted Sabbath services until 1835.[27] Intermittent preaching was held, when local clergymen could be obtained. No Sabbath School was established, nor was secular instruction given in the three R's, though in more northern prisons this was common. Parsons reported in 1830 that there was no room in the prison large enough to assemble convicts in, and the prison yard was used in good weather.[28] He wrote in 1826: "The sole object of American prisons is not reformation." The belief that through reformatory influences prisoners would be regenerated and turned out into the community good and useful citizens had produced, according to Parsons, a sickly and mistaken administration of the American penitentiary system, teaching the convicts to believe that they were merely unfortunate beings (guilty of no crime), and real objects of commiseration, claiming benevolence beyond the necessities of the poor and honest members of society, who had committed no crime, and violated no law. There had been too much of a sickly and squeamish sympathy practiced in most of the prisons, wrote Parsons.[29]

The prison served, therefore, two purposes. It was a place of incarceration and deterrence, and also of industrial activity. Even by 1805 it was felt that the convicts should work harder. Earnings were not meeting expenses. Because of the commingling, day and night, of the prisoners, the penitentiary had few terrors for the indigent. The prison was placed in 1806 under the sole charge of the governor of the State, and a new keeper appointed. By 1807, great industrial activity was recorded and profits of nearly $8,000. The chief occupations were boots, shoes, wrought and cut nails. A sales agent was appointed. For some years, profits were reported. Within ten years, however, a Legislative committee reported that penitentiary institutions, "when conducted upon the mild and merciful principle that led to their establishment" could never be depended upon as sources of revenue to the State.[30] The estimated budget for the fiscal years, 1818-1819 showed:

DISBURSEMENTS.

For raw materials	$55,000
Salaries	3,400
Removing criminals to penitentiary from jail, etc.	5,500
	$63,900

RECEIPTS.

Sale of manufactured articles	'35,000
Deficit	$28,900

[27] Jol. House of Delegates, 1835-36, Document 7.
[28] B. P. D. S., 1830, p. 425.
[29] Jol. House of Delegates, 1826-27, App. 4.
[30] Jol. House of Delegates, 1818-19, p. 150.

Clearly, therefore, the profits announced by the prison in successive years were on the operations of the industries, and not, as in Connecticut for instance, upon a net surplus, after all expenses of the prison including salaries of officers, had been paid.

In 1817 the law was amended to provide that the Governor should appoint a board of directors, and two years later all powers formerly vested in the Governor were vested in them, the Legislature however electing the superintendent, which often caused divided authority between them.

The prison seems at no time to have been on an absolutely self-supporting basis. A comparative table presented by Superintendent Morgan in 1840 throws some light on the penitentiary operations:

1816-1820.

Cash paid into penitentiary by State, on manufacturing account..		$255,405 34
On account of expenses to buildings		11,317 76
		$266,723 10
Cash paid into State treasury by penitentiary from manufacturers		157,189 58
Deficit, 1816-1820		$109,533 52

1832-1840.

Paid by State treasury for operation of penitentiary		$98,332 00
Paid into State treasury by agents	$51,630 00	
Clothing furnished lunatic hospital	20,500 95	72,130 95
Balance against penitentiary account		$26,201 05
But—		
Other work done for State by penitentiary	$32,544 25	
Balance in favor of penitentiary from 1832-1840		6,343 20
	$32,544 25	$32,544 25

The Virginia Penitentiary seems to have had little influence upon other States. Indeed, it had little to suggest, save that which should be avoided. Its architecture was faulty. No other prison built upon its design. It was not self-supporting. It made no feature of reformation. It could not successfully conduct a silent system, because of the construction of the prison. Its death rate was abnormal. Its solitary cells and dungeons were places of horror. It maintained no chaplain nor Sunday School. Its Sabbath chapel was at best intermittent. Its location was unsanitary. In comparison with Auburn, Wethersfield, or the Eastern Penitentiary, it presented but a sorry figure for the State prison of the leading State of the South.

CHAPTER XIX

THE EASTERN PENITENTIARY OF PENNSYLVANIA
1829-1844

No prison in the United States has ever been such a storm-center in the discussion and development of prison reform as the Eastern Penitentiary of Pennsylvania, which received its first prisoner on October 5th, 1829. In a previous chapter * we have described its unique architectural feature — the radial "ranges" of cells, ramifying like seven spokes of a wheel from a common center. We have described the clearcut and definite penological principle upon which the prison was to be administered, namely, the absolute separation of all prisoners at all times from each other, with the accompanying separate industrial activity of each prisoner in his own cell.

As early as 1837, the prison had already become famous as the chief exponent of what was now known as the "Pennsylvania plan," both in the United States and in Europe. The prison was not only visited by representatives of other States planning to build new prisons, but was studied with especial care by delegations of official specialists from foreign countries, as Gustave de Beaumont and Alexis de Tocqueville of France (1831), William Crawford, secretary of the London Prison Discipline Society (1832), Doctor Julius of Prussia (1835), Mondelet and Neilson of lower Canada (1834), and De Metz and Blouet from France in 1836-37. Especially from the detailed descriptions and thoughtful criticisms and deductions of the above can a peculiarly comprehensive picture of the Eastern Penitentiary be reconstructed.

Convicts customarily entered their cells upon commitment to the Eastern Penitentiary, not to emerge therefrom until the day of their liberation from prison, unless in case of punishment, illness or death.[3] Exceptions to the rule were made infrequently, as in cases in which the convict was removed to work in an adjacent shop-cell, or to exercise himself alone in a yard, or even — as with Superintendent Wood in 1834 [1] — to wait on the table in his residence. Even under such circumstances, the inflexible rule was followed that no association of prisoners or communication with each other was tolerated.

The convict on his arrival at the prison was visited by the physician, who until the year 1842 was an attending physician, but after that in residence. After the medical inspection and a hot bath, the prison uniform was given to the new prisoner, not the

---
* Chapter XI.
[1] McElwell.
[3] Main features of the following description or routine from De Metz and Blouet, p. 28.

[217]

striped or motley uniform of the prisons on the Auburn plan, but clothing without humiliating or conspicuous pattern. Experience early proved the danger of escape to be almost negligible, and the necessity of a striped uniform as a distinguishing mark was not felt.

With bandaged eyes[2] the convict was led to the central rotunda or "observatory," where the superintendent spoke briefly to him of the purposes of the prison, and of its rules and methods. Thence, still blindfolded, the convict was led to his cell, over the door of which was a number, by which he was henceforth to be known. Within the cell, his eyes were unbandaged. If he was so fortunate as to have a cell on the ground floor, he could exercise at specified periods in the little adjacent yard, corresponding approximately in size to his cell, and entered by a door from his cell. Never would a prisoner from the next cell to the right or left exercise when he was in the open air, for then there might be communication.

During the first few days in his cell he was left almost entirely to himself, save when the officer brought him his meals. Without work or book he sat and thought, overwhelmed generally by the horror of the silent, impassive, powerful, monotonous, relentless engine of punishment of which he had become a helpless part. The solitude seemed insufferable. He felt that he could never endure his sentence; that he must certainly die before his time of liberation should come.[4]

After a few days the prisoner was asked if he desired some work, an offer generally eagerly accepted. If the prisoner had a trade, he was customarily allowed to follow it in prison. In retrospect, most prisoners testified that "they would have died if they had not been permitted to work."[5] Sunday seemed interminably long, because no work was allowed on that day. Work thus became an opportunity — a favor granted by the prison to well-behaved and industrious inmates, whereas in the prisons of the Auburn type work there was a painful, daily enforced task, to which the prisoner had to be driven on pain of punishment.[6]

The prisoner at the Eastern Penitentiary was, however, obliged to choose between being placed at work or in a dark cell. There was no simple option of working *more* or working *less*. His choice was seldom long in suspense, and he chose work.[7]

The Bible also became a document of interest to the prisoner, because his possession of it was a favor during his good behavior. The infrequent visit of the moral instructor, or of some visitor from the outside world, might be lengthened or made more frequent if the prisoner would try to learn to read from the Bible as a text-book. Moreover, any visit from an officer came to have an intense meaning to the prisoner. Such visits alone connected him with the world of living beings. One prisoner was cited by the Prussian

---

[2] According to Julius the prisoner was not blindfolded, but his head was covered with a hood. Julius. S. Z., p. 190.
[4] de Beaumont and de Tocqueville, p. 197.
[5] Same, p. 188.
[6] Same, p. 24.
[7] Same, p. 40.

visitor, Doctor Julius, as saying that his greatest joy was the visit of a cricket or a butterfly because it seemed like company.[9] No communication with family or friends was ordinarily allowed the convict. Julius found, several years after Crawford's visit, that, very exceptionally, the convict might be allowed to write his family about himself, but that he was never permitted to hear from them.[10]

So absolutely was the news of the outside world excluded, that months after the cholera raged in Philadelphia in 1832, the inmates were still unaware that the epidemic had occurred.[8] Not one case of Asiatic cholera appeared in the Penitentiary, although the disease swept away numbers in the city. The sole visitors to the prisoner were the inspectors, the superintendent, the doctor, the moral instructor, the employees designated for that purpose, and the official visitors — who undoubtedly appeared seldom at the prison, and were the governor of the State, the members of the Legislature (represented by a committee who visited during the Legislative session) the Secretary of State, the judges of the Supreme Court, the attorney general and his deputies, and the mayors and recorders of Philadelphia, Lancaster and Pittsburg. The active committee of the Philadelphia Society for Alleviating the Miseries of Public Prisons visited frequently, and had the legal power of entrance.[11]

Therefore, the prison was not an institution where the convicts were absolutely isolated. Only from other inmates were they relentlessly separated. Heavy fines might be imposed upon a visitor who smuggled in a letter to an inmate, or acted as a means of communication between the inmates. No favors of food were granted; a prisoner, unless ill, must subsist only from prison rations. No tobacco, wine or beer was permitted.

The prisoner arose at daybreak, or in summer between 4.30 and 5. He went to bed between 9 and 10 in the evening. In winter he worked after dark by lamplight, if his skill were sufficient to warrant the prison the extra expenditure of light. The prisoner received three meals a day, breakfast at 7, dinner at 12, and supper at 6.[13]

Combe gave in his "Notes on the United States" the diet of the prisoners. The men received for breakfast: 1 pint of coffee or cocoa; for dinner ¾ lb. of boiled beef without bone, or ½ lb. pork, 1 pint soup and ample potatoes. For supper they had mush *ad libitum*. They received ½ gallon of molasses per month, salt when asked for, and vinegar as a favor. Sometimes they had turnips and cabbages in the form of "crout." They also received 1 lb. of bread per day, made of wheat or rye.

If the prisoner was sick, he was removed to a solitary infirmary cell, where his diet was scanty, and where there was no greater chance of communication with other inmates than in his own cell.

---
[8] Crawford, p. 11.
[9] Julius. "Sittleche Zusbaende," Vol. II, p. 252.
[10] Same, p. 191.
[11] De Metz and Blouet, p. 28.
[13] De Metz and Blouet, p. 24.

If the prisoner became very sick, the door of his infirmary cell was left open, and an attendant on watch passed from one cell to another.

All prisoners were subjected to the same regime. One day was wholly like another. No compensation was, until the year 1841, allowed the prisoner, save approbation for good conduct or good work. After 1840, over-stint was allowed. As soon as the prisoner became proficient, a moderate task, estimated at the actual cost of his maintenance was required of him. The balance of his labor was credited to him, the amount being paid on his release from prison. In 1841, $884.22 was thus expended for 31 prisoners on discharge, an average of $28.52. In 1842, the over-stint amounted to $955.54.

The inspectors of the prison were appointed for two years by Supreme Court judges; they elected their own president, secretary and treasurer. They must be property holders, and live in the county of Philadelphia. They received no salary, but were free of military and jury duty and poor duty.[14]

The stimulus to good behavior and industry was during the first eleven years (1829-1840) based on the fear of deprivation of the privileges of labor, on moral literature, and on fear of positive punishments, ranging from reduction in diet to the extremes of the straight jacket, the shower-bath and the gag. The general behavior of the convicts was undoubtedly very satisfactory. The majority of the inmates seemed "resigned, if not happy" after the first horror of separate confinement had diminished or departed.[12] The philosophy of the board of inspectors and of the superintendent was, a year from the opening of the prison, as follows:[15]

"The character of the convict is generally social, to a fault. The vices of social life have heralded the ruin of his fortune and his hopes, and, when deprived of the society of his companions in vicious indulgences and guilt, he reads and listens with eagerness, because he is relieved by the variety from the weariness of his solitude. There he can only read and hear what is calculated to make him industrious and virtuous.

"Personal vanity, which often leads the prisoner to value himself upon being regarded by his neighbors as a 'staunch man,' there deserts him, for there is no one to applaud, admire or see him. In the presence of those who are allowed to visit him, no vanity that is not praiseworthy can be indulged. Hence, this mode of punishment, bearing as it does with great severity upon the hardened and impenitent felon, is eminently calculated to break down his obdurate spirit.

"And when the prisoner has once experienced the operation of the principles of this institution on a broken spirit and a contrite heart, he learns, and he feels, that moral and religious reflection, relieved by industrious occupation at his trade, comfort and support his mental and physical powers, divest his solitary cell of all its horrors, and his punishment of much of its severity.

In 1831, during a period of three months, only two instances were recorded for which even a meal had been forfeited for bad conduct.[16] In 1834, the inspectors declared that the penitentiary

---

[12] Board of Inspectors, 1830, p. 17.
[14] Same.
[15] Board of Inspectors, 1830, p. 10.
[16] Board of Inspectors, 1831, p. 9.

system was emphatically a mild and humane discipline.[17] It was a system of privations rather than of punishments.[18] De Beaumont and de Tocqueville stated in 1832 that there was in the Eastern Penitentiary no punishment, because there was no infraction of the rules.[19] The French investigators found that in Auburn the prisoners were treated much more severely, but that at Philadelphia they were much more unhappy.[20] William Crawford, the English specialist, bore similar testimony in 1834 to the mildness of the discipline.[21] In 1835, there occurred, however, a serious Legislative investigation of the Eastern Penitentiary. Sweeping charges of cruelty and immorality on the part of the superintendent and lesser officials were made by the attorney general of the State. An investigation, extending over several months, was held by a Legislative committee, resulting in the spring of 1835 in a majority report and a minority report.[22]

The following findings were common to both reports:

No charge of immorality on the part of the superintendent was proved.

Physical punishments of a severe nature were at times employed. Buckets of cold water had been thrown in the winter time upon an inmate with filthy habits. This inmate was probably insane. The gag had been used upon a prisoner — also probably insane — and the said prisoner had suddenly died under the process. The straightjacket was used at times with refractory prisoners.

Convicts were not infrequently employed outside their cells, on operations such as cooking, breaking coal, making fires, and occasionally as waiters, and in work connected with building and construction of cells. These convicts did not work in association.

The main issue between the majority and minority reports of the committee was as to the degree of severity of the punishments employed. The majority report was extenuating and apologetic, finding the harsh physical punishments, as employed at the prison, duplicated in insane asylums and in the United States Navy. The minority report expressed horror at the frequency of the extreme punishments. The minority report regarded the majority report as a whitewash.

The investigation demonstrated that the Eastern Penitentiary administered a graded system of punishments.[23] The first and mildest punishment was a deprivation of the use of the exercise yard by the convict for a given period. The second stage of punishment included the forfeiture of a dinner for a period of from two to three weeks — in other words, a serious reduction in rations. For severer cases, the dark cell was employed; this being an ordinary cell from which light was totally excluded. Often even the single blanket was denied the prisoner. Every twenty-four hours the convict received eight ounces of bread and some water.[24] His

---

[17] Board of Inspectors, 1834, p. 4.
[18] Board of Inspectors, 1834, p. 9.
[19] de Beaumont and de Tocqueville, p. 40.
[20] de Beaumont and de Tocqueville, p. 46.
[21] Crawford, p. .....
[22] Report of Joint Committee of Legislation in relation to Eastern Penitentiary of Pennsylvania, 1835.
[23] McElwell, p. 15ff for description of punishments here summarized.
[24] According to Julius (S. Z., p. 192), one and one-half pounds bread and one pint of water every twenty-four hours.

sufferings were intense, especially in cold weather. One convict had been held in the dark cell for forty-two days, and was suffering from starvation and delirium when taken out.

The next degree of punishment in an ascending scale was the absolute deprivation of food, for a period of not over three days. A further stage was reached with the infliction of "ducking," in which process the convict was suspended from the yard wall by the wrists, and drenched with buckets of cold water, the degree of severity of which depended upon the state of the atmosphere.

The "mad or tranquilizing chair" was another instrument of corporal punishment. It was a large box-chair made of planks. The convict was strapped in the chair and his hands were hand-cuffed. For the feet there was no resting place. It was not possible to move body or limbs, and the consequent pain was intense. Arms and legs swelled frightfully. Even while in this position prisoners had been beaten.

The "straight-jacket," another punishment, was a sack or bagging cloth of three thicknesses, with pocketholes in the front for the admission of the hands. In the back there were rows of eyelets, whereby the jacket might be laced up. The jacket was forced over the head of the convict, and his hands were inserted in the pockets; a collar was fitted about the neck, but the head was left free. The jacket was kept upon the prisoner for from four to nine hours. Convicts in the Eastern Penitentiary had been so tightly laced into the jacket that their necks and faces were black with congealed blood. The torture could be made excruciating. One convict was reported to have lost the use of his hand. Men of the stoutest nerve would shriek as if on the rack.

The "gag" was the severest and most complicated of the punishments. It was under this treatment that an insane convict died, thus precipitating the investigation. The gag resembled the stiff bit of a bridle, having an iron "palet" or mouthpiece in the center, and chains at each end. It was placed in the mouth of the sufferer, and drawn tightly toward the jaws, the chains being fastened in a lock. The prisoner's hands were placed in leather gloves which had iron staples in them, through which staples leather straps were introduced, and his arms were crossed behind his back. Other straps were passed around his hands, and then passed between the chains of the gag and the back of his neck. Now his hands were forcibly drawn up to his shoulders, and his head drawn back, this tightening the gag in the mouth, and rendering the agony intolerable. The bits and chains, passing with force against the veins and arteries, necessarily produced a suffusion of blood to the head, and the sufferer, if not speedily relieved, was in great danger of death.

After the investigation, the severer physical punishments were apparently abandoned. The majority report had found the ducking process "indiscreet," but discovered no evidences of intentional cruelty. The committee stated that the cold shower-bath was frequently employed in the best establishments for the insane as a disciplinary and curative measure. The thirteen buckets of cold water with which the convict in question was drenched had succeeded in breaking him of his filthy habits.

Nor was the use of the gag unusual, the navy being cited. It was frequently used in the Eastern Penitentiary, and the committee regarded it therefore as *not unusual*. It had not been considered by the attending physician, Doctor Bache, as cruel, and therefore the gag was held to be *neither cruel nor unusual*. The gag was not naturally calculated to produce death, and therefore the relation of the punishment of the convict in question and his death was not that of cause and effect. By such reasoning did the committee exculpate the administration.

Nevertheless, the disciplinary methods of the Eastern Penitentiary should not be judged by present standards of estimating punishments. The age in which the Eastern Penitentiary was founded was one of standarized cruelty in discipline. Both the British and American navies were rigorous in corporal punishment. If free seamen were thus flogged and otherwise punished, should convicted malefactors and most desperate criminals be let off more easily? The dark cell seemed a mild and humanitarian substitute for corporal punishment. Indeed, the Boston Prison Discipline Society in the first ten or fifteen years of its existence took no clear-cut stand against the floggings and other harsh disciplinary measures of the Auburn system. Even Dorothea Dix was reluctantly obliged to concede the necessity of flogging the most refractory prisoners.

The list of corporal punishments, outlined above, is for the sensitive student of to-day most painful reading. And it is not pleasant to realize that only within the last few years, even in the State of New York, has the severer punishment of the dark cell and the "cooler," a synonym for the dark cell, been abandoned in the prisons. Less than ten years ago the writer saw men on the verge of collapse in the dark cells in the Penitentiary of the City of New York. Mr. Osborne undergoing a week's imprisonment in 1913, in Auburn Prison, in order to acquaint himself with the routine life of the inmates in that year, was put into the "dungeon" and subjected to cruelties of treatment that horrified the State when published. It is still more or less customary in some prisons to stand recalcitrant prisoners up in a cage so constructed that they cannot sit down. Corporal punishment, floggings, chaining prisoners to the wall, stringing up so that the toes barely touch the floor, and similar semi-tortures, are still from time to time announced in investigations, and in the statements of inmates or discharged prisoners.

The fact is, in many cases, that the will to administer a prison on humanitarian lines, and the intention to inflict severe discipline upon those inmates who will not conform to such humane administration, goes hand in hand. Repeatedly, wardens were found, in the prisons of a decade ago, who were men of standing in the community, men of ideals, and yet who practiced severe punishments as a part of the necessary conduct of a prison. It was not paradoxical so much as it was traditional. The customs had been handed down, and had the sanction of long usage, and frequently of law. The warden, generally politically appointed, and aware that his term was bounded partly by the fate of his political party, was not inclined to be rebellious against tradition, but on the other hand was inclined to continue the practices which, however abhorrent to him at first, were regarded by the officials of the prison as necessary and as a part of the customs of the prison that the warden must "stand for."

It was the gradual introduction of the honor system, which individualized the treatment of prisoners as no previous methods had, that by its very nature reduced the use of physical and severe punishments, because it forcibly impressed upon warden and officials alike the fact of the humanness of the inmate, and his potential capacities to be like other men. It is relatively easy to punish persons out of a mass, but hard to punish the individual when he stands clearly by himself. While to know all, in prison, has not been to pardon all, in accordance with the French adage, it is a fact that to know much more of the prisoner has resulted in the recognition that punishment is one of the most futile methods of achieving permanent change, as compared with the systematic and intelligent use of privileges and deprivations, and the stimulus of personal ambition and the desire for proper gain.

Therefore we find at the Eastern Penitentiary a generally mild and benevolent administration, coupled with the occasional use of literally horrible tortures. Samuel L. Wood, the warden, was a Quaker of high standing. Indeed, the Legislative committee found Wood even too liberal in his relaxation of the prison rules, in the cases of convicts who seemed to need exercise or outdoor employment, and when constant cell confinement appeared too arduous. The committee held that any association of a convict even with someone not a convict while at work — as with a civilian blacksmith — was contrary to the law requiring constant separate confinement.[25]

The administration weathered thus the stormy year of 1835. From this year until 1840, when Mr. Wood resigned, the discipline seems to have gone forward without serious friction. Harriet Martineau, an English woman, wrote in her "Society in America," published in 1837 in New York, that she had, in her visits to the cells at the Eastern Penitentiary, been favored with the confidence of a great number of the prisoners, every one of whom told her (not being aware of the existence of the other prisoners) that he was under obligation to those who had charge of him for treating him with respect.

In 1838 a moral instructor was appointed. The original law of 1829 had provided for an unsalaried chaplain, which office the administration found it impossible to fill because of the entire lack of provision for a salary. Despite the frequent and devoted visits

---

[25] Report of Joint Committtee, 1835, p. 22.

of several clergymen, the need of systematic moral and religious training of the convicts was repeatedly urged by the prison board and the warden. The Legislature was obdurate for nearly ten years. George Combe, the noted Scotch phrenologist, visited this prison in January, 1839. He wrote:

"No single circumstance in the history of Pennsylvania indicates the low state of general information among the people more strongly than the extraordinary fact that after erecting this penitentiary at great expense, the Legislature continues insensible to every entreaty of its legal guardians to be furnished with adequate means of moral and religious instruction of the prisoners."

When finally the salaried office of "moral instructor" was created — and filled by a former Baptist minister — many petitions of citizens urged the Legislature to discontinue the office for fear of proselyting. The excellent moral results upon the prisoners, keenly desirous of human company, caused the Legislature of 1839 not to yield to the importunate citizens.

A striking testimony to the good order and the quiet atmosphere of the Eastern Penitentiary came from an unexpected source in 1843, when two members of the board of managers of Sing Sing Prison, who had officially visited the Philadelphia institution, reported that [26]

"they were forcibly struck with the contrast and order that prevailed at the Eastern Penitentiary, and the confusion and discord that reign here (at Sing Sing). There, at the Eastern Penitentiary, are seen none of the evils which were witnessed at our prison. There was abundant opportunity for thought and reflection. No scenes of riot diverted the convicts' minds from the thought of the crimes they had committed, or the ruin they had brought on themselves.

"The humble and the penitent incurred no hazard of being compelled to transgress even in the place of their punishment. The last moments of the dying man were not disturbed by ribald songs or abominable blasphemy. The vicious held no supremacy there. No assaults upon the officers, no battles among the wretched inmates, were permitted to break the quiet of that prison house. No opportunities were afforded to the veteran criminal of extending the corruption of service among the weak and the timid.

"No inducements were held out to the hardened to defy all control and set an example of disorder and disobedience. Heaven's first law — that of order — reigned there; and while in the solitary system was seen the hazard of stultifying the mind, that evil could hardly be deemed greater than the certainty, in our prison, of corrupting the heart and destroying the moral sense."

Striking testimony of a similar character was given by Captain Maryatt, quoting a prisoner at the Eastern Penitentiary who had served a term at Sing Sing: [27]

"In Sing Sing the punishment is corporal — here it is more mental. In Sing Sing there was little chance of a person's reformation, as the treatment was harsh and brutal, and the feelings of the prisoners were those of indignation and resentment. Their whole time was occupied in trying how they could deceive their keepers, and communicate with each other by variety of stratagem. Here a man was left to his own reflection, and at the same time he was treated like a man. Here he was his own tormentor; when there, he was quite as much wronged himself. . . . At Sing Sing there was great injustice and no redress. The infirm man was put to equal labor with the robust, and punished if he did not perform as much. The flogging was very severe at Sing Sing."

---

[26] Annual Report of Inspectors of Mount Pleasant Prison
[27] Diary in America, Vol. II, pp. 264-269.

In 1844, the cultural work of the Eastern Penitentiary was extended by the addition of a school teacher, and ample time was given to moral and secular instruction.[28] A library of useful books was established. Six gardens were being constructed, thus furnishing employment for twelve invalids, half a day each. Between 400 and 500 bushels of tomatoes, for prison fare use, were one of the products. Vegetables as well as flowers were also reared by many of the convicts in their own airing yards, and were thus "made the instruments of productive and very interesting amusements."[29] Lights were allowed in the cells of inmates until nine o'clock in most cases. An innovation was introduced in the form of congregational singing by the convicts in their own cells, as an uplifting feature, but it is recorded that officers "in socks" spied in the corridors to observe and prevent any communication between convicts under cover of the sound.[30]

Richard Vaux, who was the president of the board of inspectors of the Penitentiary, wrote that the period from 1829 to 1849 was one of experiment and experience.[31] The period that we are now considering is almost coincident with that of Vaux. Let us seek to analyze the results of the first fifteen years, during which period the principles and methods of this world-famous prison had become substantially fixed. Nowhere else in the country were the friends of prison reform so philosophically inclined, or in the aggregate so humanely disposed. The Philadelphia Society for Alleviating the Miseries of Public Prisons was already an old and established society, with power to enter for benevolent purposes the prisons of the State. Its membership was undoubtedly largely from the Society of Friends. The board of inspectors was composed mainly of Quakers. The superintendent was a Quaker. Quaker influence was strong in the State Legislature. The field represented by the Eastern Penitentiary was, in short, broadly open for the development, under the most favorable auspices, of a wise and philosophically grounded prison system. The Quakers had championed the Pennsylvania system, and did not hesitate to defend it.

The establishment of the Eastern Penitentiary was followed by a curious, and in many respects a most unfortunate, development in American prison theory and methods. As we have seen in previous chapters of this study, two prison systems, the Auburn and the Pennsylvania systems, took shape, and became bitter rivals. Each system adhered to a certain basic principle, namely, that prisoners should be kept from all communication with each other, but the systems differed, in that Auburn used silence as the medium of separation, and Philadelphia used the actual physical separation of inmates at all times. This fundamental difference of method, and other differences less material, might have been made the subject of friendly and constructive discussion, and perhaps of ultimate

---

[28] Report of Inspectors, 1844, p. 15.
[29] Report of Inspectors, 1844, p. 36.
[30] Report of Inspectors, 1844, p. 23.
[31] Report of Inspectors, 1844, p. 85.

readjustment and compromise into a third system, had there not been injected into the situation, in 1826, by the establishment of the Boston Prison Discipline Society, an element of militant and contentious advocacy of the Auburn system at all costs that grew, with the founding of the Eastern Penitentiary, into a violent and acrimonious campaign against the Pennsylvania system, even before it had had a fair chance to get started.

Both Philadelphia and Boston had now societies for prison reform, but with a basic difference in constitution. The Philadelphia society was a mutual organization, in which there seemed to be a general high level of interest and intelligence. The Boston society was practically one man, the Reverend Louis Dwight, who was indefatigable, and pursued both prison reform and the Philadelphia group with almost equal persistence. The Philadelphia society was pacifistic and didn't like a fight. Dwight was a born missionary, with the militant spirit strongly developed in what he believed to be a righteous cause. The Philadelphia society published no journal of information or propaganda, relying upon the annual reports of the inspectors of the Eastern Penitentiary to interpret that system. The Boston Society's annual reports gave fine chance for pamphleteering, and Dwight was a zealous, untiring, an unreserved adherent of the system he had espoused, almost with deliberate blindness, seeing for many years no faults in a faulty system. The Boston Prison Discipline Society's annual reports were the only documents of the period in which the progress, methods and statistics of American prisons were compiled. Naturally, Dwight's personal slant on the American prison methods colored the choice and the display of the yearly descriptions of American penal institutions, and of the development of American methods.

Consequently, these annual publications, coming out of Boston, became for practically all save the adherents of the Pennsylvania system authoritative in a period when prisons were a relatively new and serious problem in all American States. Legislatures purchased copies of Dwight's reports by the hundreds, and circulated them as penal truth. The annual reports were otherwise distributed far and wide. Dwight became the high national expert on prisons. His society — which meant him himself — furnished documents wherever new prisons were being planned. There was no such counter-diligence coming out of Philadelphia. Dwight traveled extensively. He advised, and appeared before, Legislatures and committees, and wherever he went he was a bitter and outspoken opponent of the Pennsylvania system. It is probably not too much to say that this one man in large measure conditioned the form of prison structure and method adopted in many an American State, and consequently lasting down almost to the present day.

Dwight's platform on prison management was simple. Auburn, in the first place, was a model for the world. A prison should be economically built, and economically administered. A prison should support itself from the labor of the convicts. Prisons should have a low death rate. Prisons should render impossible the communication of prisoners with each other.

The opening of the Eastern Penitentiary challenged not only Dwight's sober judgment, but aroused in him nothing less than what the psychologists to-day would call an emotional complex. They were doing in Philadelphia just what he had staked his reputation on denying as a policy. The Eastern Penitentiary had proved by far the costliest of all the American prisons to build. It would, in his opinion, be equally expensive to administer. By the constant isolation of the convicts, it had raised a system that denied the supremacy of the Auburn methods. Its architectural layout was wholly different from that of Auburn. It was heretical! And so, as the years came and went, Dwight inserted into the reports of the Boston Society conclusions that were little short of deliberately misleading regarding the institution in Philadelphia.

Meanwhile, a considerable amount of literature was growing up relative to principles and methods in sound prison discipline. England, France, Germany, Sweden, Holland, Switzerland and Italy were seeking light. The conditions of promiscuous association of prisoners were similar in Europe to those in the American prisons, that the Auburn and the Pennsylvania systems aimed to abolish. There existed on the one hand a continuing correspondence between English prison reformers and representative Americans with similar interests, particularly in Philadelphia. The London Society of Prison Discipline published an annual report that was somewhat circulated in America, and carried occasional references to American prisons. The early successes of Walnut Street, from 1790 to 1800, had been enthusiastically heralded in Europe by the Duc de La Rochefoucauld-Liancourt. In England, the London Society, in France the thinkers on prison administration like Charles Lucas and Moreau-Christophe, in Belgium Ducpetiaux, and in Prussia Doctor Julius, were propagandists for some fundamental prison reforms. They were all searching for the latest and best, and so when Auburn and the Eastern Penitentiary were established and heralded as successful innovations in this complicated field, they straightway planned to visit American prisons either personally or through representatives.

They came to this country in the thirties and they found the two rival systems operating, one, the Auburn, indigenous, invented by Captain Brittin, or Captain Lynds, or Mr. Cray, all of Auburn, and on the other hand the Pennsylvania system, a product of the Philadelphians, but with the architectural plans of Haviland, an English architect, and copied from earlier English prisons.

On the return of the several representatives to their own countries, they published comprehensive accounts of their American studies. During the twenty years from 1840 to 1860 it might almost be said that the question of the relative merits of the Auburn and the Pennsylvania systems was transferred, in the matter of discussion and heated argument to Europe.[32] A new

---

[32] Foulke. Remarks on Cellular Separation, p. 2.

literature seemed to be forming. Many European authors wrote exhaustively on the subject who had never visited this country, and who had never seen the prisons they so warmly described and discussed. Finally, in 1846, a first international prison congress convened at Frankfort on the Main, at the invitation of German specialists in prison discipline. The entire session of several days was devoted to the discussion of the invariable question, the relative merits of the two American systems. This problem was regarded as fundamental, and something that must be settled for Europe, because almost all Europe was building prisons. It is amusing, in a way, to think that while it was impossible to gather in this country a group of people to determine the relative merits of the two systems in open discussion and with scientific mind, Europe became the verbal battleground for the settlement of our own problems, so far as a settlement was possible.

The two systems were analyzed acutely at this conference, as they had never been analyzed at home. Dwight of Boston was the only American present, but beyond briefly stating at one session the chief activities of the Boston Society, he took no further part in the discussions, which were conducted in German, French and English.

But we are getting ahead of our study, chronologically. In 1832, Gustave de Beaumont and Alexis de Tocqueville published in Paris their famous treatise "On the Penitentiary System in the United States," which was translated into English by Francis Lieber in 1833 and published in Philadelphia. This work, crowned by the French Academy, was the first of a number of careful and scholarly studies of American prisons published by foreign students during the period of 1830-1840, after personal investigation of our prisons.

De Beaumont and de Tocqueville visiting the United States in 1831, found that solitude, applied to the criminal in order to conduct him to reformation by reflection, rested upon a philosophical and true conception.[33] Pennsylvania had adopted a system which at the same time agreed with the austerity of her manners, and her philanthropic sensibility. The penitentiary at Cherry Hill (the Eastern Penitentiary) was a combination of the principle first tried at the Western Penitentiary in Pittsburg (solitude without labor) and that of Auburn (association in silence during the day).[34] The Frenchmen found, as a basis for the Pennsylvania system, that while there were similar punishments and crimes called by the same name, there were no two beings equal in regard to their morals; and every time that convicts were put together, there existed necessarily a fatal influence of some convicts upon others, because, in the association of the wicked, it was not the less guilty who acted on the more criminal, but the more depraved who influenced those who were less so. The prison must, therefore, since it was impossible to classify prisoners, come to a separation of all.[35]

[33] de Beaumont and de Tocqueville, p. 3.
[34] de Beaumont and de Tocqueville, p. 10.
[35] de Beaumont and de Tocqueville, p. 21.

If it was true that all evil in prison originated from the intercourse of the prisoners among themselves, it followed that nowhere was this vice avoided with greater safety than in Philadelphia.[36]

Perpetual seclusion in a cell was an irresistible fact, which curbed the prisoner without a struggle, and thus deprived altogether his submission of a moral character (by which the authors seemed to mean that there was no clash of emotions and circumstances such as would cause the ultimate yielding of the prisoner to the principles of the prison as a result of the mastery of self, through the recognition of the justice of the position taken by the prison). The French critics found that the prisoner obeyed much less the established discipline, than the physical impossibility of acting otherwise. On the other hand, the Auburn system gave to the prisoners the "habits of society" (that is, the painfulness of compulsory labor, the necessity of laboring, and the necessity of obedience to authority).[37]

While the Pennsylvania system had often been reproached with rendering labor by the prisoners impossible, and while in truth a great many arts could not be pursued by a single workman in a narrow place to advantage, nevertheless the penitentiary of Philadelphia showed that the various occupations that could be pursued by isolated men were sufficiently numerous to occupy them usefully.[38] The Pennsylvania system was expensive, but not difficult to establish, and once established, the simplicity of its methods would enable it to run itself.[39]

At Auburn, continued the French critics, the prisoners were more severely treated; at Philadelphia they were more unhappy. At Auburn, where they were whipped, they died less frequently than at Philadelphia where, for humanity's sake, they were put in a solitary and sombre cell.[40] De Beaumont and de Tocqueville did not hesitate to state their conviction that the system of perpetual and absolute seclusion, established in Philadelphia in full vigor, would prove less favorable to the health of the inmates than would the Auburn system.[44]

On the other hand, the moral situation in which the convicts were placed was eminently calculated to facilitate their regeneration. The system seemed especially powerful over individuals endowed with some elevation of mind. The absolute solitude produced the deepest impression on all prisoners.[41] They were particularly accessible to religious sentiments. It was hard for anyone enjoying the ordinary intercourse of free society to feel the whole value of a religious idea thrown into the lonesome cell of a convict.[42] Could there be a combination for reformation more powerful than that of a prison which handed over to a prisoner all the trials of solitude, while it led him through reflection to

---
[36] de Beaumont and de Tocqueville, p. 23.
[37] de Beaumont and de Tocqueville, p. 24.
[38] de Beaumont and de Tocqueville, p. 34.
[39] de Beaumont and de Tocqueville, p. 40.
[40] de Beaumont and de Tocqueville, p. 47.
[44] de Beaumont and de Tocqueville, p. 47.
[41] de Beaumont and de Tocqueville, p. 50.
[42] de Beaumont and de Tocqueville, p. 51.

remorse, through religion to hope — a prison which made him industrious by the burden of idleness, and which, while it inflicted the torment of solitude, made him find a charm in the converse of pious men, whom otherwise he would have seen with indifference, and heard without pleasure? Without doubt the impression on the criminal was deep; experience alone would show whether the impression was durable. It was to be questioned whether the sudden transition, at the end of the prisoner's term from the solitary cell to the busy outside world might not be demoralizing. Yet that disadvantage was offset by the advantage that the prisoners, not having seen each other or known each other in prison, would not know each others' faces afterwards.[48]

Did the Pennsylvania system reform? De Beaumont and de Toqueville emphasized in their answer to this question an important fact. What was meant by "reformation"? In a literal and specific sense, it meant the radical change of a wicked person into an honest man — a change that produced virtues instead of vices. *Such reformation, spiritual and all encompassing, must be very rare,* more infrequent, indeed, than even the chaplains of American prisons believed. Such thorough-going conversions might occur here and there, but there existed no human agency of proving this complete reformation.[45] Nevertheless, the French critics pointed out that at Auburn, one-third of the pardons were given on the presumption of such reformation.

"The theories on the reform of the prisoners are vague and uncertain," wrote de B. and de T. "It is not yet known to what degree the wicked may be regenerated, and by what means this regeneration may be obtained." (de B. & de T., p. 49.)

Of a different kind of reformation, less thorough, but yet useful to society, there were many instances:[46]

"Perhaps leaving the prison he is not an honest man, but he has contracted honest habits. He was an idler; now he knows how to work. His ignorance prevented him from pursuing a useful occupation; now he knows how to read and write; and the trade which he has learned in the prison furnishes him the means of existence which formerly he had not. Without loving virtue, he may detest the crime of which he has suffered the cruel consequences. And if he is not more virtuous, he has become at least more judicious; his morality is not honor, but interest. His religious faith is perhaps neither lively nor deep; but even supposing that religion has not touched his heart, his mind has contracted habits of order, and he possesses rules for his conduct in life. Without having a powerful religious conviction, he has acquired a taste for moral principles which religion affords; finally, if he has not become in truth better, he is at least more obedient to the laws, and that is all that society has the right to demand."

The French critics found, in brief, that the Pennsylvania system would afford more reformation than that of Auburn. The latter was more conformable to the habits of men in society, and effected a greater number of reformations of a kind that might be called "legal." The Pennsylvania system produced *more honest men,*

---
[43] de Beaumont and de Tocqueville, p. 52.
[45] de Beaumont and de Tocqueville, p. 55.
[46] de Beaumont and de Tocqueville, p. 59.

and the Auburn system *more obedient citizens*. The advantages of the American penitentiary system in general were summarized:

The impossibility of the mutual corruption of the prisoners.
The great probability of their contracting habits of obedience and industry, which would render them useful citizens.
The possibility of a radical reformation.

William Crawford, secretary since 1817 of the London Prison Discipline Society,[47] visited for the British Government the United States in 1832 to 1833, and investigated in particular its State prisons. His findings were embodied on his return to England in 1834 in a volume, remarkably complete as to architectural plans, facts and statistics; it was the most elaborate published in any land up to that time.[48] Crawford adhered emphatically to the Pennsylvania system. He uniformly found the deterrent influence to be very great, and such as belonged to no other system of jail management. The prisoners with whom he talked in the Philadelphia prison said that the discipline in prisons on the Auburn plan was less corrective than were the restraints of continued solitude. In the Eastern Penitentiary the segregation from the world was certain and complete. He could perceive no angry or vindictive feelings among the prisoners. A mild and subdued spirit prevailed among them. Solitary confinement seemed to him a powerful agent in the reformation of morals. Instances had occurred in which prisoners had expressed their gratitude for the moral benefit they had derived from their imprisonment.[49]

The discipline seemed to be safe and efficacious; it had no unfavorable effect upon the mind or health. He recommended for England the adoption of the Pennsylvania system for every class of offenders; for those awaiting trial, witnesses, and for those imprisoned for short terms, as well as for the convicts. Recognizing, however, the expensiveness of prisons on the Pennsylvania plan, he found himself driven to consider the alternative of the Auburn system as developed at Wethersfield, but he recommended solitude for certain classes of offenders.[50]

The effects of the Auburn system, Crawford was persuaded, had been greatly overrated.[51] The rule of silence was clandestinely broken, notes were exchanged and spectators were gazed at. Severe punishments were necessary in order to preserve the system of silence. Invariably the lash produced strong feelings of degradation and revenge. The discipline at Auburn was of a physical nature, that of Pennsylvania of a moral nature. The whip inflicted immediate pain, but solitude inspired permanent terror. The whip degraded while it humiliated, while solitude subdued, but did not debase. At Auburn the convict was uniformly treated with harshness, at Philadelphia with civility. The Auburn prisoner, when liberated, conscious that he was known to past associates, and that

---

[47] Julius, d. amerik. Besserungs Systeme, Preface.
[48] Same, p. 32.
[49] Crawford, p. 11.
[50] Crawford, p. 31.
[51] Same, p. 19.

the public eye had gazed upon him, saw an accuser in every man he met. The Philadelphia convict quitted his cell, secure from recognition and exempt from reproach.[52]

A striking statement of Crawford was that no one was more emphatic in his advocacy of solitary confinement (with labor) by day and night than the warden of Wethersfield — the prison regarded by the advocates of the Auburn system as the model prison on that plan.[53]

Francis Lieber, the translator into English of the penitentiary study of de Beaumont and de Tocqueville, was himself an erudite and painstaking student of prison discipline of his time. He was born in Berlin in 1800, and after imprisonment for political reasons by the Prussian Government in 1819 and 1824, he removed to the United States in 1827 and settled in Philadelphia, where he became the editor of the Encyclopaedia Americana (1829-1833).

Lieber citing the fact that prisons had been called hospitals for patients afflicted with moral diseases was an earnest sponsor of the Pennsylvania system, which in his opinion worked calmly and steadily, without subjecting the convict by repeated punishments, to a continual recurrence of disgrace for misdemeanors which the common principles of human nature were sufficient to induce him to commit.[54] The greatest step that a convict of the common class could make toward reformation was from thoughtlessness to thoughtfulness. Few committed to prisons were accustomed to think; it was for want of thought that they became guilty. Surrounded as they were at Auburn by a variety of objects during the day, they could not feel the same inducement to reflection as under the pressure of constant solitude. Lieber had asked many prisoners if they preferred to be placed together with others; almost invariably they considered it the greatest privilege to be left alone.[55]

Theorizing on the possibility of serious mental results from separate confinement, Lieber made the surprising statement that all experience proved how difficult it was to make any impression on the feelings of the benighted and unhappy subjects of criminal punishment.[56]

Lieber recognized the serious expense incurred in the building of the Penitentiary, but he held that other similar institutions could be built far more cheaply. But even though prisons on the Pennsylvania plan proved expensive, the reformation it effected would warrant the increased outlay.[57] Prisoners did not leave the Pennsylvania institution worse than when they entered. In separate confinement a specific gradation of punishment could be obtained as surely, and with as much facility, as by any other system.[58] Furthermore, by virtue of the greater severity of separate confinement, a greater reduction in the term of imprisonment might be

---

[52] Crawford, p. 19.
[53] Same, p. 31.
[54] de Beaumont and de Tocqueville, p. 292.
[55] Same, p. 294.
[56] Same, p. 296.
[57] Same, p. 297.
[58] Same, p. 298.

achieved. *Months* might be substituted for the *years* in sentences, as answering all the ends of retributive justice and penitential experience.[59] The cheapest method of keeping prisoners was that which was most likely to reform them.

To the United States came in 1835 Doctor Niclaus Heinrich Julius, representative of Prussia, to study our prisons. He was the leading German student of prison discipline, and was the editor and publisher of a magazine devoted to prison science, as it was developed at the time. Doctor Julius was also an emphatic advocate of the Pennsylvania plan.[60] At Auburn there was too much distraction of attention. The time of punishment could be shortened at Philadelphia because of the deeper impression produced by solitude. Auburn had a more physical and negative effect, Philadelphia a more moral and positive effect. Other factors, already cited under previously quoted authorities, were reiterated by Julius. A further advantage of the Philadelphia plan was that no central hospital was necessary, which under the Auburn plan became a place of idleness and verbal communication. If necessary, both sexes might be housed with propriety under the Pennsylvania plan in the same prison since all rooms were separate.

The Pennsylvania system was therefore the best plan in Europe or America for prison discipline and for reformation.[61] The alleged detriment to health, and the greater mortality, Julius denied. He also denied that by the isolation of convicts valuable social tendencies were destroyed. How could any association in prison of criminals with each other be valuable? Indeed, even the Auburn plan allowed no actual association. Doctor Julius stated that he found wardens of prisons on the Auburn plan who said that if they had the rebuilding of their prisons to do, they would build on the Pennsylvania plan.

While initial costs seemed greater, the Pennsylvania plan nevertheless dispensed with messhall, hospital, workshops, chapel and other buildings for congregate purposes. The extravagant architectural adornments of the Eastern Penitentiary did not need to be repeated in future prisons.[62] Private vices were no more likely to occur under the Pennsylvania system than under the Auburn system, while sodomy was rendered impossible.

To Julius a prison was always a prison. The prisoner must never for an instant forget the fact. All that the prisoner possessed belonged to the State, for the eradication of the debt that had arisen through his guilt.[63] The prison was an opportunity for atonement. Julius was strongly opposed to any alleviation in prison discipline that would make the prison anything but a place of repentance.

From France came a second delegation, consisting of De Metz and Blouet. De Metz was a counsellor at the royal court of justice in Paris and Blouet was a government architect. Their mission

[59] de Beaumont and de Tocqueville, p. 299.
[60] Julius. d. Amerik. Besserungs Systeme, p. 8ff.
[61] Same, p. 33.
[62] Same, p. 39.
[63] Same, p. 256.

was especially to weigh the relative merits of the Auburn and the Pennsylvania systems. Their report to the French Government was statistically and architecturally a monumental work. These French specialists reaffirmed the preferences of other European visitors for the Pennsylvania plan.[64] It eliminated flogging; the association of prisoners while in prison, and their mutual recognition after discharge. There was greater reformative value in solitude; classification of prisoners was unnecessary. There was no distraction in moral and religious instruction, and the solitary cell furnished to the prison officials a better chance to study intensively the individual prisoner. From the Philadelphia prison there seemed to be less chance of escape, and its separate cells permitted this type of prison to be used, if necessary, for all classes of criminals.

"In all prisons of the Auburn type, punishment is either cruel or insufficient. Silence can succeed only with cruelty. There is either cruelty or impunity."

On the other hand, the painstaking analysis of Blouet showed the far greater expensiveness in construction of a prison on the Pennsylvania plan. Estimating for France, Blouet declared that an Auburn-type prison of 480 cells could be built in Paris for 932,000 francs, or a per capita cost of 1,942 francs, or approximately $388 per inmate. A prison for 480 inmates on the Philadelphia plan would cost in Paris 1,709,000 francs, or 3, 561 francs per inmate, or approximately $712 per inmate. From the financial standpoint, the Auburn system was much more economical and safe.

Mondelet and Neilson, the Canadian commissioners who followed in 1834 the above-mentioned men in their investigation of the two prison systems, also declared for the Pennsylvania system because it offered better protection to inmates both in and after the institution, and partly because so many complaints were being made by the mechanics against the labor conditions under the Auburn system. The two Canadians recognized that the Pennsylvania buildings cost more and that the system earned less, but their recommendations in 1835 against the Auburn system were followed by the Legislature of lower Canada, and Haviland's plan for the Trenton prison in New Jersey was chosen by Lower Canada for a model of the prison they planned to construct.[65]

On the other hand, Commissioners John Macauley and H. C. Thompson, who had been sent early in the thirties from upper Canada to examine into American prisons in the United States, reported in a statement dated Kingston, upper Canada, November 12th, 1832, that they favored the Auburn system for a new penitentiary in upper Canada for the following reasons: [66]

The people of upper Canada favor the Auburn system.
There are important testimonials in its favor.
Other States have built prisons on the same type.
The Pennsylvania system is yet in the experimental stage.

---

[64] De Metz and Blouet, p. 34.
[65] Julius. d. Amerik. Besserungs Systeme.
[66] B. P. D. S., 1834.

And, finally, international approval of the Pennsylvania system came in 1846, when at the first international prison congress at Frankfort on the Main, the delegates from the leading European countries passed, by almost unanimous vote, the following resolution:

"Separate confinement can be used in general with such increasing or decreasing degrees of severity as are conditioned by the nature of the offense, and by the character and conduct of the prisoners, so that each prisoner shall be occupied with useful labor, shall have exercise each day in the open air, shall receive religious, moral and school instruction, shall take part in divine service, and shall receive the visits of the chaplain of his own religious faith, the director of the prison, the prison physician, the members of the supervisory board and of the prisoners' aid societies which may be permitted by the prison rules."

We have cited above an impressive sequence of opinions highly favorable to the Pennsylvania system. Against these formidable published decisions of men of special qualifications were arrayed practically only the annual publications of the Boston Society. Yet that organization possessed the great advantage of being always alert and on the ground. The annual reports of the Boston Society gave no opinions of foreign critics unfavorable to Auburn or favorable to Pennsylvania. In this one cannot refrain from questioning severely the ethics of Dwight. While de Beaumont and de Tocqueville had been translated by Francis Lieber, it is very doubtful whether the publications of the other Europeans had any considerable circulation in the United States.

But the great strength of the opposition to the Eastern Penitentiary lay in three objections, which were never allowed by the opponents of the system to subside. The Boston Society argued as follows:

1. The Pennsylvania system was extravagant in construction, and resulted in a serious annual financial loss to the citizens of the State in its operation.
2. The Pennsylvania system produced a higher mortality and morbidity rate than did the Auburn system.
3. The Pennsylvania system produced a higher proportion of insanity than did the Auburn system.

These were serious charges. The appeal to the pocketbook has always been potent. If other States were actually making from their prisons on the Auburn type profits above all expenses, while Pennsylvania's prison produced an annual deficit, this carried an almost irresistible suggestion to legislators in favor of the more economical system. If the Philadelphia prison was more dangerous to life and to mind, then humanity as well as economy justified the adoption of the Auburn plan.

In the years from 1829 on, a mass of documentary evidence in annual reports, and deductions therefrom, came into existence. The Eastern Penitentiary was ever on the defensive. From this often confusing, incomplete, and contradictory material we shall now endeavor to determine to what extent the strictures of the Boston Society were tenable.

1. *The Pennsylvania system was extravagant in construction and resulted in a serious annual financial loss to the citizens of the State in its operation.*

The annual reports of the board of inspectors of the Penitentiary carried no clear financial statements during the period now under discussion. Vague references to the cost of administration appeared occasionally. This failure to publish an annual financial statement seemed a confession of industrial failure, and it was legitimate for the Boston Society to proclaim the probabilities that such was the case.

An analysis printed by the State Auditor of Pennsylvania in 1897 [67] showed the follownig disbursements by the State, in the construction and operation of the Eastern Penitentiary from 1821. when the law establishing the prison was enacted to 1844:

	Erection and completion of buildings, etc.	Furniture, equipment, etc	Support and maintenance, inclusive, salaries
1821	$100,000		
1824	80,000		
1825	60,000		
1826	891,125		
1828	4,000		
1829		5,000	1,000
1830		4,000	
1831	120,000		
1833	130,000		
1835	60,000		
1836	10,000	15,000	
1838		10,000	
1843		8,000	
1844		8,000	
	$653,125	$50,000	$1,000

The cost of building the Penitentiary, which on completion provided in its 7 radial cellhouses for 586 inmates, was $653,125 up to 1844, inclusive. The extravagance was openly confessed by the friends of the institution. The wall itself cost about $200,000.[68] The Penitentiary was, according to George W. Smith in 1833 [69] the only edifice in the country calculated to convey to American citizens "the external appearance of those magnificent and picturesque castles of the middle ages, which contribute to embellish the scenery of Europe." But in the above financial statement, the annual cost of maintenance and of salaries does not appear. The law of 1829, establishing the government of the Penitentiary, provided that the expense of maintaining and keeping the convicts in the Western and Eastern Penitentiaries should be borne by the

[67] State Prisons, Hospitals, etc., Embracing their History, Finances, etc., Vol. II. C. M. Brush, State Printer, Harrisburg, Pa., 1897.
[68] B. P. D. S., p. 827.
[69] Richard Vaux, p. 56.

counties in which they should have been convicted. These charges are to-day remotely hidden away in inaccessible county documents. A citation by McElwell in 1835 shows the following typical charge for the County of Philadelphia:

For support of 114 prisoners, for various periods from January 1st—December 31st, 1834, provisions, clothing, fuel, medicines, etc., at 20 cents a day, and $2.00 a year for bedding.. $6,104 00
By amount at credit of above prisoners for labor............................... 4,355 77

(Due) $1,748 23

In short, the counties paid the differences between what the convicts cost the State and what they earned for the State. These deficits do not appear in the annual reports of the Eastern Penitentiary with any regularity. The following comments appear in the reports:

1830. The expenses of the institution, not including salaries, have more than been met by the proceeds of the prisoners' industries.
    When the prison has 300 inmates it will be entirely self-supporting, including salaries.
1831. Our convicts have, with but a few exceptions, maintained themselves.
1832. Profits for the past year have met all expenses save salaries. We hope for revenue from convicts when building is completed.
1833. Labor is attended with difficulties. Have not met expenses.
1834. Reformation of the prisoner the all-important thing. Our prison was never expected to be self-supporting. Had a reasonable grant for a capital fund been made, a different result in our pecuniary affairs might have been shown.
1835. (In the minority report of the investigating committee:
    "There has existed a too intimate understanding among individuals, a frightful blending of accounts."
1835. Deficiency, $4,998. Want of capital a bother.
1836. Pecuniary affairs never showed so favorably as this year.
1837. Considerable loss in industries. Hard times have caused decreased income.
1839. Our institution cannot expect to be lucrative to the State.
1840. Partial financial statement, showing profit and loss in the industries.

The contention of the Boston Prison Discipline Society as to initial extravagance and annual expense was thereby proved. Side by side with the unfortunate financial showing of the Eastern Penitentiary were placed the following statements:[70]

1828-1841. Auburn supported itself and paid salaries of officers except in 1837-1838, and except in those two years produced surplus of $69,460.59.
1829-1844. Wethersfield supported itself, including salaries, every year save six months in 1833, and netted $78,699.
1833-1842. Sing Sing supported itself, including salaries every year save one, and netted $119,527.24.
1831-1842. Massachusetts State Prison supported itself, including salaries, every year save two, and netted $45,593.
1835-1842. Ohio State Prison at Columbus supported itself, and netted $124,963.78.

---

[70] B. P. D. S., 184.., p. 275.

The comparison of the total cost of construction, and cost per capita, as given by Doctor Julius, was also highly unfavorable to the Eastern Penitentiary:[71]

Prison	Capacity	Cost	Per capita cost
Auburn[72]	700	$450,000	$584 42
Sing Sing	1,000	200,000	200 00
Massachusetts	300	86,000	286 66
Connecticut	232	35,000	150 86
N. Y. C. Penitentiary	240	32,000	133 33
Maryland[73]	318	184,770	581 00
Washington, D. C.	160	180,000	1,125 00
Eastern Penitentiary (with wall)	586	600,000	1,023 89
(without wall)	586	400,000	682 00
Philadelphia County Prison	408	300,000	735 00
New Jersey	192	200,000	1,041 00

Auburn-type prisons were generally built by the labor of prisoners, reducing the costs of construction by one-fourth to one-third.

2. *The Pennsylvania system produced a higher mortality and morbidity rate than did the Auburn system.*

The theoretical basis for this assumption was the proposition that constant isolation of individual prisoners was unhealthy to the body and conducive to disease. The practical basis of this claim was the yearly death rate, as compared with the death rate of Auburn and of sister prisons.

No claim based on the statistics of one year or of a few years has substantial value. There was a comparison habitually made of such short periods by the Boston Society, followed by dogmatic assertions of Pennsylvania's disadvantageous death rate.

The most adequate analysis that we have met of the mortality statistics of the Eastern Penitentiary, is found in an article "On the Effect of Secluded and Gloomy Imprisonment," published in 1845.[74] The treatise aimed to show the peculiar susceptibility of the negro prisoners to disease and death. The following were the average death rates of white and colored prisoners:

	Average number in prison	Average whites	Average colored	Deaths		Percentage Mortality		Total
				Whites	Colored	Whites	Colored	
1830	31	21.81	9.19	1	0	4.19	0	3.
1831	67	47.75	19.25	2	2	4.18	10.02	6.
1832	91	69.42	21.58	1	3	1.44	13.52	4.4
1832	123	89.30	33.70	1	0	1.11	0	.8
1834	183	123.58	59.42	1	4	.81	6.68	2.7
1835	266	154.74	108.26	2	5	1.26	4.61	2.6
1836	360	202.00	148.00	2	10	.99	6.74	3.3
1837	387	233.00	154.00	7	10	3.00	6.49	4.3
1838		240.00	161.00	7	19	2.92	11.8	
1839		245.00	173.00	2	8	.81	4.62	
1840		232.00	162.00	9	13	3.88	8.02	
1841		203.00	144.00	4	13	1.97	4.61	
1842		212.00	130.00	3	6	1.41	9.03	

[71] Julius. Sittleche Zusbaende, Vol. II, p. 239.
[72] Crawford, App. p. 32.
[73] De Metz and Blouet, p. 38.
[74] Jol. of Prison Discipline and Philanthropy, Vol. I, No. 3.

According to the tabular statement, the average rate of white deaths in the first thirteen years was 2.03. The average rate of colored deaths in the same period was 7.03. F. C. Gray, in "Prison Discipline in America," gave the average of deaths of whites for the period 1837-1846 as 2.18, and of blacks as 7.77.

The Penitentiary officials claimed that in estimating the relative mortality or morbidity of the Eastern Penitentiary as compared with Auburn or Wethersfield, the relative number and character of the colored population of the prison at Philadelphia should be considered. The colored population in the prisons of the United States in 1837 was as follows:[75]

Prisons	Total prisoners	Total colored prisoners	Percentage
Tennessee	122	2	1.93
Auburn	678	30	4.41
Vermont	92	4	4.79
Massachusetts	291	24	8.24
Ohio	392	41	10.45
Baltimore	387	73	18.86
Sing Sing	753	One-fifth	20.00
Wethersfield	190	49	25.26
Eastern Pen	386	154	31.28
New Jersey	141	49	34.75
Washington (City)	76	49	65.47

As early as 1837 the attending physician at the Eastern Penitentiary reported that the prison was burdened with a sickly, inefficient colored population, which by self-abuse became debilitated in mind and body, and diseased, making three-fifths of the prison's mortality.[76] In 1838 the prison had more colored prisoners than any other prison outside the slave-holding State. Pennsylvania was bounded by three slave States. Pennsylvania was the recipient of the discontented free blacks, worthless, slaves and runaway slaves. About forty per cent. of the inmates of the Eastern Penitentiary were colored.[77] The cases of mental disorder were mainly among the colored prisoners, and caused by masturbation.[78] The mortality of the colored prisoners was markedly greater than that of the colored population in Philadelphia.

In 1839 the physician stated that the prison received an increasingly disproportionate number of colored convicts, which accounted largely for the sickness, mortality and medical expense. In 1842, the colored convicts were described as often diseased beyond recovery, broken down with repeated imprisonment, vicious habits, debauchery, privation and exposure. They were proverbially careless and improvident, negligent of the simplest duties of the toilet, incapable of the expedients familiar to intelligent men incarcerated like themselves, oppressed with strong animal propensities, and unfortified by moral or intellectual resources."[79]

[75] Report of E. P. Inspectors, 1838.
[76] Report of Inspectors, 1837, p. 12.
[77] Report of Inspectors, 1838, p. 10.
[78] Same, 1838, p. 13.
[79] Report of Inspectors, 1842, p. 25.

Mortality statistics from the chief prisons of the country in the period under discussion do not permit of such assembling as to be properly comparable. The periods under comparison were generally too brief or unequal periods were compared. We append a number of statistical statements:

Prison	Period	Percentage of deaths	Remarks
Eastern Pen	1829–1842	2.03	White prisoners
Eastern Pen	1829–1842	7.03	Colored prisoners
Eastern Pen	1829–1842	3.9	Total population
Auburn	1824–1834	1.8	
Wethersfield	1828–1834	1.3	
Massachusetts	1824–1834	2.2	
Virginia	1800–1834	7.1	
Auburn	1823–1835	1.6	

It is apparent that the deaths in the Eastern Penitentiary occurred in a higher percentage, on the whole, than at Auburn, Wethersfield or Massachusetts, but if the negro deaths were eliminated, the proportion would have been little more than in the more northern prisons.

The following table, from the report of the Prison Association of New York for 1845,[80] bears out the preceding statement:

Prison	Years embraced	Prisoners	Deaths	Average for series
Auburn	1830–43	9,417	179	1 in 52.6
Sing Sing	1830–43	10,455	324	1 in 32.2
Massachusetts	1830–43	3,992	70	1 in 57
New Hampshire	1830–43	1,049	7	1 in 149.8
Vermont	1833–38	728	10	1 in 72.8
Connecticut	1830–43	2,523	63	1 in 40
Kentucky	1837–43	1,062	19	1 in 55.9
Virginia	1830–43	2,365	198	1 in 11.8
Ohio	1836–42	2,462	71	1 in 34.6
Maryland	1832–43	4,215	156	1 in 26.3
Maine	1830–37 and 43	698	9	1 in 74.4
Eastern Pen	1830–43	3,808	147	1 in 25.9
Western Pen	1830–43	1,488	42	1 in 35.5
New Jersey	1837–43	1,051	8	1 in 131.2

However, the death rate is but one factor in an estimation of the health of a prison — and one that can be most seriously affected by a liberal exercise of the pardoning power. The Auburn prison physician reported in 1844 that it had long been a principle upon which pardons were granted, that they were necessary to save life. Twelve pardons were granted at Auburn for that reason during the year in question. Obviously, the death rate in that year was materially reduced at Auburn, and the procedure of pardoning vitiated any employment of the death rate as an index of healthful or disease-producing conditions within that prison.

[80] Report of Inspector, p. 93.

But at the Eastern Penitentiary, also, so many pardons were granted as to affect materially the mortality statistics, in case such pardons were given in any considerable number because of grievous illness:

Pardons Given in Eastern Penitentiary 1842-1846 [81]

Year	Whites	Colored
1842	31	2
1843	15	0
1844	39	7
1845	30	2
1846	26	0
	131	11

The several prisons showed considerable variation in the statistics of pardons. The following illuminating statement was presented in the report of the Prison Association of New York for 1845.[82] The series of years from which the computations were made varied also. Thus, the statistics for Vermont, Kentucky, and Ohio, for instance, covered but a few years, and presented very incomplete and statistically unrepresentative percentages.

Prison	Series of Years	Proportion of pardons to total number of prisoners
Auburn	1831-33; 1839-43	1 in 20
Sing Sing	1831-43	1 in 22.7
Massachusetts	1830-43; omitting 37, 38	1 in 21.6
New Hampshire	1830-43; omitting 38, 39, 41	1 in 11.2
Connecticut	1830-43; omitting 38	1 in 34.6
Vermont	1843	1 in 7.7
Kentucky	1840, 42	1 in 5.4
Virginia	1830-43	1 in 21
Maine	1830-37; 1842-43	1 in 10.5
Ohio	1839, 42	1 in 81
Maryland	1837-43	1 in 18.6
Eastern Penitentiary	1830-43	1 in 28.1
Western Penitentiary	1830-43	1 in 10.9
New Jersey	1839-40; 1842-43	1 in 6.4

As to the health of a prison, who shall determine the factors whereby judgment shall be pronounced? What is meant by health? Is the prison to be judged by the average health of the outside population? What is the standard of prison health? Is the State to adopt methods that will prevent in each individual a diminution of his strength and cheerfulness? In measuring the state of prison health, what credit shall be given to the improvement in health of those admitted in diseased condition? How long after a prison has been established shall we regard it as having passed the experimental stage, and as being open to unqualified criticism? Who

[81] Gray. Prison Discipline in America, p. 95.
[82] P. 108-110.

shall give the facts regarding the state of health or disease within the prison? Even granting that the prison possesses a qualified medical officer, do not such physicians differ in diagnosis and judgment? What allowances should be made for such differences of opinion? What should be the judgment as to mental health?

The above questions, asked years later, in 1861, by William Parker Foulke of Philadelphia,[83] show very pertinently the practical impossibility of determining the relative healthfulness of a prison, without comprehensive and easily comparable statistics. The Eastern Penitentiary was from the first under the care of studious and apparently competent physicians. Their annual reports were exceptionally detailed and scholarly, in comparison with those of other prisons. Relatively comprehensive vital statistics were published annually. The very care exercised by the attending physician in the interested discharge of his duty would, when interpreted in terms of illness, easily give to uninterested or hostile readers the impression of the apparent presence of abundant illness. Furthermore, the challenge itself of the antagonists of the Pennsylvania system brought out annual reports of the physician in painstaking detail.

Doctor Franklin Bache, a great-grandson of Benjamin Franklin, was the first attending physician. De Metz and Blouet said of Doctor Bache that he was a devoted physician and student. He kept a journal of the most important facts coming under his observation. He kept a history of each prisoner, during his entire imprisonment, including his past life, his conduct, and his condition at discharge.

In March, 1837, after an incumbency of eight years, he issued the following vital statistics:

Of the 312 prisoners who had been discharged, up to the close of 1836, the results were, at time of discharge:

Health improved	78
Health the same as at entrance	164
More feeble, but not sick	17
Health not so good	15
Very much worse	4
Died	33
Suicide	1
	312

"Speaking abstractly, separate solitary confinement is not healthy; an unnatural condition of restraint cannot be favorable to health. Confinement can be relatively healthy, in substituting fewer causes of illness than our population would meet on the outside. The mortality of the inmates I believe to be lower in prison than it would be on the outside. In my seven years the average mortality has been three per cent. A certain number of cases of insanity have presented themselves, some of them existing prior to entrance and continuing; others had given signs of insanity prior to entrance."[84]

At the time of Doctor Bache's testimony, the cells in the lower tier were damp; the thickness of the walls caused slower change

---

[83] Foulke. Remarks on Cellular Separation, p. 43.
[84] De Metz and Blouet, 2d Part, p. 28.

in temperature in the stone than in the air, and congelation ensued. The population had to struggle against the evil effects of walls recently constructed, and cells unequally heated by hot water. In the winter of 1836-37, two prisoners had had their hands frozen in their cells.[85] Doctor Bache acknowledged that certain maladies could be caused by confinement in the narrow space of a cell, but that the prison physician must do the best he could with the means at his disposal. Open-air exercise throughout the day was one remedial measure.[86]

No special maladies were produced by separation. The predominant maladies were scrofulous, and lung affections, including consumption and dyspepsia. Most lung affections were complicated with diseases of the stomach and intestines, caused by indigestion and irregularity of evacuations.

Nevertheless, Doctor Bache's general impressions were that the effects of separation were highly favorable in a penitentiary system, the mortality of the Eastern Penitentiary being only one-half as much as in the old Walnut Street Prison, where it was six per cent.[87]

It is impossible, to-day, to fail to gain the impression that Doctor Bache, in his statements, was seeking to be honest with himself, and at the same time to put the best face forward for the prison. We know, of course, that the close and constant confinement was detrimental to vigorous health. We know that the close confinement would develop physical conditions that might not appear as acute diseases, but that would predispose to disease, and would weaken the system. It would have needed only a comparison with the healthy out-door farm life on the prison farms of to-day to demolish any complacement belief of a hundred years ago that the separate confinement of the Eastern Penitentiary was harmless, or relatively so, from a health standpoint. But, since prisons had to be, and the system had been adopted, it was natural to bolster it up within the limits of admissible statement.

In 1837, Doctor William Darrach was appointed attending physician. In the following year he reported that the Penitentiary was "the recipient of disease and the dispenser of health," an optimistic manner of phrasing his early impressions. Admissions in good health amounted to 55.5 per cent.; discharges in good health amounted to 75.2 per cent. Eighty prisoners, entering in imperfect health, brought in 114 terms of disease, of which 39 were syphilitic, 24 thoracic, 15 abdominal, 11 febrile, 6 cephalic, and 4 scrofulous. The diseases in the medical register requiring special notice were smallpox — an epidemic; chronic pleurisy, inflammation of the lungs, and acute "dementia," due mainly to masturbation (cases of short duration, mainly curable, among colored prisoners).

In 1839, the physician reported that what long confinement, masturbation, full animal diet and cold and damp might do to hasten the issue was worthy of consideration. In 1842, a resident

---

[85] Same, p. 125.
[86] Same, p. 124.
[87] De Metz and Blouet, 2d Part, p. 125.

physician was appointed, with consequent improvement in health, there being now more constant medical attention, with increased open-air exercise. The separate gardens were used for the employing of invalid or convalescent prisoners. The new resident physician found scrofula and consumption rare save among the colored inmates, the amount of consumption in the prison being less than was generally supposed.

During 1844 there went out from prison — after a confinement of more than two years:

		Per cent.
In improved health	4	13.3
In unimproved health	22	73.3
In impaired or less perfect health	2	6.7
Died	2	6.7
After a confinement of two years or less		
In improved health	9	15.3
In unimproved health	43	72.9
In impaired or less perfect health	3	5.1
Died	4	6.7

It could hardly be said that a prison that sent out only one-seventh to one-eighth of its inmates in improved health and discharged three-fourths of its inmates with health no better than when they came in was "the recipient of disease and the dispenser of health."

At the close of the period we are studying occurred the international prison congress at Frankfort, Germany, at which gathering the following statistics relative to health and mortality at the Eastern Penitentiary were presented by Varrentrapp, which he had himself collected and coordinated:

```
Received at Eastern Penitentiary, 1829-1845, incl................2,059
    Discharged....................................................1,715
    Of whom there had died........................................ 176
```

Length of sentences of the 2,059 inmates	Number of inmates	Per cent	Number of the 176 who died	Per cent who died
1 to 2 years	400	20	10	2
2 to 3 years	587	30	39	22
3 to 4 years	511	26	53	30
4 to 5 years	139	7	19	10
5 to 6 years	121	6	15	8
6 to 7 years	41	2	11	6
7 to 8 years	52	2	13	7
8 to 21 years	82	4	16	9

According to Varrentrapp, there died, of the 176:

```
In the first year.........................................50, or 28.4 per cent.
Second year..............................................63, or 35.7 per cent.
Third year...............................................41, or 23.2 per cent.
Fourth year..............................................10, or  5.6 per cent.
Fifth year...............................................  7, or  3.9 per cent.
Sixth year...............................................  2, or  2.8 per cent.
Seventh year.............................................  2, or  2.8 per cent.
Eighth year..............................................  1, or  1.4 per cent.
```

Varrentrapp claimed that the mortality of those imprisoned for longer periods was not greater than for those imprisoned for shorter periods. In short, there was no cumulative or increased tendency to mortality, with those of longer sentences, but rather a decreased mortality rate.

3. *The Pennsylvania system produced a higher proportion of insanity than did the Auburn system.*

We have already seen, in the quotations from official reports of the Massachusetts State Prison, and from Connecticut, that the insane prisoner had become a serious problem and a menace in the prison. Serious developments of insanity had occurred in Auburn Prison, when the experiment in solitary confinement, without labor, had taken place for over a year in 1822 and 1823, and had resulted in violent deaths, suicides, and mental aberration. Stories of madness within the solitary cells of European dungeons were in circulation in America. General Lafayette had condemned, early in the twenties, the proposed plans of Pennsylvania for solitary confinement, and the Prison Discipline Society of Boston had made much of this citation. Throughout the campaign of the Boston Society against the Pennsylvania system, the effect of separate confinement upon the mind was marked for special reference.

The effect of the discussions of the extreme principle of separate confinement *without* labor carried over into the period subsequent to the opening of the Eastern Penitentiary. From the close association of thought between such solitary confinement *without* and *with* labor, the thesis was easily developed that isolated confinement of prisoners in any event would induce a large percentage of insanity.

It is true that the advocates of the new method at the Eastern Penitentiary based their optimistic denials of probable insanity largely upon theory. Those who feared, or claimed to fear, the development of insanity under such conditions, based *their* arguments on the constant and unrelieved solitude believed to inhere in the Pennsylvania system, whereas under the Auburn system — a so-called "social system" — the inmates were alleged to obtain that change and variety necessary to preserve a normal mental state, through the daily though silent association with their kind. The supporters of the methods of the Eastern Penitentiary claimed that the prisoner would not only have as an adequate mental diversion his daily industrial tasks, but that he would also enjoy the wholesome association — even though brief and infrequent — with the superintendent and various other officers of the prison, and also with members of the board of inspectors who would occasionally visit his cell, besides the intermittent visits of the chaplain, the physician, and the representatives of the Philadelphia Society.

The annual reports of the Eastern Penitentiary were therefore studied with the keenest, and often very hostile, attention. If the Pennsylvania system tended to produce insanity, that system was foredoomed to failure. At the end of 1830, one year from the opening of the prison, it was reported that neither insanity nor bodily infirmity had been produced by the mitigated separation from other convicts. In 1832 the inspectors reported that there was a disposition in some counties to use the prison as a bedlam. That this was practically inevitable was seen already in other States, and in our chapter on "County Prisons and Jails" [98] it will appear how impossible it was to keep "lunatics" from being sent to county prisons and to State prisons save through the establishment of special institutions for their reception. The inspectors reported that prisoners had been received whose mental states made them irresponsible to the law. In short, insane convicts were being sent to the prison because there was as yet no insane asylum in Pennsylvania to which they might be sent in anything like adequate numbers. And the way was thus open, statistically, to the inspectors to make the point that if there was insanity within the prison, that insanity has existed prior to the admission of the convicts in question.

In 1835, the superintendent's report emphasized a difference of much importance in the mental cases under care or observation:

"A minute inspection of the character of the unhappy inmates of the prison has developed another interesting fact: That many more of them than was supposed are really irresponsible beings. These may be divided into two classes: First, idiots, or those who, possessing too little capacity to take care of themselves, are fit subjects for the guardianship of a poor-house.

"Second, the insane, or those laboring under such an aberration of mind in a greater or less degree as renders them unsafe members of society. Although not being answerable for their actions, they cannot be regarded as proper subjects for a prison. In some of the States provision has been made for such persons, and I should rejoice to see a similar one adopted in Pennsylvania, as we are confident that several of this description have been, and some are now, inmates of this penitentiary."

In 1837, Doctor Franklin Bache's incumbency of the office of prison physician ended. He stated at this time:

"A certain number of cases of insanity have presented themselves, some of them existing prior to entrance, and continuing, others had given signs of insanity prior to entrance. The subject of insanity in relation to prisons is a difficult problem. One must, in many instances, distinguish between criminal actions and those caused by insanity. Judges and juries are very reluctant to admit insanity in defense. In some instances, in consequence, insane persons have been sent to prison. In every prison there will be a larger or smaller number of cases of insanity. I have seen more cases of insanity in Cherry Hill (Eastern Penitentiary) than in Walnut Street."

A recapitulation of the period from 1829 to 1837 shows an excellent record, as reported by the prison physician:

Year	Average number of prisoners	Cases of insanity
1829	31	None
1830	67	None
1831	91	4, but none originating in prison.
1832	123	1, not attributable to mode of discipline.
1833	183	2, not originating in prison.
1834	266	None.
1835	360	

[88] Chapter XXII.

In 1837, Doctor William Darrach became the attending physician. He found in that year no case of insanity that had been produced by separate or solitary confinement. There were cases of "dementia," the effects of "vicious conduct" (masturbation), which occurred every year, but they usually yielded to medical remedies. Such cases of mental disorder were found to be of short duration and curable. They were mainly among colored prisoners and developed within a few months from entrance. Doctor Darrach found, on the other hand, that hundreds of prisoners had been discharged from the prison in a better state of body and mind than when they entered it.

Although 26 cases of mental disorder occurred during the year 1839 the physician asserted that the prisoners had been committed who were insane before trial, and were not proper subjects of penal treatment and punishment. He was satisfied that the separate system of discipline was not chargeable with any injurious influence on the mind. The superintendent pleaded in this year for the establishment of a State hospital for the insane.

In 1843, Doctor Darrach ceased to be prison physician. During his incumbency, the following cases occurred:

Year	Average number of convicts	Cases	Remarks
1837	387	14	12 cured.
1838	401	18	All cured but one.
1839	418	26	Only one diseased at time of report.
1840	394	13	9 cured.
1841	397	11	
1842	342	13	

For the balance of 1843, and for a part of 1844, Doctor Edward Hartshorne served as resident physician. He found that separate confinement, instead of stultifying the intellect, operated in general in the opposite direction. The causes of derangement, he said, originated either before entrance, or from causes unconnected with the method of prison discipline. Nineteen cases of defective intellect (imbecile, idiotic, demented and insane) were admitted in the single year of 1843.

Doctor Given, the succeeding resident physician, made in 1844 a noteworthy suggestion, foreshadowing the research tendencies of many years afterwards:

"From the well-known hereditary nature of insanity, it occurred to me that a careful register of all prisoners in whose families mental diseases prevailed would, in the course of time, throw considerable light upon its development in prison, and would also show the parallelism of insanity and crime. . . .

"I found that 20.2 per cent. of all prisoners received since the date of my appointment had insane relatives, all of whom, with one exception, were not further removed than uncles or aunts."

Here was a direct forerunner, in bent of mind, of Richard Dugdale, who thirty years later, in the State of New York, made the famous study of the "Jukes" family, led thereto by the discovery of the many persons by the same family name in the prisons, asylums and almshouses of New York.

The recapitulation for the years 1843 and 1844 is as follows:

Year	Average No. of convicts	Cases developed	Remarks
1843	334	5	Only one under treatment.
1844	360	5	2 of 5 entirely cured. A third improved.

The above record of the first sixteen years cannot be said to have shown a serious degree of insanity directly caused by isolated and continued cellular confinement — basing our presumptions upon the given figures. Most of the insanity existed, it was alleged, prior to admission to the Penitentiary. The physicians of the institution were alert, gifted with professional zeal, and, by the nature of the prison discipline, observant of the inmates. The contract system was not conducted with driving intensity. The charge of subordinating health and mental aberration in prisoners to prison profits could not be brought against this prison. Men were not forced to toil, though obviously physically or mentally ill, as was the case in Auburn, Sing Sing and Massachusetts.

And comparisons between the Eastern Penitentiary and other prisons were not possible, with satisfactory accuracy. The vital statistics were inadequate. However, a commissioner appointed by the New York Prison Association to make a report on the prevalence of convict insanity stated in 1846:

"Whilst inspecting the prison at Auburn, we were struck by the great number of individuals affected by mental aberration, whose cases appeared to have quite escaped the doctor's observation. Some few of the most excitable were, we understood, under treatment. . . . The experience of the last few years, and the facts observed in our prisons, tends to confirm us in the opinion that cases of mental derangement are much more frequent in the prisons on the Auburn system than are mentioned in the reports."

We turn now from the discussion of the amount of insanity to the number of recommitments to the Penitentiary, or, in other words, to the presence of recidivism. The success of a penitentiary system has always been supposed to be indicated to an extent by the proportion of inmates passing through an institution who do not again, so far as is known, get into that prison, or into some other. But it is still, in the year, 1921, impossible to secure in the United States sufficiently comprehensive prison statistics to determine with exactitude the results of any prison, in terms of "repeaters" or "recidivists." The difficulty is inherent in the fact that an inmate may never return to the same prison, after once discharged, but may subsequently appear in a number of prisons in other States or even in the same State.

Therefore, to attempt to measure the success of the Eastern Penitentiary by a measure of recidivism within that particular prison would be unsatisfactory, though arguments were made and refuted along exactly these lines. If a prison, for instance, maintained a most severe regime, or instituted some new form of discipline, it was reflected for a time in the tendency of criminals in the communities to "take a chance" as was evidenced when the Walnut Street Prison opened, and later, in the earliest years of the Eastern Penitentiary. But such deterrent effects do not tend to prolong themselves, and familiarity breeds a certain contempt for any new system.

Yet the assumption is fair that in many instances, one experience with a prison system has sufficed to cause the prisoner to determine not to commit further crime. Certainly, any large proportion of recidivism would indicate a failure on the part of the prison to function successfully, though the converse, as we have said, would not necessarily be true. The predominant cause in such a reformation might be the "radical reformation," or spiritual conversion, described by de Beaumont and de Tocqueville, or it might be the "legal" reformation, analyzed by the same authors and critics. Perhaps the dominant reason for non-return to prison might be the deterrent effect of a severe penitentiary discipline — though such severity of treatment has never appeared to be a consistently deterring factor in the reduction of crime. Or, there may not have resulted an actual state of reformation in the discharged prisoner, and so the marked reduction in recommitments may be simply an index, as we have pointed out, of the transfer of activities outside the law in other States.

The proponents of the Pennsylvania system claimed that the association of prisoners with each other, even without the power of communication, was the cardinal error of the Auburn system. The separation of the prisoners was the vital principle of the Pennsylvania system:

> "The questions of original cost, kinds of labor, or capacity to be self-supporting have no direct concern with the system of punishment. If the punishment by the separation and individual treatment of the convict secures society and protects the people; deters from crime, and punishes the offender; reforms the individual; returns him to his former social relations better, or no worse, than when he was separated from them by his imprisonment; prevents the organization of a criminal class in the community; then the principal purposes and the highest aims of punishment are obtained. . . . A congregate prison, the system of congregating prisoners for work, unless it is profit making, could not be regarded as defensible."

The basically weak point of the Pennsylvania system was, that while it was obviously humane, it could not prove itself superior to the Auburn system as a profit-maker, an institution of economy, or one markedly more able to reform the individual, maintain a lower percentage of sickness, death or insanity, or show an appreciably lower percentage of recidivism. It could in general refute the charges of the Prison Discipline Society of Boston that it was markedly higher in all these lines, but it could offset with difficulty the practical and weighty arguments that the Auburn system was a money-maker and that prisons of that type cost much less to build. Therein lay, for this country, probably the two conditioning factors that led to the erection, almost universally, of State prisons of the Auburn type. The basic question was one of money — not of humanity. Auburn-type prisons cost less and made more than did the Pennsylvania-type. That settled it!

Yet the Eastern Penitentiary made an auspicious beginning in the matter of recidivism. Up to 1833, four years after the opening, no discharged prisoner had been recommitted. They had either reformed or gone to other States. There was in the criminal community great terror of the Penitentiary. The inmate population of both the Eastern and the Western Penitentiaries was in 1835, but a little over 500, whereas in 1829 there were 629 in the Walnut Street Prison alone. In 1832, the inspectors of the Eastern Penitentiary stated that the reduction in the number of commitments to prison was due to the entire separation of the convict from his fellows, from the outside world, and from his family and friends.

By 1835, however, the recommitments were occurring. Of the 189 inmates discharged since 1829, 16 had been recommitted. In 1837, of .... prisoners received, 19 had previously been inmates. Concern was now expressed regarding the difficulties experienced by discharged convicts in finding employment. Houses of employment should be established on a large scale, near the cities and large towns, for all who were able and willing to work.

Reconvictions mounted seriously in 1838, being 47 of the 178 admissions, or 26 per cent. The board of inspectors were driven to explanations for their apparent lack of success, and stated that of the 35 recommitted inmates, 26 were convicts who had prison records in other prisons also. The board confessed that it was worrying, in that it recommended a law that would impose on each reconvicted person an additional term of imprisonment, over and above the sentence for the specific offense. In other States, said the inspectors, such additional penalties were imposed, and reconvictions were not so frequent.

The Prison Discipline Society reported that the recommitments to the Eastern Penitentiary since its opening had been 1 in 8.64 admissions. In short, the Penitentiary had already failed to meet the hopes and the sanguine promises of its enthusiastic promoters. Great initial expense, annual deficits, no adequate annual statements of receipts and disbursements, and certain obvious disadvantages of administration in a prison where prisoners must be dealt with individually, were facts staring the board of government of the Eastern Penitentiary in the face.

Seeking, other reasons for the failure to be a model prison in matters of reformation, a new argument was presented by its adherents. Before the Pennsylvania system could be said to be in full operation, each county must also possess a prison for the separate confinement of those accused and awaiting trial, as well as of those serving jail sentences. The damage and the contamination was already effected in the lesser prisons, and the convict came to prison irretrievably ruined. This argument, unfortunately, applied just as potently to other State prisons operating on the Auburn plan, and it applies to-day with all the force of this earlier statement in 1838.

The following table from Julius is interesting, bringing the statistics in collated and comparative form from a number of State prisons, but the various items are often not at all comparable. For instance, the percentage of the Eastern Penitentiary appeared most favorable, one recidivist in thirty-five being recorded, in comparison with Auburn, one in twenty-three. But Auburn's figures ran through sixteen or seventeen years, while the figures of the Eastern Penitentiary were for a space of only five or six years. Auburn had hundreds of "graduates," where the Eastern Penitentiary had but a few, in the general public. Other differences are obvious, and need not be commented upon.

Prison	Period	Total Prisoners received	Recognized Recidivists	Proportion of Recidivists
Eastern Penitentiary	1829–35	554	16	1 in 35
Western Penitentiary	1826–33	324	20	1 in 16
Auburn	1817–33	2215	97	1 in 23
State Prison in New York, and Sing Sing Prison	1797–33	7522	754	1 in 10
Massachusetts	1819–33	1355	261	1 in 5
Massachusetts	1818–35	1722	309	1 in 6
New Hampshire	1812–33	407	19	1 in 21
Vermont	1816–33	627	59	1 in 11
Maine	1824–33	469	44	1 in 12
Maryland	1812–34	2670	308	1 in 9
Virginia	1800–33	1736	85	1 in 20

CHAPTER XX

KENTUCKY

The establishment in 1798 of the State Penitentiary in the frontier State of Kentucky was the beginning of a very interesting development of a "home-made" prison system in the then "Wild West." Far removed from centers of civic influence, Kentucky was comparatively a wilderness, with a population of some 130,000. It had been admitted to Statehood in 1792, and was prior to that a part of Virginia. The settlement of the State by immigrants from the Eastern colonies was reflected in the variety of birthplaces registered in later years by the prison population. As late as 1835, the other States in the Union furnished 80 of the inmates, as compared with 82 born in Kentucky itself.

The convict in the early days of Kentucky was said to be a daring and desperate character, as was natural in a frontier existence, and he required the most rigid discipline and constant watching to keep him within the prison walls and to force his compliance with the rules of the prison. Horse-stealing and other thefts, as well as crimes of violence, were characteristic of the earlier years. The list of the more frequent crimes from 1800 to 1815 was as follows:

Horse-stealing	55	Rape	4
Felony (not specified)	46	Perjury	3
Larceny (grand and petty)	23	Counterfeiting	3
Manslaughter	23	House burning	2
Stealing slaves	6		

Virginia had established its own penitentiary system in 1796, followed in two years by Kentucky. Both States drew with much literalness upon the penitentiary system that had just developed at the Walnut Street Prison in Philadelphia. Before 1796 or 1797, at which time the act of the Kentucky Legislature made murder in the first degree the only capital crime, twenty-six felonies had been punishable by death. The widespread influence of the blood-abhorring Quakers thus reached Kentucky, and gave to the frontier State the chance to say later with frequency that in the early history of the Kentucky prison system there

"was a degree of philanthropy and sound philosophy not surpassed elsewhere in the world."

The new State, with small and scattered population, was of course poor. Popular subscriptions of money or one acre of land — which might be sold to bring in cash — were asked about the year 1796, with which to build the prison. The prison was to be large enough to hold 30 persons. The program of prison discipline was far more complete than was for a long time the prison itself. As in Philadelphia, solitary confinement during not less than one-twentieth nor more than one-half of the sentence was mandatory, and, as in other States, so here it was found impracticable to carry out the law.

Inmates were to be instructed in branches of labor. Frankfort, the capital of the State, was chosen as the location of the prison. The first convict was received in 1800. The administration of the prison was under a board of six inspectors. The annual salary of the keeper was $333.33, and of the deputy keeper $100. The first keeper was John Stuart Hunter, who had emigrated from Philadelphia in 1783, and was described as "an amiable gentleman, very sanguine, and somewhat visionary in his notions." To save money, Hunter was also appointed physician. A sample report of his treatment, reported to the board of inspectors in 1802, was the following:

April 16, 1802, T. Jones — colic.
  1 dose castor oil.
  Bled.
  Anodyne — recovered.

For some months after the opening of the prison, the number of inmates did not equal the number of inspectors. Treatment was of an intimate and individualistic character. The board voted, for instance, on October 9th, 1800, that

"Peter Winebrenner (a convict), be allowed 3 d. on each pair of shoes he makes of best quality; 2 d. for second quality. For best boots, 12 d.; for second quality, 9 d.; and those under him be allowed 2 d. per pair of best shoes, etc. The weavers to be credited 4 d. for each yard of cloth of 600 or under; for finer quality, 1 d. more."

The rules of the period give a picture of the prison routine. On the first of May and of November, two new outfits of clothes, underwear, etc., were given. The bed equipment consisted of coarse country tow linen; of a bed tick filled with straw or chaff; two woolen blankets and a bunk. The linen of the prisoners was changed once a week. Prisoners were to bathe when directed. They were to wash their hands and faces before breakfast. Heads and beards were to be closely shaven on Saturday evenings, and at the same time the convicts were to wash and iron their own clothes. Blankets were to be washed on the first Mondays of January, April, July and October. Cell walls were to be whitewashed the last Saturday in April and October, with an extra ration at the time for the convicts performing this service.

The physician was to keep a record of the sick, and lay the same before the board of inspectors twice a year. No liquor was to be introduced into the prison, under a penalty of a twenty-dollar fine. No visitors without passes were to be admitted, except officers of the prison, ministers of justice, members of the General Assembly and ministers of the Gospel. The labor hours were like those at Philadelphia. The prisoners might walk and air themselves in the yard, as the keeper should permit. No games of chance were allowed, nor any other sports save by permission of the keeper.

Convicts might read in their leisure time, and donations of books were asked. There was to be a plain, practical discourse on Sunday morning. For prisoners violating rules, there were solitary "refractory cells," and for attempted escapes there were the punishments of irons and solitary confinement. In 1802, labor accounts were opened with each prisoner, as in Philadelphia, but in 1810 this system was abandoned as impracticable.

The "days of small things" lasted at the Penitentiary for many years. Watchmen, for instance, received but $10 a month, yet might be fined $40, if it were shown that they had not used all diligence to prevent a successful escape. Convicts were credited for their work, and debited for clothing, maintenance, etc. In 1802 the agent — who was the financial and industrial manager of the prison — was ordered by the inspectors to charge each convict as follows:

For clothing per year	$20 00
For subsistence, and the expense of watchmen and agent	36 00
When there are more than 10 convicts	31 50
And so on, down to 20 convicts	15 25

In 1804, when three convicts had escaped, the rule was made that convicts should be debited with proportionate share in the expenses of retaking convicts, and five prisoners were charged an equal share of the expenses. Furthermore, the courts visited costs on the convicted prisoners, which the prisoners should pay off from their share of the profits of their labor. George Fielding, for instance, about 1807 was sentenced to the "jail and penitentiary house," for two years, with the following costs:

Clerk's fees	$9 66
Sheriff's fees	1 11
Attorney's fees	2 50
Veniremen's allowance	14 93
Called court, expenses of	10 61
	$38 81

There were frequent additional charges, as in the following case:

To the sheriff, summoning 23 men as guards	$4 83
To one rope, to confine prisoner on taking him to penitentiary	25
To distance of 17 miles, at 12 1-2 cents a mile	2 12½
To 23 guards, for traveling 17 miles, at 3 cents, going and returning	23 46
	$30 66½

Rules of punishment, some of them unique, were developed in the first decade of the nineteenth century. Any convict commencing a quarrel with another should "suffer such punishment (within the prison) as should be awarded by an impartial jury, but not over four lashes, or 10 hours of solitary confinement." Any prisoner who struck another, when the blow was not returned, was to receive on the bare back such number of lashes as should satisfy the injured person — but not to exceed twenty lashes, and not over ten a day. A retaken escaped convict should receive thirty lashes, and those convicts giving bribes thirty lashes. A convict who attempted to burn the prison in 1807 was sentenced to 10 lashes a day for ten days. In this year the ball and chain was used for the first time.

The industrial problem became increasingly complicated at the prison. Various industries were tried: Nailmaking, weaving, blacksmithing, shoemaking, etc. In December, 1808, the agent advertised that he had on hand a large quantity of nails, log chains, drawing chains, pole irons, axes, hoes, tinware, copper ware, shoes, boots, etc.

"all of which he offers at the most reduced prices for cash, or for the following kinds of produce, to wit: whiskey, brandy, cider, lacure, pork, bacon, hams and hog's lard, to be delivered in Frankfort."

The prison found it very hard, on the one hand, to get raw material like iron and coal from Pittsburg and elsewhere, and on the other hand to find a market for its products. The Legislature authorized the sale of products at any point on the Ohio or Mississippi Rivers. The agent of the prison might contract with any supercargo or shipper to take on freight cargoes to such points, taking a receipt or bond for the faithful discharge of duty. The returns from the sales were to be made within six months, and the agent was to pay the net proceeds into the public treasury. After September, 1810, the prison was to receive no further appropriations from the State, and must subsist from the labor of the prisoners. The agent was to receive ten per cent. commission from the sales.

This plan opened up a direct road to the most embarrassing results. The prison administration was forced, in order to get money to run the prison, to sell its goods. A market, often far distant, had to be sought. Nail making, which at first had appeared to be a good industry, soon found in New Orleans a successful competitor. Long chances were taken with customers whose credit was doubtful. In a land that was still a frontier, the age was one of barter. In 1811 and 1812, outstanding dues to the prison amounted to about $13,000. Long-time credit was given. Money to buy raw material for the prison was often lacking. In 1813, the State advanced $5,000 to buy nail-iron. There was no other prison of the kind west of the Alleghanies, none nearer than Virginia and Philadelphia. The problems of industrial management in prisons were new, and without clear precedents.

In 1815, a new method was tried. The keeper was to have full charge of the prison, and render an account every three months to the State auditor. The keeper was empowered to make contracts and collect debts. He was to have ten per cent. commission on all articles, when sold and paid for. The attitude of the Legislature was clearly that of handing over a troublesome problem to the keeper for solution, and telling him to run the prison the best way he could. The finances became with each year more involved. The office of industrial agent was created. The Legislature questioned why, with the convicts working ceaselessly, the Penitentiary did not pay a profit. In 1823, the Legislature found the institution very unprofitable, and the prices of articles too high.

There was talk now of abandoning the Penitentiary and restoring the earlier sanguinary laws. It is to be noted that this movement was practically contemporaneous with the agitation in the Eastern States to have a new prison system, or else revert to ancient methods. In 1825, the Legislature made a radical departure, and handed the prison over bodily to the newly appointed keeper, Joel Scott, who continued in office until 1832. He was to employ the convicts at hard labor, treat them humanely, pay the State half of the net profits accruing from the labor of the convicts, and keep the other half of the net profits in lieu of salary. He was to maintain the prisoners, and also defray all other expenses except buildings. The State was at no time to receive less than $1,000 a year from the keeper.

This procedure meant literally the wholesale leasing of the prison and its population to one man. Labor, rent, equipment, plant, heat — all were delivered over to Scott. The State was weary of the long years of unprofitable prison management. No other successful prisons were in sight, to suggest any other plan. These were the very years when the prisons in Philadelphia, New York and Boston were heavy charges upon the State. In those cities also, there was, as we have said, strong agitation to give up the existing penitentiary systems and revert to the barbarous corporal and capital punishments that the penitentiary systems had replaced.

Kentucky was watching the progress of prison matters in the East. An enlightened statement was made by Governor Adair to the Legislature in 1821, that the prominent defects in the Kentucky system were the omission of solitary confinement, the lack of any general instruction of prisoners, the absence of all rewards of merit to the convicts, and the neglect of the State to furnish any suitable provision for prisoners on discharge. The Governor urged absolute and compulsory solitude of prisoners as both punitive and reformative. Prisoners should be taught reading, writing and arithmetic. Rewards should be offered that would bring to the worthy prisoners both exemptions and distinctions, and would also shorten the time of confinement and service. The convict should on departure receive a part of his earnings. The penitentiary system should not be abandoned; it was not a money-making or money-earning project, but a magnificent plan.

We have not found evidence that the State met Governor Adair's recommendations, except in the matter of erecting an additional prison building during Scott's administration. The chief interest was that the prison should cease to be a financial burden to the State. To protect the prisoners against the desperate treatment that such wholesale leasing might easily bring with it, a board of visitors — the earliest supervisory body we have noted in any State — was appointed, consisting of the Auditor, Treasurer, Registrar and Attorney General, all State officials.

This board was required by law to visit the prison at least once a month, examine the state of the institution, note the health of the convicts, their dietary, cleanliness and treatment generally.

They were obligated to report to each successive Legislature their opinion as to the management and government of the prison. In practice this intended check on the administration of the keeper was neglected, only three reports being made to the Legislature in later years. Sneed, the chronicler of the history from which the details of this account have been taken, states, however, that Keeper Scott was a man of integrity, and allows it to be inferred that the prison was properly administered.

The financial troubles of the State were now largely past. By 1827 the Penitentiary had ceased to be an annual burden. New industries and machinery had been introduced. The keeper found no difficulty in vending his products. Unquestionably, there was long, hard, daily toil at the prison. By 1830, the average population numbered 100. The men worked from sun to sun, save for meals. Shoemakers worked until 9 or 10 o'clock at night in the winter. There were two meals in the winter and three in the summer.

Scott studied the annual reports of the Prison Discipline Society of Boston. He advocated the principles of the then noted Auburn system. He furthered divine service at the prison, and in 1829 the Legislature appropriated its first money for moral and religious instruction, not to exceed $250 per annum, for a chaplain to conduct religious services and to teach. A chapel and school room were built. There was as yet no hospital. Corporal punishment was almost entirely dispensed with. Scott's health was declining, and he refused reappointment as keeper in 1832. How much Scott made for himself during his incumbency as keeper is unclear. Apparently, the total net profits were $81,136, of which Scott would receive half. Unquestionably, the position had now become a lucrative one.

Thomas S. Theobald succeeded Scott as keeper in 1832. His administration was characterized by great industrial activity. New workshops were built in 1835, providing also a large chapel, school room, hospital and mess hall. A new prison building, to contain 250 cells, was projected and completed in 184... The prison population in 1847 numbered 114, distributed as follows as to age:

15 to 20 years	11	50 to 60 years	16
20 to 30 years	58	60 to 70 years	1
30 to 40 years	35		
40 to 50 years	13	Total	124

A Legislative committee in 1839 found that the profits of the prison for nine months had been $15,030, of which $7,515 was the State's share. The State was, however, standing half of the expense of erecting new buildings. Profits from March 1st, 1839, to November 30, 1840, amounted to $42,512. A Legislative committee reported the whole prison to be a scene of activity, the workshops clean and healthy, the health of the convicts good. They were reported to be well clothed, comparatively happy, and kindly treated, although in many instances corporal chastisement was necessary.

The average number of convicts at the prison increased rapidly. For the four years ending in 1843, the average population had been about 160. The real profits for three years and nine months had been, in 1,400 days, $62,641. Each convict paid the State, over and above all expenses, 28⅝ cents per day. A Legislative report for 1843 republished the following table from the Prison Discipline Society's report:

Tabular View of Nine Penitentiaries

	No. of prisoners beginning of year	No. of prisoners end of year	Expenses over earnings	Earnings over expenses
New Hampshire	78	74		$460.62
Massachusetts	322	331	$1,015.92	
Rhode Island	14	21	6,548.86	
Auburn	695	717		17,706.76
Sing Sing	827	811		9,640.10
Maryland	329	284	6,493.13	
Connecticut	205	214		8,065.29
Ohio	483	480		21,897.32
KENTUCKY	162	162		29,859.52

The Legislative committee made the point that Kentucky, with fewer convicts than Ohio, was making more money than any other State.

And so the committee waxed generous! As an "echo of an enlightened and benevolent sentiment," and as showing Kentucky to be merciful and not cruel, the committee recommended that in addition to the sum of five dollars which the State gave the prisoner on discharge, he also be given a suit of clothes!

The earnings from March 1, 1839, to November 30, 1842, were $100,494, of which the State received its share. Small wonder that when in 1844, it came time for the Legislature to appoint a new keeper, there was most intense political activity. The award of the highly lucrative position was made to a firm, Craig and Henry by name.

Just at the close of this period occur the first echoes of discontent among the mechanics of the State at the competition of prison labor. A legislative committee recommended in 1844 that in view thereof, the manufacture of rope and bagging, non-competitive industries, be extended to employ as nearly as possible all prisoners.

The foregoing account, gathered from the exhaustive account of Sneed, portrays a prison that was seemingly without effect or influence upon the prison reform movements of the time, and which, far removed from the Eastern centers, went on its way, developing its own methods of administration and financial management, harkening to the developments in the East, but without reciprocal relations with the Eastern prison boards of executives. It is an instance of a prison in a frontier land, discovering a successful financial method, and utilizing methods of lease and of administration discovered in no Eastern State in the same period.

CHAPTER XXI

OTHER EARLY AMERICAN PRISONS*

1
OHIO

Numerous prisons were established in this country, or reconstructed, during the period of the growth of the Auburn and the Pennsylvania systems of prison administration, but in the foregoing chapters we have given detailed attention to those which seemed to play the more important or essential parts in the development of an American penology. The prisons we are now about to describe failed to wield noteworthy influence in the development of prison methods in States other than their own. Yet in each State we find certain developments not only essential to chronicle, but also of interest to the student.

Ohio's State prison became after its transformation into a prison of the Auburn type an exceptionally noteworthy money-maker for the State — and this is its chief characteristic in this period. The first State prison in Ohio was erected in Columbus, the capitol of the State, in 1816. It was an insecure, illy constructed edifice, calculated originally for only 30 prisoners, and it stood on elevated ground, back of the Scioto River. The surface of the ground about the prison was so uneven in places that convicts could evade at times the observation of the guards. The prison was on the conventional type, with large rooms. There was a wall, 400 feet long, 150 feet wide, and 14 feet high, enclosing the yard of the prison. The cell buildings were on the northern side of the wall.

Through the prison building ran a central passageway. The prison building itself was 150 feet long, 30 feet wide and 2 stories high. The passageway was eight feet wide, and the sleeping cells were on each side, *vis a vis,* and having grated doors. The prisoners could thus communicate with each other when locked up at night. When Crawford visited the prison in 1832, he found 5 cells occupied, each of the dimensions of 9 feet by 7. At one end of the building were the kitchen and dining hall, and over the kitchen was the hospital, a room 30 by 16 feet, also used as a workroom for the shoemakers and the tailors.

The basement contained several cells for solitary confinement, 8 feet by 6 feet in size. The walls were of stone, lined with plank. These cells were quite dark, and were entered by a trap door from the ground floor above. The convicts were confined therein for short periods, according to the sentence of the court. The workshops of the old prison were small and badly arranged. There was

---
* Chapter unfinished because of author's death.

a close association of the convicts with each other, without supervision. Owing to want of room, at the time of Crawford's visit, only 75 prisoners could be employed in the workshops, and the rest were shut up in their cells. The output had not been productive, and the prison was being run at a considerable loss.

At Crawford's first visit, there were 190 convicts, made up of 163 white men and 20 colored men, 4 white women and 3 colored women. On a subsequent visit he found 203 prisoners, of whom 114 were employed in working on the construction of the new penitentiary, also in making bricks a half mile away from the old penitentiary. Whenever the convicts exceeded the number of 120, the governor of the State was forced to grant pardons in order to create room in the prison for the newcomers.

Sentences to the penitentiary were at this time (1832) not actually exceeding generally 21 months. Several persons were found sentenced for life. The prisoners associated with each other at meal times, and their moral and religious welfare was totally neglected. Much of the time of the prisoners was passed in mutual contamination and in plots to escape. The officers of the prison seldom were sure of the safety of their own lives. The Legislature of 1831 branded the prison in the official statement that

"a more perfect system for the dissemination of vice could not be devised than is to be found within the walls of the Ohio penitentiary."

Crawford reported that the State had purchased a plot of land of some eight acres in Franklinton, not far distant from the old prison, and contiguous to extensive beds of limestone. The building was in process of erection at the time of his visits. It was to contain 700 cells. This new prison, on the Auburn plan, was expected to solve the same grievous problems of prison maladministration that had affected other States.

The old prison had a keeper as the only responsible officer. The keeper appointed all deputies, the clerk, the guards and the physician. He paid such compensation as he deemed reasonable, except to the clerk, who received $400 per annum and the physician, who received $250 per annum. The deputy keeper received $400. There were three overseers in the shops, and a doorkeeper, who received $300, and 3 men on the walls received $264 each per annum. The keeper was elected annually by the Legislature and received $1,000. He made all purchases, sold all manufactured articles, paid all expenses and made a quarterly statement to the State auditor, and an annual report to the Legislature.

Two-thirds of the inmates were convicted of horse stealing, larceny or burglary. The Boston Prison Discipline Society, reporting on this prison in 1827, gave five sentences as for life, several for 15 or even 20 years, and no sentences of less than 3 years. Two-thirds of the total number of sentences were for 3 years. In the old prison there was no classification, and in winter there were four men in a room, in summer three. There was no method of warming the sleeping rooms in winter. Of moral instruction there was little.

there being only occasional preaching. The principal evils of the old prison were, the faulty construction, the unusual proportion of sickness in the hospital, the want of instruction, and the gruesome cells for solitary confinement.

In 1828 a chaplain was appointed, named James Chute, at a salary of $30 a month, which was raised out of the personal subscriptions of the ministers of the synod of the Presbyterian Church of the region. Reformation was increasingly recognized as practically impossible under the old system — the keeper sent to Boston for the annual reports of the Prison Discipline Society, the Legislature discussed the prison repeatedly, a fire in 1831 destroyed nearly all of the shops and was probably incendiary, the governor's message in 1832 was one of general condemnation of the prison, and the chaplain resigned. An instance of the primitive conditions of the prison was evidenced in the fact that at this period the women prisoners were all kept in one large room, partly underground. There was no chapel and no assembly place in the prison. The prison was designated as a "sinking fund" of $10,000 per annum.

The new prison was carefully planned. There was to be a south front of 400 feet, to be occupied, in the center, by the keeper and his family, from which building there was a general entrance by a hall, 12 feet wide, to the guard room. Beyond was another passage, having on each side, entrances to the wing building that contained the cells. In the guard room were inspection apertures to command a view of the long passages in front of the cells. There was a double range of cells, back to back, and an area of 11 feet surrounding the cells. Each wing was to contain 70 cells, and to be of five stories. The cells were 7 feet by 3.6 feet by 7 feet. When built, they were found to be deficient in ventilation.

The prison for women was detached, and in the rear, a double range of cells, 24 in number. The upper floors of this building formed a hospital. There was an airing yard for the women's prison. The workshops were in a separate long range of buildings. At the back, the prison yard was 400 feet square, and a boundary wall of 25 feet in height, and 3 feet in thickness, was the barrier from the outside world.

In October, 1834, 189 convicts were moved from the old to the new penitentiary. At this time, $47,532.25 had been drawn from the State treasury for the cost of the prison, and $30,000 more was to be asked for. A Mr. Medberry was appointed warden. In 1837 it was reported that the convicts were used not only for the construction of the new prison, but for the State Lunatic Asylum at Columbus. Their labor value was estimated at fifty cents per day. There was still no chaplain and the death rate was high.

The Prison Discipline Society of Boston, persistently campaigning against the neglect of the Lord's Day by the continued omission of church services and a Sunday School, emphasized in its annual report of 1837 that the solitary cell of a prison was a deadly place in which to put a man in to spend his Sabbaths:

"Legislators of Ohio — ye fathers, ye brothers, ye sons — will you place *men*, sustaining these relations, week after week, month after month, and year after year, in solitary cells to spend their Sabbaths? Will you place mothers, sisters, daughters in solitary cells to spend their Sabbaths? Will you do it? If you will, may the Almighty avert from you the dreadful affliction of having members of your own families placed in these circumstances! May you never know by your own experience, what it is! May you never be driven to suicide by it! May you never have your flesh and blood dried up by the slow and consuming effects of unmitigated solitude and despair!"

However, the prison began to delight the Legislature from the financial side. In 1837 the earnings were good. In 1838 the Prison Discipline Society condemned the State for earning $20,000 from the work of the convicts, but giving them no Sunday suit!

"There ought to be a rebellion in society against all prisons where convict labor is more than sufficient to defray all expenses, if the prisoners are compelled to spend their Sabbaths and go to meeting in their dirty clothes! Where is the flesh in man's heart?"

Nevertheless, the prison went on profiting extensively by the labor of its inmates, and by 1840 had established a special reputation as a productive factory. Competent judges, after visiting it, and comparing it with other penitentiaries, declared it inferior to none. In 1841 the prison made $21,897, leading all American prisons in earnings. The State penitentiary at Frankfort, Kentucky, was second in this year.

In 1843-44, Gerrish Barrett, representing the Prison Discipline Society, made an extended tour of the central States, and visited the Ohio prison. He found 350 cells, operated on the Auburn plan, in five stories, well warmed by 6 stoves, and well lighted by 2 tiers of windows. The female apartment contained 36 cells, and only 9 inmates — 6 white and 3 black. There were 500 men under proper discipline and hardly giving, according to Barrett, as much trouble as the few women:

"The women fight, scratch, pull hair, curse, swear and yell, and to bring them to order a keeper has frequently to go among them with a horsewhip. . . . One of the best planned hospitals that I ever saw is in this prison."

In the year ending November 30, 1842, 137 prisoners were received. There were in that year 78 discharges by expiration of sentence, and 66 by pardon. No one was sentenced to the prison for less than one year. In the last year there had been a net gain of $28,794, of which $945 came from the admission of visitors. There was in the prison no library, nor teacher, or chapel.

Mr. Barrett preached at the prison. The day was cold and the room used as chapel was twice as large as need be. There were two outside doors, left wide open, that let in a constant current of fresh winter air. A small stove in the middle of the room scarcely made a perceptible change in the atmosphere. The prisoners were thinly clad, and sat on loose benches without backs. Meanwhile, Mr. Barrett, with overshoes and wadded surtout, shivered with the cold.

2.
WASHINGTON, DISTRICT OF COLUMBIA

A prison, to take the place of the old jail in the city of Washington, was contemplated as early as 182... The prison was erected in 1827 and 1828, and was on a point of land projecting into the Potomac, almost south of the Capitol, and in the direction of Alexandria. The principal building was of brick, on the Auburn plan, 120 feet long, 50 feet wide, 36 feet high, and contained 160 cells in 4 stories. There were also two buildings, one on each flank of the prison, having communication with it by a small door on a level with the first gallery. These buildings were 25 by 40 feet, containing cellars, two upright stories, and lodging rooms in the roof. One building was devoted to the keeper, his deputies and his family, and the other to the kitchen, the hospital, and other purposes. A wall, 75 feet in advance of the front, and 20 feet high, enclosed an area 300 feet square. The design of the prison was the result of a visit by Charles Bulfinch in 1826, while architect of the public buildings at Washington, to other penitentiaries, for suggestions relative to the new prison at Washington. He favored the Auburn plan.

The cells of the prison were 7 feet 11 inches long, 3 feet 4 inches wide, and 7 feet 9 inches high. The cells were warmed with stoves in the area, similar to the method at Sing Sing. The windows in the outside walls were large.

The prisoners worked in association in the daytime, and in silence from sun-up to sun-down. If they finished their work early, they might read the scriptures, and also religious tracts. Silence was strictly preserved in the cells at night. On discharge from the prison, the inmates were furnished with a garb suitable for a laborer, and money sufficient to bear their expenses home. The warden found a ready market for all the articles manufactured in the prison. At the time of Crawford's visit in 1831, there were 46 male convicts employed, among whom were 25 engaged at shoemaking, 8 at oakum picking, 2 at tailoring, 2 at carpentering, one at plastering.

The punishments for being idle and for conversation were, being placed in the stocks, and in solitary confinement in cells, but not in darkness. The restricted diet of bread and water was a part of the punishment, and the period was not to exceed 20 days.

The discipline was not strict, and the agent petitioned in 1832 for the use of the whip. The warden was found by Crawford to be warmly interested in the moral welfare of those committed to his charge. The board of control of the prison was made up of three inspectors, who visited the prison weekly. The warden was not to be present at that time unless required by the inspectors.

Several years later, in 1835, De Metz and Blouet visited the penitentiary, and reported an exaggerated solicitude on the part of the warden for his prisoners. There were services on Sunday, and a school for those who could not read. The discipline was found to be relaxed. Indeed, some prisoners asked the warden to keep them at the prison after they had finished their terms. The warden, an opponent of the Auburn system, because of the necessity of keeping up rigid discipline, was a believer in the Pennsylvania system of separate confinement.

The Reverend Gerrish Barrett, representing the Prison Discipline Society of Boston, visited the prison in 1842. He found it admirable in construction and a model of neatness, with no vermin, and no impure air. There was not an invalid in the hospital. There were 80 prisoners, the chief occupation being shoemaking. Punishments were mild. The prison ran behindhand regular in the operation of the industries.

This prison, at the nation's capital, went through the storm-and-stress period of American penology without seemingly having any influence upon it. Small, mild in discipline, conducting a regime that set a remarkable health record, the prison was nevertheless inconspicuous and offers nothing to the student of the currents of American penology.

3.

GEORGIA

The State penitentiary of Georgia emerges, in the reports of the Prison Discipline Society of Boston, from obscurity in 1827, only to be mentioned as threatened with abandonment by the Legislature of the State on the ground that it was not fulfilling the mission for which it was organized in 1817. Like the other prisons of the period, it was constructed on the old and traditional plan of large night-rooms, but by 1830 the system had become so unpopular that the Legislature abolished the prison by an overwhelming majority.

The institution had been a tax of several thousand dollars a year to the State. Rigid discipline, effected by means of the "cow skin," the "slue paddle," the "wooden horse," and confinement in a dungeon, had not brought forth industrial efficiency.

But, in January, 1832, a Colonel Mills was asked to take charge of the Penitentiary. He found 88 convicts, "mostly reduced to the lowest depths of degradation and perfect misanthropes." He pitied the group, sought to raise them from their degradation, and planned to use in the process mainly moral influences. He instituted what was exceedingly rare, if not unique in this period, a system of rewards and punishments, and we find that the privileges of the yard were given on the Sabbath to such as merited the same, on account of good conduct, and also the privilege of working for themselves during the time allowed for dinner, which was ninety minutes.

None of the prisons discussed as being in the midst of the currents of prison development in this period had instituted such radical innovation — one that even in the present period of American penology is still approached with doubt by not a few wardens of State prisons. The freedom of the yard on Sundays is in this year of 1922 enjoyed in many prisons, but even as late as 1910, there could not be found traces of it in most eastern prisons.

Colonel Mills was equally forceful in his plan of punishments. He used the stocks, which was unusual, and also cellular confinement and restricted diet of bread and water until the offending inmate was humbled. He was always careful not to punish until there were thorough grounds therefor. Convicts who had been found by Mills on his arrival as warden wearing heavy clogs were released and put on good behavior, and it was reported by him that he never had to punish one of them in summary manner for misconduct thereafter.

Before the coming of Mills, missionaries working in the prison had declared the situation hopeless; that the prison "was no place to get religion." With the coming of Mills, a great religious reformation movement took place. Preaching was not only tolerated, but requested, and a Bible class of considerable size was formed. Nor was the industrial end of the institution less developed. The business of the prison was greatly augmented, and net annual gains of several thousand dollars were reported. All the convicts were organized into a Sunday School. Clergymen came into the prison from the outside to preach. Mr. Mills' policy was as follows:

"The superintendent of a penitentiary should be a monarch, but not a tyrant. It is an easy matter to drive men to degradation by undue severity; there are very few that would bear the lash, without destroying that self-respect which is all-important to moral reformation."

The death rate of the prison was extremely low. There was no death among the officers, guards or convicts from the 10th of April, 1831, to the 28th of April, 1834. Nor was there any escape.

In 1841, the Reverend Gerrish Barrett visited on his travels this prison. He described it as in the suburbs of Milledgeville, the capital of the State, on ground that was too low. It had 150 cells, occupied by 160 prisoners, among whom were 4 white women and one mulatto. The cells were on the Baltimore prison plan, but smaller. The spaces between the tiers of cells were entirely floored over. The cell doors were of wood, without any grating, and fastened with a padlock.

The chief industries of the prison were shoemaking, harness making, and wagon making. The prison did not support itself. No ardent spirits and no tobacco were allowed. Thirty of the 160 prisoners could not read and 52 could not write. There was no one save their fellow convicts to teach the ignorant to read. There was preaching once a week from a minister from the town, who received $150 annually for his services. There was no flogging in the prison, but the paddle was used. The paddle consisted of a piece of wood, 4 feet long, and 2 or 3 inches in diameter; one end of the paddle was wider than the rest, flattened, and was filled with holes. With the flat end, from 5 to 30 blows would be applied to the bare skin of a prisoner, while he was held over a block or a barrel.

The wall about the prison was of brick, too low, and so weak that the keeper stated that a man could dig through it with a shoe knife in a few minutes.

4.
TENNESSEE

In the session of 1830, the Legislature of Tennessee passed a law authorizing the construction of a penitentiary. Three commissioners together with the governor of the State, were appointed to superintend the building of the institution, and they accordingly sent a representative into Eastern States to acquire information and advice. The foundation of the new prison was quickly laid near Nashville, and it was to be 310 feet long by 58 wide, and 3 stories high. A wall 4 feet thick and 30 feet high would enclose a yard 310 feet by 300 in the rear of the main building. By 1831 the prison was finished and occupied. It was on the general plan of Auburn and Wethersfield.

A correspondent of the New York Observer, writing in 1832, described it as the best penitentiary, probably, in the valley of the Mississippi. On a level plain, one-half mile west of the city of Nashville, it stood, the yard covering 3 acres of ground. The main building when completed would contain from 200 to 300 convicts. At the time, there were but 43 convicts, who were working daily in erecting the internal buildings and shops. There was solitary confinement at night, and association of work during the day.

In 1833 the prison was relatively complete, and was said to be on the general plan of the penitentiary on Blackwell's Island, New York City. There were two buildings, 4 stories high, containing in all 200 cells, in which the convicts slept in single cells at night. There were then 65 convicts. Since the opening of the prison, three years before, there had been received no woman prisoner. The convicts worked from sunrise to sunset, with the intervals for meals.

On Sunday, the convicts were confined in their cells for about half the day. Each convict had a Bible in his cell, which was sufficiently light so that he could read in the daytime. There was a Sabbath School for all convicts. Four hours of each Sunday was given over to instruction under a clergyman, Reverend Mr. Parish, the professor of languages in Nashville University, assisted by four or five "pious young men." There was no chaplain appointed for the prison. Clergymen from the surrounding country preached. On the Sabbath, as at the time in Georgia, the prisoners were sometimes allowed a short period in the yard. At this time there had been no escapes, no insurrections, and no recommitments.

The punishments consisted of solitary confinement for not exceeding 30 days on the order of the keeper, subject to the supervision of the inspectors.

The earnings of the prison exceeded the disbursements during the next few years. The official attitude toward the prisoners was far more lenient than in the north, and we find in 1838 a law providing for an actual gratuity and privilege for the well conducted prisoners in the form of chewing tobacco for those accustomed to the weed. Incidentally, the Prison Discipline Society of Boston protested against this action of the Legislature.

The missionary, Gerrish Barrett, visited the prison in 1841. He found a prison on the Auburn plan with the keeper's house, as usual, in the center of the building, with the cellblocks as wings on each side. The cell doors were of wood, the grating in the doors small, the ventilation of the cells imperfect, and the area outside the cells 25 feet wide. The number of prisoners was 181, of whom 173 were white males and 6 black males. There were but two women in the prison.

Before the penitentiary system had been introduced into the State, in 1833, criminals were punished by whipping, cropping, hanging and other severe punishments. The punishments substituted therefor have been outlined above.

Most of the convicts were found to be employed in making hats, stonecutting and blacksmithing. The articles were sold for the account of the State, and not on contract. There was each year an excess of profits over expenses.

We find at this time, in Tennessee, a method of commutation that existed in no northern prison at the time, and was a very early precursor of the now customary methods of shortening the prison sentence through good behavior. This method was reported in the journal of Gerrish Barrett, and yet no comment whatsoever was made upon it by the Boston Prison Discipline Society, although thereby there had been spread before them the direction that in future years the entire system of reduction of sentences by reward for good conduct and industry was to follow.

For good conduct, a deduction of two days in each month was made from the term of the sentence, and conversely, for each day of punishment inflicted, 5 days were added to the length of sentence. Barrett himself passed over this revolutionary departure from the conventional methods without comment! He was much more concerned about the absence of church or Sunday School.

Visiting the prison again in 1842 or 3, he found that the earnings from the labor of prisoners, since the reception of the first prisoners in 1831, had been more than enough to meet the first cost of the Penitentiary. He presented the following social statistics relative to the 177 convicts of the Penitentiary: (*See footnote, page* 260.)

CHAPTER XXII

COUNTY JAILS

In 1911, at the National Conference of Charities and Corrections, held in Tremont Temple, Boston, Massachusetts, an elderly man, Frederic H. Wines, one of the long-time authorities in the field of delinquency and the treatment of the criminal, spoke in a manner that moved the great audience deeply. Mr. Wines was the son of Enoch C. Wines, pioneer in this country in agitation along more modern lines for the establishment of the State reformatory, the indeterminate sentence and parole. The elder Wines had organized the National Prison Association in 1870. He had been the founder of the International Prison Congress of 1872 in London. He had, in 1880, published the most authoritative volume yet issued on the "State of Prisons in the United States."

Frederic H. Wines, the son, had come nearly to the end of a long and useful life. Many of his friends sensed the fact that his strength was failing. His words that night in 1911 were an admonition to the workers in charitable and correctional fields in this country:

> "Mine is a poor, weak voice; it will not carry very far. This right arm is not the arm of a giant, nor even of an athlete; it will not deliver a smashing blow. For the sake of the human derelicts languishing in merited or unmerited confinement, I could wish that both were stronger. Still more earnestly do I wish it for the sake of our common country and its honor.
>
> "An old man suffers in many ways that a young man hardly understands. One of my secret griefs is the shame I feel, that my country has so long tolerated, and continues to tolerate, a wrong which disgraces it in the eyes of the world, and which, unless it is redressed, must sooner or later bring down upon it the vengeance of Almighty God.
>
> ". . . The only hope of enlightened progress in dealing with the problem of crime in America is the overthrow of the county jail system. . . . With the State once in command, there can be no question but it will find a way to right the wrong and remedy the evils which inhere in the present organization and management of minor prisons."

This utterance came one year after the Eighth International Prison Congress had been held, for the first time in the United States, at Washington. Universal condemnation had been expressed by the foreign delegates, numbering over a hundred, of the American county jails. The paradox of finding in the same country many examples of the most enlightened and advanced treatment of prisoners in reformatories and prisons, and, on the other side, the abhorrent neglect of lesser offenders and persons awaiting trial in county and local prisons, struck deeply into the minds of the men and women from foreign countries. It would seem that a clarion note had been sounded in 1910 and 1911 to American State and local governments, and that the next general line of attack in penological matters should be upon the county jail.

Nevertheless, in 1920, at the Semi-Centennial of the American Prison Association, held at Columbus, Doctor Hastings H. Hart, also one of the oldest and most distinguished workers in the charitable and correctional fields in the United States, challenged the members of the Prison Congress as follows:

"Men and women of the American Prison Association, I charge you with fifty years' neglect of the most hopeful and most deserving part of the prison population! I beg you to repent and, from this day forward, to attack the jail problem with the same interest and intelligence whereby such great results have been accomplishd in the reformation of convict prisons and the development of the modern adult and juvenile reformatory system. . . . .

"I have examined the twenty-six volumes of proceedings from 1883 to 1919. They contain about 14,000 pages. Of these, about 170 pages — a little over one per cent. — are devoted directly to the subject of county and municipal jails. In the nine years from 1888 to 1897, I can find only one page of direct discussion of jails. It is true that the subject of county jails is referred to incidentally in reports on prison discipline and in numerous papers and addresses, but these 170 pages are all that I can find dealing directly with the subject."

Why is it that during the century and a half, approximately, since the organization of the Philadelphia prison society and the beginning of an American prison system, the county jail has continued to be "the weakest link in the American penal system?" Why does there seem to be practically a perpetual blight upon efforts to put the county jail management upon an efficient basis? Is there any hope that, as Doctor Hart infers, there is a solution, and that reclamation may ultimately start where it logically should start, in the minor prisons and with the lesser offenders?

The study of the development, or persistency, of the county jail is not at all without interest from the historical standpoint, and out of the experiences of the first seventy-five years, the period covered by the present study, we may learn much as to the causes for the notorious position occupied even to-day by the county jail in our country. For the county jail is the basic correctional institution, out of which grew, on the one side, the prison and the reformatory, as well as the juvenile reform school and the larger local prisons, the Bridewell, the debtors' prison, and municipal institutions, on the other.

In the Colonial times, as soon as a community developed beyond the few houses originally built and occupied, there was of course need for a lock-up for the detention of offenders. As soon as a county government was instituted, a county place of detention and punishment was essential. To the county prison were sent the criminals not dealt with summarily by public punishments. The county jail became quickly, in our Colonial period, the center for the reception of lawbreakers.

The Quakers, foremost in the elements of prison reform, made the workhouse in Pennsylvania and New Jersey the basis of the early penal system. Yet it was inevitable that a county institution, whether workhouse or jail, should develop at the call of necessity.

In March, 1682, it was enacted by the assembly of East Jersey that "in each county there shall be a common gaol, which shall be for felons, vagrants and idle persons, and safely to keep all persons committed to gaol for debt before or after judgment."

The administration of the county gaol was vested in the sheriff of the county, a provision still generally existing. The Colonial gaol was a gather-all. As certain cities, like Philadelphia, New York and Boston grew to metropolitan dimensions, the gaols of those cities became in appearance municipal prisons, the city and county of Philadelphia being, for instance, coterminous.

Thus we found the British in Philadelphia, in 1776, taking possession of the local jail. In 1787, the reorganized prison society of Philadelphia was to direct its attention in greater measure to the miserable physical and social conditions of the public jails. It was the scandalous old jail at the corner of Third and High Streets in Philadelphia that was abandoned in 1790 in favor of the Walnut Street Prison, which became the first State prison. But, as we saw in the initial chapters of this study, within relatively few years the Walnut Street Prison became congested and conglomerate in its character, taking on again many of the attributes of the abandoned jails.

Then came the first effort at a division and classification of the prison population on the basis of the elimination of the lesser offenders from the State prison, and their confinement in a local jail. As we said in Chapter Five, some physical alleviation came when the Bridewell was built, on Mulberry and Broad Streets. To this institution were sent henceforth those lesser offenders whom we to-day classify as misdemeanants, or violators of local ordinances. In short, the prison had sloughed off a certain proportion of its former population — yet the Walnut Street Prison continued to be congested with felons, due to the increase of the prison population out of all proportion to the State's population.

In the city of New York a similar development occurred. We have seen how Newgate Prison of New York became a center of promiscuous association, and how the first prison system broke down. We saw Thomas Eddy, as early as 1804, recognizing that the prison in Greenwich was wholly inadequate to deal with the crime problem, and urging that a new prison be constructed to take the place of the then existing Bridewell, from which only a few years before the felons and major offenders had been received in the new prison. Both in Philadelphia and New York, as well as in Boston, the first State prison grew ultimately into a magnified county jail, so far as problems of congestion, promiscuous association, debauchery and general physical conditions were concerned.

But out of the first State prison system evolved a second system, of silence, labor, and repression, typified by Auburn and the Eastern Penitentiary. No such development came to the minor prisons, the jails, the Bridewells, the local prisons. When the

Prison Discipline Society was organized in Boston in 1825, its primary stress was laid upon the betterment of State prisons. Yet, in its first annual report it dilated upon deplorable conditions in county jails, and it is from this point on that we find systematic attention given to the horrifying indifference of the county and its residents to the plight of the denizens of county jails.

The county jails in all States south of the Potomac were destitute of court-yards, and had windows on the streets. So insecure was one jail in Virginia that all the prisoners made their escape in the winter of 1824-25. In northern States, the new prison discipline society's secretary found cells or rooms without windows, some cells in which the only ventilation was through cracks in the door. Three men were placed in one such cell, and within a few hours the keeper found them apparently lifeless. In many jails the only means of communicating with prisoners was through holes in the cell doors.

The same jail treatment was meted out to persons convicted and to those awaiting trial. A man condemned to several years for robbing the mail was found in the same cell with others who had not been proven guilty. A black man was found in a large cell, naked, with eleven other persons, also prisoners. In many jails in the larger towns no clothing was furnished by the jail authorities, and the prisoners wore such clothes as they had.

In the District of Columbia was an old jail, described as follows by Representative Thompson in Congress in January, 1826:

"Here, just under the eye of Congress, not half a mile from the hall in which we legislate, we have the worst prison on this side of the Atlantic. The building is divided by a passage from one end to the other, on each side of which are eight cells. In these 16 cells the marshal has frequently been compelled to confine 70 or sometimes 80 individuals, among them innocent individuals, against whom no bill was afterwards found; and these imprisoned not for an hour, but for months. . . .

"In one of these cells were confined . . . 7 persons, 3 women and 4 children. They were almost naked; one of them was sick, lying on the damp brick floor, without bed, pillow or covering. In this abominable cell, these 7 human beings were confined, day by day, without a bed, chair or stool, or any other of the most common necessities of life; compelled to sleep on the damp floor without any covering but a few dirty blankets. . . . I forbear to describe more minutely the uncleanliness of this abominable place."

Probably as a result of this impassioned statement, $5,000 was appropriated by Congress to repair the jail at Washington, $10,000 to build a jail in Alexandria and $40,000 to build a penitentiary in Washington.

It was at this period, in 1826-27, that agitation in several States resulted in the erection of separate institutions, called houses of refuge or houses of reformation, for the reformatory treatment of juvenile delinquents, through their removal from prisons and jails, and their care along radically different lines, stressing education and reformation, and reducing the element of punishment. A considerable proportion of lads and even boys were found in the prisons:

STATES	Whole Number	Under 21	Proportion
Maine	116	22	1 to 5
New Hampshire	253	47	1 to 5
Vermont	534	75	1 to 7
Connecticut	117	39	1 to 3
Auburn	997	148	1 to 6
Virginia	201	30	1 to 7

Children under twelve years of age were found in the prisons. "The loathsome skin, the distorted features, the unnatural eyes of some of these boys indicate the existence of unutterable abominations."
Jail fever had, within the previous three years, raged twice at the Bridewell in New York City, and from there had been introduced into the local Penitentiary at Bellevue, on the East River "near New York." This prison was an intermediate institution between the Bridewell and the State Prison, and will shortly be more fully described. The Prison Discipline Society reported that the wretched "apartment" in the Bridewell was the common receptacle of all the males who were committed to that prison. It had contained at one time 90 persons "in a common mass of drunkenness, lasciviousness, obscenity, madness, filth, lunacy and fever." The Bridewell was declared to be a common nuisance, within 20 yards of the City Hall.

"When the secretary of this society visited the Bridewell this season, he was told that it would not be safe to risk his life, even for the few moments, in the room in which most of the persons committed were immediately confined by 20's."

In Philadelphia's old county prison, the deaths in the female department in the last year had been one fourth of the population. Vagrants were confined in the hospital, diseased "in a dreadful manner which may not be named." The average deaths in the Walnut Street Prison in Philadelphia had been for six years more than six per cent.

The Prison Discipline Society, in this survey of jails in its initial year of activity, found recidivism and intemperance striking characteristics of the jails. The superintendent of the Almshouse and Penitentiary in New York City declared that nine-tenths of the commitments were from intemperance, while the similar officer in the Boston House of Correction set the number at three-fourths. A typical "rounder" or recidivist was cited:

R. L.

Received.
October 8, 1824.
January 11, 1825.
February 11, 1825.
October 12, 1825.
January 26, 1826.
April 26, 1826.
July 28, 1826.
August 29, 1826.

Discharged.
October 14, 1824.
January 17, 1825.
August 9, 1825.
November 11, 1825.
April 25, 1826.
July 25, 1826.
August 12, 1826.

Obviously, with such a stream of repeaters, vagrants, drunkards, and petty offenders flowing ceaselessly through the jails and Bridewells, there was no inducement to aim at reformation of the inmates. There was no continuity of executive management of the jails. In the county prisons or jails the sheriffs, elected by partisan politics, could not in most States succeed themselves. The physical conditions of the jails were in almost all cases primitive, if not actually repellant and abhorrent. The most degraded types of humanity were committed to these institutions and in a conglomerate mass.

Here and there, an institution for lesser offenders rose above the great mass of jails, sometimes because of its bulk and great populations, sometimes because of its exceptional management. The Penitentiary in New York City was such an institution, famed at first only for the highly objectionable conditions existing therein. It was connected with the Almshouse, on the East River, some two and one-half miles from City Hall. It was in the same yard with numerous other buildings, and to these institutions were sent the paupers, the criminals and the wretched flotsam and jetsam of the city, who were not sentenced to State prison. The number of the poor people brought together here at some seasons of the year was about 2,000. The Penitentiary was on the old plan of large rooms, sometimes holding twelve persons thus crowded together. In one-fourth of the building, cells on the Auburn plan had been recently erected, at the time of the visit of the Boston society's secretary. For a short time there was a treadmill connected with the Penitentiary, almost the only example of this form of discipline recorded among the prisons of this country, and then only for a few years.

The Penitentiary was under the same general supervision as the Almshouse, a board of commissioners; there was the same superintendent, the same physician and the same chaplain. The prisoners varied from 200 to 300 at one time. With the erection of the House of Refuge the children, formerly at the Penitentiary, were moved to the new institution. A large proportion of all the prisoners at the Penitentiary were colored. The crimes were chiefly larceny, assault and battery, and the lesser grades of crime common to a large city. Sentences did not exceed three years. Employment in the prison was very irregular, there being the treadmill, a pin factory, and the picking of oakum, as well as intermittent work on the public highways. There was no system of labor. The superintendent of the institution was wholly pessimistic as to the possibilities of reformation of the inmates:

"As well might you kindle a fire, with a spark, on the ocean, in a storm."

The county prisons were generally constructed without reference to classification, inspection by the officers, or economy. Prisoners were allowed to commingle freely, and hence to contaminate each other. Keepers argued as follows, in favor of the commingling of prisoners:

It takes more time to open many doors than it does to open a few.
There are some apartments in upper stories and it is not convenient to put the prisoners up there.

It takes more work to feed and warm the rooms when the prisoners are separated.

Prisoners wish to be in the same rooms for company.

In general there was free communication through the doors between the different cells. There was a great lack of cleanliness, as might be expected, and vermin swarmed. County prisons had far more females as prisoners than did the State prisons, for there was frequent reluctance to sentence a woman to State prison, and the county prisons were the remaining feasible institution. Often there was no matron to supervise the female prisoners. Many prisoners, both male and female, were simply held for trial, and were finally discharged, not condemned, "without bill or witness." In the county jails, among the prisoners, were many children and youths.

In the New York Penitentiary, in 1828, no change had been effected in the night-rooms or large cells, and "convicts could not lie down without mingling their limbs in one solid mass." In New York City an aged clergyman, the Reverend John Stanford, almost four-score years old, was continuing to "fulfill his numerous appointments at the State Prison at Greenwich, the Penitentiary at Bellevue, the Bridewell and the Debtors' Jail."

Statistics from the Bridewell in New York for the years 1822-25 showed the extraordinarily large number of prisoners who passed out of the Bridewell without ever coming to trial:

Years	Committed to Bridewell	Tried	Acquitted	Condemned	Discharged without trial
1822	2361	541	180	361	1820
1823	1926	599	177	422	1327
1824	1961	586	169	417	1375
1825	2168	547	161	386	1621
	8416	2273	687	886	6143

In short, of 8,416 persons committed to the Bridewell, 6,143 were discharged without trial. And from Philadelphia it was reported in 1828 that

"of about 130 ordered for trial at a late court of quarter sessions, there were about 70 or 80 against whom no bills had been found, many of whom were apparently without offense, and were of course discharged, but with tarnished characters, and probably with minds corrupted during their sojourn in prison."

The Boston Society's secretary had hardly begun his visits to jails and other lesser institutions of corrections before he became aware of the abominable conditions surrounding many persons who were imprisoned for debt. These people were not criminals, yet were forced to abide with criminals. They were not convicts, yet they were in prison, and their eyes and ears and bodies were subjected to the same abhorrent surroundings, the same filth and licentiousness as were the persons committed for some form of lawbreaking. The smallness of the sums because of which debtors were thrown into jail was shocking to the sensibilities of men and women of the time we are studying, when the facts were brought to their attention.

In one county prison, out of 37 cases of imprisonment for debt, 20 were for less than $20. In another State, the law prohibited imprisonment for a sum less than $13.33. "Such a law would diminish imprisonment for debt in Massachusetts by one half," wrote the secretary, Mr. Dwight. The amount of costs in connection with the prosecution was more than one-half the average amount of the debts themselves. In 18 cases cited, the whole amount of the debts was $155.68, and the loss of time to the debtors themselves in prison was 236 days —"which at 75 cents a day would have paid the debts."

The fruitlessness of the efforts to collect debts in this manner was more than clear. In one instance, out of 42 cases of imprisonment for debt, only two debts, totalling $16, were paid, or a proportion of $1 to $141 of the total debts. Thirteen of the debtors were imprisoned 13 months, and then discharged. In most States, the debtor was retained in prison only so long as the creditor paid a stipulated sum for his maintenance. Since the creditor was generally not going to secure his payment from a man who by reason of his being in prison had no chance to earn the sum required, it followed that such imprisonment was often solely for purposes of revenge. With the coming in of laws requiring the creditor to pay the board of the debtor in prison, the amount of imprisonment for debt was found to diminish by one half. In New York, the number of cases of imprisonment for debt in 1828 was 1,085. Debts amounted to $25,409; damages to $362,076. The amount paid by debtors in jail toward the cancellation of such debts was only $295. The Boston Society's report for 1829 estimated that 75,000 persons were annually imprisoned for debt in the United States.

In another section of the same year's report, the following estimates were cited of the extent of such imprisonment for debt, and the causes thereof:

Number of persons imprisoned for debt annually in the United States, principally from the intemperate use of ardent spirits	50,000
Costs of process in 50,000 cases of imprisonment for debt	$250,000
Expenses of courts for same number of cases	250,000
Loss of time in prison at 60 cents per day, of 50,000 for 15 days each	450,000
Board of the same	250,000
Turnkey, notifying creditor, administering oath, etc	125,000
Derangement of affairs as much as loss of time	450,000
Grand total	$1,755,000

Visitors to the jail sometimes, but all too infrequently, would discharge a debtor by paying the debt. In the Arch Street Prison in Philadelphia,

"a gentleman from Boston discharged a decent young man from close confinement in this jail in February, 1830, by paying costs $1.50 and the original debt, 25 cents. He would in all probability have remained in jail 30 days.

". . . In the part of this prison appropriated to debtors, the unfortunate inmates, white and black, were found in one hall together, with privations so great as to form a severe punishment for their misfortunes and poverty."

The estimates of the proportion of debtors in the county and local prisons, in comparison with the "criminals," are surprising. In Worcester, Massachusetts, they were 3 to 1; in Rhode Island, 4 to 1; in 17 prisons of the north and middle States nearly 5 to 1. In Philadelphia, 30 persons were in prison for debts of less than one dollar; in 30 prisons there were 595 persons imprisoned for more than $1 and less than $5; in 32 prisons there were 2,184 persons imprisoned for more than $5 and less than $20. For more than $20 and less than $100, there were 902. The number of persons imprisoned for debts of over $100 was very small, or as 1 to 7 compared with the number imprisoned for less than $20.

In 15 prisons of the north and middle States the following figures applied:

Less than one day's imprisonment	269
More than 1 and less than 5 days	323
More than 5 and less than 10 days	203
More than 10 and less than 20 days	154
More than 20 and less than 30 days	83
Over 30 days	431

There was a total of 19,987 days of imprisonment. In 17 prisons, out of 2,057 imprisoned, only 294 paid their debts. Three times as many were discharged by the creditor as paid their debts. Twice as many took the poor debtor's oath as paid their debts.

The operation of the laws relating to imprisonment for debt were very different in the northern and the southern States. In 17 prisons of the northern States, in 1830, 2,742 persons were imprisoned for debt. In same number of southern prisons, only 35 persons. In Massachusetts, the law forbade any imprisonment for debts less than $5. In New Hampshire, for less than $13.33. Massachusetts required the creditor to pay the debtor's board. One jailer testified to the Society that many cases of imprisonment for small debts would be prevented if the creditors were obliged to take oath that the debts were *true* debts. The Society found that in Kentucky and Ohio, imprisonment for debt had already been abolished. The sheriff of Hunterdon County, New Jersey, wrote:

"The laws of New Jersey provide food, bedding and fuel for criminals in the county prisons; but for debtors nothing is provided but walls, bars and bolts. An applicant for the benefit of the insolvent law of this State must make oath that he has rendered a true and perfect inventory of all his lands and tenements, goods and chattels, money and effects. This inventory must accompany his petition to the county court for the benefit of the insolvent laws. The court then appoints him a hearing in forty days after making this application. You will now perceive the debtor must subsist during these forty days upon the cold and precarious crumbs of charity, starve to death in prison, or, infinitely worse than either, live upon the avails of a foresworn conscience."

The Providence Daily Advertiser, in this same year, published a statement one day, that

"on Saturday last, upwards of 20 persons were comitted to jail in this town, for debt, or executions. . . . Among the debtors are many of our most worthy fellow citizens. One of them, Captain Samuel Godfrey, is now 86 years of age, with the loss of hearing, and nearly bent double by infirmities. We envy not the feeling of a creditor who thus exacts the pound of flesh, at an age, too, when the sources of life are so dried up, that he might venture to cut it out without the risk of drawing a drop of blood.''

In the same year, the Society received many letters from prominent men throughout the country, among which letters one from "E. P." may be thus summarized as presenting the then current view among intelligent citizens:

"Imprisonment is punishment. Punishment, if deserved, implies previous crime. But poverty is of itself no crime. Therefore inability to pay a just debt does not necessarily imply crime. Consequently, imprisonment merely on account of such inability is unjust and wrong.

"If it can be shown that the debtor has committed a crime, let him be punished for his crime, and according to his deserts. But let him not be punished for what may be merely his misfortune."

In the Society's report for 1831, certain progress was reported in some States toward more lenient debtor laws. Maine had passed a law abolishing imprisonment for debt exceeding five dollars, and punishing fraudulent debtors. In New Hampshire generous "jail yard limits" were established, being for debtors the limits of the town. In Vermont, poor debtors were allowed to take the poor debtors' oath within two hours after judgment was rendered. There was, however, nothing to prevent imprisonment for small sums. In Massachusetts a law was passed in 1831 exempting females from imprisonment for debt, and others for sums less than $10. In New York a law was to go into effect in March, 1832, abolishing imprisonment for debt. There was in New York City a society for the relief of debtors confined for small debts, but only 15 persons seemed to have been released during a given period, probably a year, whose debts altogether amounted to only $132. In Maryland a law was passed exempting all persons from imprisonment for debt who had resided in the State four months, and where the debt did not exceed $30.

However, the Prison Discipline Society of Boston reported in this year that

"in regard to our county prisons, nothing has been done in the way of reform; and we have no heart to pull down the old county prisons and build greater, while the principal cause of any such necessity arises from the fact that about 3 in 1 of all the persons committed in them are for debt, and about two-thirds of these are for debts under $20, and from one-half to two-thirds of the whole number on writ, without judge, jury or witness. The country at large does not seem inclined to enlarge its county prisons for the sake of persons incarcerated for small debts. . . . We shall therefore labor (as a society) for the present to prevent the imprisonment of persons, at least for small debts, rather than labor to enlarge or rebuild the county prisons, for their solitary confinement or more severe discipline."

We turn now to another class of inmates of the county prisons, the insane, whose indescribably wretched and unjust fate shocked the new secretary of the newly-formed Prison Discipline Society. In the first annual report, in 1826, appeared a brief outline of some of the most flagrant instances of the horrible treatment of the "lunatics."

It was estimated that in Massachusetts there were, at the time, about 30 lunatics in county prisons. One was found in a jail, in a cell where he had been for nine years. He had a "wreath of rags" about his body. Another wreath of tattered garments was about his neck. In the cell was no bed, chair or bench. There were two or three rough planks in the room on which he could sleep. In the corner was a heap of filthy straw. He had built a bird's nest of mud in the open grate of his den.

"Connected with his wretched apartment was a dark dungeon, having no orifice for the admission of light, heat or air, except the iron door about two and one-half feet square opening into it from his prison. The wretched lunatic was indulging some delusive expectations of being soon released from his wretched abode."

In one county prison there were ten lunatics.

"Two were found, about 70 years of age, a male and female, in the same apartment of an upper story. The female was lying on a heap of straw, under a broken window. The snow, in a severe storm, was beating through the window, and lay upon the straw around her withered body, which was partly covered with a few filthy and tattered garments. The man was lying in a corner of the room in a similar situation, except that he was less exposed in the storm. The former had been in this apartment six, and the latter twenty-one years."

Another lunatic had in eight years left his room only twice. The door had not been opened in eighteen months. In the midst of the horrid and indescribable filth he lived. Seen through the door, the question was: "Is that a human being?"

"The hair was gone from one side of his head, and his eyes were like balls of fire."

In another room, a cellar, were five lunatics, of whom the keeper said:

"We have a sight to do to keep them from freezing."

The treatment of the insane was, at this period, still mainly of the nature described by the few typical instances just cited. The number of instances might be increased indefinitely. Harrowing beyond all other narratives of prison treatment are many of these descriptions. In the entire United States, at the end of the twenties of the nineteenth century, there were but few asylums for the insane. An asylum had been established in Williamsburg, Virginia, before the Revolution. Kentucky had a State asylum. The private asylum, called the McLean Asylum, had been in existence in Charlestown, Massachusetts, since 1818, and the Connecticut Retreat for the insane had been established at Hartford in 1824. The private asylum of Bloomingdale was founded in New York in 1821. In Pennsylvania was the Pennsylvania Hospital, the oldest of its kind for the insane in this country, founded in 1752. An asylum in Frankford, Pennsylvania, had been established in 1817.

In these asylums, the newer and humane methods of treatment of the insane were being applied as the curative effects of kindness and the striking off of chains became evident. But practically none of these asylums was open in any large measure to the poor, and particularly to the criminal population, with the result that lunatics, feared and also regarded generally as no longer human, were dealt with by most primitive and often fearful methods. For the security of the public they were confined in county prisons, or in almshouses, where prison cells were erected for them. Or they were lodged in the yards or environs of dwelling houses, in cages constructed by the families of the lunatics, and dealt with unintelligently, and often in fear. Garrets of houses would be used as the only available place of confinement — the "lunatic" becoming almost literally the skeleton in the closet of the family — or cellars were put in use. Chained, dragging heavy fetters about with them, or fastened to huge staples in the floor, forced into paroxysms of violence, the miserable sufferers grew worse and worse, as the treatment grew cumulatively abhorrent and severe.

A report of the New York Legislature showed in 1825 that there were in the State of New York "819 lunatics and 1,421 idiots." The ratio in comparison with mentally normal people was 1 to 721. Of these lunatics, only 263 were able to pay for their own support. The other 556 were insane paupers, either confined in private families, poorhouses, or jails or roaming at large, a terror to others. Bloomingdale could accommodate by the end of the third decade about 200 patients, and a small private asylum at Hudson, New York, about 50. A committee of the Legislature recommended a spacious hospital in the State to accommodate at least 300 poor and imprisoned lunatics.

In 1830, the Legislature of Massachusetts appropriated $30,000 for the erection at Worcester of a hospital for lunatics. The erection of the institution went on rapidly. Horace Mann, one of the building commissioners, wrote:

"The proper mode of treating insanity was almost universally unknown, and the jails and houses of correction were the only places where the strictness of confinement then deemed indispensable could be enforced. . . . It is now most abundantly demonstrated that, with appropriate medical and moral treatment, insanity yields with more readiness than ordinary diseases."

He recommended a change in the State law to provide that as soon as the institution was ready, no lunatic should thereafter be committed to a jail or house of correction, and that all then confined in jails and houses of correction be transferred to the asylum. In this connection, a curious omission is apparent, for when the law was passed, it did not include the transfer of lunatics from the State prison — and, as we have seen in Chapter XIV, the presence of the insane in the State prison was almost as detrimental as in the case of the lesser prisons.

By 1833, the Massachusetts State Lunatic Hospital at Worcester was in operation. The Prison Discipline Society's report for 1836 showed that during the previous year, 113 patients had been received, 112 discharged and 111 were remaining. Of the discharged, 52 had recovered, and 23 were improved. Of the patients during the year ending November 30, 1835, whose insanity was of less than one year's duration, recoveries were reported to be 82½ per cent. Of the old cases, the recoveries were but 15½ per cent. Ninety-one applications for admission had been rejected.

"One case had been, at the time when he was brought to the institution, 28 years in prison; for 7 years he had not felt the influence of fire, and many nights he had not lain down for fear of freezing. He had not been shaved for 28 years, and he had been provoked and excited by the introduction of hundreds to see the exhibition of his ravings. He is now, and has been, comfortable in health, well clad, keeps his room remarkably clean, shaves twice a week, sits at table with 16 others, takes his meals, walks about the village, and over the fields, with an attendant, and enjoys himself as well as his illusions will permit."

The trustees of the asylum asked the Legislature for a farm.

"Shut up in our halls, or in their cells, they (the patients) are unhappy, restless, discontented, and in consequence less mild and docile, often troublesome. But when suffered to go out into the field and garden to labor, their whole nature seems changed. . . . They become cheerful and healthy."

The superintendent of the McLean Asylum, Doctor Thomas G. Lee, was cited by the Prison Discipline Society as using most enlightened methods with the insane. The superintendent recommended for the insane all the varied industries of a large farm. He wrote:

"I confidently anticipate the time when all these things will be performed in our insane asylums, and when arrangements for such labor will be considered as indispensable as the strong rooms and straight waistcoats have been in times past. . . . We have within the last eight months demonstrated not only the practicability but the great utility of labor."

Just as the Prison Discipline Society elevated as a model the Auburn Prison, for other States to follow, so did the Society seek to discover something approaching a model among the lesser prisons. The secretary sought in vain among the county jails of which he learned, in this age before railroads and telegraph. In the second year of his incumbency of the office, he traveled several thousand miles. The salary of the secretary, Mr. Dwight, was $1,000, given only on condition that he would give his entire time to the work, and defray his own traveling expenses. He visited on his first tour thirteen States and the District of Columbia, paying main attention to prison conditions. It was practically entirely his findings that annually appeared in the annual reports of the Society. He spread "prison reform" propaganda in the several States, through groups and committees, and sought to establish branches of the Prison Discipline Society wherever he went, but without much result.

Dwight's hope was that some county jail could be found that he could praise in his reports. Rumor came to him that there was a good jail in Geneseo, New York; that Bangor, Maine, was going to build a modern county jail. In Boston, the Leverett Street Jail was a scandal that cried to heaven. The House of Correction in Boston soon developed the model that Dwight was seeking. Stonebreaking for the macadamizing of the city's streets was the principal kind of labor. There never, according to Dwight, had appeared elsewhere anything like the industry, efficiency and discipline among the men in the House of Correction in 1829. The matrons were pious. The earnings of the female inmates from sewing was no inconsiderable sum. There was, however, no separate confinement at night.

Dwight noted an interesting method of dealing with delirium tremens at the Boston House of Correction. At once, on admission, liquor was refused the inmate, but a strong decoction of wormwood was given freely, "like tea." There had been only one fatality.

The Boston council appropriated, in 1831, $20,000 to alter one of the buildings among the group of charitable and correctional institutions in South Boston, in order that it should contain 200 cells, on the Auburn and Wethersfield plan. De Beaumont and de Tocqueville declared the House of Correction in South Boston to be a model for similar establishments, and the county jail in Leverett Street just the opposite. They pointed out that the discipline of the Boston House of Correction dispensed entirely with the whip; that there was a hospital and a competent physician in attendance. They remarked upon the cleanliness of the institution.

The Boston House of Correction was, indeed, an exception to the run of lesser prisons. In Middlebury, Vermont, was a county jail, for instance, of which Dwight wrote:

"If it were known to the good people of Middlebury, Vermont, that a similar dark hole were in actual existence, and had been for a term of years, in Calcutta, and could probably be purified and enlightened by sending a missionary there for the purpose, his outfit might probably be immediately furnished and his support secured in that village, so well known for intelligent kindness and benevolence."

The more Dwight traveled, the more outrageous appeared to him the treatment of lesser offenders, and those imprisoned for debt. Gross ignorance characterized the jailers and the keepers.

"In the county prisons, to a vast extent the keeper may be a farmer, a deputy sheriff, a tavern keeper or almost anything else, which requires his absence except when he turns the key. The consequence is, profane swearing, gambling, Sabbath breaking, universal disorder and idleness; and it seems not yet to have been thought that vigilance is necessary to county prisons. So long as it is supposed that any class of prisons can be managed without unceasing vigilance, so long they will remain nurseries of vice.

Taverns were frequent adjuncts to the county jails. In the old county prison at Hartford, Connecticut, there was a tavern under the same roof, warmed by stoves in the rooms. It was finally burnt — and in its place rose a jail that became the model for the Prison Discipline Society to refer to, as we shall shortly see. The old jail at Hartford caught fire because an insane female prisoner, excited over some mocking of persons, outside, kindled the fire and perished in the flames. In the new prison, to be shortly described in detail,

"no public house is connected with the jail; no spirits ever drank within its walls; no conversation is ever permitted with the prisoners, and the sound even of the keeper's voice is never heard by the secluded and unhappy men."

The proximity of the tavern to the county prison seems strange to us, when known to be under the same management as the jail, although into the most modern times there has been traced the closest relationship of cause and effect between the saloon and the jail. But in the period of a century ago,

"the county jail was the central point where were gathered the authority and business of the county. Here it was considered indispensable that a tavern should be connected with it, as thus accommodation was afforded to the judges of the county court, the jury, and because, too, without a tavern no one could be induced to keep a jail."

Returning now to the development of the system extolled as developed in the House of Correction at South Boston during the thirties, and proclaimed throughout the country wherever the reports of the Prison Discipline Society reached, we find that by 1836, the only punishment allowed by law to be inflicted on convicts for infractions of the rules of the prison was solitary confinement upon bread and water, or the deprivation of certain meals, the offender being still kept at labor. In 1837, the institution had been in operation four years, with 250 prisoners at the time of reporting.

"Stripes (floggings) have not been inflicted in a solitary instance. Only 6 keepers, including the master, and clerk, and two matrons make up the officers. There is not a gun and bayonet, sword or pistol, cowhide, cat or whip of small cords, gag, restraining chair, handcuffs, stocks, or any other instrument of restraint, punishment or torture, about the place.

"No corporal punishment is or ever has been inflicted. Solitary confinement without bed or blanket, with rations of bread and water only, has never failed to produce the desired effect, even in the most refractory."

The House of Correction was called a model of construction. The general plan was of the Auburn type, but the windows were fewer and much larger than those at Charlestown and Sing Sing. The cell doors were also better. The whole institution was characterized by neatness and by persistent industry. There was also a day school for 20 boys, two hours every day, in the three R's. There was a Sabbath School for the women, taught in turn by nearly two hundred ladies. The Prison Discipline Society reported that:

"if there are better models of this class of prisons than the Hartford County Jail and the House of Correction at South Boston, we have not seen them."

Unquestionably, the system of discipline at the Boston House of Correction was remarkable in its results, in an age when the most repressive methods were regarded in the State prisons as being the only possible means of preserving safety of life and property, and of securing from the convicts a requisite amount of work. Here was an institution of which we know unfortunately too little, where methods of government, without force or the show of authority by arms, prevailed and were successful. It has been only within recent years — a decade perhaps — that we have grown at all accustomed to hear of prisons where guns and revolvers and other arms have been even partially abandoned. It has been generally supposed that such results were due in large measure to the honor system, yet in this House of Correction of ninety years ago such results were achieved. The "master" of the House of Correction — a name wholly unknown to-day — was Charles Robbins.

We have mentioned the Hartford County Jail, in Connecticut. The old jail was superseded by a new jail, on a lot of some two acres, and was built in 1836-37 at a cost of less than $10,000. The county prison was on the Auburn plan, with thirty-two cells, each 10 feet by 5 feet by 7 feet. There were three rooms for prisoners, each 16 feet square by 8 high.

By 1838, the Boston Society reported that through the new jail there had resulted complete separation of the prisoners, easy and much more perfect supervision, reduced expenses in guarding and warming the jail, greatly increased ventilation and light, diminished danger or possibility of burning the jail, and the repayment of a large portion of the expenses of the prisoners by the avails of their labor. The three inspectors — or members of the board of managers — were Amos Pilsbury, Alfred Smith, and Nathaniel Goodwin. We can readily understand, from the presence of Pilsbury on the board, why the new county prison was built on the Auburn plan, and why the method of administration approached that of Wethersfield.

In 1839, the Hartford prison was called by Dwight "the best county prison that we have ever seen." Shoemaking was the principal occupation of the inmates. The value of having a "model jail" became increasingly apparent. There were said to be about twenty times as many people committed to county jails in the United States as to State prisons, or about 40,000 annually. Probably a tenth of those committed were discharged subsequently as innocent. Probably a fourth of all those committed to county jails were debtors. It was estimated that more than a thousand women, and between a thousand and two thousand youths, were committed annually to county prisons. The old-style county prisons were very heavy burdens to the whole community, costing a total of $600,000 for current expenses. The Hartford jail, on the other hand, nearly or quite supported itself, besides being an institution conducted on an exemplary plan. "As our county has been honored for its prisons, so it has been reproached for its loathsome county jails," wrote Dwight.

It was in the summer of 1839 that a representative of the Prison Discipline Society, probably Dwight himself, made a journey through the interior of New York State. This trip, and several others in successive years to State and county prisons in the south and central States, furnish us with a wealth of vivid description, from which we shall quote in part, that it may be apparent to what degree of callousness, actual cruelty and stupidity the management of the lesser prisons had arrived:

Albany, New York. About 20 prisoners, young and old, tried and untried, novice and hardened villain, mingled together in one space, in front of the cells, without supervision or employment. . . 15 females were in one room, with beds, so far as they had beds, on the floor. The jailer told us how many times, by day and by night, it was necessary for him to go the round of observation, and he had to do it all himself."

Schenectady, N. Y.	"A jail recently built." This is followed by a very graphic description of the plague of lice and other vermin, from which the prisoners found it impossible to escape.
Fonda, N. Y.	"A gentleman of respectability said that a prisoner, with a piece of iron hoop, could dig through the walls in an hour. He considered the erection of the jail a piece of peculation."
Whitesboro, N. Y.	"The smell of the jail was so bad in front of the house that I removed my family a considerable distance, under a shade, while the examination of the jail was made."
Morrisville, N. Y.	"There was one prisoner in the jail for murder, to be executed a week from this day. I found him weeping, and crying for mercy and the forgiveness of his sins."
Auburn, N.Y.	"The jailer was not at home. His wife unlocked the doors and a prisoner showed me the jail. It is as much better than many old jails than it is worse than the Hartford jail."
Rochester, N. Y.	"There has been a praiseworthy attempt to provide a place where the prisoners might be employed in hammering stone for the highways, and considerable labor of this kind has been done. I visited the ground selected for a workhouse and found it low, barren and uncultivated. What is needed in Rochester for this purpose is one of the good farms in the vicinity, elevated, airy, well-watered, fertile and highly cultivated, on which could be erected, first a workhouse, then a house of refuge for juvenile delinquents, and then a jail.
Canandaigua, N. Y.	"There is no regular employment, nor thorough supervision, nor systematic moral and religious instruction in this jail."
Geneseo, N. Y.	"One young man, who listened to me through a small orifice in the door of his solitary cell had thirty days' sentence to solitary confinement. His cell was a totally dark dungeon, except as a small orifice in the top of the door, about as large as the face of a man, admitted light. He could not see to read in his cell, and when he turned his back to the door, he could scarcely see his hand before his face. . . . These cells are intolerable places of confinement, either before or after conviction, . . . There has not been a religious service for several months. The Presbyterian minister of the village said he had not done his duty in the past, but would endeavor to do it."
Batavia, N. Y.	"The doors of the cells are like those in Geneseo, intolerable. The jail was extremely filthy."
Buffalo, N. Y.	"This is a prison within a prison. The inner prison is timber, shrunk, and have left a multitude of large cracks and crevices, hiding places for vermin. It was in this place that I addressed the supervisors, about forty in number. . . . Buffalo and New York seem to be the traps where transient persons are caught and imprisoned for the whole state. One prisoner told me that he was able to keep off the lice, by greasing the legs of his bedstead, and tucking up the bedclothes carefully."

On his travels, the representative of the Boston Society constantly held up as a model the Hartford County jail. In 1841 the county prison supported itself, and earned $600 surplus. The school of vice was said to have become a school of reformation. "Why not make the 75,000 convicts in county prisons earn the $1,260,000 annually that are now lost, and apply the sum to public improvements?" asked the Boston report. The keeper of the Hartford institution wrote, suggesting that a society be formed in Connecticut by farmers and mechanics for the encouragement of discharged convicts, by giving them work at low rates of wages, until they could provide better for themselves.

Intensely partisan, the reports of the Boston Society would not give fair and sympathetic attention or treatment to any institutions developed on the Pennsylvania plan, either of architecture or administrative methods. In Pennsylvania, the new county prison of Philadelphia, at Moyamensing, was built in the early thirties, the appropriation of $150,000 having been authorized by the Legislature in 1831. The institution was to take the place of the Walnut Street Prison, and was to be built on the plan of separate confinement, like the Eastern Penitentiary, with 300 cells, to receive all persons sent to Walnut Street for less than one year, and all persons heretofore committed to the Arch Street Prison.

The prison was located 310 feet on Passayunk Road, and was 525 feet in depth. It was enclosed by a substantial yard wall. It was of castellated Gothic architecture, and was built of Quincy sienite. The central building was three stories high, with high towers. On each side of the central building were wings, receding 10 feet, and about 50 feet wide. At the extremity of the wings were massive octagonal towers, from which extended the yard wall. The central building was to be occupied by the keeper and his family. The cells were built in two blocks, extending from the wings, at right angles with the principal front. There were 408 cells, each 9 feet wide, 13 feet long, and 9 feet high. There was a corridor in the center, 20 feet wide and extending the whole height of the building. The windows in the cells were 4 inches wide and 4½ feet long. They were glazed with pressed glass, making them translucent. There were two sections to the county prison, so as to keep the untried and the convicted prisoners separate from each other. The cornerstone was laid on April 2nd, 1832.

By 1836, the new county prison was occupied. Dwight makes no comment upon it in the annual report of the Prison Discipline Society beyond the above fact.

Gerrish Barrett, representative of the Boston Society, visited the Moyamensing prison in 1841 or '42. He found it a very complete and costly establishment. There were three long ranges, radiating from a common center forming three distinct apartments: (1) for male vagrants and those awaiting trial; (2) for convicted males; (3) vagrants and convicted females and those awaiting trial. In the female department were 111 vagrants and untried women, occupying 50 cells, and there were 30 convicted women in separate cells. The department for convicted males had 204 cells, in two stories. The inmates were required to work, most of them in cells, some in the prison yard and workshops. Their health was said to be promoted by their going out of their cells to work. At this time, convicts could be sent to Moyamensing for any period, but formerly there was a limit of two years.

The heat of the prison was furnished by 16 coal heaters, consuming 350 tons of coal a year. There was preaching in two departments each Sunday, but there were no attempts to teach the ignorant to read. Of the last 298 persons committed, 107 could not read and 19 could not write. During the year ending March 1, 1842, there were committed to the prison 2,123 white males, 915 white females, 1,042 colored males, and 930 colored females. A total of 5,010.

Going back now to the development of the Penitentiary in New York city, we find that by 1832 much progress was being made in the erection of the city's buildings for the poor and the criminal on *Blackwell's Island, which had been bought by the city, and which was located in the East River. In 1829 the city purchased the Island, which was approximately 100 acres in extent, and some 4 miles from City Hall. By this year, a building had been erected on the plan of the State prison at Wethersfield, to admit finally 500 inmates. Here, the new Penitentiary was being built, with a north wing of 250 cells and a south wing of an equal number, constructed on the Auburn plan. The old penitentiary building was occupied by the female convicts, and by untried prisoners and vagrants who formerly occupied the Bridewell. The female convicts convicted of State prison offenses were occupying one part of the old building, pending the erection by the State of a separate prison for women. The old Bridewell near the City Hall was now given up, and was used for the confinement of the very few remaining debtors. The former debtors' prison was abandoned, and was being renovated, to become later the Hall of Records.

In 1838, on January 19th (to cite a specific date for statistical purposes), the "count" in the Penitentiary was as follows:

	White	Black	Total
Court prisoners, male	144	97	241
Court prisoners, female	8	4	12
Male vagrants	141	18	159
Female vagrants			334

	Average number in hospital	35 to 40
	In fever hospital	31
Males.	In quarry	152
	Cutting stone	14
	Shoemakers	12
	Blacksmiths	7
	Carpenters	12
	Coopers	6
Females.	Picking oakum	77
	Sewing and spinning	40
	Kitchen	17

* In 1921 renamed Welfare Island.

Men employed in various kinds of labor and in hospitals, about 75. The Penitentiary was a place of punishment for crime; a workhouse for idlers, and a hospital for the sick, infirm and aged. The chief diseases were venereal and delirium tremens. The keeper was, in 1838, Colonel Jeremiah Vanderbilt, "many years an intelligent merchant in the city of New York, a member and officer of the Rutgers Street Church." The keeper received $1,000 per annum, dwelling on the Island for his family, and free use of all stock and products of the Island. He was appointed by the common council of the city. The hospital and the prison was supplied by Doctor Nicholas Morrell at a salary of $630.

CHAPTER XXIII

THE REVEREND LOUIS DWIGHT

We have repeatedly, in the foregoing chapters, referred to the highly influential annual reports of the Prison Discipline Society of Boston from 1826 on, and to the controlling spirit that produced them. Louis Dwight, for years the secretary of the Prison Discipline Society, possessed some of the attributes of John Howard of England, yet unlike that eminent prison investigator, he was not dispassionate, not judicial, but on the other hand was possessed of a fighting spirit and a sense of organization that the English reformer never exhibited. Louis Dwight was a promoter of prison betterment, a missionary in heart, and an impassioned fighter for what he believed to be right.

John Howard was forced into his great philanthropic service by a chance appointment as sheriff of Bedford, England, which led him first to investigate the jail under his charge, and then, horror-stricken by his discovery of local conditions, to extend ultimately his investigations to the entire continent of Europe. But Dwight was forced into his American prison visiting by bad health, which incapacitated him for a pastorate, and also by an intensely religious nature, that led him to say:

"I had rather be the honored instrument of turning a single soul free from the error of his ways, than to be the proud monarch of the universe. I had rather be immersed in prisons, contending against sin, than to receive the honors of Lafayette."

Louis Dwight was a pioneer in American prison reform, of good New England stock, and of stern Puritan morals, born of highly devout parents in 1793. He was faced toward the ministry. But a hemorrhage of the lungs, caused by an experiment in the chemical laboratory in Yale College in 1813, incapacitated him permanently as a pulpit speaker. Nevertheless, he entered the ministry, and became first the agent of the American Bible Society, and then of the American Education Society. Compelled in 1824, by feeble health, to give up this work, he sought by long journeys on horseback to recover his health. In order to serve God and man, he planned to distribute Bibles to prisoners on his route — an occupation new to him.

Thus did chance lead him to his life work. His horseback journey through the South Atlantic States in 1824 revealed the horrible and unknown conditions of jails and prisons. His first missionary act was, at the New Haven jail, to comfort by prayer and counsel a woman condemned to death. The New York City Bridewell horrified him. The further south he rode, the more desperate seemed the conditions met. Prisoners in rags and chains; sexes commingled; mere boys the victims of lecherous men; debtors imprisoned for lack of payment of jailer's fees; squalor beyond description — these were a few of the pictures of degradation and misery that he faced.

"There is but one sufficient excuse for Christians in suffering such evils to exist in prisons in this country, and that is, that they are not acquainted with the real state of things. . . . When I shall bring before the Church of Christ a statement of what my eyes have seen, there will be a united and powerful effort to alleviate the miseries of prisons. . . . I only know that these prisoners are the most miserable and degraded of the human race, and that no one in the country is doing anything for their relief."

Returning to Boston in 1825, Dwight soon founded the Prison Discipline Society, of which he remained the militant secretary until his death in 1854, after which the Society ceased to exist. This Society was not destined to be simply a Boston or a Massachusetts organization, but the conception in Dwight's mind was national, and in the earlier years of his secretaryship, he made many efforts to cause the establishment of branches of the "work" in other cities, notably in Trenton, New Jersey, and at one time in New York City. But these local developments did not continue, and when in 1844 the Prison Association of New York was founded, it was as a wholly distinct society from the one in Boston.

The annual reports of the Boston Society were Dwight's personal messages to this country and to Europe, and they were practically the only documents of the kind available. They carried a relatively large amount of fact-information, but often much out of balance, particularly in relation to discussion of the Eastern Penitentiary or other prisons operating on the "separate" system. During many months of each year, Dwight was separated from wife and family, on his visits to prisons, and at one time he wrote to his wife:

"Let us hope that your self-denial in giving me up, to continue my efforts in that which is bidden me to do, may result in salvation to those who would otherwise die in their sins."

His salary was relatively small, and out of it he had to pay his own traveling expenses. Seemingly, he never spared himself. His physician said of him, after his death, that he had worked too hard in his day. The following abstract of a letter of Dwight to his daughter from Fairfield, Connecticut, written on January 6th, 1830, is typical:

"I am exceedingly tired to-night, having been all night, on Sabbath night; most of the night, last night; all day, on each of the days, for three days past, in the cold, travelling over rough roads; and after exploring several towns today, with the commissioners for locating the workhouse, I have spent the evening addressing a large company at the Courthouse, so that I am literally exhausted. Last night after getting into the house, from a cold stage, at one o'clock, there was no fire, and putting on a buffalo skin, I could not get warm."

The reports of the Prison Discipline Society, written undoubtedly almost if not quite in their entirety by Dwight, were nevertheless wholly impersonal so far as any personal aggrandizement of the man was concerned. Rarely do we discover from the report the evidences of the constant intense activity of the secretary. Only occasionally de we find an item like the following, in the report for 1829:

> "The Society sent its agent at three different times to Connecticut; once to visit Newgate Prison alone, and ascertain its character; again, with the Commissioners of the Legislature to spend as much time as should be necessary to make a thorough investigation, and disclosure of abuses existing in that institution; at which time, after spending nearly a week at the prison, he visited the principal towns of the State and invited meetings of the principal men, that the evils might be exposed to them; and, also, made such representations to the Governor as induced him to submit the subject to the Legislature; and, finally, in acceptance of the invitation of the Commissioners sent its agent a third time, to appear before the Legislature, and make such representations as had already been made to the Governor and many respectable citizens. After which, within two or three weeks, a law was passed, with almost entire unanimity, to abandon Newgate, and build a new prison on the Auburn plan at Wethersfield."

Dwight's monuments are, on the one hand, the long series of annual reports of the Prison Discipline Society, filled with notes and facts from the prisons of the land, the county jails, the local prisons; and on the other, the constantly growing number of prisons built on the Auburn plan. He was for twenty years *the* American authority on prisons and their inmates. Never did his religious zeal forsake him. He was engaged in a holy war. The salvation of human souls was the impelling force within him. The paralytic stroke that was the ultimate cause of his death was sustained by him while in harness. Almost the last act of his long life was a sermon preached to the insane of a Boston institution. Throughout his long professional career, the insane were special objects of his compassion.

His daughter said that he was perpetually cheerful. Friends described him as affectionate, kind, of pleasing address, faithful to engagement, frank, sensitive, and of strong feelings. He was intensely devout. His enemies claimed — and in the light of these later years, correctly — that at times he distorted the truth, and misrepresented facts. It was this failing in Louis Dwight that stood in the way of his becoming a great man in his profession. Toward all that pertained to the Eastern Penitentiary he was highly biased, seemingly incapable of calm judgment, and he was persistently unfair, although his motives were in no way low or sordid, or for his own gain.

At the very end of the period that we have been considering in this study, he was severely arraigned in public by Charles Sumner, of his own Society, for the distortion and suppression of facts regarding the Pennsylvania system.

Yet, viewing his entire span of activity, he served valiantly the cause of prison reform. Battling against the constant separation of prisoners from each other, he anticipated the trend of American prison administration, which never accepted the principle of separation of inmates. To-day, in no prison of the country is the original Pennsylvania system in operation. Honor systems, self-government efforts, the trainng of both adult and youth, occur under systems of association and intercourse.

Dwight was a salient figure in his time, the forerunner of Enoch C. Wines, just as Amos Pilsbury was the forerunner of Zebulon R. Brockway. Dwight has failed of proper recognition, and is hardly mentioned in our present histories of the period. He contributed largely to the emancipation of poor debtors from the liability to imprisonment. He fought incessantly for the removal of the insane from prisons and jails to proper asylums. "He increased the security of society from the misdeeds of criminals by the greatly improved plans of prisons which he presented."

The influence of John Howard's example upon Dwight is clear. Dwight abridged and published Brown's Memoirs of Howard in 1831. In 1828, Dwight wrote to a friend:

"I am grateful to you for your willingness to give me up to the cause of the suffering and miserably guilty portion of our race; for whom there cannot be much compassion, and for whom there has been so much less exertion in this country than in Europe."

CHAPTER XXIV

THE EARLY JUVENILE REFORMATORIES, 1824—1844
NEW YORK, BOSTON, PHILADELPHIA

Inevitably, in the development of more humane treatment of criminals and other law-breakers, the miserable fate of the children inprisoned for offenses against the law attracted painfully the philanthropic attention of the sponsors of the newer methods of dealing with prisoners. The first era in the treatment of criminals by systematic methods of imprisonment, the Walnut Street era, with its imitators in other States, succeeded in establishing only the most primitive classification of prisoners, though it was recognized that more extended classification must occur than the simple separation of males from females, or felons from "vagrants." The first era, therefore, hardly did more than put the felon in one institution, the State prison, and retain the lesser offenders in the houses of correction, the Bridewells and the county prisons. And not even that classification was carefully carried out. So that at the end of the first era, in the early twenties of the nineteenth century, with the almost complete breakdown of the first prison system, the State prisons still contained the young and the old, the white and the colored, the novice and the old-timer. Lodged in large rooms, associating promiscuously, the prisoners were inevitably steeped in the habits and lore of crime.

But in the rapidly growing campaign against the degenerated State prisons, a new note was struck, one that had not been heard when Walnut Street was the prison held up as the example for the world. The tender years of many of the prisoners now appalled the prison reformers. Some children were found only 12 years old, who had been many months in prison.[1] Their wretched physical condition and their fearful moral corruption were conspicuous and horrid facts:

"The loathsome skin, the disturbed features, the unnatural eyes of some of these boys indicated, with a clearness not to be misapprehended, the existence of unutterable abominations."

In the Prison Discipline Society's report for 1827 appeared the following statistical table:

Proportion of Inmates Under 21 Years of Age in Different State Prisons

	Total Prisoners	Under 21	Proportion to Total
Maine	116	22	1 in 5
New Hampshire	253	47	1 in 5
Vermont	534	75	1 in 7
Auburn	997	148	1 in 6
Richmond	211	30	1 in 7

[1] B. P. D. S., 1827, 18.

There was no unclearness in the minds of the philanthropists of this period as to the immeasurable viciousness for the young of the prison surroundings. Edward Livingston wrote in 1822:

"It would be more reasonable to put a man in a pest house, to cure him of a headache, than to confine a young offender in a penitentiary, organized on the ordinary plan, in order to effect his reformation."

It was in New York City that the first organized, constructive movement to solve the problem of the juvenile delinquents developed. There met at the home of Joseph Curtis in the winter of 1815-1816 some fifteen prominent citizens, who resolved to investigate thoroughly the sources of crime and poverty.[2] Out of this gathering grew the Society for the Prevention of Pauperism, whose highly important report in 1822 we have discussed in Chapter Nine, in treating of the rise of the Auburn system.

In the group of men thus gathered together were Joseph Griscom, a professor of chemistry and natural philosophy, and Thomas Eddy, who had been the leading spirit in the establishment of the State prison (Newgate) in New York in 1796. Griscom made in 1818-1819 a tour of the British Isles and the Continent, giving special attention to charitable institutions. He found in England that in 1817 there had been founded a society for the improvement of prison discipline and for the reformation of juvenile depredators. A juvenile reformatory of this Society was visited by Professor Griscom.

It was an asylum for the children of convicts, and for those children who had been trained to evil courses. Mechanical trades were taught. Boys and girls were housed in separate buildings. After being trained, the boys were bound out as apprentices for a certain number of years. The main effort of the asylum was industrial rather than scholastic. At a suitable age, the girls were also placed out at service, and the boys were sent to the colonies or to America. Unquestionably, this reformatory, as well as other European juvenile reformatories, was in Griscom's memory, when in 1819 the young Society for the Prevention of Pauperism emphasized the lack of separation of adult and juvenile offenders in the local New York State prison:

"Here is one great school of vice and desperation; with confirmed and unrepentant criminals we place these novices in guilt; these unfortunate children, from ten to eighteen years, who from neglect of parents, from idleness or misfortune, have been doomed to the penitentiary by condemnation of law. . . . And is this the place for reform?"[3]

"*Who, from neglect of parents, from idleness or misfortune, have been doomed . . .*" Thus did the Society for the Prevention of Pauperism recognize and proclaim that in the case of the children, their criminality was, to a considerable extent, the result of environmental forces beyond their own control. Society, after contributing by its own actions or its own neglect to make them

[2] Memoir of Joseph Curtis, pp. 63ff.
[3] Half Century, etc., p. 39.

criminal, sent them to prison, to be exposed to "a fruitful source of pauperism, a nursery of new vices, a college for the perfection of adepts in guilt."[4]

Society's propensity to help in rehabilitation and reformation seems to be somewhat in proportion to the degree of responsibility of the sufferer or the victim. The last to enjoy the advantages of reformatory influences in prisons have been those deemed fully responsible, and therefore assumed to be in crime through deliberate choice. The first to enjoy the aid of reformatory methods have been those who have appeared least responsible for their plight — the children. In cognate fields of philanthropy, the sick have been regarded as not responsible for their sickness, and therefore the philanthropy of the community has been expended upon them. The treatment of the insane changed fundamentally, as the conception grew that insanity was not the will of God, but a grievous form of illness. Diminished responsibility in the individual has, in short, gradually meant increased responsibility of society, and to-day, when it is held by many that all criminals are to a greater or less extent the victims of their environment and their own physical and mental equipment, the natural corollary is said to be that the prison should shoulder an increased responsibility for their redemption and their rehabilitation.

At first, the Society for the Prevention of Pauperism recommended simply a division of the inmate population of the State prison, and the erection of a separate building for juveniles within the prison enclosure itself. But this plan was not long urged. Other suggestions for helping delinquent children were already current. As early as 1803, Edward Livingston had addressed a letter to the Mechanics' Society, in which he urged them to found an establishment to provide work for the discharged and pardoned convicts, among other persons. Thomas Eddy carried this idea over into a plan for an institution for young discharged convicts. Eddy also, during the years when the plans for a reformatory for juvenile delinquents were being developed, emphasized the necessity of embodying in the new institution preventive as well as curative methods.

It was therefore natural that by 1822 the Society for the Prevention of Pauperism should urge the founding of a juvenile reformatory, to which children might be sent rather than to State prison:

"These prisons should be schools of instruction rather than places of punishment, like our present State prisons. The youth confined there should be placed under a course of discipline severe and unchanging, but alike calculated to subdue and conciliate. . . . The end should be his (the youth's) reformation and future usefulness."

The Society appointed a committee, of which James W. Gerard was chairman, to report on the feasibility of establishing a juvenile reformatory.[5] The committee, after study of all sources of advice,

---
[4] Report of Society for the Prevention of Pauperism, 1821.
[5] Half Century, p. 44.

both American and foreign, recommended on February 7, 1823, the erection of a building, entirely separate from the State Prison, for the imprisonment of young offenders both before and after trial. The proposed house of refuge should also be the place of refuge for young delinquents after discharge from prison. Such an institution would appeal to judges and jurors, to whom the thought of a State prison sentence for children was repugnant. Between one hundred and two hundred persons, from seven to fourteen years of age, were annually brought before the police on charges involving various degrees of crime.

The next step was to appoint a committee to prepare a plan for the "house of refuge," and Professor Griscom was made chairman of the committee. Mindful of the European juvenile asylums, he said that such an institution would in time come to seem simply a decent school and manufactory; from which the aspects of a prison should be as far as possible removed. All the groups of citizens, public and private — judges, jurors, juries, district attorney, and philanthropists were enthusiastically united in this first civic campaign to save the criminal and delinquent children.

At a meeting on December 19, 1823, at which the Griscom report was read, $800 was raised, and in a short time $18,000 was secured from private subscriptions — the first instance of a large fund being raised from citizens for institutional prison reform for children. So important was the movement, and so keenly did the Society for the Prevention of Pauperism believe that the chief cause of poverty and crime was to be found in the delinquency of childhood, that the Society was reorganized as the Society for the Reformation of Juvenile Delinquents [6]— and that society exists to-day, and still conducts the House of Refuge in the city of New York. A board of twenty-five managers was appointed until the Society should be incorporated, which occurred on March 29th, 1824.

The State then conferred upon the Society for the Reformation of Juvenile Delinquents powers that were extraordinarily broad.[7] Heretofore, in the prison field, some State, county or municipal body or board had managed the correctional institution. But now, there was given over to a private group the power of imprisonment and of treatment. The Society was authorized to maintain a house of refuge. Legal custody of the inmates was given to the Society, to which was left by the State their management and superintendence.[8] The ultimate authority lay in the entire body of subscribers, who elected the board of managers, thirty in number, who in turn appointed the superintendent and other officers of the institution. The managers were not required to submit to State authority beyond the filing of an annual report, and were therefore subject solely to the control of public opinion.

---

[6] Half Century, p. 63.
[7] Act of Incorporation, Chapter 126, Laws of 1824.
[8] de Beaumont and de Tocqueville, p. 110.

Two distinct classes of inmates were to be received by the Society: (a) Those children convicted and sentenced for crime, and (b) the children who were *not* convicted of crime, but who were destitute or neglected, or both, and who were in imminent danger of becoming delinquent. No age limit was set for admission, but boys might not be held by the managers beyond majority, nor girls beyond the age of eighteen years. The institution was thus to be curative, educational and preventive. Commitments to the House of Refuge might be made by police courts, those of special or general sessions, or by the commissioners in charge of the Almshouse. Boys and girls were to be sent to the House of Refuge who were dangerous to society and to themselves; orphans who were vagrant, children abandoned by their parents and leading a disorderly life. In short, all those who would infallibly become guilty if left to themselves.[9]

It is of special interest to-day, a century later, to see how, in the formation of this first House of Refuge, the founders set up unerringly the arguments for the reformative treatment of children that fifty years later were set forth as pertaining to young men, out of which agitation developed the State reformatory system of this county, initiated at Elmira. And now, a hundred years from the time of the founding of the House of Refuge, we find the principles then laid down as applicable to children largely accepted as also applicable to a considerable proportion of the population of the State prisons — and to-day the modern State prison accepts in large measure the principles of treatment, and methods of discipline applied a century ago in the first institution for delinquent children.

"In most instances they have no inveterate habits to extirpate," wrote the Society for the Prevention of Pauperism in 1822. "No moral standard of conduct has been placed before their eyes. No faithful parent has watched over them, and restrained their vicious propensities. Their lives exhibit a series of aberrations from regularity, a train of accidents that has rendered them the victims of temptations, and the sport of adversity.

"They have been sent from place to place, subsisted by various means, or been left to combat with poverty, want, and the inclemency of the seasons, by the exercise of their own ingenuity. Everything about them has been various and unsettled, and in the unfortunate hour of temptation, while under the pressure of want, they have offended against the laws and been sentenced to the State prison. There are exceptions to these remarks, in a few solitary instances of premature and settled baseness; but the view has a very extensive application to the cases of juvenile offenders, in our large cities and towns. In the interior it is very rare that boys are indicted for crimes."

The wisdom of the promoters of the new institution, as well as that of the law-making body, was manifest in the provision of law that sentences to the House of Refuge should be indefinite, and not fixed. That is to say, there should be no fixed and settled limit to the sentence, upon the termination of which the youth should be discharged. The fixed sentence was characteristic of commitments to the State prison, and in general of all commitments of adults. In the case of the long sentences to State prison, we have seen the pardoning power operate to shorten the sentence, and we have repeatedly observed in this study that the long sentence to prison

---
[9] de Beaumont and de Tocqueville, p. 111.

has been shortened by the only means available — the act of the chief executive of the State, often leading to flagrant abuse of the power of pardon.

But now, for the children, a revolutionary step was being taken. These same children, if sentenced to prison or jail, would receive a fixed sentence. But since the House of Refuge was to educate children for an honest life, and teach them a trade, it was essential that they should be retained long enough in this school to learn the trade, at least to the extent of being equipped to be apprenticed out to their masters for the period of their minority.

The decision, therefore, by which children were committed to the House of Refuge had generally neither the solemnity nor the forms of a judgment. The court simply committed the delinquent to the House of Refuge, which from that moment acquired all the powers of a guardian.[11] This guardianship endured only through the minority of the child. The charter of the Society required that the rules and regulations of the Society should not be inconsistent with the Constitution of the State and Nation. Through the power of *habeas corpus* the courts might inquire into the commitment and detention of any child. The managers had the right to restore to liberty any inmate at any time.

Even after the managers had indentured a child, they still retained the legal right to recall the child to the institution and to employ most rigorous means, if necessary, in so doing. In short, there was given to the Society the power of parent, together with disciplinary means to achieve the difficult task of reformation and control of juvenile character. It should be noted that the Society had thus not only the advantage of the indeterminate sentence, bu also what in later years was the power of parole (in the case of the House of Refuge called "indenture"), with which was coupled the power of return to the institution, as in the case of parole in later years.

It was natural that in the early years of the institution vigorous protest should have been made against the employment of such drastic power by a private body. Only the highly intelligent handling of a new enterprise, based upon the most humane motives, enabled the managers of the House of Refuge to continue to command the support of public opinion. It was claimed that their power was contrary to the constitution of the United States; that the power of the managers to shorten or to prolong, at their pleasure, the duration of detention of the youthful inmates was arbitrary, and should not be tolerated.

The status of the House of Refuge in the correctional system of the State was interpreted in citations from the annual report of the House of Refuge of 1839, when two decisions were quoted, one relative to the House of Refuge of Philadelphia (a similar institution), and the other a decision rendered — probably in a matter of the same institution — which affirmed that the House of Refuge was not a prison but a school.[10] Reformation and not punishment

---

[10] Supreme Court of Pennsylvania, December Term, 1838.
[11] B. and T., p. 112.

was the aim of the institution. The court recognized the position of the House of Refuge as *"parens patriae,"* the "common guardian of the community." The right of parental control — which some of the plaintiffs claimed probably was paramount — the court held to be a natural right, but not an inalienable one. Not only was the restraint of the person of the child committed to the House of Refuge lawful, but the court held that it would be an act of extreme cruelty to release the child to improper parents.

The second decision quoted [11a] held that the greater or less degree of restraint which was imposed by the superintendent must depend upon circumstances and could not be made the subject of any precise estimate. So long as it was governed by a regard for the best interests of the young, it had perhaps no other limits, and must be discretionary.

In short, the Houses of Refuge in New York and Philadelphia were an entirely new type of educational correctional institution. In theory, and to considerable extent in methods, they differed from the prisons, in protest against which they had their origin. The chief differences may thus be summarized:

	HOUSE OF REFUGE.	STATE PRISON.
Policy	Reformative and Educational	Punitive.
Population	Children	Adults and children.
Degree of Crime	Any delinquents	Felons.
Ages	Maximum, boys 21, girls 18, no minimum	No limit.
Sentences	No minimum. Maximum boys 21, girls 18	No limit.
Nature of sentences	Indefinite	Definite.
Method of release	Indenture	Discharge.
Nature of release	Provisional during good conduct	Absolute.
Supervision after release	Correspondence with employers, visits	None.
Power of recall	Yes	No.
Government	Private board	Public board.
How appointed	Self-perpetuating	Legislature or Governor.

The New York House of Refuge was the first of its kind to be established in America or Europe.[12] The juvenile asylums established earlier in Europe received children not by court commitment, but through voluntary applications and admissions. Therefore, the early European reformatories failed to possess such broad powers as did the American House of Refuge.

A location was granted by the city of New York at the junction of the Bloomingdale Road and the Old Post Road, where now Madison Square is located. This site of four acres was about one mile north of the then habitable portion of the city, and two miles from city hall.[13] Federal government buildings used as barracks were ceded and then renovated. On January 1, 1825, six boys and three girls were received as the first inmates.

From the outset, the Refuge engaged strong public approval. Within a year from the opening, the city's district attorney stated that its influence was most benign in the diminution of the number of juvenile delinquents. The most depraved boys had been withdrawn from the haunts of vice. In 1825, Governor Clinton stated

---
[11a] Opinion of J. R. Ingersoll, Washington, January 7, 1835.
[12] Half Century, p. 68.
[13] Half Century, p. 72.

in his message to the Legislature that the House of Refuge was the best penitentiary institution that had ever been devised by the wit of man, and established by his beneficence.

A field without precedent lay before the first superintendent, who was Joseph Curtis, the New York citizen in whose house had met nearly ten years previously the little group of men to discuss the treatment of poverty and crime. Curtis was a man quite out of the ordinary. We find at the outset, in charge of the House of Refuge, a man who sought to introduce the methods of love and kindness into what had been a system of horrible, cruel treatment of children in the prisons. A little biography of the man, Joseph Curtis, published in 1858,[14] called him a "model man." Under him, "order was the first law of the institution; unswerving justice was maintained and love was the keynote."[15]

The methods of Curtis were those of rewards and deprivations, and his treatment was based on personality. His appeal was to the human nature and the natural emotions of the children. To those children for instance, who had been good throughout the week, he gave cake and coffee on Sunday morning at eleven. Any boy that finished his work by Saturday noon in summer could go for a swim and have the afternoon at liberty. A former pupil, writing many years afterwards about his former superintendent, said that in no case did an escape occur, under such circumstances.[16] Any boy that behaved particularly well was allowed to go "to the city" to visit his friends. If a boy ran away, but came back of his own free will, he was forgiven.

During the play hours, Curtis would romp with the children, play baseball with them, make kites, play marbles, and run with the little inmates.[17] But at table they must be silent, holding up a hand if they wanted water, a thumb for vinegar, three fingers for bread, and one finger for salt. In the long winter evenings, narratives would be read, and there would be singing and the telling of stories. Seated around a long table, the children might ask him questions on any subjects occurring to them.[18]

Yet Curtis was tenacious in disciplining when he believed it to be necessary. A form of mutual disciplining was invented whereby the boys tried each other by jury, Curtis being the judge. Each boy made his complaint, and if the one complained of was found guilty, the number of stripes was named by the foreman of the jury and Curtis administered the punishment.[19] Corporal punishment was highly distasteful to him, but principle was all-governing.

The former inmate, whom we have already mentioned, wrote of Curtis:

"Many a time, at midnight, have I seen the good Samaritan with noiseless tread move from couch to couch, bathing a heated forehead, here moistening

---
[14] Memoir of Joseph Curtis. C. M. Sedgwick, N. Y., 1858.
[15] Memoir of Joseph Curtis, p. 66.
[16] Same, p. 72.
[17] Same, p. 80.
[18] Same, p. 88.
[19] Same, p. 70.

the parched lips and fevered tongue of another, and all with a gentleness unsurpassed by women's gentleness." [20]

Yet the superintendency of Curtis lasted hardly more than a year. It was an intensely personal administration. His chronicler stated that the break came between Curtis and the board of managers when he refused to lash a boy who had run away and had voluntarily returned. Though the board yielded to Curtis's position, the strained relations led to his resignation in May, 1826.

The board of managers wanted to see a definite system of rules and regulations established and administered. According to a narrative of the first fifty years of the House of Refuge,[21] the year of Curtis's superintendency was marked by restlessness and efforts to escape, and a constant guard was rendered necessary. This was said to be due to the miscellaneous nature of the daily work, which was indefinite and unsystematic. It was said that "the most conspicuous items in the first volume of the daily journal were those relating to attempted or successful escapes." [22]

But Curtis maintained that the institution could not be managed like a factory.

"Many things may be done that to a casual observer may seem inadmissible, but still, rightly managed, are productive of good."

The case of Joseph Curtis was of a social significance far greater than could be appreciated at the time. He seems to have instituted a theory of administration that would subordinate system to personality, as a method of education. He chose by far the harder method, but the one offering the possibility of rich rewards. He aimed to develop the individuality of the child, bring out his powers of self-expression. He believed in the development of character rather than routine. He made his board of managers nervous, just as all other executives of institutions who have adopted insurgent or novel methods have made boards of managers very nervous. We have but to think back, in this study, to Caleb Lownes and his colleagues, and the earliest days of Walnut Street Prison, when, for a few years, a most humane discipline excited the admiration of visitors. But it failed, shortly, and severer methods came in. We recall Warden Goodell, at Auburn Prison, whose mild and individualistic methods brought about alleged restlessness and trouble among the inmates. We saw Amos Pilsbury chided by a Legislative committee for trusting prisoners outside of Wetbersfield, in the earliest days. And, shortly, we shall see the superintendent of the Boston House of Reformation in a still more daring effort to normalize the education of childhood, and the reaction of those in authority to his methods.

Honor systems, self-government methods, and any other innovations in correctional institutions have had to fight for their continued existence. It has been characteristic that coupled with the development of methods of fostering self-expression and individ-

[20] Memoir, p. 91.
[21] Half Century, p. 87.
[22] Same, p. 87.

ual treatment has gone often a certain temperamental attitude of mind in the executive, because of which strained relations have shortly developed between the controlling body and the executive. The controlling body — board of managers, common council, Governor — have wanted regularity, system, something applying to all inmates, something making for efficient routine, something measurable, easily understood, "normal." The insurgent executive has wanted the power to deal with all cases individually, set up innovations, perform experiments, often without having the foresight to recognize the inevitable difficulties in an institution filled with inmates not gifted in logic, but strong in emotional and illogical state of mind.

To Joseph Curtis, family life and the rule of a loving but determined *pater familias* were the chief desiderata in institutional management of children. "Institutionalism," as this condition of systematic and monotonous adherence to rules is termed that governs most easily the greatest number, was evidently objectionable to Curtis.

We would here deviate from the chronological history of the early years of the House of Refuge in New York, to outline a similar but even more striking career of a "personality" at the head of the House of Reformation in Boston, in the person of the Reverend E. M. P. Wells, a young Episcopal minister. In 1826, the Massachusetts Legislature gave to the Boston city council authority to send juvenile delinquents, who under the former law had been committed to State prison, to such an institution as the council should provide at South Boston,[23] about two and one-half miles from the city. A commodious building was provided in an extensive field of from 30 to 40 acres. The government of the House of Reformation was by a board of seven directors, and the city of Boston assumed entire support of the institution, thus making it a public reformatory, in contrast to the privately managed House of Refuge in New York.

There came to the Boston House of Reformation as superintendent in 1826, the above-mentioned Mr. Wells, a serious episode in his college career at Brown College throwing light undoubtedly on his attitude toward the little inmates of the House of Reformation over which he was to preside. While a student at Brown, he was called before the faculty to give information as to the participants in a student prank of some magnitude. He stated that he had not taken part in it. When he refused to give the names of the participants — among whom was his own roommate — he was threatened with expulsion, and on still refusing to bear witness against his college mates, he was expelled. In later years, Brown gave him an A. M. degree, probably in part atonement for the college's harsh action toward him.

One of the rules of the House of Reformation, under Wells, was that no boy should be required to give information of the faults of another, nor should he be allowed to do so, unless he was apparently

---

[23] B. P. D. S., 1826, p. 47.

conscientious in so doing.[24] Thus did one of the earliest reform schools go on record as intolerant of "snitching," and of government through stool-pigeons.

This rule was, however, but one of a series of remarkably enlightened regulations, which placed the House of Reformation in Boston temporarily at the forefront of American institutions in the matter of insurgent administrative methods. The young clergyman's philosophy of boyhood was the following:

"Most people imagine, when they see or hear of bad boys, that they are a worse kind of boys, worse by nature than others. If my observations be of any value on this subject, it is not so, for though at first there be strong sproutings of evil principle and passion to be lopped off, we often find him as good a stock, and as rich a soil, as in other cases. . . . However bad a boy may be, he can always be reformed while he is under fifteen years of age, and very often after that age; and he who has been reckoned and treated as incapable of anything like honesty and honor, may be worth the most entire confidence. . . . We live happily together as a family of brethren, cheerful, happy, confiding, and, I trust, to a greater or less degree pious."[25]

The administrative methods of the Boston House of Reformation were amazingly enlightened in a period when repressive and even punitive treatment of children would have been natural, and easily justified by the public customs and opinion of the time. But corporal punishments were entirely excluded from the House. *By vote of the children,* one after the other of the instruments of physical punishment had been abandoned, and last of all the ferule, and they offered as a substitute their own word of honor to behave.[26] The children, said de Beaumont and de Tocqueville, who visited the institution, were treated by the superintendent as though they were members of a free society.[27] Nobody in the House could be punished for a fault not provided for by divine law, or by those of the country or of the House itself. Nobody should be punished for a fault sincerely avowed. A book of conduct was kept, in which each child had his account of good and bad marks, and each child, at the close of the day, in the evening assembly, was called upon to judge himself, and to assign his own marks of merit or demerit.

It was stated by the French observers that the children always judged themselves more severely than they would be judged by others, and that not infrequently the marks had to be corrected.[28] Twelve little jurymen, from among the children, pronounced condemnation or acquittal of the accused, in cases of morality or other offenses. The children elected their own monitors, and nothing was said to be more serious than the manner in which these electors and jurymen discharged their function.

Children whose conduct was good enjoyed great privileges. The system of gradation provided for three "Mal Grades" and three "Bon Grades." The classification was as follows:[29]

---
[24] B. and T., p. 119.
[25] Mary Carpenter, "Juvenile Delinquents," London, 1853, p. 212.
[26] Memoir, p. . . . .
[27] B. and T., p. 118.
[28] Same, p. 119.
[29] Same, Appendix.

First Mal Grade: Those who are positively inclined to do wrong.
Privations:
1. Deprived of play and conversation, except with members of the same grade, or when necessary, with those with whom they work.
2. Not to go to superintendent's room.
3. Not to vote at elections.

Second Mal Grade: Those positively and regularly inclined to do wrong.
Privations:
1. Those of First Mal Grade.
2. Not to converse with any boys, except when necessary about their work.
3. Not to speak to superintendent except when permitted.
4. Deprived of regular seat, and kept constantly under an inmate sheriff, and never dismissed from such surveillance except in bedrooms.
5. Deprived of cake and other extra food.

Third Mal Grade: Positively, regularly and continually inclined to do wrong.
Privations:
1. Those of First and Second Mal Grades.
2. Food: Bread and water. Must wear bracelets or a visor, and be kept in solitary room.

Thus, in descending scale, was discipline sought by a systematic withdrawal of privileges, until the limit of such privileges was reached, and positive punishments, but not of a corporal nature, were administered. The salient and fundamentally important feature of the gradations was that it was optional with the inmate whether he ascended or descended. Had a superior authority arbitrarily imposed the punishments or deprivations, the rebellious and emotional spirit of the child could have secured foothold for the nourishing of a sense of injustice or of martyrdom. Punishments under such conditions could be but the forerunners of rebellion or of a permanently anti-social spirit.

On the other hand, under the above methods, not only was the sense of justice but of personal interest appealed to, and responsibility was shifted entirely to the young inmate himself. If he was bad, it was because he, knowing the consequences, chose the bad, and not because it was forced upon him by the administration. The spirit of the place was based upon the knowledge and anticipation of the pleasures awaiting the one who maintained good conduct, privileges ever before the inmate of the so-called "Bon Grades," of which the following are a summary:

Third Bon Grade: Positively to do right.
Privileges:
1. Any that the Mal Grades offer.
2. To go to the city under a monitor, when 25 marks have been acquired.
3. To walk about grounds, under a monitor.
4. To go to gymnasium and reading room.
5. To use the books and papers in the assembly room, by permission.
6. To hold offices, by election.

Second Bon Grade: Positively and regularly trying to do right.
Privileges:
1. Privileges of all previous grades.
2. To go to the city, for twenty-five marks acquired, without monitor, if it is the third time.

3. To be entrusted with keys of secondary importance.
4. Capable of holding offices of appointment.
5. Permitted to take books from the reading room.
6. Also to use papers in assembly room, without permission.
7. Other things being equal, to have preference before all inferior grades.

First Bon Grade: *Positively regularly and continually trying to do right.*
Privileges:
1. Those of all previous grades.
2. To walk about the stockade without a monitor; to sail and swim without monitor.
3. To go to one's room without permission, and into dining room when necessary.
4. To leave one's seat in the assembly room without permission.
5. Other things being equal, to have preference before all lower grades.
6. To have the use of the recreation room.
7. To be entrusted, when necessary, with the most important keys.
8. To have one's word taken on all common occasions.
9. To have one's birthday celebrated.
10. To wear undress uniform.

It was made easy to the bad inmate to begin to climb back up the ladder of conduct into the better grades, but the higher he climbed the harder it was made for him to go higher. In other words, promotions from grade to grade were possible, as follows:

Grades.	Minimum Stay in Same, Before Promotion to Next Higher Grade.
Third Mal to Second Mal	One Day.
Second Mal to First Mal	One Day.
First Mal to Third Bon	One Week.
Third Bon to Second Bon	Two Weeks.
Second Bon to First Bon	Four Weeks.

Demotions from grade to grade might occur at any time, by the attaining of a certain number of bad marks.

At the very entrance into the House by the new inmate, the self-government features of the establishment were apparent. After the customary physical examination, bath, etc., the newcomer was introduced to the other lads, and received a copy of the "Laws," if he could read. He was then placed in the Second or Third Mal Grade, where he remained for a week on probation. If his conduct was good during this period, it was so reported to the boys, and a vote was then taken as to whether he should be received into the community. If one inmate of the First Bon Grade, two inmates of the two highest Bon Grades, four of the first three Grades, or five inmates altogether voted against the newcomer, he was sent back into further probation. If he was a lad of peculiar circumstances, extra age, or one committed from the municipal court, he was kept in solitary confinement one or more weeks before being presented to the other boys. If the conduct of a community member were extraordinarily bad, he was expelled from the community, and could be readmitted only after a period of probation.

Monitors were appointed from among the boys at the beginning of each month, and the head monitor presided over the institution in the absence of the officers. There were thus two inmate keepers of the keys of the institution, who rang the bells and opened and shut the doors. There was an inmate sheriff and two sheriffs' deputies, to take charge of the second and third "Mal Grades." One of these three officers must be always on duty, except during the institutional sleeping hours; there was an inmate steward who should attend to the marketing, the boys' meals, and the provisions; there was also a monitor of police, who was to have two or three boys under him, to clean and arrange each day the boys' part of the house. Other monitors were those of the wardrobe, of the rooms, of the floors. The monitors of divisions and of the First Grade were elected by the boys of such divisions, and conducted the divisions at all marching times, and saw that their personal appearance was satisfactory.

Wells' policy of emphasis on physical development, and on academic training, to an extent not found in the Houses of Refuge of New York and Philadelphia, was manifest in the daily schedule of hours:[30]

6.00- 6.45	Recreation.
6.45- 7.30	Religious Exercises.
7.30- 8.00	Breakfast.
8.00-10.00	School.
10.00-12.45	Labor.
12.45- 1.30	Recreation.
1.30- 2.00	Dinner.
2.00- 4.45	Labor.
4.45- 5.30	Recreation.
5.30- 6.00	Supper.
6.00- 8.00	School.
8.00- 8.30	Religious Exercises.
8.30- 9.30	Going to Bed.

The time of rising was naturally earlier in summer than in winter.

The daily schedule thus gave 5½ hours to labor, 4 hours to school, 2¼ hours to recreation, and 1½ hours to meals. Religious exercises consumed 1¼ hours. The day time was divided fairly equally between labor and academic instruction. The school gave mainly primary school subjects and the manual labor was much the same as in prison, save as to quantity and intensity.[31] In the games, Wells took part, believing that physical and moral qualities arose from such sports.

Having read, for several hundred pages of this study of the persistent application in the early American prisons of repressive and cruel measure of discipline, we naturally ask ourselves how this very radical plan of Wells was regarded by his contemporaries. De Beaumont and de Tocqueville, expressing keen interest in this experiment, stated that they did not regard it as an infant republic in good earnest.[32] The system seemed to them, however, to be remarkable in its originality. They stated that there was more depth in these political plays, which agreed so well with the institutions of the country, than would be supposed at first glance. The

[30] B. P. D. S., 1829, p. 246.
[31] B. and T., p. 114.
[32] Same, p. 120.

impressions of childhood, and the early use of liberty, seemed to them to contribute perhaps at a later period to make the young delinquents more obedient to the laws. Despite the great novelty of the Boston system, de Beaumont and de Tocqueville liked the New York system better, because simpler and less remarkable. (This was a system that followed the system of Curtis, which we have described.) In Boston it was not the system that was the cause of success, but the remarkable man at the head of the institution.[33] There would be great difficulties in putting such an administration as the Boston one into practice, if the superintendent were inefficient. The Boston system was the more elevated, but more difficult. It was possible to discover superintendents for Houses of Refuge like those conducted in New York and Philadelphia, but one could not hope often to meet a man like Wells.

Francis Lieber, himself a student of prison discipline, held that Wells was one of the most peculiar, most interesting and most heart-cheering men that had ever come to his knowledge. He wrote:

"We know of no instructor who has been deeper into the human heart, and knows more thoroughly to what principles of the human soul he may apply."[34]

Doctor Julius found in the Boston House of Refuge rules that looked excellent on paper, but which it was impossible, he said, to carry out.[35] By this time, Wells had, however, left the House of Reformation, and had established a private school, of which we shall shortly make mention. Julius declared Wells to be the most fitted man in America for work with juvenile delinquents, just as he found Wood of the Eastern Penitentiary the best equipped warden for adult prisoners.

But Wells was very hard for a committee of the Boston Common Council to understand, who visited officially the House of Reformation in 1832. They found the devotional exercises excellent, but the scholastic instruction poor. The superintendent, in explanation, said that the *mechanical* part of education, such as arithmetic, writing and spelling, held the lowest place among the purposes of the House of Reformation.[36] Poor returns were also being had from the labor of the children; they were earning little toward their keep. The committee held that the institution was intended to be one of rigorous moral and physical discipline. It had, said the committee, for its object "convertible practical utility, and not *recreation* and *show*." Boys should receive more care and attention. They were not properly employed. There was found no settled plan of systematic and productive labor. Various mechanic arts should be introduced. Furthermore, the boys were sometimes detained too long for their own good.[37] In short, the committee obviously felt that the boys were not earning enough, working enough, and were not docile and inconspicuous enough to conform to the standard of training of those days.

---

[33] de Beaumont and de Tocqueville, p. 120.
[34] Same, p. 120.
[35] Julius. Sittleche Zusbaende, Vol. II, p. 362.
[36] Report of Standing Comm. Common Council, 1832.
[37] Same, pp. 31-33.

A break between Wells and the controlling powers was inevitable. The Common Council's committee wanted system, and Wells wanted self-expression and the development of personality. Wells resigned shortly. Some thirty years later, Frank Sanborn, the Secretary of the Massachusetts Board of State Charities, wrote of Wells, that the latter, when in the flush of his youth, "showed the true magnetic power of drawing youth into virtuous paths; but he was called to other work.[38] This "work" was of Wells' own making, for he established a private school in South Boston for the moral discipline of boys. This institution Julius declared was without equal at the time in America, and without any precedent.[39] The school received not only unruly boys, but those for whom the special kind of curriculum seemed fitting. The tuition fee was $3.00 a week, and there was capacity for 40 boys. The daily schedule, clearly an outgrowth and development of Wells' experience at the House of Reformation, and an indication of what he would have aimed to institute at the House of Reformation, had he been permitted to work out his program, was of such insurgent character in an era of dogmatic principles of "schooling," that it deserved recording:[40]

Summer.	Winter.	Occupation.
5.00	6.00	Getting up; silent prayers, making beds, washing, cleaning teeth.
5.15	6.15	Singing, New Testament, prayers in unison.
6.00	7.00	Gymnastics, games, running.
6.45	7.45	Breakfast (tea or coffee, wheat bread and butter).
8.00	8.15	School. (Reading, speaking, writing, composition, arithmetic, grammar, history, geography, natural history, natural philosophy, ethics, botany, Latin, Greek, French, phrenology, music, drawing, bookkeeping, riding, fencing.)
10.00	10.15	Recess till 11.30. Then running.
11.45	11.45	Quiet occupation for each student, of such nature as he chooses.
12.15	12.15	Gymnastics, games, etc., as in morning.
1.00	1.00	Dinner. (Twice a week fresh meat, once rice, once maize pudding, once beans, once chopped meat or fish.)
1.30	1.30	Quiet occupation, as in morning.
2.00	2.00	School.
4.30	4.30	Gymnastic games, as in morning. Running.
500	6.00	Supper, like breakfast.
6.00	6.30	Court. Judging conduct of each during day, and presentation of marks for the day.
6.30	7.00	Prayer and song.
7.15	8.00	Bedtime, separate prayers, as in morning, and the overseer reads aloud until all boys are asleep.

The above schedule allotted 4½ hours to school, about 4½ hours to play and regulated gymnastics, only one hour to "quiet occupations," and about two hours to religious observances. With Wells it seems to have been deliberately a matter of letting the individual

[38] Report, Board of State Charities, 1865, Lxviii.
[39] Julius. Sittleche Zusbaende, Vol. II, p. 367.
[40] Julius. Sittleche Zusbaende, Vol. II.

child find himself, through a maximum of playtime and hours of self-exploration, coupled with an abundance of schooling over a wide range of subjects, and a total absence of compulsory and supervised industrial training. It was obviously the plan of this clergyman-educator to get as far away as possible from traditional educational and former prison methods in dealing with children. Could we know what Wells' scholastic and recreational methods were, we should probably find an elementary approximation to Pestolozzi and Montessori. And in penological philosophy he was clearly a forerunner of William George and his George Junior Republic, and of Thomas Mott Osborne, with his Mutual Welfare League.

Wells was obviously far in advance of his time. The age demanded system — and the subordination of individuality in institutional management. And in both New York and Boston, system was secured, by the successors of Curtis and Wells. To the New York House of Refuge came N. C. Hart in July, 1826, a successful high-school teacher [41] of medium height, very stout and of becoming countenance. He proved not only a most amiable superintendent, but also a good organizer and disciplinarian.

"The lightning with him was made to do its work without the thunder."

He formulated a code of rules,[42] from which few changes were made during the succeeding half century. A system of grades and badges was inaugurated.

From this time on, and within a little over a year of the opening of the House of Refuge, the presence and influence of a well-defined organization was manifest at the House of Refuge. By the end of 1825, indeed, a separate building had already been opened for the girl inmates.[43] The Legislature in 1826 authorized the reception of children from any county or city of the State. The financial support of the Refuge, at first gained through private contributors, came within a few years from State and city almost entirely, as we shall shortly see.

Much of the excellent success of the Refuge came through the devoted and constant participation of certain of the managers, particularly of three important committees, the indenturing, school and executive committees. Special efforts were early made by the indenturing committee to find positions for the older boys in the mercantile and the marine service. Many boys were apprenticed to sea-farers, on long whaling voyages.[45] Sea-faring was regarded as among the best trades to enter. By 1831 the Refuge could report that

"a large number of boys (formerly inmates) have returned this season — dressed without exception when they came to see us, some with watches in their pockets. The greater part returned to the same industry."[44]

---

[41] Half Century, p. 117.
[42] Half Century, p. 122.
[43] Half Century, p. 97.
[44] Annual Report, 1831, p. 8.
[45] Half Century, p. 105.

Great care was taken by the indenturing committee to make suitable placements of the boys and girls. These gentlemen served without compensation, no member of the Board of Managers being allowed to receive any payment for his services. The committee met always once a week, and frequently several times a week, their sessions occupying the greater part of the day. All applications for apprentices were investigated by the committee. Tutelary supervision was maintained over the bound-out children, and not infrequently, children were transferred to other masters, if the first placements did not seem successful. The committee conceived it a part of its duty to become personally well acquainted with the boys in the Refuge.

A ladies' committee gave similar attention to the girl inmates, at least once a week throughout the year.[46] Almost without exception the girls were indentured into "housewifery," or as we would call it, domestic service.

By 1834, 1,480 children had been received and 1,148 bound out as apprentices. Correspondence was always kept up with the person to whom the children were bound, and also with the children themselves.[49] The managers claimed that these 1,148 had been snatched from crime and infamy. By 1836, the Society for the Reformation of Juvenile Delinquents announced that the number of converts from vice to morality, from idleness to industry, and from despair to hope, had been greater than could have been secured by any other means, and more than sufficient to justify the continued patronage of the State and city authorities.[47] By 1840, the bulk of the indentured boys were being placed out with farmers, and the tendency to send boys to sea had disappeared.

Fifteen years' test had now been given to the results of the Refuge. Since the system had been established, the number of juvenile convicts coming before the courts had diminished by nearly one-half, and in some years by more. Of those discharged from the Refuge, very few were ever recommitted.[48] One year of residence at the Refuge generally was sufficient discipline and training before indenturing. As the years went by, scarcely a week went by without some former inmate visiting the Refuge as a friendly and successful young citizen. By 1844, practically twenty years had elapsed since the opening. A cross-section presented by the abundant statistics in the annual report gives a picture of the institution, its population and activities. During the year, 262 inmates were received, as follows:

From New York Police Office	114
From the Court of Sessions	55
From Commissioners of the Almshouse	18
From other counties	29
	216
Returned after having been indentured or released to friends	46
	262

---

[46] Annual Report, 1831, p. 21.
[47] Annual Report, 1836, p. 7.
[48] Same, 1840, p. 21.
[49] Same, 1834, p. 9.

The number of inmates brought back to the institution (46) from apprenticeship or the supervision of friends was reasonably small, judged by comparison with the parole-violation statistics of the present day, being in 1844 18 per cent.

The distribution of population by color was as follows:

	In Institution January 1, 1844	Received during Year	Disposed of during Year	Remaining end of Year
Boys, white	214	160	165	209
Girls, white	62	54	67	49
Boys, colored	36	41	38	39
Girls, colored	9	7	6	10
	321	262	276	307

Racially, the population, which in the first years had been predominantly the children of American parents, had changed, and Irish children were in the majority:

Irish............... 88	German............ 14
American........... 47	Scotch............. 5
English............ 22	French............. 1

The children were being received at very varied ages. Of the 216 received for the first time in 1844, there were:

7 at the age of 8	19 at the age of 13
2 at the age of 9	41 at the age of 14
7 at the age of 10	35 at the age of 15
11 at the age of 11	40 at the age of 16
12 at the age of 12	22 at the age of 17

Average age of all the children, 13 years, 11 months.

During the year, indenturing had been mainly to farmers (116 boys), housewifery (68 girls), boot and shoe makers (14 boys), and smaller numbers to many different trades.

The New York House of Refuge was an institution that was firmly determined to train children in habits of industry. Curtis, the first superintendent, fell out, as we have seen, with his board of managers because of alleged unsystematic conduct of the Refuge. His successor, N. C. Hart, developed a program that to-day would seem stiff indeed:[50]

Sunrise	Getting up, assembly, prayers, parade in open air.
Until 7.00	Breakfast.
7.00	School.
7.30-12.00	Labor.
12.00-1.00	Dinner.
1.00-5.00	Labor.
5.00-5.30	Supper.
5.30-8.00	School.
8.00	Bed, after prayers.

In short, the children were compelled to work 8 hours a day, and in addition to that they were given four hours of schooling each week day. Into this day, already filled to the extent of 12 hours,

[50] Annual Report, House of Refuge, 1831.

came a bit of play, necessarily very brief, for those who had finished their morning work early. The labor of the children was, as far as possible, let out to contractors, but the labor was done at the institution. In 1828, the fee given *per diem per capita* by the contractors was 12½ cents for 8 hours work:

"This method has been adopted as on the whole the most advantageous. Free from losses and risks attendant upon carrying on of trades for the account of the Society it enables the officers of the institution to bestow more time and greater attention on the moral government of the children." [51]

In 1831, the Society received for the labor of the children $2,953.36. The chief occupations through this decade were the making of brass nails, the manufacturing of cane seats for chairs, whip stocks, as well as weaving, willow working (covers for bottles and demi-johns) and shoemaking.[52]

In 1837, there was but four months' labor in the shops, because of the business depression throughout the country. Contractors would not take the boys, even without compensation. In 1839, the boys were reported as being occupied for from 6 hours to 7 hours at some light mechanical employment, and as having produced in the last year a total of $1,787 for the institution. In 1841, 120 of the boys were being employed at from 9 cents to 12½ cents a day.

The causes of juvenile crime were increasingly studied in the annual reports. The environmental theory of the causes of delinquency had been discussed, stressed, even before the Refuge was established. Neglected and abandoned children fell naturally into evil ways. Of the first 513 children received by the House of Refuge:

135 had lost their fathers.
40 had lost their mothers.
67 were orphans.
51 were little criminals because of parental neglect or misconduct.
47 were children whose mothers had married again. [53]

The name "House of Refuge" had been chosen because it might suggest misfortune only, and not punishment. The Society was conscious of a great distinction between the little inmates and the adult inmates of a prison.

"With a criminal, whose corruption is inveterate and deeply rooted, the feeling of honesty is not awakened, because the sentiment is extinct. [54]

But it was believed that the feeling still existed in the youthful breast. Griscom said in 1826:

"A child might be made quiet and industrious by beating, but it seldom happened that kind-heartedness, morality and intelligence were induced by whipping." [55]

Therefore, on admission the lad was informed that he was not in a prison. The crimes he might have committed before entrance would be forgotten, and his career in the Refuge would depend upon

---

[51] Annual Report, House of Refuge, p. 10.
[52] Annual Report, 1835, p. 47.
[53] de Beaumont and de Tocqueville, p. 11.
[54] Same, p. 123.
[55] Half Century, p. 120.

his present and future conduct. And, while the lad was getting his training for life, the Society was studying the causes of his delinquency.

Intemperance was proclaimed in 1836 one of the chief causes, and described as a hydra-headed monster. The Society found little incentive to crime occasioned by want, but it asked:

"If we could but abolish drunkenness, where would we find candidates for admission into our prisons?" [56]

The temptations offered by petty pawnbrokers' shops were another important cause of crime. These shops were "fences," for the receipt of stolen goods. The report advocated the opening of several offices under the direction of a board of managers like those of a savings bank or of the House of Refuge, with rates of interest simply sufficient to meet the operating expenses. Institutions, said the report, had already existed in Europe like these. Nearly a century later, the Provident Loan Society, a philanthropic pawnbroking society, was established along similar lines in New York City.

In the following years, theatrical performances came in for severe criticism as a demoralizing influence upon the children of the city. Several new minor theatres had opened, and the boys stood in throngs outside the entrances, begging for the "return checks" that would admit them. Failing these, or stimulated by the gay life within the theatre, children would steal from parents or employers, or get money from the pawnbroking "fences." The pits in the theatre brought the lads into contact with strangers, pickpockets and the like. Out of 130 instances of delinquency, 59 were attributed to this cause.[57]

There were 2,850 dram shops licensed in the city, a large proportion of which were kept open on Sunday. The day was profaned. The penalty for vending strong drink on the Sabbath was practically a dead letter. A natural consequence of intemperance was the striking degree of licentiousness in both sexes.

In 1838, the Society recommended a strengthening of the "patrol," or police force. Three-fourths of the petty thefts were being committed by minors. Juvenile peddlers should be licensed. There was a most serious lack of attendance at schools; 4,000 children under the age of 14 were not going to school. In 1839, the Society discovered another factor in making young criminals, the New York fire department. Children, known as volunteers, were first at the fire houses, on an alarm of fire, and furnished part of the motive power. There was the well-known strife to get to the fire first. There was additional fatigue induced thereby, and the thirst for stimulants. Free access to merchandise in the burning or destroyed buildings, and the total absence of older persons of authority gave to the children almost irresistible temptations. The Society appealed for a paid fire department.

[56] Annual Report, 1836, p. 15.
[57] Annual Report, 1837, p. 17.

The hawking of papers, and the erratic life of the canal boats, were cited also as leading to crime. There was noted, too, the orphanage of immigrant children, whose parents had died on the voyage across from Europe. Fathers, moreover, were cited who had left their families, and husbands who had gone west to seek work. The children of the Refuge were, more than half of them, foreign-born or the children of foreigners.[58] Many families were being supported largely by the begging methods of their children.[59]

"Who, among all the sons and daughters of Adam, if subjected to the same ordeal that tries the morals of these children, would come forth unscathed? It is not always the act alone that decides the turpitude of the offense; there are 10,000 circumstances that come in to heighten or palliate the criminality of the transaction."[60]

The mortality record of the institution was almost always excellent. During the first four years there was but one death, and that not from natural causes. The record of illnesses showed what in those days were considered the "usual summer maladies," such as intermittent fevers, dysentery, and in a number of years distressing "opthalmia," which was contagious, and was probably trachoma.

In the first ten years of the institution's career, there were but 15 deaths, among 1,478 children, of which ten deaths occurred in the "cholera year."[61] The resident physician furnished no evidence, in his annual reports, of any serious study or concern as to the causes of disease in the institutional inmates. In 1834, the city was creeping up toward the institution, and the opening of streets and the erection of an embankment for the railroad led the physician to state that the effluvia from the stagnant water and the new soil told on the children's health. Bad water from new wells was given as a cause of dysentery.

Only 29 deaths occurred in the first 16 years.[62]

"Many children are sent to the Refuge who are worn down by disease (the offspring of their own folly), who by careful medical treatment, aided by wholesome restraint, are soon returned to health and a sound constitution."

As already stated, the inception of the House of Refuge was due to private philanthropy, and the financial support of the undertaking came at first from contributed funds. At the meeting of the Society for the Prevention of Pauperism on December 19th, 1823, $800 was subscribed, and shortly afterwards $18,000 was readily secured,[63] the city being divided into canvassing districts. For $6,000, the Federal Government ceded, at the junction of Bloomingdale Road and the Old Post Road (the present Madison Square) a site of some four acres, with large barracks, and a house suitable for the superintendent and his family.[64] Of this sum, $4,000 was subsequently remitted by Congress.

[58] Annual Report, 1839, p. 9.
[59] Annual Report, 1840, p. 22.
[60] Annual Report, 1841, p. 13.
[61] Annual Report, 1834, p. 13.
[62] Annual Report, 1840, p. 29.
[63] Half Century, p. 57.
[64] Same, p. 74.

The State Legislature in 1825 provided for an appropriation of $2,000 annually for the term of five years, beginning in 1826. In 1829, greater support by the State was obtained, for an annual appropriation of $8,000 was authorized, to be paid out of the surplus accruing from the moneys received from the head-tax on immigrants, and used primarily for the maintenance of the Marine Hospital on Staten Island.[65] Furthermore, the excise commissioners in the city of New York were directed by law hereafter to pay to the Society for the Reformation of Juvenile Delinquents $1.50 from every tax received for licensing any tavern, grocer or "ordinary," or public garden.

Theatres and circuses were taxed $500 and $250 respectively, for the benefit of the House of Refuge. In 1831, the excise act was amended, to provide for an appropriation of a definite sum of $4,000 annually. In 1839, a penalty of $500 was placed upon the neglect of a theatre or circus to secure a license, the said sum to be collected by the Society. Theatre and circus licenses were also still to be paid to the Society.

A typical financial statement was that of the fiscal year 1831:

Income.		Expenditures.	
From labor of children	$2,953 36	Balance due treasurer	$2,242 67
Marine Hospital Fund	8,000 00	Clothing	1,492 50
Tavern licenses	1,250 00	Food	4,807 56
Tax on 4 theatres	2,000 00	Coal, wood, oil, stoves, etc.	1,100 76
Excise fund	4,000 00		
Sales of chair bottoms, etc.	2,524 82	Furniture, beds, bedding, etc.	961 29
Cash, donations, subscriptions, etc	281 83	School and hospital	189 12
Balance due	1,046 10	Salaries	3,346 45
		Chair shop	2,489 83
		Building, repairs, etc.	2,582 54
		Paid finance committee	6,737 73
		Premium, interest	111 60
		Printing annual report, stationery, etc.	110 72
		Horse, cows, etc.	447 84
			$26,620 61
	$22,056 11	To balance	$1,046 10

The Society received in 1834 a donation of $5,000 from the Manumission Society toward the erection of a building for colored children. The lot of such delinquent children in the city was very hard. They had the same temptations to commit crime as did the white children, whereas on the other hand the opportunities for apprenticeship were not open to them. Both the colored parents and their children were densely ignorant.

By 1835, the Society had expended about $80,000 for buildings,[66] workshops, walls and the like. The new building for the colored children was burned in 1836 by one of the girl inmates, who was promptly sent to State prison. In 1838, a new location was chosen for the Refuge, at Bellevue, on the borders of the East River, at the foot of East Twenty-third Street. Near this location was the

---
[65] Laws of 1829, Chapter 302.
[66] Annual Report, 1835, p. 16.

Almshouse. A new building, 150 feet long and 42 feet wide, three stories in height, was erected for the girls, and the fever hospital was converted into a dormitory for boys.[67] In 1839, the board of managers reported that the Refuge supported, schooled, and furnished books and clothing at $1.27 per capita per week. This included all expenses, save insurance and repairs to buildings. Further weekly *per capitas* were announced as follows:[68]

	Average.	Per Capita.
1836-37	243 Children	$1.24
1837-38	209 "	1.50
1838-39	229 "	1.15
1839-40	209 "	1.26

The cost of the new female building, and of the alterations on the fever hospital, shops, stables, wall, etc., was $52,968.64, of which the city of New York paid $40,000.

The treasurer's report for 1844 varied little in nature from that of 1831, above cited. Disbursements were very similar, the income being from the following sources:

From labor of children:		
Due 1843, received in 1844	$1,447 29	
Due in 1844	5,583 55	
		$7,030 84
From State Treasury (instead of Marine Hospital Fund)		8,000 00
Licensing of theatres and circuses		3,194 00
Excise fund		4,000 00
Finance Committee		573 15

Returning now to a consideration of the history of the Boston House of Reformation during the first twenty years of its career, we find that the Boston House of Reformation had its origin in an act of the Massachusetts Legislature, which in the winter session of 1826 gave to the city council of Boston authority to send juvenile delinquents, who under the old law would have been sent to State prison, to such place as the city should provide at South Boston.[69] The House of Reformation was in consequence established some two and one-half miles from the city, near the House of Industry. A commodious building was located within a yard of from 30 to 40 acres. The boys worked in the secured enclosed field at times, under supervision of the superintendent.

The House of Reformation and the House of Industry were under the same unpaid board of managers, seven gentlemen from Boston. The early staff consisted of a superintendent, school teacher, and the overseer of the shoeshop. The institution was supported entirely by the city of Boston, at a cost in 1827 of about $3,000.[70]

The garb of the boys was a plain uniform, a "jockey"-blue jacket and white trousers, the cost of the suit being about one dollar.

We have already seen, in describing the system under Mr. Wells, that the general purpose and administration of the Boston institu-

---
[67] Annual Report, 1838, p. 6.
[68] Same, 1839, p. 42.
[69] B. P. D. S., 1826, p. 47.
[70] B. P. D. S., 1827, p. 133.

tion was similar to that of the New York House of Refuge. Boys and girls were received from the courts, trained, and then "identified." The whole number received from September 20, 1826, to April 30, 1828, was 143, of whom 26 were girls. By 1829, the average number of inmates was 100, with about ten per cent. of them girls. Their commitments were for the following delinquencies:[71]

Stealing	47
Vagabondage	29
Stubborn and disobedient	49
Leading idle life, and being neglected by parents on account of drunkenness and other causes	11
Wanton and lascivious conduct	4

The average age of the children was 11 years and 10 months. Their employments in the week of January 4th, 1829, were the following:

Occupations	Boys	Girls
Hat making	16	....
Basket making	15	....
Hair work	27	....
Police duties	15	....
Monitors	3	....
Oakum	10	....
Office	1	....
Office and at home	1	1
House work	....	1
Sewing and knitting	....	8
In solitude	3	1
	91	11

By 1831, the annual cost of maintenance had increased to about $6,000. Children to the number of 303 had been received, and 204 discharged, of whom 155 were reported to be doing well. Only two deaths had occurred in 4 years and 9 months, and in 15 months only one case of sickness. In 1832 — the last year of Mr. Wells' superintendency — the need of a new building was felt. Details of the House of Reformation are deplorably few, because no annual reports were published.

Practically coincidentally with Mr. Wells retirement from the Boston House of Reformation, an "association of gentlemen of great respectability" purchased in 1833 Thompson's Island in Boston Harbor, containing about 120 acres of good land, and proceeded to erect on the island suitable buildings for a farm school for the education and reformation of boys exposed to extraordinary temptations, and who were in danger of becoming vicious and dangerous.[72] Another charitable association, the "Boston Asylum," had been incorporated as early as the year 1814 to "receive, instruct, and employ indigent boys of Boston," and orphans in particular. The Asylum had power to receive those children whose parents neglected them. Places as apprentices were obtained by

---
[71] B. P. D. S., 1829, p. 192.
[72] B. P. D. S., 1834, p. 836, and Dorothea Dix, p. 92.

the Asylum for the children. Legal power was given to duly authorized persons to take these children from their neglectful parents.[73] This institution was the oldest of its class in Massachusetts, and one of the oldest in the world.[74]

The Boston Asylum and the new Farm School on Thompson's Island merged in 1835, under the title of "The Boston Asylum and Farm School for Indigent Boys." The society was strictly a private corporation, and received boys who had not yet committed crime. It was believed that no stigma would be attached to Farm School boys. The Farm School was to give to children an open-air and agricultural training, as well as schooling — a program suggested in 1831 by Ralph Waldo Emerson, when he was a member of the Boston School Committee, but his recommendation was not acted on.[75] On Thompson's Island there was farming, much exercise in the open air, and sea bathing, as well as "innocent sports." Each boy had a flower garden to cultivate. The boys learned domestic service also. In the summer, they worked one week upon the farm, and passed the next week in school. Men from the city came over on Sunday to address the children. Between 1835 and 1836, about 400 boys were received, and 37 had been apprenticed.[76]

During the winter, 6 hours of schooling were had each week day, and also from dark until prayers. The boys slept in a dormitory, 60 by 36 feet, the berths being "double-deckers," one above the other. The supervisor slept in the dormitory.[77]

The year's expense sheets cited by the Prison Discipline Society's report of 1837 are of interest:

Food, 110 boys per week		$64 43
Salaries, per week:		
Superintendent and family	$19 17	
Schoolmaster and family	8 65	
Three females at $1.75	5 25	
2 men at $15 a month	7 00	
One tailor	2 00	
One assistant	1 50	
		$43 57
Fuel, soap, wear and tear, bedding, etc.:		
Fuel per year		$300 00
Soap		75 00
Wear and tear		1 50
Clothing each boy per year		11 00

This new movement — with its broader institutional conception, and its support by private philanthropy — caused diminished public interest in, and a reduction in the number of inmates of, the Boston House of Reformation. From now on, until the end of the period we are considering, the House of Reformation offers no specially interesting features. The children were removed

---

[73] Memorial of Society for Prev. of J. Del., to N. Y. Legislature, in Docs. of House of Refuge, 1832, p. 34.
[74] Report, Massachusetts Board of State Charities, 1865, p. 97.
[75] Annual Report, Board of State Charities, 1865, p. 102.
[76] Dorothea Dix, p. 92.
[77] B. P. D. S., 1837, p. 154.

temporarily in 1833 or 1834 to Fort Warren in Boston Harbor, while the House of Reformation was being renovated for use as a House of Correction,[78] and they were then moved back to one wing of the renovated structure, an entirely unsuitable and cramped arrangement.

By 1836, a "new and noble edifice" was occupied by the House of Reformation. The boys were making 850,000 brass nails a day. The girls were sewing and learning housewifery.[79] Six hours of contract labor and four hours of school were the daily program. The contractor paid 10 cents a day for each boy's labor. The boys not thus occupied picked oakum, netting the institution 10 to 15 cents a day.

In 1836, colored children were first admitted. The ages of the inmates ranged from 8 to 21; the causes of commitment of the boys were as follows: [80]

Larceny	33
Stubbornness and disobedience	21
Vagrancy	15
Drunkenness	1

The girls were committed for the following causes:

Larceny	4
Stubbornness and disobedience	8
Wantonness and lasciviousness	3
Vagrancy	2
Obtaining money under false pretenses	1

About 1841, the House of Reformation became a branch of the House of Industry, and under the same management as the latter institution. The children were kept under constant but mild discipline.[81] Their hours were:

Labor	6 hours
School	4 hours
Recreation	2 and ½ hours
Mending, sweeping, cleaning, making beds, etc.	3½ hours
Sleep	8 hours

The east wing of the building was by 1847 occupied by the "Boylston School," numbering about 100 boys, between the ages of 6 and 13, who were of humble origin, but of promising capacity. They pursued the usual common school branches, and were placed out at the proper time as apprentices.

The example of New York and Boston, in establishing separate institutions for juvenile delinquents was soon followed by Philadelphia. By 1827, $15,000 had been raised by private subscriptions, and the Pennsylvania Legislature had voted $40,000 for the completion of a House of Refuge.[82] The Refuge was opened on November 29th, 1828, and received the first inmates in December.[83] More than $86,000 was ultimately expended in construction and

---
[78] B. P. D. S., 1834, p. 836.
[79] Same, 1836, p. 53.
[80] Same. 1837, p. 153.
[81] Dorothea Dix, 1847, p. 90.
[82] B. P. D. S., 1827, p. 136.
[83] B. P. D. S., 1829, p. 324.

outfitting.[84] The institution was situated on a hill near Philadelphia, and was a large building with surrounding gardens. The building cost $38,035, the main building being 92 feet long, the center of the building containing a room for library, and for the use of the managers and the families of the institution officers. The wings of the structure comprised the dormitories for boys and girls, and several large school rooms. Separate cells (called dormitories), were provided for entire separation at night, the dimensions being 7 feet long, by 4 feet wide (slightly larger than the cells at Auburn Prison, and much smaller than those at the Eastern Penitentiary). Each cell was furnished with a small bedstead and shelf, was well lighted, and well ventilated, and exposed at all times to supervision.

The workshops were located in an extensive area, surrounded by a high wall. A hospital and a chapel were provided. The first annual report showed 57 boys and 23 girls as inmates. The trades were:

Boys.	Girls.
Bookbinding.	Sewing.
Basket weaving.	Washing.
Wicker working.	Ironing.
Tailoring.	Mending.
Carpentry.	Cooking.
Shoemaking.	General housework.

The daily program was:
4.45 Rising bell.
5.00 Dormitories opened.
5.00-7.00 Morning worship and school.
7.00 Breakfast.
7.30 Work.
12.00 Dinner, then a lecture or talk.
1.00 Work (½ hour of play, after completion of work in afternoon.)
5.00 Supper.
5.30 School.
7.45 Evening prayers, then bed.

The contractors paid 12½ cents a day for 8 hours labor of the able-bodied children, which was a sum entirely inadequate for maintenance. The baleful effects of a childhood passed without schooling were emphasized by the Pennsylvania Society for Promotion of Public Schools in 1830, when it asserted that there were at least 400,000 persons in Pennsylvania, between the ages of 5 and 14, and that of these not 150,000 were in all the schools of the State.[85]

Juvenile cases fell off materially in the Philadelphia courts after the establishment of the House of Refuge. This applied to the white children only. Colored children, who were not admitted to the House of Refuge, continued to come before the courts in large numbers. The managers early found that the younger children were far more receptive to reformatory treatment, and urged in their first annual report that only children under 16 should be admitted.

---

[84] Julius. Sittleche Zusbaende, Vol. II, p. 359.
[85] Mary Carpenter, "Juvenile Delinquents," 1853, p. 210.

In the same year we find the first record of a benefaction to a private institution for delinquents, Frederick Kohne leaving to the House of Refuge $100,000 in his will.

In 1831, the receipts were:

Life and annual subscriptions, donations, and from labor of inmates	$4,434 98
County treasury	10,000 00
	$14,434 98
Expenses:	
Provisions, clothing, fuel, salaries, repairs, interest	$15,605 86

The deficit was therefore, in this year, $1,170.84. The city of Philadelphia gave from $10,000 to $14,000 a year in support of the institution.[86]

The statistics of population for the year 1831 were:[87]

Received	Boys	Girls	Total
From courts and magistrates	87	24	111
Returned after escape	1	...	1
Returned after indenturing	11	...	11
	99	24	123
Discharged			
By indenture	39	10	49
By age	6	8	14
Not proper subjects	7	4	11
Returned to friends	14	3	17
Sent to almshouse	3	...	3
Sent to sea	2	...	2
Died	2	...	2
	73	25	98
Remaining January 1st, 1832	113	44	157

The lads were indentured more to farmers than to any other occupation. The girls all learned "housewifery." The average age of the boys was 14½, of the girls 15, on reception. The time of discharge was at majority.[88] The managers of the Philadelphia institution stated in 1833 their attitude regarding juvenile delinquency. Juvenile delinquents, and particularly those of tender age, had not acquired habits of crime, but were on the way to acquiring them. Their first offenses were to be considered symptomatic, showing temptations, evil counsel, bad examples, or parental neglect. The purpose of the establishment was essentially parental, and children were bound out from the Refuge without stigma and without difficulty. Masters took them into their homes and placed them on a footing with the other apprentices. Masters, however, would not take the oldest boys, because there would not be sufficient time left before the boys' majority to afford compensation for the unrequited expenses of the earlier period of apprenticeship. An

---
[86] Julius. Sittleche Zusbaende, Vol. II, p. 360.
[87] B. P. D. S., 1832, p. 578.
[88] Julius. Sittleche Zusbaende, Vol. II, p. 362.

"incorrigibly vicious" boy was not bound out. The Refuge was not a prison, nor really a place of punishment. The administration was not in any sense vindictive.

The managers in this year announced a new cause of juvenile corruption — the children's theatres, in which the players were minors of both sexes. These show-houses were established in obscure places, and were conducted with unlimited license. They were visited by children in stealth, and often the entrance fees were dishonestly acquired.

It was regarded as a notable fact that in the "cholera year" of 1832 in Philadelphia, not a single case of cholera developed in the House of Refuge.

CHAPTER XXV

THE STATE OF PRISONS IN 1845

The year 1845 marks an especially convenient time at which to pause and summarize the state of American prisons, and to conclude this study of the formative era of American penology. It was in the year 1844 that the Prison Association of New York was founded, bringing into the field of prison reform an organization of representative citizens of New York, who adhered to neither the Auburn nor to the Pennsylvania system, but sought to understand the essentials of adequate prison management, and also to effect the betterment of prison conditions. In the year 1845, the Massachusetts Society in Aid of Discharged Convicts was formed, which co-operated with the State Agent in the relief of prisoners released from prison. In 1844 and 1845 appeared the first two editions of Dorothea Lynde Dix's "Remarks on Prisons and Prison Discipline in the United States," an acute analysis of prison conditions for the general reader.

The Pennsylvania Society for the Alleviation of the Miseries of Public Prisons inaugurated in 1845 the publication of a quarterly magazine, thus abandoning their passive and almost sacrificial attitude toward the vicious and persistent attacks upon the Pennsylvania system, made in the annual reports of the Boston Prison Discipline Society, and particularly by the Reverend Louis Dwight, its militant and highly biased secretary. It was in this period that for the first time Mr. Dwight was called severely to account for his constant championship of the Auburn system, and for his bitter opposition to anything that came out of the Pennsylvania system. The first serious attack from within the Boston Society was being led by Doctor S. G. Howe and Charles Sumner, who challenged not only the wisdom and the judgment of Mr. Dwight, but also his intellectual honesty and his veracity.

In 1846, the first international gathering of those interested in or specializing in penology was held at Frankfort on the Main. The world's attention was being co-operatively directed to the problems of prisons. In the antipodes, the daring experiments of Maconochie, with self-government in limited measure and with a broad interpretation of the honor system, had already been tried out. Obermaier in Bavaria had accomplished extraordinary results through trusting to the honor of prisoners. In short, a distinct penological literature was being built up, less in America than in Europe. Germans, French, Belgians and English were plunged into both academic and practical controversies over the relative merits of the Auburn and the Pennsylvania systems, and the battle was being fought on the other side in a far more scholarly and thorough manner than had been the case in the land of their origin. In our own country, principles had become fairly well established; methods were fairly well fixed; traditions had already formed. It was now more a period of development of the details of prison discipline rather than one of hardy experimentation. Terms of daily use within institutions had grown definite. Prison life was a concrete fact; prisons had come to stay; new institutions were springing up in the newer States, and the daily routine of prison life was made up of fixed and carefully regulated hours, tasks and motions. The roots of prison methods were striking well down into the soil of customs and traditions.

In short, in New York, Boston and Philadelphia, the three centers of interest in prison reform, these movements above-mentioned marked the end both of the experimental period and of the one-man domination of the prison reform field, which since 1826 had been virtually ruled by Mr. Dwight, through his tireless controversial activity, his visits to institutions, his pamphleteering, and the wide circulation of the Boston Society's annual reports, which had circulation not only throughout the United States, but among the prison reform groups of Europe. The new era would mean a searching study of existing prison conditions, and a definite unwillingness to receive any longer predigested facts. The initial annual report of the Prison Association of New York exhibited a scholarly tendency to go to the root of all available facts. The new era marked the end of the dominant attention given to administrative details by students of the subject, and therefore marked the beginning of the period of fact-study, of the evolution of broad principles, and of the independent thinking of different groups, culminating within a quarter century in the coming of Enoch C. Wines, of Zebulon R. Brockway, of Frank Sanborn, and of the first meeting of the National Prison Association in Cincinnati in 1870, after which grew rapidly the movement for the establishment in the United States of the reformatory system of treatment of young men, initiated in the New York State Reformatory at Elmira in 1876.

This decade from 1840 to 1850 is therefore the period of the rise of a third conspicuous wave in prison reform. The first period had extended from 1787 to approximately 1820, and it was marked by the establishment, in 1787, of the Philadelphia Society for the Alleviating of the Miseries of Public Prisons, the opening of the Walnut Street Prison in 1790, and the establishment of the State Prison in the city of New York in 1797. The first period had been marked also by the philanthropic interest and activity of men like Benjamin Rush, Caleb Lownes, William Bradford of Philadelphia and Thomas Eddy of New York. The Walnut Street Prison in Philadelphia standardized the construction and administration of the first State prisons, as to night-rooms, separate punishment cells for solitary confinement, prison labor, compensation of prisoners, silence at work, boards of inspectors, officials, etc. Out of the example of the Philadelphia prison developed, in close imitation, the first State prisons of other States: New York, 1796; Virginia, 1800; Massachusetts, 1804; Vermont, 1808; Maryland, 1811; New Hampshire, 1812; Ohio, 1816, and Auburn prison in New York, 1816, in its first architectural plan.

This earliest period brought the beginnings of a systematic prison reform movement in the founding of the Philadelphia Society for the Alleviating of the Miseries of Public Prisons in 1787, followed by immediate and personal attention to these "miseries." There ensued considerable prison reform propaganda, through pamphleteering by the Society's members, and through actual participation in the administration of the Walnut Street Prison.

The first "sag" in this earliest period was not slow in coming, occurring as early as 1800 in Philadelphia, and in the case of the other prisons within a few years of their openings. Although many principles and methods evolved by the Philadelphia philanthropists were marked by common sense, the commingling of the prisoners in the large night-rooms, added to the inevitable congestion of the prison population, as the State's population increased, precipitated the downfall of the first prison system. The prisons reverted quickly to the abhorrent conditions of idleness, debauchery, extortion and extravagance that had marked the local prisons of the pre-reform period, antedating the founding of the Walnut Street Prison. In Philadelphia and New York, outraged public opinion led to violent protests, and also by 1820, to the possibility of a return to the sanguinary and public capital and corporal punishments of the earlier days, for which prisons were to have been a substitute.

The second wave of prison reform swept over the Eastern and Middle Atlantic States during the twenties of the nineteenth century. This ten-year period from 1820 to 1830 was marked by the evolution of the two separate systems of prison discipline, destined to become subjects of heated discussion and intense rivalry. The period also brought with it the erection of the four most conspicuous prisons in early American prison history — the renovated prison at Auburn, from 1819 on; Sing Sing, known as Mount Pleasant, in 1825; the Connecticut State Prison at Wethersfield, in 1827; and the Eastern Penitentiary of Pennsylvania, from 1829 on.

The desperate moral and physical conditions in the old prisons at the end of the first period (1790-1820) led easily to the extreme penological antidotes for the abuses and excesses of the past, and there developed the two prison systems above mentioned, those of Auburn and of Pennsylvania. The basis of both systems was the prohibition at all times of verbal or other communication between prisoners. The fundamental difference in the systems lay in the methods employed to secure such separation of prisoners from each other. The Eastern Penitentiary housed its prisoners in large cells, one in a cell, and never allowed them to leave those cells save for extreme illness or on discharge. The Auburn system housed its prisoners separately, but in small cells, and brought the prisoners together in the workshops during the day under strictest rules of absolute silence. The Pennsylvania system required its inmates to work in their cells, apart from each other.

In construction, therefore, the two systems differed. The Auburn plan meant primarily a prison cellhouse of several tiers of small cells, built back to back, encased in an enveloping building. The cells were incredibly small. The Pennsylvania plan required rooms of adequate size for uninterrupted occupancy.

The second period of prison reform, just outlined, brought, as did the first era, the establishment of a prison reform society, this time in Boston — the Prison Discipline Society, conducted under the militant and often highly biased leadership of the Reverend Louis Dwight. Arguing successfully on the grounds of the greater economy, safety and simplicity of the Auburn system, and on the appealing ground of the constant utilization of the inmates at productive labor, the Boston prison society played a dominant role in persuading the States of the Union, almost one after the other, to adopt the Auburn plan. Only in Pennsylvania, New Jersey and Rhode Island did the Pennsylvania plan find adoption, and in the two latter States the system was abandoned, at least in part, within a few years.

In the succeeding decade, 1830 to 1840, there developed no such "sag" and failure as had marked the first period. The time was one of experiment and development, but there had now been found a fundamental basis upon which to build. The prisons had become "going" institutions. The first traditions, so essential in the conduct of a well-systematized institution, were being fixed. The proponents of each system, at Auburn and Philadelphia, were claiming signal success in their efforts to establish a thoroughgoing prison discipline. The Auburn system speedily reduced the expenses of maintenance to the State, and many prisons actually began to produce surpluses. The silence, rigid discipline and security were a wonderfully grateful relief to the harassed civic nerves of many States, after the excesses of the previous disorganized and debauched prisons. On the other hand, the champions of the Pennsylvania system praised similarly their results, and particularly the complete absence of any contamination of prisoners through physical association.

But, along with the acknowledged successes of these systems, there developed serious faults, visible as time went on. The self-supporting or surplus-producing prisons of the Auburn type incurred, or ran the danger of incurring, the angry hostility of the "mechanics," who found themselves faced by the competition of prison-made goods. Particularly in New York was the claim violently made by the labor groups that the competition of the prisons was unfair and damaging. Furthermore, the unbroken silence in Auburn-type prisons could, in most instances, be maintained only by the inflicting of severe corporal punishments. Floggings became so atrocious in Auburn, and especially in Sing Sing, as to stagger public opinion when finally revealed. The machine-like regularity of prison life under the Auburn system led also to the handling of prisoners in the mass. Efforts at reformation were sacrificed to the struggle of the State to make money out of the prisons. The taxpayers were led to concern themselves primarily with the question whether the prisons cost the State money, or brought money to the State.

Prisons on the Pennsylvania plan were not without weaknesses. Far more expensive to construct, and far more costly to maintain because of the impossibility of permitting the associated labor of convicts, the Eastern Penitentiary was with increasing frequency charged with a higher rate of deaths, disease and insanity than was alleged to occur in prisons of the Auburn type. Punishments were milder, to be sure, because most infractions of rules in prison arose from the contact of prisoners with each other, or from the desire to communicate.

Hence arose the belief, by 1840, that the prisons were failing to fulfill their earlier promises. Particularly disturbing were the scandals that broke out in New York through the disclosures of appalling cruelties at Sing Sing Prison early in the fourth decade of the century. Out of this, and other serious conditions, grew the third wave of prison reform, dating from approximately 1840. The visits of Dorothea Lynde Dix to prisons in the early forties revealed especially the deplorable and ignored conditions in the secondary prisons, such as jails, workhouses and houses of correction, and also the wretched negligence of most States toward their insane prisoners.

Moreover, the Prison Association of New York came into existence in 1844 through the suggestion of a humane member of the board of managers of Sing Sing Prison, who sought private help for discharged prisoners whom the State released with a bare pittance, after a miserable and disintegrating prison life. From this proposed field of activity, the Prison Association quickly swept on to a general concern about prison conditions, and about the plight of prisoners before, during and after imprisonment in correctional institutions. At the same time, the Quakers of the Philadelphia Society threw off the pacifistic tolerance that had inhibited any aggressive resistance to the attacks of the Boston Society upon the Pennsylvania plan, and started propaganda of their own, for their system in particular, and for a philosophical attitude toward the problems of prison reform in general.

This third era, in the midst of which our study of prison administration closes, affords us therefore an especially favorable point from which to attempt a more general survey of prison conditions a half-century after the opening of the first State prison on Walnut Street. We find the two great systems, namely, the silent system of Auburn, and the separate system of Pennsylvania. The best types of the separate system were the Eastern and the Western Penitentiaries of Pennsylvania. In the secondary institutions, the separate system had been best developed in the county prisons in Dauphin County, and Chester County, Pennsylvania, and in the

Moyamensing prison in Philadelphia County. The best types of the separate system were Auburn, Wethersfield, and Charlestown, Massachusetts, and perhaps Baltimore. The silent system was also well represented in the county jails of Hartford and New Haven in Connecticut, and in the House of Correction at South Boston in Massachusetts.

The *State* prisons were practically the only correctional institutions in which management had actually developed into system. County and local prisons were almost without exception the centers of callous, unsystematic and ignorant confinement of inmates. In the State prisons themselves, there were varying degrees of efficiency and humanity. Industrial productiveness was found, under the Auburn plan, coupled often with bloody atrocities and moral corruption, as at Sing Sing. The basic principles of the two systems, in the prisons of Auburn and Pennsylvania, were not of themselves inhuman, in the light of the time, and an alleged, though subordinate, purpose of the prisons was reformation; but the modes of daily operation were conditioned by the nature of the administrative authorities.

Striking differences in methods of management prevailed. In the House of Correction at South Boston, not a blow had been struck upon a prisoner, it was claimed, for over a decade, and no weapons were carried by keepers. The Connecticut and Massachusetts State prisons were operated with a minimum of corporal punishment. On the other hand, Sing Sing Prison gave, in some months of 1843, as many as 3,000 lashes a month. The larger the prisons, the more likelihood, and apparently the more necessity, there was of rigorous punishments, because of the far greater difficulty of preserving constant order and silence.

But the trend of all prisons was strongly toward the reduction of the use of the lash, and toward an increase in the relatively more humane solitary confinement in dark cells. The "shower bath" or ducking came into more general use. The "gag" was seldom used, but at Sing Sing, where the lash was not used upon women, the gag was sometimes employed upon women; straight-jackets were employed upon refractory prisoners. Reduction of meals to a bread and water diet was common.

Public opinion upheld corporal punishment, but not its development to an extraordinary degree. Floggings were customary outside of prison, in the navy, the schoolhouse and the home. Complete abandonment of similar practices in the prisons was not advocated, and yet certain wardens prided themselves upon their ability to get along without the use of the "cat." Even Dorothea Dix conceded that for especially refractory cases the lash had to be used as a last resort.

Security against escape by inmates, and productiveness of labor of inmates, were the two main demands of the law-making and appropriation-making bodies. The self-supporting prison was praised, and the prison that returned a surplus was held up to public admiration. Encouragement of this attitude of the public mind was fostered regularly by the Prison Discipline Society's reports from Boston. The achievement of these two ends led, in the prisons operating under the silent system, to the constant rigorous guarding of inmates, and to a constant driving of the inmate forces to the one end of turning out the maximum of commercially valuable products. The two chief phases of prison administration, therefore, were those connected with security and industry. The public must be protected from the criminal, and the taxpayer must be protected from any unnecessary drain upon his pocketbook.

Security against criminals was to be obtained by imprisonment, by severity of treatment, and by the deterrence of potential criminals on the outside. All phases of imprisonment were therefore surrounded with factors to excite dread and horror. Public opinion branded the criminal as an outcast, a definitely different person from the great body of law-abiding citizens. Religious dogmas proclaimed the eternal damnation of the wicked — and the criminals were all wicked. Hence, the naturalness of severe and even terrible treatment of criminals.

The prisons were built according to forbidding, and often monumental, architecture. The facade of the Eastern Penitentiary of Pennsylvania was at the time of its construction the most imposing architectural effort of its kind in the United States. High walls surrounded almost every prison, save Sing Sing, and the walls were patrolled by armed guards, who would shoot to kill. The public saw nothing of what passed inside the prison, save when admitted at regular hours upon payment of a small fee, which permitted them to gaze upon the inmates as upon the members of a human menagerie.

Security also demanded heavy masonry in prison buildings. Stone was the common material of construction. Cells, in prisons of the Auburn type, were "constructed for the one great object of securely packing, in the most economical manner, the greatest number of human beings in the smallest possible space." The most elementary sanitary requirements were neglected — but the prisoners were thus held safe against escape. The solid masonry of the cells sweated trickling streams of moisture on damp mornings, after a night of unventilated and noxious imprisonment of hundreds of human beings in catacomb-like "apartments," 7 feet long, 3 feet 6 inches wide, and 7 feet high. But society was thus protected against the escape of wild criminals. The darkness within the cells was such as to bar the reading of books when day-light had passed — but the intervening bars prevented the outbreak of the enemies of society. The gross ignorance of the age as to the principles of ventilation led to miserably unaired, disease-breeding, clammy cells — but the dangers of escape were thus minimized.

The necessity of perpetual security led also to the government of the prisoners at all time *en masse*. All movements were made in numbers, when possible. At all times, when prisoners were in groups, as in the workhouses, the supervision was vigilant and unrelenting. Separation of the individual prisoner from any possible contact with his neighbor was regarded as imperative. Hence the rule of perpetual silence. Hence the feeding of the prisoners in their cells. Some prisons, as in the case of Auburn, used a common messhall, but this was considered to be fraught with greater danger, and even in these messhalls, the benches were so arranged that all prisoners faced in the same direction. No conversation was tolerated, and severe punishment attended any attempt at communication. But talking was never stamped out. Mass movements of prisoners were reduced to a minimum. Humans were driven like animals. The march to and from the workshops and the cells was the only exercise had by the inmates. The idea of recreation had not penetrated into most prisons in any form.

In prisons on the "separate" plan, like the Eastern Penitentiary, this mass movement naturally did not occur. Exercise — regarded as necessary in the Eastern Penitentiary — was had in the little separate yards attached to the ground-floor cells, or in adjacent cells on the upper floor. But the New Jersey State Prison, the erection of which began in Trenton in 1833, was without provision for exercise yards. The guarding of prisoners in institutions of the separate type was far easier than in the Auburn-type prisons. The escape of a prisoner from any prison, in the era from 1825 to 1845, was extremely rare.

Security and intimidation demanded, further, the inhibition of any special mental activity of a secular nature. The prisoner was barred almost absolutely from knowledge of the outside world. It had practically ceased to exist for him when he entered the prison. Thus would he fail to have disturbing influences to plot escapes; thus would he appreciate the dire fact that the wages of sin were a living death; thus would the world outside understand the horrible consequences of crime. No letters reached the prisoner. Rarely were his most intimate friends allowed to visit him. Never might he talk with his visitor without the presence of an eavesdropping guard. Never was news of secular events allowed to penetrate into the prison. The prison world was cut off from the world outside. At long intervals the prisoner might write to a member of his family, but no return letters were allowed him.

In short, two test questions applied to all activities of the prisons of the Auburn type. Is the prison safe? Is the prison economical? Economy built cells without running water or water-closets. The bare necessities of existence were admitted to the cells, although the inmate passed approximately fourteen hours a day cooped up in these extremely small places. Beds were of wood, and infested often with vermin. Sheets and pillow-cases were rare. Blankets were filthy and insufficient. Heating was done mainly by stoves in the corridors. Extremes of temperature were inevitable in winter. Some cells were hot and stifling, and some were cold, frigid and wholly uncomfortable. The windows in the prisons being closed to save the heat, ventilation conditions were frequently intolerable. Prisons of the Pennsylvania type were generally heated by iron tubes containing hot water or steam from a central source.

The inmate in prisons of the Auburn type suffered from a perpetual round of inconveniences. The absence of running water in his cell reduced his chances of adequate washing of face, hands and body. Intensely disagreeable body odors were a frequent cause of complaint in the cell houses. The water supply in most prisons was quite insufficient. Sing Sing Prison never had pure water in this period. The Rhode Island State Prison allowed a warm bath once in three months. Occasionally, when the prison might be located on the water front, as at Sing Sing or Charlestown, Massachusetts, the inmates were allowed at intervals a plunge. Inmates washed in the shops. No water was carried into the cells save for drinking purposes — and very little of that. Bath tubs were rare in prisons. Crude shower baths were sometimes available. In the Eastern Penitentiary, however, in addition to cold water bathing in the cells, where each prisoner had a tub, a wash-basin, soap and towels, there was provision for a warm bath once a week by steam-heated shower baths in separate cells.

In most prisons of the Auburn type, inmates ate in their cells. The food was served necessarily luke-warm or cold. The cells became infested with vermin, because of the accumulated dirt and crumbs. Most disagreeable odors became common. There was little airing of bedding or clothes, and less washing of them.

This was the day of crude lights. Individual cells of prisons were not lighted. Candles were allowed in the Eastern Penitentiary as a privilege, or when additional labor had to be done after dark. Oil lights hanging in the corridors in Auburn-type prisons, made the darkness almost more visible. Hence the custom of working prisoners from sun-up to sun-down, six days in the week, the only alternative in the prisoner's life being the idlness of the cell. Those who could read, and desired to, found their only available time the intervals of meal-times during the day, and the Sundays, unbroken save for the chapel services or Sunday school. The libraries of the prisons, when existing at all, possessed a few moral and often antiquated volumes.

The prisoner's clothing was crude, but generally sufficient, although little attention was given to his garb. The inmates, marched at times of necessity through rain and snow to and from the shops and cells, had no changes of garments. They dried their wet garments in the narrow cells, or in the corridors, with resulting dampness and intolerable odors.

A distinctive garb was worn, whether of alternate black and white stripes, or a parti-colored costume. For a distinctive mark, the half of the head was sometimes shaved.

The chief positive daily activity of the prisons was the manufacturing of products for sale in the open market. All prisons aimed to reduce by this means the costs of maintenance and improvements. The most lucrative method of employing convicts was through the letting out of the labor of the convicts to contractors who paid a fixed sum for the labor of the inmates, supervised the manufacturing, furnished the materials, and received the finished product. Another method of utilizing the labor of inmates was by the piece-price system, whereby the prison sold the completed article to the contractor at a stipulated price. Some prisons sold their own products in the open market, by what is now called the State-account system. Kentucky's State prison was leased out to one man to operate, and later to a firm.

The prisons of the Auburn type showed higher earning capacity, due to the utilization of the inmates in workshops. From 1828 to 1841, Auburn Prison produced enough to support itself, pay all salaries of officers, except in 1837-38, and except in those two years produced a total surplus of $69,460. Sing Sing, Massachusetts, Ohio and Connecticut made very favorable financial showings, and, on the other hand, the "separate prisons" were far from self-supporting, a fact that was forever "rubbed in" publicly by the reports of the Boston Prison Discipline Society. The Eastern Penitentiary failed even to publish annual financial statements.

Serious objections, from the economic standpoint, were raised in the State of New York during the thirties and early forties against contract labor of prisoners, but even there with little effect upon the practice. The "mechanics," the forerunners of organized labor, objected on the ground that contract labor lowered prices, created an oversupply in certain industries, established unfair competition, and crowded out free labor into other occupations. Also it was claimed that the prisons favored with considerable financial profits in this manner the lucky contractors, gave opportunity for favoritism in the letting of contracts, taught convicts trades to the detriment of free mechanics, and developed apprentices out of the criminal classes.

Successive legislative committees in New York tried to argue away or to gloss over the issues. It was held that the competition of prison labor with free labor was much overestimated; that the prison trades were few which competed; that the mechanics themselves had the opportunity to bid for contracts; that the mechanics desired to stifle all industry in prison (which was in a way the truth); that the public in general demanded that prisons pay their way; that inmates should learn in prison to be self-supporting, in order not to revert later to crime; and that idleness would be the worst and most inhuman treatment of prisoners. The mechanics, it was said with reason, offered no practical constructive suggestions in line with the humane treatment of prisoners, and proposed either transportation, which was impracticable, or the abandonment of practically all industry and the setting-up of general idleness and consequent disorder and demoralization.

Concessions to the mechanics were made in the State of New York, first in 1835 by restricting somewhat the variety of prison occupations, making the letting of contracts more public, and limiting the number of convicts to a trade. Foreign industries of silk-growing and weaving were to be introduced. No material change occurred, however. Again in 1845, a new prison was established in Dannemora in the Adirondacks, not far from Plattsburg, called Clinton Prison, where only mining operations were to be conducted, as non-competitive with the mechanics. But in other States than New York, the broad problems of contract labor, later to be among the most complicated and troublesome of prison problems, had hardly risen by 1845. At this time, the prisons had been in successful financial operation but relatively few years, and the pressure of convict labor was not yet an acute issue.

The general public knew little of prison conditions and problems. The abolition of convict labor was little urged for any reason of its competition with free labor, and for its injustice to prisoners. To-day, in 1921, convict contract labor is opposed chiefly because it is a form of slavery — a method of selling the actual daily labor of prisoners in servitude to the highest bidder, and for private gain. It is opposed, also, because it brings into the prison the contractor, who to an extent divides authority over the convicts with the prison executive. The strong argument of the present day, that prisoners are not duly recompensed for their labor within prison walls, was not urged in 1840 to 1845. There was a total lack of interest on the part of the prison reformers and the public in any regular wage-scale compensation of prisoners, for the following reasons:

It was held that punishment, to be sufficient, must not involve any remuneration for the suffering endured. The measure of punishment once defined, there should be no alleviating circumstances to that punishment. Since the prisoner had not been willing to work honestly for a living with the inducement of wages on the outside, he should work involuntarily within prison for *no* wages. Otherwise, there was the same incentive to work inside the prison as on the outside, and the deterrent effect of the prison would be lost. The convict was sent to prison "at hard labor." Few suggestions of financial compensation to prisoners are to be found in the history of this period. Not since the earliest years of the first State prisons — Walnut Street, Newgate in New York, and Baltimore — had substantial efforts been made to establish a wage-scale in prison.

The prisoner's time was forfeit to the State. His labor was a part of that forfeit. He was the slave of the State. He had forfeited citizenship. He was an outcast. Furthermore, grave doubt prevailed as to the desirability of any sizeable sums accruing to the convict on his discharge from prison. Such money would aid dissolute criminals, after discharge, to perpetuate further crimes, and would enable them to exist without the immediate application to work and to the earning of an honest livelihood, that was essential if released convicts were not to be quickly tempted back into crime. Therefore the State was not interested in establishing regular compensation for labor performed, but paid to the prisoner on discharge a pittance of a few dollars to enable him to reach the community from which he had been committed.

However, the necessity felt by the contractors to speed up the convicts led early to the establishment of the "overstent" or over-stint for overtime work. This bonus, paid to the convicts who thus did extra work after the completion of their stint, was of very varying amount. Prisoners left their institutions with from a few dollars to several hundreds, according to ability and length of imprisonment. There was relatively little inducement to prisoners to lay by large earnings through over-stint. No commissaries were maintained, at which inmates might make purchases to supplement the prison food or equipment. Two principles in particular governed the administration of the prisons on the Auburn plan. First, that force should be recognized as the only successful means of government, and secondly, that all prisoners should be treated alike. Therefore, no privileges of purchase, or of favoritism through the possession of money, should be set up. Moreover, the connection between the prisoner and his family that had been left behind was almost severed, and he had little to remind him of his social obligation to contribute toward their support. Indeed, he had practically no responsibility, and the whole prison regime was seemingly devised to eliminate or crush out any feeling of individual responsibility within him, save to obey the rules that were made, not for him alone, but for all.

However, compensation of another kind, for good conduct and for industry, became practically a system in all American prisons. I refer to the granting of pardons to prisoners by the governor of the State. The reasons for such granting ranged from legitimate rewards for industry and good conduct to the responses to political machinations, or to the apparent necessity of clearing out the congested prisons in order to give a place to newcomers. The abuse of the pardoning power had been emphasized, criticised and denounced for more than a half century, at the end of the period that we have been considering. The pardon was the goal or the bait, ever before the prisoner's eyes. One in every nine persons was pardoned out of Auburn Prison between 1824 and 1829; one in 18 from the Virginia State Penitentiary between 1820 and 1829; one in 17 from the Massachusetts State Prison between 1820 and 1829, and one in 15 from the State Prison of New Hampshire in the same period.

Statistics of given intervals in the thirties and forties of the nineteenth century showed wide variations in these acts of executive clemency. The larger prisons, like those of Auburn, Sing Sing and Charlestown, showed pardons in ratios of from 1 to 20, to 1 to 35. Vermont, on the other hand, pardoned in 1843 1 to every 8; Kentucky in 1840 and 1842, 1 to every 5; Ohio in 1839 and 1843, 1 to every 11. The average of all prisons, and of many different intervals between 1830 and 1843, showed a pardoning of 1 inmate in every 19. Since this method of discharging was not the only method of release, but was employed in addition to regular release through expiration of sentence, it played an important part not only in reducing the prison population, but also in furnishing an incentive to the prisoner to good conduct and good work.

The average length of sentences to State prison was considerable. Taking the years 1839, 1840 and 1841 as a basis for statistics, we find the average length of sentences ranged from 2 years and 5 months in the Eastern Penitentiary of Pennsylvania to 7 years and 3 months in the Connecticut State Prison. The Prison Association of New York showed by statistics in 1846 the great disparity of sentences for the same offense, but regarded this as not so great an evil as the length of many of the sentences. The average length of sentences, from the figures of 18 prisons, and applying to the period between 1840 and 1846, was 4 years, 11 months and 18 days. The shortest sentence was three months. The longest sentence was of course for life. The customary minimum sentence was for one year. Sentences from 10 to 42 years were shown to be the maximum definite sentences, outside of life sentences in the several prisons. There was no exceptionally large number of life-term inmates in prison, partly because the pardoning of a life-termer was actually more probable, after a span of from seven to ten years, than the pardoning of an inmate who had been sentenced to 10 or more years of imprisonment.

The pardoning power of itself was not only not an evil, but was a necessity in an age without the use of the principle of the systematic commutation of sentences in accordance with law. But the abuse of the pardoning power was a serious and often demoralizing evil.

What about the results of prison treatment, in the period we are considering? The test of a prison's success has generally been held to be the proportion of inmates, who, through the nature of the prison treatment, are deterred from further crime. Cure has been held to be demonstrated, negatively, by the subsquent non-appearance of the said inmates in any correctional institution. Affirmatively, by the proved activity of the discharged prisoners in leading an apparently honest life, and in continuing to be self-supporting. The return to prison for a subsequent crime is called "recidivism."

The tests of prison treatment, in terms of subsequent appearances in correctional institutions, were extremely faulty. Statistics of recidivism were painfully incomplete, largely because they could not from the nature of the case be obtained. There existed not only no system of recording physical measurements or marks of identification of inmates, but there was also naturally no central bureau of records, and no adequate records. The era was one of building up the elements of prison discipline and routine — not one of analyzing prison results by fine tests and research. Only those statistics based on the recorded experiences of a single prison could be prepared regarding recidivism in that one prison, and even then the evidence was largely "hearsay" or subjective. Convicts might have served previously in several other institutions, and might have lived a long life of crime and still appear in prison statistics as first offenders in the prison under consideration.

The Massachusetts State Prison showed by intermittent statistics between 1820 and 1843 a total of 3,037 receptions and 147 recommitments; the Eastern Penitentiary 2,818 receptions and 139 recommitments. Such figures have only a misleading effect. Indeed, statistics compiled at various times throughout the nineteenth century show not only the widest variations, but also elements that make them hard of comparison with each other. It would be most difficult even to-day to prove by any statistics of recidivism the success or failure of prisons in the United States in the absence still of a complete central bureau of identification.

We need not then give lengthy consideration to the seriously inadequate statistics of the early periods. Indeed, the term "reformation" connoted several different things, but usually the word meant a thorough spiritual conversion of the prisoner, as well as the intention to lead henceforth a law-abiding life. Elam Lynds, the warden of Auburn and Sing Sing prisons, did not believe in the permanent reformation of any adult convict. Reports from many prisons, between 1830 and 1840, testified to the presence of only occasional "reformations." No studies of scientific thoroughness were made, to determine results. An occasional survey of the lives of discharged prisoners was made, as at Auburn prison between 1825 and 1830, when, by letters to postmasters, district attorneys and others, Warden Gershom Powers learned that of 160 prisoners released, 112 were decidedly steady and industrious, while 12 others were "somewhat reformed."

Dorothea Dix, in 1845, knew of no person who had uniformly kept in view so large a number of discharged convicts as 50 or 100 after their "enlargement" from any prison, for two, three, or five years. In general, reformations were assumed to have taken place, if the prisoners failed to return to prison. We must, therefore, frankly abandon any effort to determine from the statistics of "reformations" the relative values of either the silent or the separate systems, or of individual prisons that employed these systems. Moreover, the judgment of the times as to the relative success of the competing systems was based mainly, not on possible reformations, but on such tangible, or apparently tangible facts, as the routine administration, the relative proportion of sickness and death, cases of insanity, provision for mental and moral instruction, humane treatment, discipline, industrial productivity and the like.

We have thus far described those factors of prison discipline which were employed to assure security and intimidation, obedience, and industrial productivity. In this review, the prisoner has appeared as a slave of the government, a thing to be used, a person without civic rights, a convict to be kept from escaping and continuing thereby his crimes, a person to be punished for any infraction of a rigorous system of discipline. He was provided in general with the minimum of creature necessities, threatened by harsh and often ingeniously cruel punishments, harassed by numerous and frequent positive discomforts, driven to work from sun-up to sun-down every day in the year save perhaps the Fourth of

July, Thanksgiving, and Christmas, locked into desperately unsanitary and disease-breeding cells for thirteen or fourteen hours a day, and for practically all the time from Saturday night to Monday morning, cut off from the world of friends and people and events, merged into a body of outlaws, and ostracized and hated by society in general.

To what extent did the prisons, as representatives of society's reaction against convicts, make provision for the inmates of prisons as reclaimable human beings? What measures of health, of education, of religious consolation, of other civilizing forces were utilized? Let us consider first the provisions of health.

Society was in no way vitally interested in the extent to which the prisons of the period made provision for the prisoner as a reclaimable human being. The illness or the health of the convict meant little to the world outside. But the administrator of a prison was interested in maintaining a favorable health rate, because the prison labor contractors paid the State only for the services of the able-bodied. Auburn, Sing Sing, Massachusetts, and other prisons drove inmates to work who claimed to be ill, or who were suspected of feigning insanity. Many of the most terrible records of cruelty in this period center about such practices. Deaths within a few hours of the final abandonment of work testify to the horrors of the practice.

Little systematic medical service was rendered to the prisoners, and still more infrequent were any careful studies of the medical problems of prisons. Doctor Franklin Bache at the Eastern Penitentiary, Doctor Woodward at Wethersfield, and Doctor Coleman at Trenton, were exceptions as prison physicians, emphasizing by their very concern about morbidity, mortality and their causes the very low general average of medical services in prisons. The "doctor" came for a few hours, and irregularly; he was on call at other times, but often failed to arrive in time to save life. Prison hospitals were mainly hit-or-miss places of segregation of the severely sick, who were attended by inmate "nurses" in the intervals between the visits of the physician. Of these "nurses," gruesome stories of callousness and brutality were frequent. Drugs were administered by poorly qualified "apothecaries" or by inmates. The physician's salary was small, he was held to no professional standards, and his scientific interest was generally slight or wholly wanting. It may safely be said that to most of the physicians, the task of medical and surgical service to the convicts was not stimulating.

The hospital was regarded by the prisoners as a goal to be attained if possible, but only because their ordinary existence was so intolerable. At the hospital a slightly different diet could be had. Here they could talk — in the prisons of the Auburn type — with each other. Here, lewdness and immorality flourished. To counteract the tendency to attain the hospital, severe penalties were affixed to feigned illness, and admission to the hospital was granted only on proof that was often so adequate as to bring about also the speedy death of the patient, because of the delays in proper medical or surgical treatment. Resident physicians were rare, and in the relatively enlightened Eastern Penitentiary there was no resident physician until 1842. Hospital records in most prisons were so inadequate as to give a wholly imperfect picture of prison morbidity and mortality.

Several facts concerning the prevalence of diseases stood out prominently. Consumption, rheumatism, coughs and colds were the prevailing diseases in the winter months, and "intermittent fevers," typhoid and dysentery were frequent in the summers. Over one-half of the deaths in Auburn prison from 1817 to 1844 were from "some form of diseased lungs." Many forms of "scrofula" developed, and were attributed by the Prison Association of New York in 1845 to the deplorable lack of ventilation in the cells.

But despite the grossly insanitary physical equipment of the prisons, and the strikingly inadequate medical service, both Dorothea Dix and an investigating committee of the Prison Association of New York in 1845 and 1846 held that, on the whole, imprisonment tended to increase rather than decrease the chances of life. Regular hours, regular diet, and the entire absence of chances for dissipation, coupled with necessarily long hours of sleep, seemed to more than offset the evils of bad ventilation, cramped and clammy cells, the extremes of temperature in the several parts of the prison, and the wretched physical condition of many of the inmates on admission. Dorothea Dix, after several years of prison visiting, stated that the prisoners seemed to be in quite as good condition as those men who worked in similar trades at free labor.

The percentage of deaths, in most prisons, was considered low. For many years the Auburn-type prisons registered approximately from one to two per cent. of deaths annually. Virginia's prison ran an abnormally high death rate, due to local conditions. The Eastern and Western Penitentiaries registered a somewhat higher death rate than did Auburn, Wethersfield or Massachusetts. However, a most important factor was omitted from all of these calculations. The number of inmates pardoned out for serious ill health, and not recorded at the time of the compilation of mortality or morbidity tables, often made the published statistics wholly unreliable as an accurate picture of health facts. Furthermore, a much higher percentage of negroes in the population of the Eastern Penitentiary and of the State prisons of Maryland and Virginia contributed to the higher mortality rates, and threw out the possibility of comparing similar statistics.

Bitter controversy arose as to the morbidity, mortality and insanity percentages in prisons of the two rival types. The Auburn-type prisons scored somewhat lower mortality rates, but housed fewer negroes. Cases of illness were less prominent in Auburn-type prisons, but at the Eastern Penitentiary the exceptionally well-trained physician, Doctor Bache, displayed scientific interest in his work, and gave detailed reports of his studies in the annual reports of the prison. At the close of the period that we are now considering, both the Boston and the New York prison societies were doubtful as to the relative healthfulness of the two systems, when conducted under the best conditions, while the Philadelphia prison reformers were convinced of the good morbidity and mortality records of their local prison. The leading prison administrators and students of Europe, who had, in the main, made long-distance studies of the two systems, were practically a unit in urging the adoption of the separate system of confinement. The warfare, which for twenty years had been vehemently waged by the Boston Society against the Pennsylvania system, with health facts as perhaps the chief supporting argument, apart from the financial facts or hypotheses, had not eventuated in much more than a drawn battle.

There was similar unclearness of statistics regarding the presence and seriousness of insanity in the prisons. Not until toward the end of the period we have discussed in this study was any earnest effort made to remove from the State prisons the insane, though agitation for their removal had been a leading feature of the program of the Boston Society for many years. Only in Massachusetts was there by 1845 a good system of the transfer of the insane from the prison to the State asylum. Insanity was little understood as yet even by the medical profession; its treatment through kindness, the striking off of chains, and the abolition of physical punishment, was new and not well established. Laymen knew the ailment only as it was manifested in "crazy people." Many private families still kept their insane in cages on their own property, or in their own homes. Wardens reported to the Boston Society, in response to a circular letter, that only "here and there" was there a lunatic in their prison population. Some prisons stated that they had not had a single lunatic in their entire history! Pennsylvania treated its insane in the separate cells of the prison, to which cells they were admitted on entrance.

Unquestionably, there was much unrecognized insanity in the prisons. "Feigned insanity" was a frequent diagnosis for the actual disease. Brutal corporal punishments were applied as curatives for supposed malingering in contract-labor prisons. Tragedies innumerable and unrecorded occurred without question among the imprisoned insane. Much of the incentive to brutal punishments arose undoubtedly from the inability of the mentally sick to obey the prison rules, and perform satisfactorily the stints of work set for them, stints that were frequently severe, even for the able-minded.

The Eastern Penitentiary was made a target by the Boston Society as an insanity-breeder, on the assumption that "solitary confinement," if long continued, produced madness. Two fallacies, however, were embraced in this conclusion. First, the Pennsylvania system provided for separate, but not solitary, confinement of its inmates. Visits of some frequency occurred in the cells of the Eastern Penitentiary, not only from the prison officers, but also from the representatives of the prison reform society of Philadelphia. Actual solitary confinement had occurred in Auburn prison in 1822 and 1823, and had produced madness. But in the Eastern Penitentiary, the second fallacy of the Boston argument was made clear by the fact that only in the annual reports of the Eastern Penitentiary had a careful and scientifically-minded physician recorded and discussed with apparent sincerity and faithfulness the manifestations of mental disorder within the institution. This very honesty and frankness furnished good ammunition to hostile critics, who failed to emphasize the lack of similar thorough analysis in institutions of the Auburn type.

Nevertheless, the unbiased student of the period must derive a cumulative impression from the assembled facts that the permanent segregation of inmates in separate cells, as in Philadelphia, rendered the prisoners more prone to mental disorders than did the alternate association and separation of inmates in Auburn-type prisons. But insanity was a very troublesome matter to all intelligent wardens, by the fifth decade of the nineteenth century. In Sing Sing, in November, 1844, 31 of the 688 convicts were recognized as insane. In 1843 and 1844, 27 convicts had been admitted to the Eastern Penitentiary while insane. There was no other place to which criminal insane persons could readily be sent. Private and public hospitals for the insane were few, congested, and did not take criminals. The prison was the only "safe" place to which to send the criminal insane.

Prison life — made up so predominantly of silence and separation from one's fellows — induced masturbation to an appalling degree, broke down health, developed prison psychoses, and undermined the will. In many inmates of the prisons, the environment inevitably produced mental diseases. Moreover, the presence in the prisons of a mentally deficient group, not insane, but "lacking," the feeble-minded and often incorrigible, was coming to be recognized. And there was as yet no proper place for their treatment.

The above-outlined efforts to reduce illness, insanity and death were determined probably not so much by any special solicitude for the prisoner as a man as by the prison's need of able-bodied inmates. Prisons had grown to be organized institutions because the abolition of the death penalties for many crimes had made prisons indispensable. They were to be places of punishment, dread and hard labor. Only gradually, and often reluctantly, did the prisons give recognition to the demands of the prison reformers that the Gospel and the chaplain should have a definite place in prison discipline.

Chaplains, if on the staff of the prisons at all, were low-salaried intermittent, and often quite inefficient. They were not held to be among the indispensable officials, like the warden, the principal keeper or even the physician. Many prisons had no regular church service on Sunday; few prisons held daily chapel services. Often, in the absence of the chaplain, some clergyman from the vicinity officiated. Sunday schools were established in some of the more highly organized prisons, like Auburn, Wethersfield, and Massachusetts, in which religious instruction was given mainly by volunteer citizens. Dorothea Dix summed up the situation in 1845 by saying that except in the Eastern Penitentiary, general and moral teaching in the State prisons was insufficiently provided for.

The chaplain was the missionary — and often the only one — of the prison. He conducted the service on Sunday. When there was a Sunday School, he directed it. In a number of States the law required him to make daily visits to the prison, and to converse with the convicts in their cells. His eyes were to be fixed on spiritual things; he was not to be actively concerned about discipline or abuses. His presence was undoubtedly often tolerated by the warden, rather than desired. The warden himself seldom played the part of an active reformer of his inmates. Administrative matters mainly engaged the attention of the warden. Only wardens with exceptional personality were much concerned with the reformative treatment of their prisoners. At the outset of the Auburn system, Elam Lynds set a standard of relentless severity of treatment. His successor, Gershom Powers, had his first heart-to-heart talk with the inmate after he was discharged. On the other hand, some wardens, like Amos Pilsbury, combined determined disciplinary methods with interest in their charges. But even at Wethersfield, the chaplain in the early forties dared to urge the warden to give more consideration to the souls of the inmates, and less to the making of money for the State out of their bodies.

The chaplain was also practically the only teacher within the prison, in an era (1825-1845) when prisoners were rarely taught even the three R's. The end of our period under review marks in the main the beginning of a systematic effort to secure schooling for prisoners. The Connecticut chaplain was suggesting two hours a week for regular moral and general educational teaching. The Bible was the customary text book for teaching spelling and reading. No class-room instruction was held. The evening period was the only available time for instruction, and the picture is vivid, to the student of prison history, of the chaplain standing in the semi-dark corridor, before the cell door, with a dingy lantern hanging to the grated bars, and teaching to the wretched convict in the darkness beyond the grated door the rudiments of reading or of numbers.

In any prisons that permitted occasional communication of convicts by letter with their friends, the chaplain wrote the letters. Prisoners were furnished only with slates and slate pencils. The chaplain also organized the prison library, if there was one. A considerable proportion of convicts in northern prisons could read and write — 536 out of 861 in Sing Sing in November, 1844; 210 others could read but not write. A Bible was generally supposed to be in every cell. Only the better organized prisons maintained libraries. Connecticut had a small library; each prisoner was furnished also with a weekly temperance paper, and a religious paper. Massachusetts had a prison library of several hundred volumes, initiated by a donation of $50, "sent by the mother of a life prisoner to her son, to furnish him with proper reading." The prisoners in the

Massachusetts prison made frequent donations for the library out of their earnings. The State appropriated, in the early forties, $100 annually for the increase and greater variety of books.

Books were distributed at intervals of several weeks, in prisons possessing libraries, at the discretion of the warden and chaplain. The freer the use of books, the fewer were said to become the cases for discipline. Small collections of books were occasionally donated by citizens. The Western Penitentiary of Pennsylvania at Pittsburg recorded in 1845 the regular study by some prisoners (in their separate cells) of arithmetic, geography and history.

It was a natural and almost inevitable step, for some of the chaplains, from the treatment and study of the individual prisoner to the study of the causes of crime. The chaplains were, in general, the earliest social statisticians of the prisons. They were the daily recipients of the tales and confidences of the prisoners. Yet not until the late thirties do we find, as a kind of pioneer among socially-minded chaplains, the Reverend Gerrish Barrett publishing his analyses of the characters of the prisoners and the causes of crime.

As early as 1832, Jared Curtis, the chaplain of the Massachusetts State Prison, prepared statistics noteworthy in an age almost destitute of such compilations. He found in "rum" the chief cause of crime. Other external and environmental causes were found by him to be ignorance, lack of training for a trade, bad companions, runaway habits, lack of parents' care, orphanage, and Sabbath-breaking.

Indeed, inquiry into the causes of crime were not infrequent from the earliest years of the first period. The Quakers, before 1790, believed the public sanguinary punishments and the public employment of prisoners on the streets of Philadelphia made for increased crime, besides rendering callous the hearts of the onlookers. The abolition of promiscuous and debauching associations of prisoners in a common prison was effected, in order to reduce one of the chief causes of crime, the abominable intermingling of the prisoners of all classes and kinds. Common jails were designated as a prolific cause of crime. Doctor Benjamin Rush of Philadelphia held, as early as 1787, that every crime had its cure in moral and physical influences. William Bradford, in 1792, held that it was from the impunity of crime, and not from the moderation of punishments, that crimes proceeded.

Throughout the entire period that we have been studying in this volume, we have found causes sought for the dread presence of crime in society, and we have noted that practically all of the causes have been environmental, or those recognized as "standard." Thus, the period of the first prison system (1790-1820) brought out, apparently, the crime-causing tendencies of the congestion of population in prisons, the abuse of the pardoning power, the lack of classification of prisoners, the attendant idleness, and particularly the contact of juveniles with adults, hardened offenders in crime. Partisan politics, and the frequent rotation of wardens and superintendents of institutions, as well as the appointment of untrained and often unprincipled wardens and subordinate officers, were all given as causes of crime. Thomas Eddy, founder and first warden of the State prison in New York, found the increase of crimes at the turn of the nineteenth century due to the rapid growth of New York's population and wealth, with its attendant luxury and corruption of manners, and also to the great number of indigent and vicious immigrants from Europe and the West Indies. Eddy also laid special stress, as causes of crime, upon the dram shops, taverns, intemperance, theatres and other external and environmental influences.

So, throughout the period, we have found little attention given to the intensive study of the individual — hardly to be expected in an age in which so obvious a form of mental maladjustment as the insane was hardly understood, and only infrequently treated by methods that to-day appeal to us as rational. And it was natural, therefore, that we should find in prisons practically no traces of recreational alleviations of the relentless monotony of prison life. Only in Massachusetts have we found a relatively enlightened viewpoint toward the introduction of the simplest recreational features. In that institution the library was fairly well developed — but contained only morally uplifting books. Musical instruments were allowed — a rare exception in prisons — but were used for music on the Sabbath. On Saturday afternoons, something approaching a glee club was permitted to practice in the chapel, but only in preparation for the morrow's service. Even a mutual improvement society was formed among the convicts, with fortnightly discussions of ethical topics — but it can be assumed that this great alleviation of the deadly routine of prison was conducted on a highly moral and didactic plane. Nowhere do we find attention given to the importance of continued and reasonable physical exercise. In no case do we find in a prison of this period the permission to play any kind of game — though in the juvenile correctional institutions, such as the House of Refuge and the House of Reformation in Boston, games and sports had been introduced in the twenties, collateral with the establishment of the institutions, as a part of the curriculum.

Nor have we found traces of anything save the most sporadic and individual instances of a trusty system. It was an era of the maintenance of prisons as human menageries, with all the possible danger of an outbreak of the human wild beasts. Not the slightest evidence of a theory of an honor system has come to light, nor, of course, any conception of the possibilities of self-development among the inmates through the enjoyment of privileges beyond the occasional instruction in reading, or writing, or arithmetic. No self-government theories are found, although again in the House of Reformation in Boston, under Mr. Wells, an advanced system of self-government was introduced as early as the first years of the thirties, but only for children.

Meanwhile, prison customs were hardening into traditions, growing stronger and more difficult to change because of their acceptance through the years. Wardens and members of boards of inspectors came and went — learning so far as they could their new duties, but sensing that their tenure of office was liable to be short. Adherence to the customs and principles that had appeared to their predecessors safe and sound was but natural. There were few men whose personalities thrust themselves above the mediocrity of the average warden. In this period there projected the figures of Elam Lynds, Gershom Powers, Samuel L. Wood of the Eastern Penitentiary, Moses and Amos Pilsbury of Wethersfield, and Samuel Parsons of Virginia, followed in that State by the conscientious Morgan. The names are few and among them only those of the Pilsburys have endured. At the very close of the period we find Zebulon R. Brockway, who was to be in his long life the devoted student of the methods of Amos Pilsbury, as guard in the Connecticut State prison, then associated with Pilsbury at Albany in the county penitentiary, then manager of the Detroit House of Correction, then founder, with Enoch C. Wines and others of the New York State Reformatory at Elmira, then for many years its superintendent, to become the greatest practical administrator in this country of the reformatory type of institution — all the time growing as a philosopher in penological and criminological matters, to become finally the "grand old man" of the wardens and the superintendents of the United States, and finally, to die peacefully at the age of 93 at his home in Elmira, New York, in October, 1920.

Brockway, the sole figure that linked the distant past, which we have studied in this volume, with the present, in which still far too many of the conditions herein described have perpetuated themselves, and in which still many of the theories and statements we have found and studied are maintained and repeated, as if original and having the value of new discoveries!

The writer of this volume closes his study here in the year 1845, the first of the activity of the Prison Association of New York, the organization of which he is, after three-quarters of a century of the Association's activity, the general secretary. Between the end of our study, and the present day, lie over seventy-five years, a period rich in daring experiment, as well as in the evolution of already developing methods of humane and wise treatment of prisoners. He (or she) who may write the second, and final volume, of the history of prison methods in our country will live, during an extended period of study and exploration, in a field of wonderful interest, the field of the growth of the reformatory, the indeterminate sentence, parole, the specialized institutions, the juvenile courts, the practice of probation, the prison reform and prisoners' relief organizations, the honor system, the farm colonies, the individualization of punishment and of discipline, the rise of conferences and congresses on prison methods, and finally, the growth of the belief that in the community itself, long before the so-called criminal finds his ultimate way into correctional and penal institutions, lie many of the causes, and consequently lie many of the responsibilities for the presence of crime.

Yet, in this second great period, the period upon whose threshold we pause, we doubt if there will be found greater interest, and more stimulating exploration, than in the first and far less clarified period which we have studied. In the progress of our study, the forms of men long gone have risen repeatedly before us — Lownes, Bradford, Livingston, Eddy, Lynds, Powers, Brittin, Hopkins, Wood, Parsons, the Pilsburys, Combe, Doctor Bache, and many others. Who of all the readers — if there be such of this history — have known many — or any — of them before. We have gained them as our acquaintances through our study, and we are the richer therefor. They have been men of varying capacities and temperaments and methods. Some of them have been cruel disciplinarians, some have been persistently humane, some have been theorists, and have touched only slightly in practical ways the prison field. Yet they all have contributed to the great prison systems of the present day — and it is with a feeling of gladness that the writer believes that, to an extent, their contributions to what we possess to-day have been for the first time somewhat fully defined for modern students, and their services recorded and made available to the present day.

And it seems fitting that we turn at last to that woman who in so many ways went about doing good in the prison field, in those crucial days, Dorothea Lynde Dix, the woman who has given us the most cogent and graphic outline of the prisons in the period at which we close our study — eminent fighter for the betterment of the conditions of the insane, the pauper and the prisoner. We quote, in conclusion, from her some words that at the end of this study are wholly pertinent, and which for many of us have the same application that they had for Dorothea Dix, seventy-five years ago:

"Sincerely do I regret that I have so little leisure to give to the illustration of these important subjects, upon which volumes might be written, showing the origin, progress and prospects of a reform so eminently affecting social order, and the civil institutions of the Republic. Years of unintermitted labor and vigilance are necessary for producing practically beneficial results, through the influences of these disciplinary institutions.

"Society, during the last hundred years, has been alternately perplexed and encouraged, respecting the two great questions — how shall the criminal and pauper be disposed of, in order to reduce crime and reform the criminal on the one hand, and, on the other, to diminish pauperism and restore the pauper to useful citizenship? Though progress has been made, through the efforts of energetic and enlightened persons, directed to the attainment of these ends, all know that society is very far from realizing their accomplishment. We accord earnest and grateful praise to those who have procured the benefits at present possessed; and with careful zeal, we would endeavor to advance a work, which succeeding generations must toil to perfect and complete."

BIBLIOGRAPHY.

Account of the Massachusetts State Prison, by Board of Visitors. Charlestown, Mass., 1806. (Also Rules and Regulations of the Massachusetts State Prisons, in Appendix to Account of the Mass. State Prison, 1811.) S. Etheridge, Boston.

Account of the Principal Lazarettos in Europe, An. John Howard, Warrington, England, 1789.

Biographical Sketch of Amos Pilsbury. William Hunt (Albany, 1849, Joel Munsell, printer).

Boston Prison Discipline Society. Annual Reports, 1826, 1845. (Twenty-ninth Annual Report, 1854: ''A Review of Thirty Years.'')

Brief Account of the Construction, Management and Discipline of New York State Prison at Auburn. Gershom Powers (Doubleday, New York, 1826).

Brief Sketch of Origin and History of State Penitentiary of Eastern District of Pennsylvania. Robert Vaux (McLaughlin Bros., Philadelphia, 1872).

Bulfinch, Charles, Report of. Directed by the President of the United States to visit prisons for the District of Columbia. (Green, Washington, D. C., 1829.)

Corrections and Prevention. Fred G. Pettigrove. Vol. II. (Boston, 1904).

Description and Historical Sketch of Massachusetts State Prison. 1816. Board of Directors of Mass. Prison (Etheridge, Charlestown).

Die Gefangnissbaukunst. Karl Krohne (Hamburg, 1887).

Die Neuren Strafe und Besserungs Systeme. Rudolph von Julius (Berlin, 1843).

Description des Prisons ameliorees de Gand. Sir T. F. Buxton (Philadelphia).

Des Prisons de Philadelphie. Francois Alexandre Frederic, duc de La Rochefoucauld-Liancourt (Par un Europeen, Second Edition, Amsterdam, Holtrop, 1799).

Encyclopaedia Americana (Prison Discipline). Vol. X. 1832.

Enquiry how far the punishment of death is necessary in Pennsylvania, An. William Bradford. (With an account of the gaol and penitentiary house of Philadelphia, by Caleb Lownes.) Philadelphia, T. Dobson, 1793.

Essentials of a Penitentiary System as Seen by Ducpetiaux. Preface VIII.

Fifty Years of Prison Service. Zebulon R. Brockway (New York, 1912).

Governor's Message in Journal of New York Assembly, 1819.

Ideale and Irrtume Ruckblicke und Ausblicke auf die Entwikslung des Gefangniswesens. Karl Krohne (Berlin, 1908).

Inside Out, or an interior view of the New York State Prison. W. A. Coffey (New York, James Costigan, 1823).

John Bremm, His Prison Bars. A. A. Hopkins (New York, 1888).

Journal, House of Delegates. Years 1818 to 1845. Virginia.

Journal, House of Delegates. Years 1822 to 1836. Maryland.

Journal of Prison Discipline and Philanthropy. Vol. I. Pennsylvania.

Juvenile Delinquents. Mary Carpenter (London, 1853).

Lehrbuch der Gefangniskunde unter Berucksichtigung der Kriminalstatistik und Kriminalpolitik. Karl Krohne (Stuttgart, 1889).

Letter from Gershom Powers in answer to a letter of the Hon. Edward Livingston in relation to the Auburn State Prison. Read in the Legislature of Pennsylvania, Jan. 23, 1829. (Albany, Croswell and Van Benthuysen.)

Laws of the Commonwealth, Boston, Mass., 1829.
Life of Thomas Eddy. Samuel L. Knapp (London, 1836).
London Society for Prison Discipline. Report of the Committee for 1820. Rules for Gaols, 1821.
Memorial of Society for Prevention of Juvenile Delinquency, New York Legislature, Document of House of Refuge, 1832.
Memoir of Joseph Curtis, a model man. C. M. Sedgwick (New York, 1858).
Minutes of Testimony taken before John Q. Wilson. Hartford, 1834.
New York Assembly Documents. Years: 1831, 1834, 1835, 1840, 1841, 1842.
New York Assembly Journal. Years: 1819, 1820, 1821, 1822, 1823, 1824, 1825, 1827, 1833.
New York Senate Documents, 1834.
New York Senate Journal. Years: 1827, 1828, 1829.
New York Laws. Laws of 1824, Chap. 126. Act of Incorporation. Laws of 1829, Chap. 302.
Notes on the United States of North America. George Combe (Edinburgh, 1841).
Notes sur les Prisons de la Suisse. Francis Cunningham (Barbezar et Delarue, Geneve, 1828).
Notice statistique sur l'apptication de l'emprisonnement cellulaire en Belgique, 1857. Ed. Ducpetiaux.
Notices on the Original and Successive Efforts to Improve the Discipline of the Prison at Philadelphia and to Reform the Criminal Code of Pennsylvania. Robert Vaux (Philadelphia, Kimber and Sharpless, 1826).
Observations on Penal Jurisprudence. William Roscoe (London, 1819). Additional Observations on Penal Jurisprudence (London, 1823).
On the Penitentiary System in the United States and of its Application in France. Gustave de Beaumont et Alexis de Tocqueville (Paris, 1832). Translated from the French by Francis Lieber (Philadelphia, 1833).
Pictures From Prison Life. An Historical Sketch of the Massachusetts State Prison. Gideon Haynes (Boston, 1869).
Preamble to Amendment to Penal Laws, Virginia, 1789.
Prison Association of New York, First Annual Report, 1844.
Prison Discipline in America. Francis C. Gray. (In Vol. III. of the collected volumes of the Boston Prison Discipline Society, Boston, 1847.)
Proceedings of the State Convention of Mechanics, 1834, 1841. Mechanics Magazines, New York.
Rapports sur les Penitenciers des Etats Unis. F. A. Metz et Guillaume Blouet. (Paris, 1837.)
Recollections of Windsor Prison: Containing Sketches of its History and Discipline; with Appropriate Strictures and Moral and Religious Reflections. John Reynolds (Boston, A. W. Wright, 1834).
Remarks on Cellular Separation. W. P. Foulke (Philadelphia, 1861).
Remarks on Prisons and Prison Discipline in the United States. Dorothea Dix (Philadelphia, J. Kite & Co., 1845).
Remarks on the Form and Construction of Prisons with Appropriate Designs. Published by the Committee of the Society for the Improvement of Prison Discipline. (London, 1826.)

Reports:

    Connecticut: Report of Committee on State Prisons, 1833 and 1842.
    Connecticut: Report of Directors, Wethersfield, 1835 and 1844.
    Connecticut: Report of Legislative Committee, 1832.

Connecticut: Report of Directors, Hartford, 1841.
Maryland: Journal, House of Delegates, 1822 and 1836.
Maryland: Report of Committee appointed by Board of Directors of Maryland Penitentiary, 1828. to Visit the Penitentiaries and Prisons in the City of Philadelphia and State of New York.
Maryland: Report of Select Committee on the Penitentiary, 1836.
Maryland: Report of the Committee on Prison Manufactures, 1842.
Massachusetts: Report of Massachusetts Commission on State Prison, 1817.
Massachusetts: Report of Board of Visitors, 1823.
Massachusetts: Report of Standing Committee Common Council, Boston House of Refuge, 1832.
Massachusetts: Report, Board of State Charities, Boston House of Refuge, Annual Reports, 1831, 1836, 1865. Special Report on Prisons and Prison Discipline, 1865.
Massachusetts: Senate Documents; Years 1830, 1834, 1843, 1844.
New Jersey: Report of Joint Committee, Votes of Assembly, 1830, 1837, 1838.
New Jersey: Report of Governor's Message, January, 1837.
New York: Annual Reports of Society for Reformation of Juvenile Delinquents, for Years 1835, 1838, 1839.
New York: Annual Reports of New York House of Refuge, for Years 1834, 1835, 1838, 1839, 1840, 1841.
New York: Annual Report for 1815, Newgate Prison, New York City.
New York: Report of Inspectors, Auburn, 1822.
New York: Report on the Penitentiary System of the United States, Crawford, New York, 1834.
New York: Report of Agent of the Mount Pleasant State Prison, No. 92, in Senate, New York, 1834; also 1843.
New York: Report of Select Committee of New York Senate, 1831.
New York: Report of Society for the Prevention of Pauperism, 1821, 1822.
Pennsylvania: Report of Joint Committee of Legislature of Pennsylvania, relative to Eastern Penitentiary, Harrisburg, 1835.
Pennsylvania: Fourth Report, Inspectors of Eastern Penitentiary, 1832.
Pennsylvania: Annual Reports of Board of Inspectors of Eastern Penitentiary, for Years 1830, 1831, 1834, 1837, 1838, 1842, 1844.
Pennsylvania: Report of Committee appointed in 1816 to consider subject of the State Prison of Massachusetts and to inquire into the mode of governing the Penitentiary of Pennsylvania, 1817.
Pennsylvania: Report of Charles Shaler, Edward King, and T. I. Wharton, a commission created by the Legislature in 1826 to study prison discipline.

Sketch of the Principal Transactions of the Philadelphia Society for Alleviating the Misery of Public Prisons. From Origin to Present Time. (Philadelphia, 1859, Merrihew and Thompson.)
Society in America, Vol. II. Harriet Martineau (London, 1837).
State Prisons, Hospitals, etc., Embracing their History, Finances, etc. Vol. II. C. M. Brush, State Printer (Harrisburg, Pa., 1897).
State of Prisons in England and Wales, The. John Howard (Warrington, England, 1780).
Torture and Homicide in an American State Prison. Harper's Weekly, Dec. 18, 1858.

Travels in North America in the Years 1827 and 1828. Basil Hall (Philadelphia, 1829).
Travels Through the Northern Parts of the United States in the Years 1807 and 1808. E. A. Kendall. Vol. I.
View of New York State Prison in the City of New York, by a member of the institution. New York, 1815.
Visit to the Philadelphia Prison. Robert J. Turnbull (James Phillips & Co., London, 1797).
William Penn as a Lawgiver. H. L. Carson (Pennsylvania Magazine of History and Biography, Vol. 30).
Within Prison Walls. T. M. Osborne (D. Appleton & Co., New York, 1914).
Works of Edward Livingston, Vol. I.
Writings of Thomas Jefferson, Vol. I and IV. Edited by P. L. Ford (New York, 1892-1899).